Love and Iced Tea

LESLIE FINEGAN

ISBN: 978-1-4834-3230-4 (sc)
ISBN: 978-1-4834-3232-8 (hc)
ISBN: 978-1-4834-3231-1 (e)

Library of Congress Control Number: 2015908555

Lulu Publishing Services rev. date: 10/13/2015

When a stone skips over calm water, ripples appear.
Beneath those ripples, changes happen
in ways that, at the time, we can neither see nor know
but happen they do, all the same.

To Vreni
Thank you.

Chapter 1

If you didn't know that the old swing was once sparkling white, you would have thought it was meant to be speckled. For three generations, people had discussed painting the swing. No one had actually done it. Despite the creak that cracked with every swing like a tree limb snapping in the wind, no one had oiled it either. Mae rarely noticed it as she slowly rocked back and forth. Born and raised there, she had lived all her life in the ivy-covered, red -brick house that her grandfather, W.D. Hoover, had built. Her father had been born in the big house too. He then brought his new wife home and lived out his life there. Mae swore that sometimes if the air was just right and very still, she could hear peals of laughter left over from times long past, mixed with cries drenched in salt from evaporated tears.

When she was a child, Mae worried whether she would ever grow tall enough for her feet to hit the ground while sitting in the swing. Her hair used to be a rich, dark brown, full of unruly curls, but when she was thirty-five, her hair suddenly turned gray and then snow white. Gravity claimed victory over Mae's tight, voluptuous body. Her large bosoms now dangled at what was left of a waist, while her bottom crept upward, downward, and sideways. Time and life could not take away Mae's laughing blue eyes or the joy in her high-pitched voice, which sounded like giggles of water gliding over rocks in a stream.

The weather in Oklahoma was wont to change suddenly. The minute an undercurrent of warmth beckoned in the breeze, Mae and Herschel, a big, white, shaggy sheepdog that looked like a walking mop, made themselves comfortable on the front porch. Mae perched on the swing, while Herschel slept at her feet. When the evenings were nice, she and

Booty Crutchfield were known to escape to the porch after dinner. Their neighbor, Ellanor Tree, would saunter over, and the three of them would spend the evenings together like they had for so many years. Booty, Mae, and Ellanor grew up together on the same tree-lined block in the same big houses their grandfathers built, right next door to each other. Little had changed over the years. The old brick streets remained. The sidewalks were now weathered and cracked. If their grandparents had returned from the dead, they would have recognized everything (and complained about the state of the sidewalks).

The Crutchfield family was African American. Booty was named Julius after his father. Officially he was Julius, Jr. Somehow he acquired the nickname Booty, and no one remembered how he got it. The best guess was that his grandfather called him Booty and it stuck. Everyone who remembered Booty's grandfather said that, so it must be true. Booty had been called Booty for so long that people would have to stop for a moment and think what his real name was. He was a large man with a strong, handsome face and a deep, booming voice. Silver streaks now ran through his once-black hair. Booty's grandfather, Able Crutchfield, and Mae's grandfather, W.D. Hoover, had been the very best of friends.

Able and W.D. were born in Cedar Springs, in what was then called Indian Territory, before Oklahoma became a state in 1907. They had grown up together, picking cotton. The two gathered quite a reputation as hard-drinking toughs and the best poker players in Oklahoma. They played in the back room of Hoover Drug Store, where W.D. learned pharmacy from his father. He wasn't a real pharmacist; he just called himself one, which was good enough at the time.

Hoover Drug Store was prosperous from being the only place to buy textbooks and school supplies, ladies' makeup, toiletries, and other personal supplies, plus, of course, drugs and prescriptions. It was a long wooden building with a high tin ceiling and big, whirling fans. Originally, there was a lunch counter, but it closed when the Whiz Bang Cafe opened down the street. But the real money wasn't made in the front of the drug store; money changed hands in surprising amounts in the back-room poker game. That's where Able Crutchfield made enough money in his poker winnings to buy up enough land and mineral rights to make him the richest man in that area and one of the richest in the state.

W.D. knew that liquor oiled the poker game as well as the players. The state of Oklahoma was dry, which made W.D. an ardent supporter of the Baptists. He needed to keep Oklahoma dry, because he ran the liquor distribution to a string of bootleggers he employed. With the money W.D. made, Able let him buy into some oil wells owned by Crutchfield Oil Company. Even though Able was richer, W.D. made a damn lot of money. The men found wives and started their families.

Railroad tracks ran across the end of Main Street in Cedar Springs. One side was the white part; the other side of the railroad tracks was Colored Town. The Indians lived outside of town with their own school. Everybody in town expected Able and his new wife to build their big house across the tracks on the colored side, where the respectable white people, except for W.D. and his wife Rose, thought they belonged.

Many of Cedar Springs's nicer ladies considered Rose socially beneath W.D. because she came from one of the poorer families in town. Her mother had been a telephone operator. W.D. met Rose when she sold movie tickets in the booth at the new movie theater, which sported a band accompanying the silent films. Rose was not invited to the social ladies functions except those big parties where husbands attended. Rose did not take too kindly to those women, so when W.D. wanted Able to live next door in what was becoming the new and better part of town, Rose was all for it. The rest of the town was aghast when W.D. and Able bought two prime lots in the center of a block and then bought all of the land across the street from their lots. The vacant land was turned into a park for the town. It also gave W.D. and Able an unobstructed view of Main Street, which is what they really wanted. This way, they could keep an eye on what was going on about town. The Ku Klux Klan was very active in those parts, and it was an absolute necessity to see if there were any gatherings on Main Street.

W.D., Able, and Rose had broken a cardinal rule. Blacks did not live in the white part of town. Poor Jeanette, Able's wife, was scared to death; she didn't want any part of the move. She was worried sick they'd get their house burned to the ground. When she married Able, if she had

3

the slightest idea that he would do such an unheard-of thing, she would never have married him. All she wanted was a quiet life, and living among segregationists was not what she called a *quiet life.* Jeanette's nerves couldn't take it, and she grew to hate Able. After she presented him with a son, she made him build her a big Victorian house in what she called "her part of town," where she lived for the rest of her life.

Able built a big, white southern-colonial mansion with a wide front porch and graceful white columns running across the porch. Next door, W.D. and Rose had a large red-brick house built with a portico where the curved driveway led to a two-story brick garage with an apartment. A covered front porch became the gathering spot, where they enjoyed the cool of an evening on the porch swing. Ivy eventually covered the house and portico. By the time Mae and Booty sat in the front-porch swing, the pecan trees W.D. and Rose planted had matured, giving them a canopy of much-needed shade in the blistering Oklahoma sun.

Ellanor Tree's grandfather was among those furious to have his side of town—and especially his block—sullied with the likes of the Crutchfields. It was bad enough having the Hoovers next door, who made their living selling liquor. The Tree family owned the hardware store. Grandfather Tree put every dime he had into stock of a then-growing oil company that turned out to become international and one of the biggest in the country. He ended up owning so much stock that the chairman of the board came all the way from its New York City headquarters to Cedar Springs for his funeral. Grandfather Tree built an Italian-looking villa with a tile roof next door to the Hoover house. Everyone in town agreed that it was hideous, including members of the Tree family—except Grandfather Tree, who loved it. Ellanor, his brother Lorraine, and their first cousin Geneva McLish lived in the house. When she was thirteen, Geneva's father bought a brand-new Chris-Craft boat, in which he loved zooming around the lake. Everybody said that he was going to kill himself in it, and that's what he did, taking his wife with him. They were drunk—although no one would dare say that—and on the way back to the boathouse, they hit a sandbar. Her father went through the boat's windshield, slashing his jugular vein, and her mother flew overboard and drowned. After the accident, Geneva moved in with the Trees.

Cedar Springs slowly shrank from a once-thriving community of seven thousand souls to maybe one thousand, counting the people living relatively close on ranches and farms. There used to be two picture shows, a Kresses, a jewelry store, the Tree's Hardware Store, a clothing store, and a few other stores. All that was left of the original stores were Punky's Gas Station and Garage, Grovner's Grocery Store (which housed the post office), and the Whiz Bang Café. The first death blow came when the State of Oklahoma decided to build a new four-lane highway that bypassed the town. The nail in the coffin was a Wal-Mart built in Athens, the county seat fifteen miles away. Athens flourished as the local establishments withered and died, including the W.D. Hoover Drug Store.

★ ★ ★ ★ ★

Booty, Mae, and Ellanor visited on the front porch as the eye-piercing sun inched its way down the flat horizon. Silhouetted by the bright rays of the sun, the trees bent north from the ever-blowing south winds. Sometimes the sun appeared just like an orange with a pink-red hue. At other times, it resembled an egg yolk as it crept down the edge of the earth.

At the end of one particularly scorching August day, an orange-pink glow colored the air as the late summer sun gradually sunk down the horizon. Mae and Booty rocked slowly in the old swing, sipping tall glasses of iced tea while Herschel snored away under the swing. Ellanor sat in an old wicker chair with yellow chintz cushions. He was a tall man, and his feet easily rested on the brick railing on the porch. Mae always said that he was a nice-looking boy who had turned into a handsome man as he got older. Ellanor's curly black hair was turning silver-gray, and as much as Mae tried to fatten him up, he remained thin. A glass of iced tea rested on a round wicker table next to Ellanor as he gazed blankly toward Main Street. The day's news and gossip was already discussed and dispatched, so the three of them sat in the comfortable silence that only those who truly know each other enjoy. Birds flapped their wings overhead, their songs seemingly orchestrated with the oncoming evening. A cardinal was perched on a limb of a Japanese maple tree at the side of the porch. His head swiftly jerked around as if looking for something before he suddenly flew away.

Mae opened her eyes and looked around, awakened by something. "I heard someone."

"Who?" Booty asked.

Ellanor sat up in the chair and stared at Main Street. "What in the world?"

Suddenly a holler swept through the air. A man stood in front of a well-worn Honda sedan screaming at it.

"Who is that?" asked Ellanor.

"Who in the world can that be? I don't recognize the car. Do you, Booty? Who has a car like that around here? Surely, there are plenty. I just don't happen to recall one from here," said Mae.

Booty stared at the man and car and then shook his head. "I don't know who that is."

Without thinking, the three of them got up and started to stroll across the park with Herschel following.

"He's mad at the car," said Mae. "Why would he be mad at a car? I've been mad at my battery dying—in fact, I thought it was going to give me a flat-out nervous breakdown and made me late to the beauty parlor. Do you remember that, Booty?"

"I do," replied Ellanor. "You made me drive you over there because Booty had gone somewhere."

"That's right. Booty had gone to Oklahoma City just when my battery died. Mercy me—that man is certainly making a lot of noise."

The man leaned over the hood of the silver Honda, screaming obscenities. Occasionally he kicked one of the front tires. "Why do this to me—here of all places? Why? All these years nothing and ... What in the God damn hell happened? I hate you! Do you hear me? I hate you! You just stop? Here? In the middle of nowhere? You hate me, that's it. I'm being punished. Why now? Why *here?* Why couldn't you break down someplace civilized? Where I can get you fixed? God damn it! Where the fuck am I? God damn it! And it's hot! I'm hot! The hood is hot. I hate you! You did this on purpose. I know you did!"

He hauled off and slugged the hood as hard as he could. "Fuck! Ouch! God damn it! Ouch! I've broken my fucking hand! Ouch! Shit! God damn it! This is just great. My hand's broken! I'm hot! It's your fault.

Now I'm stranded with a broken hand. And I thought I'd like to drive the back roads. What a stupid idea! Never, ever again am I going to decide to sightsee. Why? Why here? God hates me, that's it."

He kicked a front tire as he screamed, "I hate you! Ouch! God damn it! I've broken my God damn toe! This is your fault!" He tried his cell phone again, and that didn't work either. Broken in spirit, hand, and toe, he put his head upon the hood and moaned, "God hates me. That's it. God hates me. My hand is broken. My toe is broken. The hood is scalding. Ouch! So what? It's okay; I'll just scald to death."

As they listened to the man's tantrum, Booty, Mae, and Ellanor unconsciously picked up speed, hurrying across the park.

"Booty …" said Mae.

"I still don't know who that is, Mae," answered Booty.

"No—no. I wasn't going to ask you that. Booty, who cuts the grass in this park? Does Pedro cut this grass? It needs cutting. This is a disgrace. Look at those flowerbeds. You can hardly tell where the flowers are because of the weeds. Remind me to walk over here more, because I couldn't see how bad it was. Children play here. Do you want children to play in a jungle?"

"Children play all the time in jungles in the Amazon," said Ellanor. "They're perfectly all right."

"Ellanor, I am not talking about children in the Amazon. Booty, who cuts this grass?"

"I don't know who cuts the grass," answered Booty. "Call Lucille. She'll know."

"I don't want to call Lucille. You call her."

"No."

"Okay, fine, be that way. I'm calling Pedro first thing in the morning to get over here as soon as he can and do something about this health hazard."

"Who's going to pay for it? The town doesn't have any extra money," said Booty, studying the man prostrate upon the hood of the Honda.

"Me, God damn it," exclaimed Mae. "It will be my personal charity."

"Fine," said Booty. "Come on, Ellanor, let's find out what's going on."

Ellanor and Booty picked up their pace, leaving Mae to bring up the rear.

"Hey!" Mae called after them. "Wait for me!"

The men walked up to the car, closely followed by the dog.

"God damn it!" moaned the stranger, not noticing the men and dog standing next to him.

Mae hurried up to Booty and Ellanor, panting and out of breath. "My God, it's hot. Let me catch my breath. Now … who is this man?"

Mae's voice got his attention. He turned his head and looked at them. "Thank God *someone* lives here."

"Of course someone lives here. Where do you think we would live?" asked Mae.

"My car's broken down," he whined. "I can't get my cell to work. Why won't my cell work?"

Ellanor had on an ancient pair of Bermuda shorts and an equally old Lacrosse shirt. "The cell tower is being built. It's not finished yet, but soon. I wrote to the president of the phone company and told him we needed service here."

"Ellanor," said Mae, "I didn't know you wrote a letter to the president. Isn't that nice? Did you get an answer? He must be awfully busy."

"What's wrong with your car?" asked Booty.

The man gazed at the car and then at the tall black man neatly dressed in an Oxford cloth white shirt open at the neck, an expensive and well-cut navy blazer, equally expensive khaki slacks, and brown Italian loafers without socks.

"You're Oriental," said Mae.

The thirty-year-old man looked at the short, plump woman with unruly curly white hair, bright-pink cheeks, and sparkling blue eyes. She wore a light-blue linen dress that brought out her eyes. Her voice was high-pitched and happy-sounding. He took time to actually look at the three people staring at him.

"My car broke down," he whined.

"Where are you from?" asked the woman. "The only Orientals I know of run the Chinese restaurant in Athens, and I really think they're Vietnamese—not real Chinese at all."

"What? My car broke down."

"Where are you from?" insisted Mae.

"Is it always this hot here?" he asked.

"You're certainly not from around here, honey, if you think *this* is hot. This is nothing. Why, you can fry an egg on the pavement some days." Mae put her hands on her generous hips while looking at the man.

"All I want—" he started to say, practically in tears.

"—Is a drink," interrupted Ellanor. "Let's go back to your house, Mae, and have a drink."

The Oriental man glared at Ellanor like he would enjoy killing him. "No. I was going to say—all I want is a mechanic." He stopped himself from screaming.

"Yes, I thought that's what you wanted," said Booty.

The man looked at Booty, grateful for the only sane one of the group to whom he could talk.

"Yes," he gasped. "I want a mechanic. Is there one here?"

The three of them answered, "Yes."

Mae and Ellanor said, "There's Punky."

Booty said, "There's me."

After Booty said that, both Mae and Ellanor stared at him with their mouths open.

"What?" said Mae. "Who did you say?"

"Me," answered Booty with great authority. "I can repair his car."

"Since when?" asked Ellanor.

Booty glared at Ellanor. "Why do you think I keep a garage for repairs at Punky's? How can you say that to me after all these years?"

"Easily," said Mae.

Booty didn't bother to respond to Mae. He held out his hand to the man. "Booty Crutchfield. This is my friend Ellanor Tree and my wife, Mae."

The man stared at Booty astounded. "Your wife?" *The well-dressed man was married to the plump, nosey woman? Amazing.*

Mae straightened up and glared at the man. "And why not, I ask you?"

He was tired and hot and mad. All he wanted was to get his car fixed and get out of this town.

He looked at Booty, shaking his hand. "My name is Eiji Takezo."

"What?" exclaimed Mae.

"It's nice to meet you," answered Booty. "I'm sure you'd like to get your car to the garage so I can get started on it."

Eiji wanted to weep in relief. He found someone who could help him. "Yes."

"What kind of name is that?" asked Mae.

Relief swept through him as he realized a reprieve from being stranded here was at hand. He almost felt giddy with the prospect that maybe by tonight, he could be on his way.

"What?" Eiji asked Mae.

"I asked you, what kind of name is that?"

It took a moment to understand what Mae was asking. "Japanese."

Immediately Ellanor said, "I saw *The Seven Samurai*. There was a Japanese film festival on PBS. Are the Japanese always committing suicide like the Swedes? Slicing across your stomach such a mess—don't you hope they do it outside? And just think of the smell …"

Mae interrupted. "Ellanor, please—no one wants to think about smells. So what did your grandfather do in the war?"

"Mae!" exclaimed Ellanor. "I can't believe you asked that!"

"Really, Mae!" Booty agreed. "This is a guest. How could you ask a thing like that?"

Eiji was so shocked at Mae's question that for a moment, he forgot about the car.

No one had noticed the tall, lanky, gray-blond man stroll up. "What happened to your car?" Lorraine asked.

"Good God, Lorraine!" said Mae holding her heart. "You like to have scared me to death. Don't creep around like that. You could have caused me a heart attack."

"This is Lorraine Tree, Ellanor's brother," said Booty. "Lorraine, this is Eiji Takezo."

"Ah," said Lorraine. "Japanese. What did your—"

Before Lorraine had a chance to ask, Booty interrupted and took charge. "Okay, let's get this car to the garage and see what the problem is. I'll just go up the street and get a tow truck, and we'll get your car to the shop."

"I'm sure Punky's there. He's always there because of the poker game," said Lorraine.

"We don't need Punky," said Booty. "I'll take care of the car."

"What?" Lorraine couldn't understand why Booty would say such a thing. He was prepared to say exactly that when Booty interrupted him again.

Booty steered Eiji over to Mae. "Mae, why don't you take Eiji home? I bet he'd like some supper. Wouldn't you? Wait until you taste Mae's cooking. Have you eaten dinner? You go with Mae and Ellanor. Lorraine, are you going with them too? Don't worry about a thing. I'll get the tow truck and look over your car once it's at the garage. We'll find out what the problem is."

Eiji looked desperate. He didn't want to be left alone with Lorraine, Ellanor, and Mae. "I'm fine. Why don't I go with you, Booty? Maybe there's something I could do to help."

"No. No. No. Don't worry about a thing. You've had a hard day. The sun's going to be going down in a bit. You go on home and let Mae get you some of her good fried chicken we had for dinner. You'll like it, I promise. Relax a little bit, and I'll be back in a while. Mae, you all take him home and take good care of him—and *no* talking about World War II. Do you hear me? He's tired and hot. Probably a nice shower would help, then a good dinner. You'll feel all better later. Where's your bag?" Booty opened the back seat and grabbed what appeared to be an overnight bag.

"I think he needs a drink," said Ellanor as he took the bag from Booty. "God knows I do."

"I'll join you, Ellanor," said Lorraine, strolling over with them across the park. "Mae, is the bourbon on the front porch, or do I need to go in the house to the bar?"

Mae glanced over at Lorraine like he was crazy. "Is the sky blue, Lorraine? Of *course* there's bourbon in the wicker cabinet. Honest to God, you've been in your bedroom too long."

Eiji watched helplessly as Ellanor held his bag. "I don't think I'll need that."

Mae put her arm through Eiji's. "Of course you will; don't be silly. You surely don't want to sleep in those dirty clothes." She led him through the park to the big red-brick house covered in ivy as Herschel trotted alongside them. She then deposited him in one of the wicker chairs with yellow chintz cushions on the front porch. "There you go. Now you get nice and comfortable. Ellanor, why don't you take the bag back to Grandmother's cottage? And Lorraine, do you think you can see fit to make this poor thing a drink while I fix his dinner?"

Both men did exactly as Mae directed. Ellanor opened the front door and headed through the house and the back yard to the cottage, while Lorraine strolled over to the wicker cabinet next to the round wicker table. Mae scurried into the house followed by Herschel.

"What would you like to drink?" asked Lorraine, looking through the liquor cabinet.

Eiji fell into the comfortable chair and realized how tired he was. "What is there?"

"Whatever you want."

"Vodka?"

"Sure. I think I'll have Jack Daniel's myself. How do you want it?"

"Over ice with tonic, if she has some."

"How about just over ice. The tonic must be inside in the bar."

But Eiji didn't have time to say anything. Before he knew it, Lorraine thrust a tall glass of vodka over ice into his hand. He flopped down in the chair next to him with his drink. "Cheers."

Eiji wasn't used to drinking vodka straight; he almost gasped when he drank it. "Good God, this is strong!"

Lorraine had no problem swigging down the bourbon and was rattling the ice in his glass. "This hits the spot. I feel better."

Just as Eiji managed to get his down, Lorraine grabbed his not-quite-empty glass and refilled both drinks. "There you go," he said as he handed Eiji the glass. Eiji looked at the full glass and didn't feel well. It had been a long day. He was hot and tired and hungry. All he had eaten was a hamburger from someplace he had stopped early in the day.

Mae came out holding a silver tray. "Here you go, honey. I know you're hungry, and this will make you feel all better. Can I get you something to drink? Iced tea? Or would you rather stick with your drink?"

"No, iced tea, please." Eiji stared at the plate, which looked delicious. Sitting on the plate was fried chicken, mashed potatoes covered with cream gravy, green beans, and a fresh homemade roll dripping with butter. He dug in as if starving. It tasted wonderful. Eiji had never tasted such food. He loved it.

Ellanor walked out the front door as Eiji started eating.

Lorraine asked him, "Do you want a vodka over ice?"

"Sure," answered Ellanor.

"Here you go," said Mae, handing Eiji's vodka over ice to Ellanor.

"Thanks," said Ellanor as he sat on the wicker chair on the other side of Eiji from his brother. "Mae, did you make your chocolate pie?"

"I certainly did, but I want to give our guest a little more food before we have dessert. Here honey, let me get you just a tad more."

Eiji consumed a second helping of everything before Mae handed him a piece of chocolate pie with meringue.

"Oh dear God, you make the best chocolate pie, Mae," Lorraine exclaimed as he wolfed down his piece.

Once Ellanor and Mae took care of the dishes, everyone sat on the porch, replete. It had gotten dark, and Booty still wasn't back. Eiji leaned back into the comfortable cushion, feeling well fed and sleepy. He didn't know if it was the vodka, the wonderful dinner, or Mae's soothing take-charge attitude in regards to his well-being, but whatever it was, Eiji felt decidedly better. Originally he thought he was going to have a nervous breakdown being stranded in this place with a broken-down car. Now, it wasn't so bad—at least not for one night.

Surely by tomorrow, he hoped, Booty would have his car up and running. *Maybe I'll stop in the next large town or wait until I got to a city and finally get rid of the old Honda,* he thought. He had had it since undergraduate days and through Harvard Law School. He should get a car more appropriate for an investment banker at his family's New York City bank, which specialized in Pacific Rim countries.

Except he was not an investment banker at the moment. He did not have a job. He had refused a transfer to the home bank in Japan. After graduating from law school, he went directly to the New York bank where he had been—until he got into a fight with his father. All of his life, Eiji obeyed his father. His father chose the boarding school and then told him he had to go to Harvard, which he did, never arguing. Eiji knew he was being groomed to succeed his father as the head of the family bank in New York. He would have membership in the same clubs and donate to the same charities.

He knew the real reason for the transfer. He would learn about and meet the correct people at the home bank. His uncle would make sure he established a relationship with the right business and political leaders in Japan. Living there would perfect his language skills. All that was true, but the real reason was that his father expected him to make the appropriate marriage. Eiji's heir must be Japanese if he were to head up the bank. His father followed his grandfather's demand by marrying and bringing to America the correct Japanese woman. She knew her duty, too: she produced Eiji. Then she divorced, left the infant Eiji with his father, and returned to Japan, having nothing to do with either of them again.

This was perfectly fine with baby Eiji's father, who then married a good-looking, socially well-connected blonde from Greenwich, Connecticut. They produced their own family, where Eiji felt like a visitor.

This time it was too much. When his father told Eiji that he was being transferred to the home bank in Tokyo, run by his uncle, Eiji refused. His father was furious, his stepmother was furious, his uncle was furious—in fact, the whole family was furious. He had two choices: go to Tokyo or quit the bank. To everyone's surprise (including his own), he quit. Until that moment, Eiji had fully expected to follow in his father's footsteps, but something happened. He suddenly had the realization that before he agreed to spend his life at the family bank with the chosen Japanese wife, he'd better discover what he wanted. He walked out of the bank on Wall Street, went to his apartment, packed a bag, got into the Honda, and drove out of New York City with no idea where he was heading.

"Ellanor," said Mae quietly, "I think we need to get this boy back to the cottage and into bed."

Mae took Eiji's arm and led him through the backyard to a surprisingly charming cottage nestled among a bunch of big pecan trees behind the house. It was covered with climbing roses and looked rather out of place in Oklahoma. The cottage seemed more suited for an old English village. Mae's grandmother had seen the cottage in a movie and wrote to the movie company asking for pictures. The movie company sent pictures, and she had it duplicated at the back of the large backyard.

He entered a quiet, air-conditioned house and dutifully followed them into the bedroom. Mae turned down the queen-size bed and fluffed the down pillows. Ellanor put Eiji's bag on a luggage rack. Eiji sat on the bed watching Mae put fresh towels in the bathroom and ready the house for him.

"I think you have everything you need," said Mae. "Come on up to the house in the morning whenever you wake up. 'Night. Come on, you all, and let him get a good night's sleep. You'll feel better in the morning, honey."

It took a while after they left for Eiji to get the energy to get up from the bed and take a nice, long shower. He was asleep the minute his head hit the pillow.

★ ★ ★ ★ ★

It was a little after ten when Mae saw Eiji strolling across the St. Augustine grass that looked like a rich carpet. Squirrels played chase through the limbs of the old pecan trees, jumping from one tree to the other. The shade of the trees cooled Eiji in the dense heat as he walked from the cottage to the ivy-covered house.

"Good morning," said Eiji. He stood in the kitchen, not knowing what to do.

"Here, honey." Mae pointed him toward the oval dining table and matching chairs that had developed a warm patina from decades of loving care. Long windows going nearly from floor to ceiling overlooked the backyard. "Let me get you some breakfast."

"I'm fine—really. I don't think I'll have time for anything," replied Eiji.

"Nonsense. I've baked these cinnamon rolls this morning." She placed a basket of fresh rolls in front of him. A place was set and waiting for him. A silver service set with butter dish, a creamer and sugar, and salt and pepper shakers sat in front of him. An old-fashioned, very English-looking plate covered with painted pink and red flowers with a matching cup and saucer waited to be filled. She poured coffee and asked, "Can I fix you an egg, honey?"

Eiji reached for a cinnamon roll, which felt warm to the touch, and took a lob from the softened stick of unsalted butter. He plopped a large bite into his mouth and muttered, "Oh, my God."

"Scrambled or fried?" asked Mae, to which Eiji could only nod with his mouth full of the cinnamon roll.

After a breakfast of scrambled eggs, bacon, and three cinnamon rolls, Eiji felt like he had to be rolled onto the front porch, where Mae wanted to sit a spell.

The covered porch was cooled by big, twirling fans and shaded by trees and a huge crepe myrtle bush filled with raspberry blossoms. Colorful pots overflowed with white geraniums and purple and pink petunias, with white alyssum falling over the sides. Hanging baskets of flowers dotted the ceiling. Wicker furniture that looked as old as the house with its yellow chintz cushions invited one to stay awhile. Mae led Eiji to a wicker chair, and once he was seated and comfortable, she strolled over to the wood swing. Herschel took his usual place under the swing and promptly fell asleep. Eiji propped his feet on the brick porch railing, barely able to breathe, he was so full. He could have fallen asleep except for the ear-splitting creak of the swing. He thought that if had the energy, he would get up and oil the damn thing, but he didn't have the energy. He was too full to move. The swing and the songs of the birds accompanied by the whirl of the fans were all he heard until even the hideous noise of the swing could not keep him awake any longer.

He woke up with a start to see a tall, thin man coming up the porch stairs. Mae sat on the swing (which thankfully was not moving), talking softly to a man sitting next to her in a wicker chair. The dog was no longer under the swing. He had moved inside the air-conditioned house and was sitting at one of the long windows, watching the happenings on the front porch. Eiji recognized both men from last night but couldn't recall their names. He was groggy from his nap and hot.

"Mae, you need to water your flowers," Lorraine said, strolling up the stairs. "What are you all doing sitting outside? Herschel is the only one with any sense—he's inside. It's too damn hot out here."

Mae looked at Lorraine. "This must be a record. Out of your bedroom two days in a row? And I wasn't about to leave our guest alone outside."

"I don't see any reason to sit out here and roast just because there's a guest," said Lorraine heading to the front door.

"That's just what I've been trying to tell Mae," Ellanor agreed. "Come on, Mae. Let's get inside before we all melt."

"Hello," Eiji said softly as one does when they first awaken.

"Oh good, he's awake," said Ellanor, walking over to Eiji. "Come on. We're heading indoors to cool off before we all die of heatstroke."

"Ellanor," said Mae, getting out of the swing heading into the house, "that's not likely to happen."

Each fell into the closest chair he or she could find, which happened to be in the living room. Forget making it through the big house to the den—the living room was there and comfortable.

Eiji's skin burst into goose bumps going from the heat of the sun into the cold of the living room. He felt chilled as he sat down in the blue silk chair. Suddenly he wished he had a sweater to go with his pink Polo shirt, his khakis, and brown Italian loafers without socks. He had gotten up dressed to hit the road in his car and so far had not even made it to his car—yet.

Everyone except Eiji was used to going from the glaring heat into the dark cold in the house. All had taken their seats either upon the couch or a chair, enjoying the pleasant cold chilling their skin.

"I've been up at Punky's," said Lorraine.

Mae shot a quick look at Lorraine that said, "shut up!" but it was too late.

Eiji remembered Punky's was the name of the garage. He immediately sat up, taking an interest in the conversation.

"Did you?" he asked. "How's my car coming along? Is it ready?"

"Dear me," said Mae in a worried tone. She nervously patted her curly white hair and straightened her skirt.

Eiji was so focused on Lorraine and his car, he didn't pay any attention to Mae.

"Well ..." Lorraine stammered.

Suddenly Eiji felt completely refreshed and not in the least bit chilled.

"I don't see any need to sit around any longer. I appreciate everything you have done, but I need to be on my way. I'm going on to Punky's and settle up. Thank you so much." Eiji almost jumped out of the silk chair and was on his way out the front door.

"Wait a minute," said Lorraine.

Mae's hand covered her mouth, and her eyes got big. She looked back and forth from Lorraine to Ellanor to do something.

"Where are you going?" asked Ellanor.

"Punky's," answered Eiji.

"You don't know where Punky's is," Mae reminded him.

Eiji was out the door, down the steps, and aimed toward Main Street, which meant crossing the overgrown park, with Lorraine, Ellanor, and Mae in hot pursuit. Mae was in the rear because she had the shortest strides and because she had to get Herschel back into the house. He had to stay in the air-conditioning. Mae deemed it entirely too hot for a long-haired, shaggy dog, and he was commanded to remain at home.

"Wait for me," she called out as she hurried as fast as she could across the park.

"You don't know where you're going," proclaimed Lorraine.

"This is a small town. I'll find it." Eiji headed across the park with Lorraine and Ellanor walking with him and Mae holding up the rear.

They got to Main Street, where Eiji stopped, so they stopped too. He looked up and down the street, trying to spot a sign for the garage. His hands went to his hips in frustration.

Looking both ways and not seeing any hint of a direction, he huffed. "Well, God damn it!" He glared at them. "Okay, where's Punky's?" He started to turn.

"It's not in that direction," said Lorraine. He was taller than Eiji, and with his long nose, gave an impression that he looked down on him.

Eiji was in no mood for any silliness. "Where, then? Must be this way?" He jerked his head in the other direction.

Before anyone answered, Eiji zipped around, heading in the direction of Punky's Garage. Lorraine and Ellanor followed close behind with Mae following.

"You all!" she shouted breathlessly. "Wait up before I have a heart attack in this heat. Must we walk so fast? It's too hot to walk this fast. You all slow down."

No one slowed down to wait for Mae. Rather, the odd-looking troop stormed up Main Street, which fortunately for Mae wasn't that long. A sign, most unprofessionally hand-painted in big red letters on what had now become a dirty white background reading "Punky's Gas and Garage" stood in front of them.

"There!" exclaimed Eiji.

"Uh ..." uttered Lorraine.

"You all wait up. Wait for me!" Mae's small feet worked as hard as they could to catch up with them.

"Uh, Eiji," said Lorraine, "you can't expect Punky to stop his poker game just for a car."

"I don't give a damn about a poker game—besides, Booty said that he was going to fix my car."

Two ancient gas pumps straddled the cracked cement drive under a drooping cover at the once-white gas station. A tilting tin sign, hung in the filthy window, advertised Dr Pepper in flowing script. The station looked abandoned. Eiji walked into the front office, hastily followed by the rest of the group, with Mae in the rear. The office looked like it had never been cleaned. Decades of dirt and dust covered everything. A dusty roll-top desk with yellowing papers stacked all over the place took up most of the back wall. A wood swivel desk chair, permanently leaning back, sat in front of the desk. Over the desk, a calendar with a picture of a pretty, smiling blonde girl leaning back in a one-piece bathing suit and an open white mink coat teased the viewer with an ice-cold Dr Pepper in her hand. The page had never been turned past January 1959. Against the filthy front window stood a grimy glass counter, littered with assorted junk. A door stood ajar behind the office. Waves of thick cigarette and cigar smoke mixed with the smell of whiskey continuously lapped from a back room. The loud clunk and chug of the hard-working air conditioner could be heard among the clamor of men's voices and poker chips.

Eiji looked around in revulsion at the room and the odors as Mae, Lorraine, and Ellanor took the lead. He followed them through a side door from the filth of the office into a large, immaculately clean, and air-conditioned garage. Eiji felt like he had entered into a sterile operating room, because everything was so pristine and bright. Mae, Lorraine, and Ellanor just stood there as Eiji looked around the garage for his car. It took a moment for him to realize that the neatly arranged parts placed so carefully in concentric circles were the remains of his car. The skeletal body graced the center of the circle. It could have been some bizarre modern artwork, except it wasn't. It was the Honda—or what was left of it. Eiji's hands leapt to cover his mouth in horror. His eyes bulged wildly.

Eiji, who always was in control no matter what, suddenly lost it. He started screaming hysterically and then did something he had never done in his entire life: he fainted dead away. Fortunately, Ellanor was standing close by and caught him before he slammed into the concrete floor. He gently laid Eiji down.

Mae immediately rushed to Eiji all in a flutter. "My God! What have you done to this poor boy? Is he alive? You could have killed him. Yes, you could have. This is all your fault, Booty. All! I told you, don't you *dare* experiment on his car. I said as clear as day to get Punky, but noooo, you wouldn't listen. You were so sure you knew exactly what to do and refused to listen to me. Yes, you did. You flat-out refused. You didn't listen to one word I said to you last night. I knew you wouldn't. I knew it as well as I know my name. And now look what's happened! At least he's still breathing."

"I'm shocked," Ellanor agreed.

"What are we going to do? I am worried sick." Mae wrung her hands. "What are we going to do? Should I call an ambulance to come over from Athens? We don't know anything about him! Wonder if he has a heart condition? On the other hand," she said, considering her options, "let's look on the bright side. If he had a heart condition, don't you think we'd already know, because he'd be dead? What are we going to do?"

"I don't know," said Ellanor.

"Nothing," Lorraine interrupted. "He's fine except for the shock."

They stood over him, pondering the situation and shaking their heads. Booty, however, was staring down at Eiji with a confused look upon his face.

"I don't understand," said Booty. "What's wrong with him? I don't get it. Why is he so upset? It's just a car. It can be fixed."

"Do you think he's in shock?" Ellanor asked Mae.

"I don't know," said Mae.

"Why is he so upset?" Booty said. "I thought I had done a good job! I did do a good job. You have to take things apart before you can put them back together again."

"I told you so, Booty!" exclaimed Lorraine. "When I saw this mess this morning, I told you he was going to be upset. I said that Eiji is really, *really* going to be upset. Didn't I tell you that? Yes, I did tell you that, and I was right."

Ellanor looked at the prostrate body and said, "Well, Booty, now let's think about this for a moment. I may be rash, but I believe that when people take their car in for repair, they expect it to be returned to them in one piece. I think you surprised the boy."

"*Surprised* the boy!" Lorraine agreed. "*Surprised the boy.* That's the world's greatest understatement. It's amazing he didn't drop dead of a stroke or heart attack or something."

"Bless his heart. He took it awfully hard," said Mae. "Don't you think so?"

"Took it awfully hard?" Lorraine said. "His car is scattered all over the garage in pieces."

"It's not scattered," said Booty firmly. "I know where every piece is located."

"I'm sure you do, dear," Mae said and patted Booty's arm. "You did a good job taking everything apart so neatly."

"Thank you," said Booty. "I tried to be careful. I noted where every piece was."

Eiji remained flat on his back on the cool cement of the garage floor, muttering, "It's a disaster. What am I going to do? What am I going to do?"

Ellanor leaned over Eiji. "Do you have a headache?"

"Horrible. It's horrible," Eiji answered in a weak voice.

"Your headache is that bad?" asked Ellanor.

"That too," moaned Eiji.

"He's got a headache," Lorraine agreed.

"My car," Eiji whimpered.

"Yes. It is your car," Booty said proudly.

"My car is ruined," said Eiji.

"Your car is not in the least bit ruined," said Booty. "I know where everything is."

"His car is in pieces all over the floor. What do you think he's going to think?" exclaimed Lorraine.

"I know where every part is," Booty repeated firmly.

"Shut up, Lorraine," Ellanor commanded. "You're just upsetting the poor man."

"I'm not upset," said Booty.

"I wasn't talking about you. I know you're not upset. I was talking about Eiji. He's upset!" snapped Ellanor.

Eiji whimpered. Tears rolled down his face. "I am going to die," he muttered. "Maybe I already have died. Maybe this is hell. Maybe I've died and gone to hell! What did I do to deserve this? What?" He was pounding his fists upon the cement floor. "I even stayed a virgin after …"

Sudden silence descended upon the room. All ears turned toward Eiji. He felt the strength of their glare. Slowly Eiji turned his head and peeked at Ellanor, Lorraine, Booty, and Mae through his bloodshot eyes. They were leaning down intently, waiting for his next words. Eiji peered up at them as a turtle would dart his head to see above his shell. "Aha!" he exclaimed. "Now I have your attention!"

"How dare he tease us like that! We've been tricked," Lorraine fussed, clearly offended.

"So what happened? You remained a virgin after what?" asked Ellanor, trying to be casual and failing.

"Aha!" Eiji said again. "You're not interested about my car. You're interested in my virginity!"

"Not really," said Lorraine.

"I am," said Mae.

"I'm certainly interested," said Booty. "I love your car. I'm going to do everything I can to put it back together again."

"I bet that's what all the king's horses and all the king's men said when they tried to put Humpty-Dumpty back together again," said Ellanor. "We love that egg, and we are going to do everything we can."

Booty slammed his hands on his hips and whipped around to Ellanor. "How dare you presume that I cannot put this foreign—"

"Really, really? *Foreign?*" Lorraine interrupted.

"Shut up, Lorraine. Don't you even think about upsetting this poor young man any more than you already have," said Mae.

"I didn't mean to upset him!" exclaimed Lorraine.

"Shut up, Lorraine!" said Mae.

"Don't tell me to shut up! You're always telling me—you, of all people—to shut up. I'm not going to shut up."

"Typical," said Mae.

As if Booty had not been interrupted by Lorraine and Mae, he continued, "This foreign *car* will go back together again."

"No one is paying the slightest bit of attention to me," Eiji said before he burst into tears. "Why won't anyone listen? Why?"

"Oh my," Mae said with great concern, "I don't think he's feeling the least bit well. Perhaps we should get him some medical care?"

"My car … my car …" Eiji repeated and repeated. He occasionally interrupted his chanting about his car with fits of screaming.

"I think he's hysterical," said Booty.

"You know, there is an excellent vet on the road between Cedar Springs and Athens," said Lorraine.

"That's Herschel's vet," interrupted Mae. "He's wonderful. What a bedside manner! Why can't doctors have such bedside manners? Sometimes I honestly wonder if my doctor knows what my name is if he didn't see my face with it. I told the vet that he ought to treat humans, and he told me he couldn't because he was a vet, like that has something to do with it."

"I've been trying to get him to treat me for years," continued Lorraine. "He does have a wonderful bedside manner. He took such good care of Puppy. I'll never forget when he neutered Puppy. I don't think Puppy ever forgot it either. I nearly had a nervous breakdown. I begged him for tranquilizers, which he refused to give me. I never understood why not. Why couldn't he slip me a few? Why not? He said that they were for animals. So what? I reminded him that I was an animal! Didn't I rate? And the vet said no! I thought it was the end of me until I remembered Ellanor. Thank God Ellanor keeps Valium around to sleep. I don't know what I would have done."

"So! It was *you* who took all of my Valium!" said Ellanor. "You lied to me. You told me that Puppy had eaten them. I wondered why that dog didn't die."

"He did die." Lorraine was almost crying.

"He died of old age," said Booty.

"My little Puppy," whined Lorraine.

"You needed a pole vault to get into the living room. That dog loved to lie at the front door," said Ellanor.

"You never liked Puppy!" cried Lorraine.

"Yes, I did," said Ellanor. "It was just that you didn't prepare me for his size."

"I want to go home. Please. Please fix my car," Eiji was weeping. "It's in pieces all over the floor."

"We know it's in pieces all over the floor, dear," said Mae. "We can see that."

"I know where every piece is," said Booty proudly.

"You see, dear," said Mae, "it's all right. Booty knows where every piece is."

"How did I know you were so ignorant about dogs? It's not my fault you didn't know how big an Irish wolfhound was." Lorraine screamed, "I loved Puppy. I still love Puppy. I'll never get over his death. Never!" Lorraine started to sob. "I'm going to get another one."

"No, you're not," Ellanor said calmly.

"I can't believe it. I can't believe it," moaned Eiji.

"Believe it," said Mae. "I don't think that Ellanor will ever allow Lorraine to get another Irish wolfhound; although, I have been wrong about Ellanor and Lorraine's doings before."

Eiji looked up at Mae with anger in his eyes. "I was talking about my car."

"Why don't you get a normal-size dog?" Ellanor snapped at Lorraine. "It is not necessary to have a dog you can ride. Just put a horse in the living room and be done with it."

Lorraine sobbed louder. "I loved my Puppy. It's my money, and I can buy whatever I want to with it."

"That's right, dear," Mae comforted Lorraine. "If you want another Irish wolfhound, you go on and get it. Ellanor was just kidding."

"I was not!" said Ellanor.

"Shut up, Ellanor," said Mae. "Puppy was Lorraine's only companion. That dog was the only thing that ever loved Lorraine. Now if he wants another one, he can have it. So you just hush up. Do you hear me?"

Eiji had begun to pull on his hair, moaning, "Why me? Why me?"

Mae unclenched Eiji's hands from his hair. She said, "You're going to mess up your pretty hair if you keep this up."

"I want my car in one piece. Please!" said Eiji. "Is that asking too much? Is it?"

Mae bent over him and patted his back. "Honey, let's change the subject, shall we? You're getting awfully upset, and you could get yourself sick with worry. Did you ever have a dog growing up? Did your dog love you like Puppy loved Lorraine?"

Upon hearing Mae talk about Puppy, Lorraine sobbed. "I am getting another dog. I am, no matter what you say, Ellanor. I never liked you, and I loved Puppy."

Eiji sat straight up, nearly knocking Mae over. "What are you talking about?"

"All I ever had was Puppy, and he died."

"Of old age. The dog died of old age," Ellanor interrupted. "And as a point of interest, I don't like you either."

"God help me. God help me," moaned Eiji. He had returned to his prone position on the floor. "I'm in an insane asylum."

"The only person I can think of that has been in an asylum—and we like to think about it as 'going away for a little rest'—is Mother," said Mae thoughtfully. "I think that's all, although one can never be absolutely sure with people from Cedar Springs. They tend to suddenly disappear and then reappear later."

"They usually term it 'taking the cure,'" said Booty.

"That's right," Mae agreed. "Taking the cure."

"Your mother is the only person I can think of at the moment," Ellanor agreed. "Don't hold me to it that she's the only person from Cedar Springs. I'm quite sure, in fact, that she's not."

"I want to go home," moaned Eiji. "I want my car fixed, and I want to go home."

"Just a moment, dear," Mae said to Eiji. "I have to talk to Lorraine and Ellanor. How is it I remember your mother was one of those that suddenly disappeared and then pop— reappeared? I recall quite distinctly that you said at the time that she had just gone away for a little rest. And didn't she *accidentally* die with the car running in the garage shortly after she returned? I was just wondering that's all. Seems a little too coincidental to me."

"No!" Lorraine interrupted. "It wasn't her fault. Anyone could forget to open the garage door. It happens."

"Oh, really?" said Mae. "That's not what Geneva told me, and she was very much there at the time."

Eiji started crying.

"How dare Geneva talk out of school like that!" Ellanor's face turned red. "My mother took her in when her parents got drunk and killed themselves—"

Mae's hand immediately went to her open mouth. "Ellanor Tree, that is the worst thing I have ever heard! How can you say a thing like that about Geneva's parents? Really! I am shocked—*shocked!* You know better than that. Her parents *accidentally* got drunk and got into a boating *accident* where they *accidentally* got killed. It was not their fault."

Ellanor glared at Mae. "They died! How about that? Anyway, that wasn't my point. My point is, this is the way she thanks us, by gossiping!

You just wait 'til I get home. I have something to say to Miss Geneva McLish, and don't think I don't."

"Now come on, you all," Booty interrupted, speaking to Mae and Lorraine. "How many years have we gone over and over about this? Poor Mrs. Tree died. How she died, I think, we can agree to disagree and let it go."

Eiji quietly whimpered. "I've had a nervous breakdown. I've gone crazy. That's all there is to it. I'm crazy."

"We should all be so lucky," Lorraine said to Eiji.

All of a sudden, Eiji was overwhelmed with anger. "Why am I here?"

"Because you are, and that's all there is to it," said Mae.

"Makes perfect sense to me," Booty said.

"We have all asked ourselves the same question. Why are we here?" Ellanor wondered. "And how did I get stuck with this crazy family, none of whom I like, including you, Lorraine?"

Eiji said, "I accidentally drove into some madhouse. Why didn't I just stay on the main highway? Why? AAA could have taken the car and me to a proper mechanic, and everything would have been all right. Fine. Fixed. Done."

"Well, that's a fine thing to say after all the work I've done," Booty interrupted. "Your car is going to be better than new when it leaves here. The worst-case scenario is that we sell it for parts and get you a new car."

"My car!" shouted Eiji. "It's my car, and it's ruined—lost in some hinterland in Oklahoma. That's it."

"I wouldn't go quite that far, dear," murmured Mae. "You're not lost in Oklahoma. You're here with us. We know where you are."

"I don't want pieces of a car. I want a car."

"Of course you do, dear," answered Mae. "There's nothing to worry about. Everything is going to be all right. If Booty can't put your car back together again—"

"Which he can't," interrupted Lorraine.

Mae whipped around, glaring at Lorraine. "God damn it, Lorraine! Shut up! Now, hush!" She returned to Eiji, and in a soothing voice, continued. "As I was saying before I was so *rudely* interrupted, if Booty

27

can't put your car back together again, he'll buy you another one. Won't you, Booty?"

"Certainly. I wouldn't leave you out to dry," said Booty.

"Booty wouldn't leave you out to dry," echoed Mae.

"I don't feel well," said Eiji.

"I'm sure you don't," said Mae. "Let's get you back to the cottage and to bed. You'll feel all better in a couple of days. You've just had a slight shock. You're going to be fine. And who knows? Maybe Booty can get the car back together again … although I wouldn't hold my breath on it. Come on now. Let's get you up and out. A little air will do you good and then some nice bed rest. A shock can be a very emotionally draining thing. I know. I can't tell you how many shocks I've had in my life, and look at me. I'm just fine. You'll be fine too."

Eiji barely remembered being led by Ellanor and Lorraine on either side of him with Mae, as usual, taking up the rear, to the rose-covered cottage where he was about to spend several days in bed, in shock.

Chapter 2

After three days in bed, with Mae hovering around attending to his every need, Eiji emerged from the cottage. He did not feel any better about being stranded in Cedar Springs. Mae told him to treat this like a little vacation. He tried but found it hard to do. To Eiji's surprise, the library at the house was jammed from floor to ceiling with books he actually wanted to read. It was also where they watched TV. While Mae did whatever she did during the day, Eiji lay on the leather Chesterfield couch, either reading or watching a baseball game. Lena, who did for Mae, came daily during the week for however long she wanted or needed to keep the house clean. Many a day, she joined Eiji in what everyone called the den (but what Eiji called the library) to watch baseball games with him. Lena smoked, and whenever she wanted a cigarette, she would say that Herschel needed to go to the backyard. Poor Herschel went outside a lot, which he did begrudgingly in the heat.

Many an afternoon, Mae would come home after doing errands, and the three of them would enjoy an afternoon watching baseball instead of Lena and Mae's usual soap operas. Lena and Mae were old friends. Lena's mother had done for old Able Crutchfield after her aunt got too old. Although the neighbors never accepted an African-American family daring to live on their block in the white part of town, it was perfectly all right for the black help to be there in their crisp white uniforms. When Lena, Booty, Mae, Ellanor, and Lorraine were little, she used to come over with her aunt from what was then called Colored Town. She played with the kids while her aunt did for Mr. Able. By the time Eiji joined Lena and Mae in the den, they had known each other a long, long time.

For many years, the Crutchfield Oil Company was run out of three floors at the bank building downtown. When stores started closing in Cedar Springs, including the bank, Able had to make the terrible decision to move the company to Athens. He hated leaving Cedar Springs and decided he wouldn't go. Instead, Able built a long, two-story, red-brick building with Crutchfield Oil Company in large gold letters next to the glass double doors. It was on what was then the outskirts of Athens toward Cedar Springs. He put T. Bob Starkey, Sr. in as his president, but he kept complete control as CEO. The heart of the company was run out of part of the first floor of the southern colonial house that Able had converted into an office. When Booty returned home to run the oil company, he took everything Able had in Cedar Springs over to Athens to consolidate the company in one place. At the mansion in Cedar Springs, Booty started and ran the Crutchfield Foundation.

T. Bob Starkey, Jr. succeeded his father and ran the Athens office. Blair Mason worked as Booty's secretary and second in command in Cedar Springs at the foundation. Since Booty became so consumed with Eiji's car, T. Bob and Blair took care of all the business.

One day, when Booty was home for lunch with Lena, Mae, and Eiji, Eiji asked over dessert, "Booty, how is the work going on my car? Have you asked Punky to come in and help you, like you said you would?"

Booty looked insulted. "I don't need Punky. Why do you think I would need Punky to do something I can do?"

"How are you doing?"

"Fine."

"Any chance the car could be ready by the end of this week? I really need to get going."

Lena had gotten up to get the bowl of whipped cream. "Here, honey," she said while putting a dollop on Eiji's strawberry shortcake. "You're going to like this. These are fresh strawberries Mae picked up at the farmers' stand. Do you like strawberry shortcake?" She put dollops of whipped cream on the others including hers, and sat back down.

"Hmm? Booty, what's going on?" Eiji was close to begging.

Lena interrupted Eiji. "I asked if you liked strawberry shortcake. Do you? Do you have it where you're from? I always wondered if they ate it in the East, haven't you, Mae?"

"Yes, I have. Do you think they make it with Bisquick, like we do? Do they?" asked Mae.

Eiji realized they were talking to him. "What?"

"Booty," asked Mae, "you going over to Athens this afternoon?"

"No!" interrupted Eiji. "He's not. He said that he would work on my car. I don't think you understand that I *have* to leave. Is my car going to be put back together again or not? If not, I have to go wherever it is you go and get another car—like now."

"I do need to run over to the office. T. Bob, Jr. called this morning, and there are things I need to look at and discuss with him. Why?"

"Wait a minute! You said that you were going to work all the time on my car!"

"I bet you want some of that good barbecue, don't you?" said Lena. "Marvin does the best barbecue."

"Why don't you run over to Marvin's," said Mae, "and get us some brisket and biscuits, their potato salad, and what else? Oh—don't forget to get a lot of their sauce."

"Wait—" Eiji tried to get a word in and failed.

"Don't forget their cole slaw," said Lena.

"Oh, that's right," Mae agreed. "Do pick up cole slaw. What about their peach cobbler?"

"Wait—what about my car?"

Mae patted Eiji. "Honey, your car is just fine. Don't you worry about one thing. Anyway, where are you going that you are in such a hurry to get to?"

With Mae's question, everyone stopped and stared at Eiji, who looked back at them in complete surprise. He had no idea that they were actually listening. Then, when Mae asked his destination, Eiji's mind went completely blank.

"Well?" Mae asked.

Eiji looked at Mae, Booty, and Lena waiting for his answer. He felt like an idiot, because nothing, absolutely nothing came to his mind. It was as blank as a blank wall. "Uh …"

Mae crossed her arms and waited a moment. Her curly white hair bobbed with her tapping toe. "There. You see? You don't know, so we might as well decide about dessert. Now, do you mind having strawberry shortcake again—Lena, is there enough for tonight? Or do you want peach cobbler?"

Lena shook her head. "Pick up the peach cobbler. I think I'll take the strawberry shortcake home to Jack for dessert tonight."

"But, wait a minute," begged Eiji. He needed to think of something. He couldn't just leave it this way with him not answering about a destination.

"Okay," answered Booty as he got up, "I'll see you all later."

"Don't forget anything," Mae reminded him. "If you think you're not remembering everything, just give me a call."

"Wait!" pleaded Eiji.

"Don't forget the peach cobbler," Lena said as Booty walked out the back door.

"Bye," he said as the door slammed behind him.

"Oh my God," whined Eiji. He put his head down on the table and moaned.

Mae puckered up her pink lips and shook her head. "Really! I don't understand you. I don't understand you at all, not one little bit. You said you were driving around the country, and that's exactly what you're doing now—except the driving part, of course."

Eiji nodded, "But—"

"I'm going down to the cottage and get your clothes to put in the wash," Lena said as she headed toward the back door. Herschel, thinking she was going out to smoke, started to get up to go with her. "Herschey-boy, you just stay where you are. I'm just going to the cottage and will be right back."

"Wait a minute! You don't need to do that. I still have some clean clothes," said Eiji. "I'll be leaving soon." But Lena either wasn't listening or didn't care, because she walked on out the door anyway.

Eiji watched the large black woman in the starched white uniform head for the cottage. Mae left the table heading toward the den, where she expected Eiji to follow.

Eiji looked around the table, alone. Even the dog got up and followed Mae out of the kitchen. He couldn't believe what just happened. What was he going to do? What about his car? Here he was in wherever-he-was in Oklahoma, stranded. There was a phone, but who was he going to call? His father was too mad at him for leaving the bank and taking off on what he called a "foolhardy trip." His father was not about to come get him someplace in Oklahoma. He crossed his arms, staring blindly out one of the back windows. He saw Lena heading toward the house with an armful of clothes. He sighed, pushed away from the table, and slowly followed Mae into the den.

★ ★ ★ ★ ★

Late summer evenings were filled with sounds of birds, insects, and the incessant calls of frogs. A crepe myrtle bush overflowing with raspberry-colored flowers covered the corner of the house. Mae kept a cut-glass pitcher filled with iced tea on the wicker table. Also on the table were cut-glass bowls of sugar, sweetener, sprigs of mint, and plates of sliced lemons and oranges. A gray cooler that looked like a Greek column filled with ice sat on a smaller wicker table next to the larger one.

A Japanese maple danced in the light breeze, while a cardinal hopped through its branches. Blue jays busily flew around and then stopped on a branch of a tree, only to take off again. Somewhere, doves were cooing, and the smell of freshly cut grass floated through the air. Eiji, Mae, and Booty sat on the front porch as they usually did after dinner, enjoying the evening cool. Herschel took up his position under the creaking swing. Sooner or later, Ellanor strolled over. Since Eiji arrived, Lorraine would also come to complete the party on the front porch. The evening star finally twinkled as dusk set. Mae had commanded Pedro and his crew to clean up the park, including the baseball field. Now there were the sounds of kids squeaking during the final game of the day in the fading light.

"Don't you think the honeysuckle smells nice? I love the fragrance of honeysuckle." Mae pulled off a flower from a branch growing up a porch column and around the porch railing. "We used to do this as kids. Don't you all remember when we did this?"

Ellanor had taken his chair on the porch next to Eiji. "Mae, you still are doing it."

"Ellanor, you know what I mean." Mae wanted to ask Eiji, except she had a terrible time pronouncing his name. Every time someone corrected her, she immediately forgot. He had without doubt the most difficult name to remember, much less pronounce, of anyone she had ever met. It was terrible trying to talk to someone whose name you couldn't pronounce. She couldn't keep saying "you" or nodding to him. Plus, it was getting embarrassing. She decided something had to be done about his name and to keep him in Cedar Springs.

Mae was sure that this Oriental man had to stay here. Having his car in concentric circles at the garage Booty rented from Punky helped matters considerably. At first, Mae didn't consider him staying, and then it occurred to her that he was, which was when she decided something had to be done.

She had a nice long chat with Booty about it, and he took it from there. Last night in bed, Booty reported what had been arranged and left it up to Mae to do the rest—like inform Eiji. That was why Mae was so fidgety. Booty knew how nervous she was and sat back and enjoyed it. He told Mae she was sticking her nose into their visitor's business and that he wanted to leave. "No—he doesn't," Mae told Booty firmly. So Booty sat back and watched.

"Who wants some more iced tea?" asked Mae.

Everyone mumbled that they were fine.

Lorraine lazily pointed back in the direction of the iced tea. "Mae, we'll get it. You've got a full pitcher there."

Mae looked over at Booty and gave him what she called "her look." He simply smiled back.

"Okay, fine," she said to Booty as she hopped out of the swing, startling Herschel.

She put her hands on her hips. She wore a pretty light-blue summer dress. The light blue in the dress accented her sparkling blue eyes. In her high, innocent-sounding voice, she said, "Well, I don't know about you all, but I need a drink."

"What?" a chorus of Eiji, Ellanor, and Lorraine replied.

Booty continued to smile, not saying a word.

"Booty!"

"What?" he asked Mae. He knew she was waiting for him to do something, like help her.

"All right for you," she said to Booty and then smiled at everyone else. "How about a splash of bourbon in your iced tea?"

"Okay," said Eiji.

Mae went over to the wicker chest that housed the outside liquor and opened it. "Who finished off the bourbon out here and forgot to tell me so I could bring out some more?" She glared at Lorraine and then to Ellanor and back to Lorraine. "Hmm?"

"I don't know," answered Lorraine. "Probably me."

"Yes, I'd say probably you too," said Mae. She stormed into the house and grabbed a fifth of bourbon from the bar in the den.

Lorraine and Ellanor stared after Mae.

"What in the world is going on with Mae?" Lorraine asked as she zoomed into the house. "Did someone die and I don't know it? It has to be someone I like, or I'm not going to the funeral. Mae knows I won't go."

This wasn't like her at all. She drank but she never *announced* that she *needed* a drink! Something was going on. Lorraine and Ellanor wondered what it was. Ellanor sat at the end of the line of wicker chairs in another ancient Lacoste shirt, Bermuda shorts, and loafers without socks. Next to him was Eiji in what had become his uniform: a Polo shirt with the shirt tail out, blue jeans, and sandals. Closest to the corner railing of the porch sat Lorraine in a white Oxford cloth shirt, blue jeans, and brown lizard cowboy boots. Eiji did not know this was out of character for Mae and wondered why everyone was surprised. A drink certainly seemed like a good idea to him.

Booty decided he was pushing it with Mae. He got up to hold the door open as she flew out with a fifth of Jack Daniel's. She zoomed over to everyone's chair and if their glass was too full, poured iced tea over the porch railing into the grass, and filled it with bourbon.

"Thanks," said Eiji as Mae grabbed his glass out of his hand. She poured more than half of his iced tea over the railing and then quickly filled it to the brim with bourbon.

"What a good idea," said Lorraine.

Mae went over to the wicker table and grabbed some sprigs of mint and plopped them into the glasses. "Here," she said to Eiji, Ellanor, and Lorraine; then she strode over to the swing, where she did the same for Booty and herself. After slugging down a good half of the drink and then refreshing her glass with more bourbon, she sat back.

"Now that's better," she announced to no one in particular.

Ellanor looked over at Mae. "Mae … what's going on?"

She smiled a coy smile.

Lorraine immediately picked up on that and sat up in his wicker chair. "Okay, Mae, what is it?"

"What is what?" asked Eiji, oblivious to what was happening.

"We need topping off. I'll get it," said Ellanor, getting up and heading to grab the Jack Daniel's. "Somehow I think we're going to need it."

Everyone sat for a while enjoying their drinks, just about to resume enjoying the evening sounds. Just about—until Mae decided it was time.

"Here's what I was thinking," said Mae a little too loudly.

Lorraine leaned into the other two men. "Here it comes."

"Here what comes?" asked Eiji.

Booty smiled like a Cheshire cat.

"Well, I was thinking …" Mae started again.

Ellanor shook his head. "Oh, God! Mae's plotting. When she said that we needed drinks, I knew it. I knew something was up. I can't believe I'm actually asking this. Mae, what have you been thinking?"

"Here's what I was thinking. I can't pronounce your name," she said, pointing to Eiji.

"My name?" he asked.

"Yes, your name. It is entirely too difficult, and I'm sorry to say this and hope I'm not hurting your feelings … but it must be changed. And that's all there is to it. There. I feel all better—don't you? You see, Booty, I told you this wasn't going to be difficult, and it wasn't the least bit. He understands perfectly—don't you?"

Ellanor, Eiji, and Lorraine all sat up and stared at Mae like she was crazy.

Eiji looked at the other men. "What is she suggesting?"

"Mae," said Lorraine, "that is the dumbest thing I have ever heard."

"Lorraine, I am sure that's not true. You have heard much dumber things, but that is irrelevant. The point is this man's name that I can't pronounce must be changed."

"Why?" asked Eiji. "Why does she want to change my name?"

Ellanor could not figure out what Mae was talking about either. "Why? Mae, who really cares that you can't pronounce Eiji's name? You're the only one. The rest of us are doing fine."

"Ellanor, you simply don't understand. I don't give a damn about that. It's not my fault it is so … foreign. But you see, it *is* so foreign. I suppose it could be worse, although nothing pops into my mind what it could be. Maybe something Russian or one of those long Slavic or Polish names or from someplace that doesn't believe in vowels. I can't ever figure out how to pronounce those. The point is his name is simply not easy to say, and that is that. Who knows how to pronounce it? I don't."

"We do," answered Lorraine.

"You don't count," said Mae very firmly. "You know him."

"I don't get what she is talking about," said Eiji. "Mae wants to change my name? There's nothing wrong with my name, and anyway, I'm not changing it. I don't even know why we're having this conversation."

Mae rocked in the noisy swing. "Well, your name certainly isn't John Smith. Now that's easy to pronounce."

"What?" asked Eiji. "John Smith? What does John Smith have to do with it?"

Mae's face turned a slight shade of red. "None of you are listening to me. I don't understand why you don't understand. Really! I am surprised at all of you except Booty, who knows exactly what I'm talking about—don't you, Booty?"

Ellanor looked at Booty, pleading, "Come on, Booty, help us out here. What the hell is Mae talking about?"

Booty realized that he had to enter the conversation if it was to get anywhere. "Eiji is going to teach at Lincoln School."

"What!" exclaimed Ellanor. "I have never—Mae, you've had some crazy ideas, but this one tops everything. Mae —"

"That is the craziest thing I have ever heard," interrupted Lorraine.

Ellanor nodded in agreement. "It certainly is."

"What's Lincoln School?" asked Eiji.

Lorraine looked at Booty and nearly shouted, "How could you let her do this?"

Booty shook his head. "You know Mae. Once she has her mind made up, nothing is going to change it. Believe me, I tried. I told her, but forget it."

Ellanor joined in. "Booty, the school board allowed that harpy Marva Wrightsberg to talk us into hiring her no-good son Bobby to be principal, of all things. Now you want us to hire Eiji—who has probably never taught school in his life, and—" Suddenly Ellanor turned to Eiji. "Have you ever taught school?"

"What? No! I haven't taught school, nor have I wanted to teach school, nor have I thought about it. Why are you people talking about this? I never asked anyone about a teaching job in my life. Teaching? Where did that come from?"

Ellanor continued as if Eiji had not said one thing. "You have a college degree, I assume."

"I told you I went to Harvard, then to Harvard Law. I don't understand what you are talking about. I'm a lawyer and a banker. I work in my family's bank, or I did, and might again. I don't know!"

"That's why we have to change his name," said Mae. "If I can't pronounce his name, children certainly won't be able to."

"Jesus Christ, Mae!" said Lorraine. "This is ridiculous."

Ellanor nodded in agreement. "It certainly is. Booty, I don't understand how you could have allowed this to happen."

"Children?" said Eiji. "What children? Why did she say children? I don't know any children, and all the children I knew are grown up. If I ever would consider teaching, it would have to be at the college or graduate level. I might consider that, depending on what it is."

Booty shrugged. "I told you I tried. I said that, and Mae wouldn't listen."

Mae jumped into the fray. "Since he's staying anyway, I told Booty that he might as well do something, and this would be a perfect opportunity for Lincoln and for him."

"Stay? I'm not staying!" pleaded Eiji. "The minute my car is fixed, I'm leaving. Who said I was staying? I didn't say I was staying. I never meant to stay. I never meant to break down here either—that was the last thing I wanted to do."

"But you see, dear," implored Mae, "you *are* here."

Ellanor looked at Eiji. "Lincoln is a grade school."

Eiji's horrified eyes grew big. He stifled a scream. "Oh my God!"

Ellanor continued, "It's where we all went and our parents and grandparents for that matter." He casually pointed in the direction of the school. "I suppose it was nice enough as grade schools go—I guess. I really am not one to comment upon grade schools."

Lorraine drank the rest of his drink. "You're right, Mae. We did need a drink. For the record, I think we'll need a little more." He got up and did his best to walk in a straight line to the bottle, which he grabbed. He made it back to his chair after pouring more into each drink. "There, that's all better. Lincoln hasn't changed one bit, except the new windows and the air conditioning, which was an act of mercy. Oh, there's the new auditorium. I can't quite recall what else, because I don't give a damn, although the air conditioning was an absolute necessity."

"I'm leaving," announced Eiji. "Don't you hear me? I'm leaving. I'm leaving."

"No, you're not, dear," said Mae quietly.

Lorraine asked Mae, "Why Lincoln? How did you ever get the idea of his teaching at Lincoln?"

Ellanor interrupted by pointing out, "Mae, Eiji doesn't have a teaching degree." Turning to Eiji, he continued, "You're a lawyer. Since when does a law degree count as a teaching degree?"

Eiji looked at each of them like they were daft. "Wait a minute! I did not kill myself making Harvard Law Review to teach in some grade school. You can't imagine how hard it is to make the Law Review. It was God damn hard. Forget about having some sort of social life! Well, I did, but it was God damn hard. You just don't know. What am I doing? Why am I explaining this? Oh my God—this is too much, just too much. I don't ever want to teach in some grade school. Why would I accept a job teaching in a grade school when I didn't want to be sent over to the bank in Tokyo?"

Mae sat up when she heard that. "Ah! That's it. There you go. You didn't want to go to Tokyo, so here you are."

"Here I am what?" asked Eiji. "Jesus! This is making my head ache."

"No," shrugged Lorraine, "the bourbon is giving you a headache. I may be getting a little headache myself. Maybe I should hop inside the house and find some aspirin. Although I'm really not sure I can get up."

"So how is he going to teach grade school with a law degree and banking experience?" Ellanor casually asked Mae.

"Really, Ellanor. You don't have to be so rude. Don't you think I've considered all this? Number one, Lincoln is a private school, if you remember. The state had the nerve to close our school. I'll never forgive who decided to do that. It was terrible—terrible! Then, to make matters worse, they announced everyone had to bus over to Athens. Well, that was not going to happen. Everyone with half a brain knows that a town without a school dies, and that's the truth. Naturally, you never bothered to attend the town meetings."

"Yes, I did too!" interrupted Ellanor. "Lorraine refused to attend because he refused to recognize Cedar Springs as a town."

Lorraine leaned over in his chair, pointing at various people as he spoke. "If you recall, I said to hell with Cedar Springs. Let the God damn town die or fence us in, because there's nothing but crazy people here anyway."

"Now that's the truth," said Eiji. "There are nothing but crazy people here. Just fence the God damned place. That's where I've ended up. Me, who killed myself to be on Law Review. It's pitiful."

"Now don't say that, Ellanor—and you too, Lorraine," said Mae. "How can you say that? I'm ashamed of you. I'm glad your mother is dead."

Lorraine nodded in agreement. "So am I."

Mae shook her finger at Lorraine. "Now you listen to me! Billie Rae was one of the sweetest women I ever knew. How she put up with that bore of a father of your all's I'll never know. She was a saint—maybe a slightly crazy one, but a saint no less—and anyway, no one is perfect. Who are we to call anyone anything like crazy?"

"Crazy seems the right word to me," moaned Eiji. "This is crazy."

"Don't be silly," Mae said to Eiji. "Now, as I was saying before I was so rudely interrupted by whoever it was—don't you all remember how the town took over the school, and that law firm in Oklahoma City who handles a lot of Booty's stuff did whatever they did, so now Lincoln is a private school that all the kids in the area can attend for free like a public school, except it's private? It saved our town. Like I said before and I'll say it again—a town without a school dies, and it does."

"Let it," burped Lorraine.

"Shut up, Lorraine," snapped Mae. "You're drunk."

"I am not!"

"Hush!" snorted Mae. "Now I've forgotten what I was saying!"

"About the kids ... oh, I don't know what!" said Booty. "I think we should all go to bed."

"No," said Mae, "I know what my point was. He is perfectly capable of teaching grade school because I have all of Blanquitta's teaching journals and stuff. All he has to do is just read what she did and simply do that. Blanquitta taught for years. She knows everything. If he can read, he can teach."

"Where's Blanquitta going?" asked Lorraine.

"She's pregnant."

Lorraine nearly fell out of his wicker chair. "You're kidding? Is he blind?"

Mae completely ignored Lorraine. "Blanquitta and the nice, skinny, rather unattractive choir director from Athens with that terrible lisp—you know, what's-his-name—are getting married, and she told Lucille that she wants to stay home and raise a family. It's what she's always wanted, bless her heart. I'm so thrilled for her. No one thought she would ever find a husband with that overbite of hers, but she did. I always wondered if Blanquitta had some sort of thyroid problem, because her eyes were kind of popped, but she's all right, sort of. I wish her hair was better, and her nose and skin aren't too good either, come to think of it. Her personality isn't the best, I'm sorry to say. She's always so cranky. I don't know why. Other than that, she's fine."

"Please," snorted Lorraine, "I don't care what you did to her hair. It wouldn't help that much. I'll tell you what—one look at Blanquitta, and you can't question evolution. She is the spitting image of a fish with those big bulging eyes. However, she does play the organ well. I'll give her that."

"Lorraine, really!" exclaimed Mae.

"Who is Blanquitta?" asked Eiji.

"Blanquitta Nelson," answered Booty. "She teaches sixth grade."

Ellanor continued, "She's part of the Pawn clan. Her mother was somebody's sister. I can't quite remember. It all gets convoluted since everybody around here seems to be related to someone somehow."

"It's a wonder we all aren't walking around with two heads," said Lorraine. "Why don't I refresh our drinks? Mae, I assume there's more bourbon in the den? I really don't think I can make it all the way down to the basement where you keep the cases."

"How sweet of you, Lorraine," said Mae. "You know where the bourbon is."

Lorraine got up and poured off the rest of the fifth into Mae and Booty's glasses then walked as best he could into the house. He returned shortly with a full fifth, which he finished opening and pouring into Ellanor's, Eiji's, and his glasses. He then pulled out a bottle of aspirin from a pocket and handed it to Eiji. "Here."

As Lorraine poured bourbon into Eiji's glass, Eiji looked up and said, "I think they're trying to get me drunk."

Lorraine nodded. "Harvard paid off for you."

"So my point is," continued Mae, "he—whose name I can't pronounce—doesn't need a teaching degree to teach in a private school. There you have it. It's perfect."

"I don't even know children," said Eiji.

"So what," answered Mae. "No one does—maybe someone does. I really don't know. You'll learn, that's what. Don't worry about it. I'm certainly not."

"Why do you think I'm staying here?" asked Eiji.

"I haven't the faintest idea, but you are. What do you have to do that's so important that you can't stay here?" asked Mae.

"I don't know," answered Eiji. "But that's not the point. I don't want to stay here and teach at a school that contains children."

Ellanor leaned over to Eiji. "I'm sorry to break this to you, but all grade schools contain children."

"So what? You know what I meant." Eiji leaned back in his seat. "I'm tired. I need to take a little nap."

"Oh, no you don't," said Mae. "We need to get you a name."

"Who cares?" answered Eiji, obviously finished with the conversation.

However, Mae wasn't at all finished with the conversation. "I've been thinking."

"Oh, God," moaned Lorraine. "I should have known she had a name all this time. I may be drunk, but not that drunk. Okay, I'll play. What is it?"

"Eli Take," announced Mae. "It keeps the first initial of both of his names so it won't be that drastic and it is easy. Everyone knows how to pronounce Eli and Take as in, for example, to take a drink, which I think I will."

"I don't want anyone to change my name," announced Lorraine.

Mae glared at Lorraine. "Well, someone should have!"

"I'm not doing it," murmured Eiji.

Lorraine sat up as straight as he could in the chair. "Just what do you mean by that?"

"Think about it," suggested Mae.

"I have thought about it, and there's absolutely nothing wrong with my name. It's an honor to be named after my Grandmother. Better than being named after great aunt Ellanor like Ellanor is, who we all remember because no one thought the old bag would ever die. I don't remember grandmother very well but so what? My mother remembered my father's mother. She said that I'm named after the social doyen of Cedar Springs. Mother was quite proud of that. I don't give a shit, but Mother liked it. It's better than my middle name, Alfred."

"Lorraine, for Christ's sake, stop being so God damn huffy! Does everything have to be about you? I wasn't talking to you. I was talking to the Japanese man whose name is going to be Eli Take. Isn't that a nice name? It has such a nice short ring to it. Eli Take. Yes. That's just fine. I like it."

Eiji groaned. "A Japanese man. That's what you're calling me now?"

"Just think about it. Please. Eli Take is a good name, and I don't know anyone else who has it. It's very easy and pronounceable. Anyone can say it. Just consider it. That's all I ask," said Mae.

"No, it isn't," said Booty. No one seemed to hear him except Mae, who shot him one of her looks.

"I have to take a nap," said Eiji very slowly.

"Me too," Lorraine agreed. "I'm tired or drunk or both, whatever. I need just a little nappy."

A loud snore erupted from Ellanor. His arms were folded with his feet propped up on the railing and his head back against the cushion, sound asleep.

Mae had her mouth open to say one more thing. Before she had a chance, Booty said, "Let's let this rest for a while. Don't you think so?"

"No," said Mae, looking straight at Booty.

"Yes," Lorraine agreed. "Mae, we're tired."

Mae crossed her arms over her breasts and huffed.

Eiji leaned back in the old wicker chair and slowly looked around. Quiet descended upon the front porch. Mae accepted that for tonight, her argument was over, and she sat back in the swing with Booty.

"Might as well enjoy the evening," she quietly said to Booty.

He looked at her and kissed her head. "Might as well."

Multiple snoring sang from the chairs along with different murmurs.

Night overtook evening, but it was hard to tell since a bright full moon lit up the world in silver. Everything was so clear, a light wasn't needed to get around. Sounds of insects battled with frogs as stillness overtook the front porch except for the crack and creaking of the swing slowly rocking back and forth.

★ ★ ★ ★ ★

The Whiz Bang Café, Grovner's Grocery and Post Office, and Sister Ringer's were the remains of the local gathering places. Sister Ringer's beauty parlor held claim as the temple of all newsworthy gossip. The Whiz Bang and Grovner's were on their third generation of owners. Each had been passed down to either a son or daughter like a marathon baton. Sister opened her beauty parlor so many years ago that no one could quite remember when it happened. Everyone went to Sister's, and they were all concerned about Sister's bad knees. Because of those knees, her older daughter Merl was being forced to take over the shop. Even though they all loved Sister, the general consensus was that Merl was the all-around better beautician.

Anytime anyone new showed up, the whole town knew it. That's why the noon crowd at the Whiz Bang was abuzz. Of course, everyone knew about the Oriental man who was fool enough to let Booty work on his car. Naturally the car was in ruins; everyone knew that too, to no one's surprise. Booty Crutchfield could certainly make money, but repairing cars—which he claimed as his hobby—was quite another matter. This was the first time that anyone actually had a close look at the man living in the cottage behind the house. Everyone agreed that he wasn't bad looking at all—for an Oriental—and he was taller than they expected.

Along with the surprise at getting to see the Oriental, there was also the surprise of seeing Lorraine Tree. My God, no one had seen him much out of the house for years. Maybe an errand here and there, but as a rule, he stayed in his bedroom doing God-knows-what. Not that anyone cared. Still, it was a surprise to see Lorraine out. Everyone agreed that he didn't look white as a sheet like they thought he would from living inside for so long. He had good color, considering. Some people didn't realize he was still alive; they hadn't seen him in so long they thought he was dead.

Mae, Booty, Eiji (who Mae still insisted upon calling "Eli"), Ellanor, and Lorraine in one of the old, red vinyl booths were quite the sight to see. Seeing Lorraine again and supposing about the Oriental man livened up the Whiz Bang immensely. Dot sashayed over to the booth to take the group's orders.

Dot and LaMont got married right out of high school, and both worked at the restaurant. Dot's parents had inherited from her father's parents, and now Dot and LaMont owned it. Their grown kids worked there, along with a few older grandchildren.

Everyone thought Dot was the sweetest thing in the world, and she was. She smiled all the time. Her hair was dyed black, ratted up in a French twist with so much hairspray, a tornado wouldn't make a dent in it. Despite having so many kids, she never lost her figure and looked just as young as ever in her light-green waitress uniform.

LaMont started working at the Whiz Bang in high school and never left—except when he got drafted during the Vietnam War. Dot ran the Whiz Bang, holding a baby on her hip, until he returned. One of his daughters was helping him in the kitchen now. The beef came from one of the local ranches outside of town. Mae said that because LaMont and Dot kept everything as local as they could, everything was so good. Arguments abounded as to which was the best: LaMont's meat loaf or his fried-onion hamburgers. Mae agreed that LaMont made excellent meat loaf, but hands down, the fried-onion hamburger was the best she'd ever tasted.

"Hi, y'all," Dot said as she licked her yellow stub of a pencil and got her pad ready to take orders. "Ellanor, how on earth can you stand that long-sleeve shirt? It's so hot outside, you can fry an egg on the sidewalk. LaMont's made his coconut cream pie, so y'all be sure to save room for dessert." She turned to Eiji. "How are you honey? How are you enjoying our hot Oklahoma heat?"

"Uh ..." stammered Eiji, not knowing what to say.

"Ellanor," said Dot, "there's one piece of meat loaf left with your name on it. People came early today."

Ellanor smiled. "You know I can't pass up your meat loaf. I'll have iced tea. I don't want sweetened today."

"Okay," replied Dot as she looked around the table, waiting for the next order. "Mae, you want the onion burger cheese or no cheese?"

"Oh, I'll have cheese, and lots of pickles and mustard. How about onion rings and a chocolate milkshake too. Eli, I'm ordering you the same thing. Believe me, you have never tasted anything so good as LaMont's onion burgers. People from all over come here for that. The onion rings are homemade, just like the french fries and everything else here. Wait 'til you taste the milkshakes. Those Hamilton blenders have to be older than we are; I remember them when I came here as a kid. Dot, he'll have the same thing."

"Okay, that'll be just fine." She stopped a minute and held out her hand. "Isn't that nice, your name being Eli? I never knew that to be an Oriental name too. I thought it was from the Bible."

Eiji stared at Dot for a moment before it hit him that she was talking to him. "It's *not* an Oriental name."

"Oh?" said Dot, not really knowing what to say but trying her best to be welcoming. "Well then, where are you from?"

"New York."

"New York?" said Dot. She was obviously surprised by his answer. "Well, I'll swear I thought you were from someplace else like China. New York, isn't that nice. Is it hot there? I'll bet not like here. Nothing is as hot as here. It gets so hot here, you can't hardly stand it. So how long are you going to be staying with us?"

Eiji absolutely did not know what to say. Should he say that he's leaving as soon as possible, or would that hurt Mae's feelings? "I've got to—"

Booty jumped in, not wanting Eiji to finish his sentence. "Dot, I'll have the same thing they're having, except no onion rings."

As much as Dot wanted to continue questioning this strange visitor to their town, she'd have to wait. "Okay, Booty, what about french fries instead?"

"No, I'll just have the onion burger and a Coke."

"Lorraine, it's good to see you out and about. Haven't seen you in an age. What'll you have today? The chicken-fried steak is awful good."

"Dot," answered Lorraine, "I haven't had chicken-fried steak in a dog's year. Talked me into it. I want sweet tea."

"Okey dokey. Be right out for you all." She turned and headed to hand in the order.

"Have you ever tasted an onion burger?" Booty asked Eli.

"I've never heard of one."

Ellanor threw his head back and laughed. "You are in for a real treat. Wait. Just wait. You're about to taste a true American experience that'll bring the word *indigestion* to a whole new level of meaning."

"Ellanor," said Mae, "you're going to make this poor boy think that's true."

"It is true," replied Ellanor, "but who cares? It's worth it."

"Oh," said Eiji, worried about the prospect. "Indigestion? I really do get terrible indigestion. I have since I was a kid."

"Ellanor is just being ugly. Don't pay any attention to him," answered Mae. "You'll love it."

"Also, Mae," Eiji continued, "the waitress thinks my name is Eli, and it's not. People are going to think that is my name."

"They already think it," Booty interrupted. "You tell Dot something, and you've told the whole town. The Whiz Bang is almost as bad as Sister's."

Mae sat up at that. "Booty, it is not."

Lorraine nodded in agreement. "That's right. If you haven't heard it at Sister's, then it hasn't happened. The Whiz Bang pales in comparison."

Mae gave Lorraine and Booty one of her looks. "You all hush up. You don't know what you're talking about. Anyway, I wasn't talking to you. I was talking to Eli."

Eiji glared at Mae. He considered getting up and walking out. On the other hand, where would he go without a car? "Mae, damn it! Don't call me that! It isn't my name. It never has been my name, and it never will be my name. If you refuse to say my name, then just point."

Mae had her mouth open to say something back to Eiji. Booty decided the subject needed changing. "Who's that blonde girl over there with Bobby?" he asked. "I don't know her. What's she doing with Bobby? He's too old for her. He's the principal for the school. He shouldn't be with a woman that young. It doesn't look good for the school at all. Bobby looks old enough to be her father. What are the parents going to think, seeing the principal with a woman that young? I'm going to have Lucille call his mother. Who is that woman anyway? I think I've seen her before."

"You have seen her before," answered Mae. "She's a teller over at the bank in Athens. She always flirts with the men and talks a blue streak to everybody. Somebody told me who her family was once, but I can't remember."

"Well," said Ellanor, "that's not going to please the bank manager, because I've seen her out with Bobby too. She's not going to take kindly to one of her employees going out with the same man she's going out with."

Mae watched the couple as she talked. "That's probably why they're having lunch over here and not in Athens. Who's going to know they're here … except the entire town? The bank manager doesn't live or work over here. She could easily not find out unless someone tells her, and she doesn't go to Sister's. She could not find out."

Eiji wasn't the least bit interested in the man, who—in his opinion—didn't look old enough to be the blonde's father. He didn't know what the fuss was about, nor did he care. The guy seemed perfectly fine, conceited perhaps, but okay, as was the woman. The restaurant was full, mostly with women, and teeming with loud talking. With nothing else to do and not even thinking, he allowed his eyes to sweep slowly around the restaurant, more out of boredom than interest. He saw a paper already shuffled through and read sitting on a shelf above one of the booths against the wall. He thought about jamming his way out of the booth and getting it but then decided against it—too much trouble. His eyes continued to wander aimlessly, wishing lunch would hurry up and arrive so they could eat and leave. Women's laughter erupted from one of the tables where Dot was standing and talking. Eiji's mind snapped at her for wasting time and not getting out the orders. *It is a wonder anything gets done here with the slow pace people work,* he huffed to himself. *None of these people would have made it in the fast world of New York.* Maybe that was where he wanted to return, except he couldn't if he intended to stay at the bank. He had to go to Tokyo for an undetermined number of years. Maybe he should go on to Tokyo. Why not? What did he have to lose? And he had everything to gain, moving up the ladder in the family business.

Out of the corner of his eye, he noticed two women in a booth. One was older than the other, and judging by the way she talked to the younger woman, she was probably the mother. She was certainly telling her something that appeared important, at least to the older woman. Her hair was dyed too dark for her aging skin. Her eyelashes were too heavy. Were they false? Why would a woman her age wear false eyelashes? She was small and thin and focused upon what she was saying to the younger woman. Eiji's eyes went to the younger woman, and that is when something happened. He felt like he had been shoved or something. He wasn't quite sure, since he had never experienced anything like this before

49

in his life. Whatever it was, he forcibly stopped himself from gasping. What was happening to him? Yes. The woman was the most beautiful he had ever seen, with black hair, ivory skin, and flashing blue eyes. Internally, he felt quite shaken and he didn't know why.

"Who is the pretty woman with the black hair sitting with the older woman at that table?" he asked.

"I just don't like it," said Booty. "It's not good for Lincoln to have the new principal showing off at the Whiz Bang with that young woman. Now, why would Bobby do that? At least keep her over in Athens and not at the Whiz Bang, for God's sake."

"Booty, school hasn't started yet, so I don't know what the big deal is. I can't see what difference it makes to anyone except Precious and Maeva, and Maeva isn't here. Bobby's an adult—granted, an idiot one—but he's still an adult, and so is the bank teller. What girl, honey?"

"That woman sitting with the other older woman in the booth, over there." Eiji stopped from pointing but just barely. "The woman with the long, black hair pulled back at the nape of her neck."

"Mae," said Lorraine. "He's talking about Blair Mason. My God! There's Precious. I haven't seen her in an age. She looks good, and she's not an older woman. I'll have you know that 'older woman' is our age, so she's not *older*, because we're not older people. I don't consider us older. Do you, Ellanor? Have we become the older people? I don't feel like an older person."

Dot interrupted by putting each drink in front of the correct person. "There you all go. I'll be right back with everything."

"Thank you," Ellanor said. "Lorraine, when we were Eiji's age or about, we thought people our age were older because we're probably his parents' age, and they're older than he is. It's all relative. Think of Aunt Ida. She's nearly one hundred years old."

Lorraine said, "Ellanor, she *is* one hundred years old. The old bitch turned a hundred last year. I always said she was too mean to die, and she's proving me right. Anyway, Precious is keeping herself together. I'm glad to see that."

"So who is she, Mae?" continued Eiji. "Her name is Blair?"

Dot returned with an armload of plates, just as Eiji said that. "Who are you talking about? Blair Don?" Dot chatted as she placed the dishes in front of people. "Precious is mad as a wet hen, seeing Bobby with that girl from Athens. He should be ashamed of himself, bringing her here for the world to see. Here you all go." After finishing with the dishes, she quickly pulled a bottle of ketchup out of her apron pocket and placed it on the table. "Now, I think that's it. You all want anything else? Here, honey, let me help you." She leaned over the table and grabbed the tall, frosty, stainless-steel container and poured a thick chocolate milkshake into Eiji's tall glass. "You got a bunch left. Here you go." She handed him and Mae straws and iced-tea spoons.

Everyone looked at their plates, suddenly starving. Lunch looked and smelled wonderful.

"I think that's it, Dot," answered Mae. "We'll let you know if we need anything. Thank you."

"Sure thing," answered Dot, already heading away from the table.

"So who is she, Mae?" Eiji asked again.

Mae, like everyone else at the table, had started on lunch. "Honey, you have got to taste this."

Eiji took a bite, spurting grease down his chin. The cheeseburger was cooked with loads of fried onions. He had never tasted anything like that. "Mae, this is delicious."

"See, I told you you'd like it. How's your milkshake? It's a real old-fashioned honest-to-God milkshake."

Eiji could barely talk from eating, so he nodded.

"I'm so glad we decided to come here for lunch," said Lorraine. "I can't remember the last time I had chicken-fried steak and how much I love it. Now this is Oklahoma haute cuisine at its finest, with the real mashed potatoes smothered in cream gravy with the chicken-fried steak and a nodding of Le Sueur peas. Next time we come, Eiji, you have got to try this. Oh, my dear God, there is a heaven, and it is the Whiz Bang—with the exception of your house, Mae."

"You better have said that, Lorraine, or you wouldn't have been invited over again," said Mae with grease surrounding her mouth. "Aren't these onion rings to die for?" She dipped an onion ring in a bunch of ketchup on her plate, savoring every bite.

"Mae," said Eiji with his mouth full, "tell me about the woman with the black hair."

While plunging a forkful of meat loaf into mashed potatoes, Ellanor said, "She just lives down the street."

Eiji's eyes lit up. "She does?"

Ellanor's mouth was full, so he nodded and continued eating.

"Honey," Mae said while trying to mop up some of the grease on her face, "Blair Don lives at the house on the other side of Booty's with her mother, Precious. Precious is such a bitch, I can't begin to tell you."

"Mae," interrupted Lorraine, "that's not at all nice to say. I like Precious."

"Lorraine, you've always liked Precious. You don't count. Believe me, little Miss Precious loves one thing and that's money and social. That's why she's trying to get Blair Don set up with Bobby, God forbid."

"Oh, Mae," moaned Booty, "please don't tell me that."

"Well, it's true. I heard Maeva say so herself over at Sister's how much she and Precious would love to see them together. In fact, Maeva said just that—that she told Bobby how much she had always expected them to marry. I don't believe it. Anyway, I was disgusted. Honest to God, those women ought to leave well enough alone. I'm telling you Precious is crazy."

Lorraine snorted. "She is not!"

"Okay, fine, Lorraine. You've always been in love with Precious and blind as a bat when it comes to her. Go ahead and stick your head in the sand. I don't care."

"I don't want to talk about it," said Lorraine a little too quickly.

Eiji was determined to find out about this woman. "So she's not married?"

"Divorced," said Booty with his mouth full of one of Mae's onion rings. "She works for me at my house. She handles all the Crutchfield Foundation business and is smart as a whip. She's too good for Bobby Wrightsberg. Worked for me since she came back here after her divorce. I tell her she's too bright for here. She needs to move some place where there are people, and I don't mean Athens. She's got to be bored silly here. I mean away, but she's not interested. I think the fight has gone out of her. Precious wore her down, and I hate like hell to see it."

Mae finished off her cheeseburger and pushed the onion rings over to Booty to finish. She used her water glass as a finger bowl, sticking her fingers in the water and then drying them with a fresh paper napkin. "Precious Blair married that sweet stupid Don Mason, who I always liked. Why he married Precious, I'll never understand."

Booty interrupted Mae, "How about Don loved her?"

"Really, Booty—I thought you had more sense than that. How about Precious got herself pregnant?"

Lorraine gasped when Mae said that. "I don't believe it! Mae, you have gone too far. I'm surprised at you, saying that about Precious."

"Why?" asked Ellanor. "It's true."

Lorraine glared at Ellanor. "I don't believe it. You all don't like Precious, and that's why you're saying that."

"Fine, Lorraine," said Mae. "You just go on thinking that and don't find it the least bit strange she had a full-term baby and told everyone it was premature. Suddenly in the middle of her and Don's sophomore year at the University of Oklahoma, there's a quickly organized wedding. Come on, what were we when that happened? Seniors in high school? Do you remember, Booty? Oh, no of course you wouldn't remember—you were at boarding school in the East, but *I* remember."

"So do I," said Lorraine. "Don't you remember, Ellanor?"

"No."

"So she's divorced," said Eiji.

"No," answered Lorraine. "Precious is a widow."

Eiji looked at Lorraine like he was crazy. "I wasn't talking about Precious."

"I am," said Mae. "She wore a white wedding dress with bridesmaids and everything. I can't remember where the reception was, probably over at the country club in Athens because of the Mason family. Anyway, after Blair Don was born, I remember visiting with Precious. I'd gone over to see the baby, and I'll never forget Precious saying how glad that she got initiated into her sorority because now little Blair Don was a legacy. Give me strength! And then, what do you know, Don—who has always been healthy as a horse—is out walking on the ranch and out of the blue, drops dead of a massive heart attack. I'll tell you, it was shocking. There wasn't any history of heart problems ever in his family. When it's your time, it's your time, and that's all there is to it. So there's Precious left a widow with a two-year-old. Well, Precious moved back into town with her parents from living out at the ranch. She's been at the old Blair family home ever since."

Booty finished off the onion rings. "I know one thing: Blair Don told me that when her mother sold her father's portion of the ranch she inherited back to the Mason family, she didn't get the money she thought she should have gotten."

"Typical," sniffed Mae.

"Absolutely delicious." Eiji put his empty milkshake glass down. "Why don't they just call her Blair?"

Ellanor smiled. "People love double names here. I think they feel empty with only one name. Mother was Billie Rae. Why not Billie or just Rae? No, had to be Billie Rae. Now that's typical."

Booty looked over at Blair Don. "She's too good a girl to be stuck here. I tell her that, too. While you're still young, get out of here and go have a good time. Go back to Dallas or Oklahoma City. You know people there. Go have fun."

"You all finished?" asked Dot as she cleared off the empty plates.

Lorraine looked at Dot. "The only things we haven't eaten are the plates."

"You all ready for dessert? LaMont's coconut cream pie is awful good. One of my girls made chocolate ice cream this morning, and I can tell you for a fact, it is delicious. How about a little coconut cream pie and a scoop of chocolate ice cream? She also made strawberry pie with fresh strawberries. The peach pie is all gone. It's all good. You know that. What do you all want?"

Eiji was sure he was going to explode. He was so full, and everything had been so good, he didn't think he could get one more thing down. He was particularly surprised when, in spite of being stuffed, he ordered the strawberry pie.

"Coconut for me," said Booty. "No ice cream."

"Just the ice cream for me," said Mae.

"Me too, ice cream," Ellanor agreed.

"I can't believe I'm saying this. I'm so full, but I have to have the coconut cream pie," said Lorraine.

Finally, with everyone feeling stuffed, they headed toward the door. As they edged past a table with four women, the one with grayish-brown curly hair and bright brown eyes stopped them.

"Mae, honey, I'm so glad to see you," she said. "We're just all dying to meet your visitor. You've been hogging him all to yourself."

Eiji gazed at the group of women.

The woman didn't wait for Mae. She held out her hand, which Eiji shook. He was surprised at her strong, firm grip. "Honey, I'm Bunny Lou Hughes. Your car is all over the floor at my husband's garage. It sure looks like a big mess to me. What are you thinking about doing?"

Mae chimed in before Eiji could answer—not that he knew what to answer. "Oh, Bunny Lou, how's your foot doing? I saw you at the beauty parlor with your foot propped up, but I didn't have chance to say hello." She turned to Eiji and said, "Bunny Lou was out mowing her lawn and cut off a couple of toes, bless her heart." She returned to Bunny Lou. "But honey, you are doing just fine. I know how much you love to play golf. I sure hope it doesn't hurt your golf game."

Bunny Lou sighed. "I'm going to be off my golf for a little while, but I'm going to be fine. Would have been worse if I'd taken my big toe. I'm just doing fine. I've got my grandmother's snazzy cane here with a gold top, and I'm ready to go. Now, are you going to introduce us to your visitor or not?"

Just as Eiji was about to introduce himself, Mae jumped in. "You all, I want you to meet Eli Take. He's visiting us here from New York City, and I think he'll be staying a while. He might take over Blanquitta's place at Lincoln."

As Mae went through the women to Eiji, he missed their names entirely. He could not believe Mae had introduced him as that name he couldn't remember. To make matters worse, she told them he was staying and might teach school. He couldn't decide if he wanted to kill Mae or turn around and walk out the door. He could feel the heat rise in his face, stunned that she would do that to him. He didn't think he could talk civilly. That did it! He was for sure leaving this place as soon as he could. Booty had bought his car from him and put the money in the bank in Athens. He was going to tell Booty to take him to a car dealer in Athens. Then he was out of here.

Eiji turned to Mae, trying to control his anger. "Mae!"

Mae smiled at him, which made him madder. "Eli—Bunny Lou is Blair Don's aunt."

"What?" Eiji gasped.

"You were asking who she was," answered Mae. "I thought you'd like to know Bunny Lou is her aunt. You'll always be Bunny Lou Blair to me, Bunny Lou. I think we'll always think of each other by our maiden names. I don't care if you've been married a hundred years or a hundred times. It doesn't matter one bit. You'll always be Bunny Lou Blair to me."

Bunny Lou smiled. "Isn't that sweet. We'll have to make sure you all meet. Although you know her mother and Maeva are doing their darnedest to be matchmakers with Bobby and Blair Don."

"Are they really?" asked Mae, knowing full well that they were.

"How are you all?" asked Bunny Lou. "It's good to see you out and about, Lorraine. Seems like it's been an age since I last saw you."

Booty knew Eiji was mad. Mae had gone too far. He had to get them out. "It's nice to see you ladies. We better be going."

Ellanor, Lorraine, and especially Eiji were relieved to hear Booty retrieve them and get out of the restaurant.

While Bunny Lou and Mae were visiting, to Eiji's eternal horror and without the slightest warning, a huge, unmistakable, booming fart exploded from him. At first, he couldn't believe that he just emitted that. How did that happen? He would never do such a thing, and in public of all things with these women. He couldn't believe it. His first thought was thank God his stepmother wasn't there. He wondered if she had farted in her whole life. She was so controlled and proper.

Surely everyone had heard. How could one miss that unless they were deaf? But Mae and Bunny Lou's conversation did not miss a beat. They continued talking as if nothing happened, and he continued listening as if nothing happened. Eiji allowed his eyes to flash straight to a fat woman at the table wolfing down an onion cheeseburger with grease dripping down her double chin, who also appeared unaffected by Eiji's eruption. Hopefully, staring at her would divert their attention from him as the culprit. He could only hope.

Booty mercifully nudged the group to the door.

Bunny Lou looked at Eiji and said, "It sure has been a pleasure meeting you, Eli. I'll look forward to us seeing you again."

Eiji was still so mortified by his horrible fart that he forgot what Mae named him. He knew she was talking to him. He mumbled something about it also being a pleasure to meet them and nearly ran out of the door.

Eiji missed dinner that night, saying that he wasn't hungry, which he wasn't. However, the pain in his chest got so bad as he was lying in bed that he had to get up and get help. He walked as quickly as the pain would let him over to the house, where he discovered Mae and Booty still sitting on the front-porch swing. Fortunately, neither Lorraine nor Ellanor was there.

Herschel barked a moment as Eiji slowly walked out the front door. When the dog saw who it was, he returned to his nap under the swing's seat.

Mae spoke first. "Hi, honey, how are you feeling? Can I get you a little something to eat?"

Eiji stood there. When he heard the mention of food, he almost gagged. "No, thank you. I'm not hungry."

"Neither was I," answered Booty. "There's some tuna left. That's what we had—sandwiches. I could make you up a tuna sandwich. It's light."

Eiji stood looking at them and announced as calmly as he could, "I'm having a heart attack. I have to go to the hospital right now."

Booty and Mae stared at him until Mae finally answered. "You're not having a heart attack."

"Yes, I am," said Eli.

"No, you're not," said Booty. "You just need some Pepto or something. You'll be fine in a while."

"I have a terrible pain in my chest, and not to be too dramatic about it, I think I am dying. I am asking you to either take me to the nearest hospital or to let me take one of your cars and point me in the direction."

"Eli, I really don't think you are having a heart attack," said Mae. "Why don't you sit down, and I'll get you some ginger ale."

"Mae," said Eiji, doing his best not to lose his temper or start crying from the pain, "I am asking you to take me to a hospital. Do I have to call an ambulance?"

Booty and Mae realized that he was serious, and before Eiji knew it, he was on his way to Athens. They took Mae's big white Cadillac so Eiji could lie down across the back seat. He tried not to moan all the way, but each bump of the highway threatened to hasten his expiration. Mae went in with him at the emergency room door, while Booty parked the car. By the time Booty got to the emergency room, Eiji had gone back with the nurse.

He sat down with Mae to wait. "They certainly got him back fast. That's good."

She looked at him, shaking her head. "It's because he told them he was having a heart attack. That did it. The staff went into high gear and got him to cardiac. He didn't want me to go with him."

"We'll probably be here all night. Do you want me to see if I can find us some coffee?"

After about three hours, maybe a little longer, they were heading back to Cedar Springs. This time, Eiji sat up in the back seat with his arms folded. No one said a word on the return trip. When they arrived home, Eiji got out of the car first and headed toward the cottage.

As he strode across the yard to the cottage, Mae shook her head. "I told him it was heartburn."

Chapter 3

Even though Herschel thought it was too hot to sit outside and preferred to remain inside with the air conditioning, Eiji thought outside was nice. He sat under the whirling fans in the shade of the front porch. There always seemed to be a pitcher of iced tea in the refrigerator, which Eiji helped himself to. The pitcher, along with a glass of melted ice with some iced tea, sat next to Eiji on a wicker table. He couldn't remember the last time he had nothing to do and no place to be. His cell phone lay on the dresser, turned off and unused since his arrival. He could have made calls, since the cell tower was up and running soon after he arrived. Truth is, Eiji didn't care. Who would he call? And more importantly, why? No. He would just as soon sit on the front porch and read. Books were crammed into the bookshelves that ran across the walls, floor to ceiling in the den. Everything was comfortable, and that's what captured Eiji.

There was a whole bunch of mysteries, which Eiji was enjoying reading. Mae would ask him if he wanted to go with her someplace. So would Booty. No, he didn't. Lena was there during the week if he wanted to visit. He also had Herschel for company, except when the dog got capricious and wouldn't consider going outside until evening, except to do his business. Sometimes Ellanor or Lorraine would drop by, but mostly during the day, Eiji sat on the front porch. Many an afternoon, he'd watch the kids playing baseball, listening to their screams of excitement, or women strolling with the babies and small children across the street in the park. Or he'd simply stretch out on the wicker couch and take a nap.

All Eiji's life, he had been busy, going to school fall, winter, spring, and sometimes summer, or to camp as a child, or traveling, or something but always going and doing. At his family's rambling house overlooking the ocean in Maine where the water was cold and seals sunned on big rocks in the ocean, something was always happening—fun things, but things still. This was different. Here he knew only a few people, not the generations of people going to the same schools, the same places, sharing much of the same history. His world was rather like Cedar Springs—how people knew each other for generations and sharing much of the same history. In Cedar Springs, though, he was in a different world with none of the same people and none of the expectations. There was the big difference. It was why Eiji felt comfortable.

Mae drove into the driveway in her white Cadillac. Eiji smiled at the sight of Mae—who was not a tall woman—driving the big car. She called it her "tank," and it was. She zoomed all over the place in it. She waved at Eiji as she headed to the portico. Eiji got up to help her unload her purchases. He wandered through the house, heading to the side door and to her car.

Mae had the back door of the car open, grabbing packages. "I told you! You should have come with me to Athens. Booty and I went to this new place that just opened. I don't know what it supposed to be, to tell you the truth, I think it's Vietnamese, but they had Chinese food too. It was one of those buffets. I think it would have helped to get there early while the food is still fresh, although they did keep refilling. I had some lettuce-leaf something that you roll up in the lettuce leaf. Honey, I ate a bunch of those lettuce rolls. Did you see the ham sandwiches I left for you and Lena?"

"Yes. Lena and I had them for lunch."

"She was going to polish the silver, and I told her not to think about making lunch because that would be way too much trouble, especially doing the silver. No point in it at all, especially with that big ham sitting in the icebox. Just make sandwiches, I told her."

"She did. And potato salad."

"Perfect. That good butcher over in Athens got in some fresh lamb, so I got us a leg. We'll eat that tomorrow. If you don't mind, I'd just as soon finish off that ham tonight. I'm tired."

"That's why Lena made a bunch of potato salad and coleslaw, because she said you wouldn't want to cook. She said to finish off the pound cake. There's fresh strawberries and whipped cream for it."

"Okay. Oh, honey, I have done some shopping. I got a tad out of hand, but I couldn't help myself. It's not often you find things that just fit and you like. Mostly it's one or the other. You either like it and you can't get your fat ass into it, or you don't like it and damn it if it doesn't fit like a glove. But today things fit and I liked them. So what do you do? You get it, that's what. There's this really nice ladies' store where I thought I'd just drop in to see what they had out of curiosity—you know. It carries just as good stuff as you get in Oklahoma City at those expensive ladies' stores there or Neiman Marcus down in Dallas. Not everything, but enough."

Eiji helped her carry her things in, first to unload the groceries and then upstairs to the bedroom. He put the clothes and packages on the bed, and she said she'd take it from there. Eiji returned to the front porch and the mystery he was reading. A little while later, Mae joined him with a fresh pitcher of iced tea, which she put on the wicker table. After pouring herself a glass, she went over to the swing, plopped down, took a drink, then put the glass on a little wicker table, and immediately went to sleep.

It was awhile later when he heard Mae say, "Oh my goodness, I seem to have fallen asleep." She glanced at the watch resting on her almost-plump arm. "Booty will be home soon."

Eiji placed a bookmark in his book and closed it. "He drove in a little while ago and waved while walking over to the office."

Mae patted her curly white hair, which remained as unruly as ever, but she tried for some organization.

"Well now, tell me something. Are you sure it's all right we're all going over to the school tomorrow?"

Eiji knew she was going to ask that. She had kept asking over and over since he finally agreed to meet Bobby and just talk. That's all, just talk about teaching sixth grade. She felt guilty, and it was obvious.

"I feel like I've dragged you into this. Booty said I did, and probably I did, as I think about it, but like I told him and you too—why not? Your car's here. Well, your car is always going to be here, so it looks like that doesn't count. You know what I mean. You can always go get another car. Where were you going anyway? But since your car is here, why not stay here with your car? That's what I was thinking. It seems convenient to me. You've never taught sixth grade, and you know all about being a lawyer and a banker, and you don't know anything about teaching, so why not give it a try? Anyway, I feel awful about making you do this. Am I making you do this? Oh, I hope not. I would hate to make you do this. I can't stand people who make people do things they don't want to do. My mother did that to me all of the time, and I would just die if I was doing the same thing to you. It would be terrible, and I mean it. So—don't let me do that, you hear? You can say 'Mae, no,' and I would listen. I'd go straight to the phone and call Lucille and cancel our appointment lickety-split. I absolutely would, and that would be the end. The way I figure it is, what the hell? Look at it as doing research on the natives. Your family's bank in Tokyo isn't going anywhere. You can always go there. For that matter, we're not going anywhere either. I don't know if that's a good point or not. That's not the point. I'm not sure what the point is … except you've done that, and this is something different."

It was Mae's argument that this was different which tantalized Eiji. The reason he took off driving around the country was to find something. This certainly was something—not the something he imagined or could possibly have imagined, since Eiji didn't know this existed. So he allowed Mae to persuade him into just going to talk to Bobby; that's all, just talk. Eiji figured he could just talk. He had not seen a grade school's interior since he was a student in one. At the very least, he would see what one looked like.

So, why not? What did he have to lose? Nothing. If he couldn't stand anything, all he had to do was to use the money Booty already gave him, buy a car, and drive out like he drove into Cedar Springs—without looking back. Seemed like an easy enough thing to do.

★ ★ ★ ★ ★

The next morning, Eiji rode in the back seat of Booty's black Range Rover around the corner and down the brick streets to Lincoln School. Houses ranging from the turn of the 1900s onward lined the streets. Most of the houses were brick. All had cared-for green lawns full of flowers and bushes. Everything was well kept. Both sides of the street were lined with big, old elm trees, giving much-needed shade. A few ancient people sat in painted metal chairs or rocked on swings on their front porches, watching the world go by. Mae and Booty knew everyone and waved to them, commenting on each.

"Oh my goodness," said Mae as she waved. "Mrs. Harrell is out of the hospital and back home. Isn't that wonderful! Everybody thought this time she was a goner for sure." She turned to Eiji in the back seat. "It was one of those things where the operation was a success and the patient died. Well, that damn near was true. She got this horrible staph infection. Her own doctor wouldn't go into the hospital room. Can you believe it? I know this is true because one of her daughters told me so—she had staph so bad that the doctor refused to step into her room. He talked to her from the door. He really cared! Bless her heart. She survived in spite of the doctor and the hospital. They don't call that hospital in Athens 'the killing fields' for nothing. I've always thought it has got to be the carpet. What hospital has carpeting? I don't think that's the least bit clean."

"My God! Miss Marie. Look at her in the swing. She takes up the whole thing. I heard that she had gotten fat as a toad. She looks like a turtle on that swing with a big round body and a little-bitty round head. I'm surprised she hasn't keeled over from a heart attack. No wonder I heard she rarely leaves her bed. She can't get out of it." Mae pushed the button, and her window glided down. She waved. "Hi, Miss Marie. How are you? It's good to see you outside taking air."

Miss Marie had been staring at the car as it drove down the block. She picked up what looked like a flipper (but was her hand) and waved back. "Hi Mae. How you all doing? I see you've got that nice boy in the back seat. He's going to teach school. Isn't that nice. They sure do need him with Blanquitta gone."

Eiji's eyes grew big when he heard Miss Marie. "My God! Does everybody in town know about me teaching at Lincoln? I haven't decided whether I'm going to or not. Everyone seems to have decided for me."

"Bye, Miss Marie. You take care. It's going to be a hot one, so don't you get too hot."

As Mae rolled up the window, Miss Marie waved again and returned to her swinging.

The drive was maybe five blocks. Booty parked in visitor parking in front of a well-kept one-story, yellow-brick school building. The building had tall windows with small panes and was shaded by graceful old oak trees. Grass that was once green had faded by the end of the hot summer, looking tired and sun-bleached.

"Well, here we are," Booty said.

Eiji sat in the back seat, staring at the school. The tall windows looked dark and empty. What was he doing? He didn't want to go into a school—especially a grade school—and teach. It was absurd. He knew nothing about teaching and even less about children. He pressed his back into the leather seat, not wanting to get out of the car. This was daft. Granted, he stayed with Mae and Booty and met some of their friends, but that did not constitute knowing them. Accepting a job teaching—which he could not imagine doing—meant staying in Cedar Springs, Oklahoma—which he could also not imagine doing. What did he know about Oklahoma? Nothing, that's what, other than the song from the musical. This was maybe the craziest thing he had ever done. *It's hot here, really hot, as in scorching hot.* This certainly wasn't in his plan. Never. It wasn't even in his universe. Yet when Booty came around and opened his door with Mae already out of the car and standing next to Booty staring at him, he got out of the car. Why?

Booty looked apprehensively at Eiji. "Are you sure you want to do this? Go inside? Don't let Mae force you. I mean it. This is sudden. When Mae makes up her mind, she can be headstrong about it, but that does not mean you have to do it."

Mae looked around Booty. "I can be a tad headstrong sometimes, you know."

Booty continued, "I'll be happy to go inside and tell them you're not interested, and that will be that. No one will get mad or disappointed. No questions asked."

"I won't be mad," said Mae.

Booty turned around and looked at Mae. "Or disappointed."

"Or disappointed," she repeated.

Booty continued, "You also know that we will introduce you as Eli Take."

"It is the easiest thing to remember and say," interrupted Mae.

Eiji could barely talk, his mouth was so dry. Why he let Mae choose that name, he'd never know. If he had to change his name, he should have had some say in it. Of course, he had never considered changing his name. It was a little late now, though.

Eiji took a deep breath. He looked at them, and then at the school, and then back to them. He took a deep breath again and this time sighed. Shrugging his shoulders, all he could think was that he might as well go inside, make Mae happy, and then say no to the job and leave. *Easy. This will be easy.* Go inside. Meet whomever he was to meet. Say thank you very much, but no thank you, and leave. Easy.

"Okay."

"You sure?" asked Booty.

Eiji nodded, and the three of them headed up the one step to the wide cement porch and through the brown metal double doors, which slammed behind them. Booty had told Eiji a sports coat, tie, and slacks would be fine, and that's what they both wore. Both wore navy blazers. Both wore Oxford cloth shirts. Booty's was white and Eiji's light blue. Both had the appropriate ties and instead of the linen slacks Booty wore, Eiji had on khaki. Mae decided on a new peach-color linen dress with a matching linen jacket, which was one of her purchases from the store in Athens. The three of them walked down the empty hall. Their footsteps echoed off the floor. An air conditioner rumbled from somewhere, pushing chilled air through the vents. No one felt like talking, not even Mae. When they arrived at the door that said Principal's Office in gold lettering on the glass, they looked at each other. Booty opened the door, and Mae headed the procession. As Eiji walked into the outer office, his stomach took a back flip. He couldn't believe he was so nervous. Why? He wasn't a kid being called into the headmaster's office. He wasn't ever called into the headmaster's office; he was too careful for that.

A woman with the smallest teeth Eiji had ever seen on an adult sat at a computer, typing away like mad. There was a bun full of gray-brown curls sitting right on top of her head. When she got nervous, which was often, she would tighten her bun so that it almost hurt to look at her face. She wore some makeup with pink cheeks, a touch of mascara, and lipstick that was barely red anymore since much had been eaten off and not replaced.

She wasn't what one would call *pretty*. On the other hand, she wasn't unattractive either. *Nondescript* might be correct. She was busy, very busy, and she let everyone know that.

"Hello, Lucille," said Mae. "Eli, I'd like for you to meet Lucille Pawn. Lucille, this is Eli Take."

Eiji walked to her desk and shook her hand. "Hello."

"I heard you were Oriental." Lucille smacked her lips. "At least you are an American one. You are, aren't you? We don't take to foreigners and illegals."

Eiji was taken aback and didn't know how to answer other than, "Huh?"

Booty relieved Eiji. "Lucille, as you are aware, we're here to see Bobby."

"He's in his office, probably on his cell phone. He's on that thing all the time, either talking or texting if he doesn't want me to hear. I figure that's why he texts, so I can't know what's going on. Maeva's one of my very best and oldest friends, but I don't know, Booty. I told her that and you too, if you remember. I don't know." Lucille smacked her lips and shook her head. "The last thing in the world I would ever want to do is hurt Bobby's mother's feelings, but I don't know. I have my hands full. I'll let him know you're here. Have you seen him lately? Be prepared, that's all I'm saying." She smacked her lips again and yanked her bun tighter.

"No need to announce us, Lucille," said Booty. "He knows we're coming."

"Suit yourself. I'd give him warning, if I were you," Lucille replied, returning to her work at the computer, again smacking her lips. "Don't say I didn't warn you."

Eiji looked at Mae with trepidation. Her eyes showed concern. "Oh, dear."

Booty opened the door into the principal's office and strode inside with Eiji and Mae following.

A good-looking man with an air of conceit emanating from him sat behind a dark, polished-wood desk. His crossed feet were propped up on the desk, and he leaned back in the comfortable dark-brown leather chair, busily texting. His head was down in concentration. He barely heard them come in. Two dark-brown leather chairs sat in front of the desk. Over to one side of the large office was an oval wooden conference table with brown leather chairs surrounding it. The air of his sweet cologne was almost overpowering.

"Bobby," commanded Booty, "we're here for our appointment." He pointed to the two chairs sitting in front of the desk for Eiji and Mae, as he grabbed one of the conference chairs and positioned it next to Mae.

The man had rich, deep auburn hair and brown eyes with fair skin and almost pretty features. He had a great smile and charm, and he knew how to use both. Bobby finished typing his text, sent it, and then put the cell phone on his desk.

He stood up, leaned over the desk, and shook Booty's hand. "Hi, Booty. It's nice to see you."

"Bobby, you know Mae."

"Of course I do. How are you, Mae? It's good to see you."

"This is Eli Take."

Before Booty had a chance to say anything else, Bobby gave Eli his full attention, just as he had Booty and Mae. He put out his hand. "Bob Wrightsberg."

Eiji sat up a little in his chair to reach Bobby's hand. Suddenly, he blanked on his new name. "How do you do." This guy was charm personified. Eiji couldn't figure out what Lucille was talking about.

For a moment, they sat and looked at each other. Each waited for the other to start. Bobby looked at Booty. Booty refused to say anything because he wanted to know if Bobby had any idea why they were there. He certainly didn't appear to remember the appointment. So Booty simply looked at him, waiting.

Bobby looked at the three of them, smiling. "Mae, your flowers look just as beautiful as usual this year. I was over visiting Blair Don and couldn't help but notice. My mother always said that you have the prettiest lawn and flowers."

Mae knew good and well that Maeva would no more compliment her yard than jump off the Brooklyn Bridge. She had known Maeva all of her life, and all of her life, Maeva barely gave her the time of day if she wasn't being downright rude. Maeva, Precious, and Lucille, along with a few chosen others, were two years older than Mae and constituted the popular group of girls with whom everyone dreamed of being friends and wasn't. *This boy is slick,* thought Mae. From what she heard about Bobby, she didn't trust him. Now she knew she didn't trust him. Mae smiled and let him squirm. She wanted to see just how he was going to smooth his way out of this.

Eiji looked at both Mae and Booty, wondering what was going on. Then he looked at Bob and realized he had no idea why they were sitting in front of him.

Bob leaned back into the leather chair. "Well, Booty, what can I do you for?"

Just at that moment, Bobby's cell rang as it sat upon the desk. He picked it up looked to see who was calling. He smiled to himself a little and considered taking the call. He decided against it since Booty, the president of the school board, sat in front of him and was staring. He really wanted to take this call. "Booty, would you mind—"

Without waiting for him to finish the sentence, Booty interrupted, "Yes, I would mind."

Bob frowned at Booty. He was accustomed to getting what he wanted. "Okay."

"And turn off your cell," said Booty, becoming impatient. "You made this appointment."

For a split second, Bobby gave it away that he had no idea what was going on, then slick as can be, he recovered. "Right." Bobby jumped out of his chair. "I need to go talk to Lucille." He rushed out of the room so quickly that all anyone could do was follow him with their eyes. After several minutes, he rushed back into the office carrying some papers. "Okay," he said returning to his chair. "There we go. Okay. Now. Okay. Let's get this show on the road. So Lucille tells me you want to teach Blanquitta's class." He searched among the papers. "Ah, here we go. Okay. Now. Let's see. Yes. Here's your transcript. Lucille said that your transcript was here, and sure enough there it is. Well, my God, this says that you went to Harvard. Did you go to Harvard?"

Eiji stared at him like he was an idiot. "Yes."

Bobby laughed. "How's their football team? Nothing like the University of Oklahoma's."

Eiji said nothing. Nor did he laugh. Nor did anyone else.

Mae was so disgusted that she was about to get up and leave. She felt terrible about dragging Eiji here and having him send the required information (according to Lucille, who ought to know since she ran the school). She glanced at Eiji, who appeared furious, which made her feel even worse. She chided herself with a feeble, "What did I do?" before she picked up her purse from the floor, getting ready to go.

Bobby didn't pay any attention since he was too busy reading Eiji's information. "My God—you went to Harvard Law. You were on Law Review. You ought to go to Oklahoma City and get a job. What do you know about oil-and-gas law? I was in what is considered to be the best law firm in Oklahoma City. I still know people. I probably could still return there if I wanted to."

Mae rolled her eyes hearing Bobby say that. Everybody in town knew that the senior partner at the law firm had caught Bobby in the middle of having sex with his wife and doing cocaine.

Before Booty could say anything, Eiji said, "I understood I was here to talk about teaching."

Booty smiled and sat back in his chair, enjoying this. Mae still wanted to leave and started to fidget.

"Teaching?" Bob looked at Eli stupidly.

"Teaching here was my understanding."

"Teaching?" Bob's cell phone rang. By habit, he looked to see who was calling and smiled.

Booty was joining Mae in being disgusted. This was a waste of time. He was sorry he let Mae talk him into this. He was sorry for Eli being dragged into this. All in all, Booty was not pleased and was furious at Bobby. Lucille was right: he was an absolute, conceited fool. "I told you to turn off the God damn cell phone. Turn it off!"

Bob was not used to being scolded. He glared at Booty as he turned the phone off. Smiling at Eiji, he said, "You're my first job interview. The teachers never leave here. Blanquitta is pregnant and quit on us. I have to say the salary here is much better than public schools. You're better off teaching at Lincoln than there. I think you would like it here. We're a small school but a good one. Yes, this is a good little school. I went here, and so did my mother and father. Everyone goes here. It's private, you know."

Booty couldn't stand it. "I don't know what Bobby means by that, and I don't think I want to know. Lincoln wasn't a private school when he or any of us went here. Lincoln accepts all of the children first through sixth grade who live here and in the area. The only reason the school is private is to keep it going because the State of Oklahoma closed it. We wanted to keep the children here, and this was the only way to do it."

"Yes," said Bob, "that is exactly what I meant. So would you like to join our little family and teach here?"

Eiji could not believe it. This wasn't a job interview. This man knew nothing about him except what his transcript showed. "Is this a job offer?"

Bobby flashed a smile at him. "It sure is."

"You are offering me a job to teach—"

Bob interrupted, "The sixth grade. That's Blanquitta's class. Blanquitta taught one class and Mary McKeen the other. Small classes. Lincoln's not a big school. A good chance to get in there and teach. I'm not sure about how many kids will be in your and Mary's classes. Lucille takes care of that, but it's not large. Good student–teacher ratio." He flashed a smile at everyone.

"Can I teach whatever I want?" After Eiji asked that, he wondered why. He had no idea what he wanted to teach. He didn't know if he wanted to teach, much less what.

Mae sat up in her chair and pounced upon the subject. "I have Blanquitta's daily teaching plans, the ones she's used for years, so they are tried and true. All Eli has to do us stay one day ahead, that's what Blanquitta told me."

Somehow Eiji found himself getting wrapped up in this. He couldn't imagine why. Yet, he was. He thought he would walk out. To his complete surprise, not only did he not walk out, he stayed. He heard himself accepting the job and was horrified at that. "Is that the contract?" He pointed to an obvious contract on Bobby's desk.

Bob looked down at the papers upon the desk and found the contract. "Yes, it is." He slid it across the desk to Eiji with a pen.

Eli signed the contract, which was for one year—and he even signed it Eli Take. He slid it back across the desk to Bob, who looked at it.

"Fine," said Bob. "I guess that's it then. Good. We can make it an early afternoon."

Mae and Booty stared at Eli, astounded. After such a stupid job interview, Eli actually signing the contract was the last thing they expected. Yet sign it, he did. The person most astonished was Eli. He couldn't fathom what he had just done, much less why. He committed to one year of teaching, which he had never done nor wanted to do, in a place he never thought he would be living in, in a cottage behind a house of people he had known for a couple of weeks. Had he gone mad? He could only assume that he must have lost his mind. Why else would he do such a thing?

The next thing Eli knew, everyone was standing and shaking hands. Then they were escorted out of Bob's office into Lucille's.

Bob patted Eli on the shoulder. "Welcome to Lincoln. Nice to see all of you. Mae, you're looking as lovely as ever. Thank you for coming. Good-bye." With that, Bobby returned to his office and closed the door, leaving the three of them standing and staring at Lucille, who stared back at them.

"What in the world was that?" asked Lucille.

The three of them looked back to the closed door and then back to Lucille. They were rather shell-shocked by the whole affair.

"I haven't the faintest idea, except that I felt like we were being escorted out of some party," answered Mae. "Booty, do you know what just happened?"

"Eli," said Booty, "are you aware that you just signed a contract to teach at Lincoln?"

"Strange, isn't it?" answered Eli.

Lucille slapped her hands on the desk. "Boy, have you ever had any teaching experience?"

Eli glared at her. "If you are referring to me, no."

Lucille shook her head. "I didn't think so." She quickly flipped through some papers on her desk. "Ah, I see there are only nine kids in your class this year and nine in Mary's. That's a good size to get real personal teaching, which I hope to God you'll figure out how to do. Really, Booty, I don't see why we had to hire someone with no teaching experience. On the other hand, we hired someone as a principal with no school experience, so who am I to question? I'm the only one who knows how to run a school, and by God, that's just what I'm doing. I told you, Booty, that Bobby was a waste of air on this earth. Did Bobby tell you he was a lawyer and worked in an Oklahoma City law firm?" she asked Eli.

"Yes."

A creepy smile crossed her lips. "Did he tell you why he wasn't there any longer?"

"No." Eli wondered why she asked that.

"He got caught snorting cocaine in bed with his law firm's senior partner's wife. And guess who found them? The senior partner. Whoops! He was not supposed to return until the next day, except it *was* the next day. It seems they had lost track of time. So old Bobby gets fired, and the wife got sent away for long-term drug treatment. This is our new principal, isn't it, Booty? I should have gotten the job as principal. I deserve it. I earned it, but Bobby got it. Didn't he, Booty?"

"Lucille," answered Booty. "You were at that board meeting. You had your say and so did Maeva, who begged us to take Bobby. We wouldn't have done it, except you insisted. Don't you remember? You said that we should hire poor Bobby and give the boy a chance. I clearly remember you saying that everyone deserves a second chance, and we should give him one. I think your exact words were that it would be the 'Christian thing to do.' So we did, and now, you're stuck with him. I don't want to hear how you should have been principal and instead of applying for the job, pushed Bobby for his mother."

Lucille sneered at Booty. "I changed my mind."

"It seems a little late for that, dear," said Mae. She took Eli's arm. "Come on, you all, let's get going and let Lucille get back to work. Bye, Lucille."

Mae practically shoved Eli out the door.

He looked at her dumbfounded. "This was crazy."

"Yes, dear, it was," said Mae as she went into the hall.

Booty quickly followed. They scurried down the hall and out the doors, hearing them slam shut behind them.

As they headed home, Eli blindly stared out of the window. "What have I done?"

Mae answered to no one in particular. "I haven't the faintest idea."

★ ★ ★ ★ ★

Eiji (who now tried to think of himself as "Eli," since that was his new name) studied Blanquitta's lesson plans as if trying to locate the Holy Grail. He spent afternoons poring over the plans and notes while Mae went to Athens to get whatever school stuff Eli wanted. Neither Ellanor nor Lorraine could believe Eli was actually doing this. They told him repeatedly that he was nuts, and Eli agreed. He must be crazy to do this. That was the only reason he could possibly divine, especially after studying the lesson plans. There was always the thought that he could run away. As the start of school got closer, the idea of running became more appealing. He knew Mae and Booty would understand. What he couldn't understand was why he didn't run.

★ ★ ★ ★ ★

A butterfly bobbed between the flowers and then flew away into the evening. Ellanor, Lorraine, Eli, Mae, and Booty assumed their usual places on the front porch. A fresh pitcher of iced tea sat on the wicker table, awaiting anyone interested. Everyone, replete from finishing off Mae's peach pie, was quietly digesting, interrupted every so often by someone's need to chat.

"There's nothing like fresh Oklahoma peaches," Mae said. "There are some things that Oklahoma just does well, and growing peaches is one of them."

Murmurs of agreement were heard all around, followed by another spell of silence.

"Well, good Lord," Mae said, once again interrupting everyone's musings.

About the same time, Lorraine joined in. "Good God, will you look who's coming? I don't believe my eyes. Is Precious actually taking a walk? Since when does Precious go outside?"

"My God, Precious can actually walk. It must be a miracle," Ellanor said.

Eli followed their eyes in looking up the block. Two women were strolling down the block. One was the beautiful woman with the black hair, ivory skin, and blue eyes. The other was a small woman with short curly brown-dyed hair. She seemed a live wire. You could almost feel her vibrating, where the younger woman was soft. It was more like she floated than walked; at least that's what it appeared to Eli, who experienced the most surprising feeling. It was as if he had been shoved in his chest. He didn't know what to make of it; he had never experienced a feeling like that. He knew who they were. He saw them at the Whiz Bang the day he poisoned himself with the onion burger.

Booty looked at Mae. "What do they want? Blair Don said that her mother was nagging her about taking evening walks, and she couldn't imagine why."

"I can bet why," Mae answered quietly.

"In all my years, I don't recall seeing Precious take a walk. I've seen Precious drive next door rather than walk. I doubt if she ever considered walking. I didn't believe Blair Don when she told me. I told Blair Don I could not see her mother suddenly deciding to exercise, and to Precious, a stroll has to be considered exercise. She wouldn't do it otherwise."

Mae watched the two women approach. "Oh, yes she would."

Booty looked at Mae. "Oh, Mae, you don't have to be so suspicious. Precious may actually be taking an evening stroll. Blair Don said that she wanted to, and it looks to me that's what she's doing."

Mae simply said, "I don't believe it."

Booty gave her a look and shook his head. "Really, Mae, you could give her the benefit of the doubt."

Ellanor looked at Lorraine. "What is she doing?"

"Damn it, Ellanor," Lorraine said. "I like Precious."

Ellanor rolled his eyes. Since Eli sat between the two, he wondered what that was all about. He thought Blair Don was absolutely beautiful. He was quite taken by her. He didn't care about her mother.

Precious suddenly stopped in front of the house. Blair Don almost continued walking until she saw her mother halt so abruptly. She stopped and looked curiously at her mother.

"Hi y'all," said Precious. Her voice sounded raspy, like she smoked too many cigarettes or drank too much whiskey or both. There was a toughness about her. "We thought we'd get out of the house and take some air. It's a nice enough evening. How's everybody?"

"Everybody's fine," Ellanor answered. Lorraine glared at him.

The women stood there a minute, and there was nothing for it. Mae had to invite them to join the group on the front porch. The only times Mae could think of that Precious came over to the house were when somebody died, and that was to bring a casserole out of guilt, not because she cared.

"You all want to join us for a glass of iced tea?" Mae asked, as nicely as humanly possible.

Booty tried to contain himself from staring with shock at Mae. She sounded so nice and sincere. Booty knew this wasn't right, not right at all.

In her gravel voice, Precious said, "Why we'd love to."

As the two women walked up the porch stairs with Precious leading the way, Lorraine flew out of his chair. He said, "Precious, there's this wicker couch. Why don't you and I take that and let Blair Don have my chair?"

Precious smiled and sashayed over to the couch with Lorraine. Blair Don walked over to the now-unoccupied wicker chair next to Eli.

Eli started to stand as she sat. "Eli Take, I don't think we've met."

"I saw you when I was with Mother at the Whiz Bang. Blair Mason."

Lorraine rushed around like a frantic host, pouring iced tea for the women. "What would you all like in your iced tea? How about bourbon, since this is such a special occasion having you all out? Seems to me cocktails are in order, don't you think so?" Lorraine knew that Mae kept a fifth of bourbon in the wicker cabinet. "This is like a party seeing you again."

Mae could have killed Lorraine. This was not a party. She did not want Precious to stay, but there was nothing she could do but smile. "What a lovely idea, Lorraine."

Booty didn't know what to do, so he didn't do anything. He also smiled, knowing that he had always thought Precious a racist as she sat drinking his whiskey on Mae's family's front porch. He almost would have laughed, had it not been such an affront with her there. Precious's family vigorously opposed the Crutchfield family moving next door. They did everything they could to stop them and never forgave the Hoover family for demanding it. W.D. Hoover, Sr. was a hated man in the Blair family except when they needed liquor. They had no qualms ordering from one of his bootleggers when the state was dry.

Lorraine tore open the box of brand-new monogrammed cocktail napkins Mae had just got from Neiman Marcus. Now she really could have killed him. He plopped a sprig of mint in each drink and delivered one to Precious and then one to Blair Don. After that, he grabbed the other glasses to add bourbon. If someone's glass was too full, Lorraine simply poured the excess iced tea over the porch railing. He was the perfect host—except, of course, he wasn't at his house. Mae could feel her face getting red, so she fanned it with a cocktail napkin. The wonderful dinner she'd cooked and the peach pie turned sour in her stomach. She yearned to demand Precious get off her front porch; instead, she *smiled* and tried not to chug her drink.

Booty savored the moment of Precious sitting on the front porch with him in a social situation. He had always heard that her grandfather and father, the self-righteous Judge Blair, were members of the Ku Klux Klan.

What a laugh; her now sitting on the front porch with him. Her father and probably her mother must be rolling over in their graves in horror. As mad as Mae was, Booty relished every moment. He wished his grandfather was here to see this. He had had such a wonderful sense of humor. He would have loved this. Booty simply smiled, waiting to find out why Precious was here. There was certainly something she wanted.

"I like your new napkins," Booty teased Mae.

If looks could kill, Mae's look at Booty certainly would have. She was in no mood to be teased. This was her home and her front porch, and she wanted Precious gone. She didn't know how to do it politely, so she simply smiled.

"Oh, Lorraine," Precious said in a too-cute voice that didn't go with the gravel sound, "you make a good drink."

Lorraine was thrilled. "Thank you." He actually blushed, to Ellanor's disgust.

"Your big old crepe myrtle bush is so pretty, Mae, and full of lovely raspberry blossoms," Precious chatted. "Adds such nice color."

"Yes," answered Mae. "It does that every year."

Precious continued, "Maybe I should have left my old crepe myrtles instead of having them pulled out. Now, I don't think I've had the pleasure to meet your visitor. My sister Bunny Lou told me all about meeting you at the Whiz Bang. She said you all had the nicest chat. Precious Mason." She held out her hand expecting Eli to get up, which he dutifully did.

"Eli Take," he said, shaking her cold hand. Precious was smaller than Eli had first thought. There were deep smoking lines around her mouth, etched into her deeply tanned, sun-leathered skin. Everything about her seemed leathery and tough. *This was a woman to be avoided as much as possible,* he wisely surmised.

"You've met my daughter, Blair Don," she said motioning with her hand.

"Yes, we just met."

"Good. I understand that you will be staying in our little community, teaching school. You're taking Blanquitta's place."

"Yes, I am."

"Bunny Lou and I were rather hoping our cousin—oh, and Lucille's cousin too—Fran would be taking that job. She's taught for years over in Athens and would have loved to stop the commute, but that's the way it is, isn't it?"

"I don't know," said Eli as he returned to his chair and took a drink.

"Of course, *she* didn't go to Harvard," Precious continued. "Just the University of Oklahoma, where she graduated at the top of her class. My mother wouldn't allow us girls to go back east to school like you and Booty did. She said that those schools were full of Communists. So you plan to be with us for a little while? Lorraine, I was so glad to see you out this evening. It's been an age. I thought we were going to have to go over to your house and drag you out of your bedroom. I told Geneva we were going to blast you out because we've missed seeing you. I hope we can drag you out some more because I would love to show you some new things in Athens I bet you haven't seen."

Lorraine melted into the teenager who had so madly loved Precious. Actually, he had fallen in love with her at Lincoln and pined over her ever since then. He was thrilled she was glad to see him. That she asked him to go with her to Athens was almost too much to bear. He could barely talk. "Yes."

"Oh, good," Precious said, batting her eyelashes at him.

Ellanor thought he was going to be sick. "I need another drink."

"Don't we all?" Mae said.

While Ellanor gathered the glasses, Mae smiled at Precious. Quickly, she turned to Blair Don. "Eli hasn't seen much of the area since he arrived. He's been pretty much housebound here with us. I bet he'd enjoy being with someone his own age and seeing the surroundings. What do you think, Blair Don?"

She looked surprised and then smiled a warm, inviting smile. "Why, I'd love to."

Eli also looked surprised. He loved Mae's suggestion. "That would be great. When?"

"How about tomorrow? Booty, there isn't that much work. Would you mind if I took the afternoon off?"

"Take the whole day off," Booty replied. "You never take time off. This will be good for you."

"Wonderful. How about I pick you up about ten o'clock and we see where we end up?"

Eli couldn't have been happier. "Great."

Precious was not happy. This was not what she intended—not at all. This man was an Oriental of an unknown nature. She didn't know if he had any money or not. Where did he come from? Who was his family? All she knew was what Lucille told her, which was not very much. She knew he went to Harvard and Harvard Law, and that was it. Bobby Wrightsberg was a lawyer too, and she knew all about him. This visit had taken a most unexpected turn. At the moment, she didn't quite know what to do about it. She decided to focus on Lorraine, which was why she was here in the first place although she really wanted to question this Oriental fellow.

Precious was in a quandary. This boy better not mess up her plans. In fact, she'd better nip this in the bud before he got any silly ideas.

"Blair Don," her mother said in a you-better-listen-to-me tone, "are you sure you should take tomorrow off? We're going to be needing to go to Oklahoma City for a few days, and I don't want you to impose on Booty. Do you? Booty, I don't want you to think Blair Don is taking advantage of you. Booty's been so nice and generous to you. I'm sure this nice man wouldn't mind doing it another time. What do you think?"

Everyone sitting there knew exactly what Precious meant, except Lorraine, who was so taken with her that he couldn't think at all. He stared adoringly at her with glassy eyes.

Blair Don was furious and humiliated; she didn't know which one she felt more. How could her mother embarrass her like that? She was an adult, and her mother treated her like a child. She felt her face blushing, which embarrassed her more. If she could have died right on the spot, she would have. Her stomach churned. The good time she was having suddenly vanished. All she wanted to do was go home.

She popped out of her chair to the surprise of all (except Lorraine, who wasn't paying any attention to Blair Don). "I have to go home," she said quickly and with a little too much force to be casual. She looked straight at Eli. "I'll see you tomorrow at ten then."

Eli looked back at her with surprise. He knew very well that her mother wanted her to have nothing to do with him. She made that evident, but if her daughter wanted to buck her, why not? He wanted to go with Blair Don, and he didn't care where. Blair Don was going to pay a price for this, he figured, because Precious was not graceful about not getting her way. He wanted to go.

"Absolutely," Eli answered. "I look forward to it."

"Great," said Blair Don. She had to get out of there before she started crying. "See you tomorrow." She rushed off the porch toward her upper-floor apartment in the old family home.

Precious sat straight up and glared. "Blair Don!" she called, but Blair Don did not appear to hear. She ignored her. Precious patted her hair and smiled at everyone. She shrugged her shoulders and tried to joke. "Kids today."

Ellanor turned to Precious. "She is no kid and hasn't been in a long time."

Precious gave one of her false giggles. "Oh, you know what I mean! She'll always be a child to me; that's what mothers are like. I don't care how old I was, my mother always treated me like a child."

"Mine didn't," Mae said.

"Neither did mine," Ellanor joined in.

"My mother wasn't even in the same country," Booty said dryly.

"Booty." Precious tried to keep her voice nice, except it didn't work. She sounded snappish. "Are you really going to let Blair Don take the day off tomorrow? I don't think you should."

"I already did, Precious." Booty smiled at her.

To Lorraine's dismay, Precious got up from the wicker couch. "Well, I think I better be going."

"Oh, now, you don't need to leave," said Lorraine. "You just got here. Sit down and stay a little while longer. You don't need to get back. Stay a bit more. We're having such a good time."

She batted her false eyelashes at Lorraine. "Oh, Lorraine, I'd love to, but I really do need to be getting on home and see what Blair Don is doing."

Lorraine grabbed her hand. "Oh, come on and sit down. Blair Don is a big girl. She can take care of herself. We were having such a good time. I don't see why you have to leave."

"Lorraine, I'd love to, but I better be going." Precious turned to leave.

To everyone's surprise, Lorraine popped up right after she did. "Okay," he said. "I can't let you walk home alone."

He was the only one who didn't get that she wanted to go home alone to talk to Blair Don. However, since her whole purpose in coming down was to see Lorraine, she relented. She could talk to Blair Don later. "Why sure, Lorraine. I couldn't think of anything nicer than you walking me home. It's been such a long time since I've seen you."

Lorraine was thrilled and dutifully followed her off the porch.

"Thank you for the drink. It was nice to see you all. I don't know if Blair Don will be able to pick you up tomorrow for you all's little ride, as nice as that would be. I wouldn't count on her being here. Don't cancel any other plans you might have, you hear? Bye, you all. Sure good to see you." She strode off the porch and headed home with Lorraine walking next to her.

Everyone on the porch watched Precious sashay up the street with Lorraine. They saw her put her arm through his and watched his step grow into a bounce. He was so involved looking at and listening to Precious that everyone on the porch gasped when he tripped over an uneven part of the old cement sidewalk. Fortunately, Lorraine caught himself before completely losing his balance and falling on his face. He righted quickly, bouncing all the way to her front door, where he followed Precious inside. At that point, it seemed those left on the porch exhaled at the same time. Ellanor, Mae, and Booty shook their heads, while Eli looked at them in dismay.

"Am I going with Blair Don or not tomorrow?" he asked.

Mae looked at Eli and shrugged. "Honey, I haven't the faintest idea. I hope so, but who knows when Precious gets on the warpath?"

"Why is she on the warpath? About me? Why? What have I done to her? Nothing. I don't even know her!"

Booty glared up the street toward the Blair family home. "She's a bitch. Always has been and always will be a real bitch. And Lorraine is an idiot, but then Lorraine has always been an idiot, especially when it comes to Precious. Jesus—what a fool. All those girls were snobs, except maybe Bunny Lou who married Punky. She disgraced the family when she came home from OU and married him."

"I'll never forget it," Mae interrupted. "You would have thought there was a death in the family, the way they reacted. White trash, that's what they called him. 'Bunny Lou married white trash from the wrong side of the tracks.' To this day, I see Bunny Lou's car over at the Blair house, but not Punky's truck. I wouldn't be surprised if Precious wouldn't let him in the house, even after all these years they've been married and all their kids, except maybe her big parties. I guess she has to then. I'm sure she holds her breath that he doesn't come in his overalls smelling like cigars."

Eli pleaded, "But is Blair Don picking me up tomorrow?"

Ellanor downed the remainder of his drink. "I figure the odds to be seventy-thirty that she doesn't make it away from Precious. What do you think, Booty? Old Precious runs a tight ship when it comes to Blair Don. Made her come home from Dallas."

Mae interrupted. "I heard Precious broke up her marriage to that nice dentist—that's just what I heard, but it sounds true to me. Precious would do that. Of course, we weren't invited to the wedding. On the bright side, we didn't have to buy her a gift or be bored at the wedding reception with no one talking to us."

"Lorraine and I were invited, but we didn't go. Geneva did, naturally, and talked about how lovely it was. Why go to the trouble and expense of a big wedding if Precious was only going to do her best to break up the marriage later? Doesn't make sense to me, but there you have it. Lorraine hasn't left yet. How long is he going to stay there?"

"Once she has her clutches in him—who knows?" Mae said. "My money is on she'll get him to marry her."

Ellanor turned white. "Oh no! Mae, don't say that, even in jest. That's not funny, not one bit. Oh my God, what a disaster. Surely not Lorraine! Surely he'll never get married. He barely leaves his bedroom. Get married? No … not Lorraine. I can't see it. He may be crazy but not that crazy. Lorraine get married? Never. He barely coped when he had his dog, much less get married. Oh Mae—that is absolutely absurd. Lorraine married? Oh my God—never! Oh please! I don't know whether to laugh or cry."

Mae had a curious little smile on her face. "We'll see."

"Do you think we could talk about me for one minute?" Eli asked.

"Of course, dear," Mae said. "What would you like to talk about?"

"Is Blair Don picking me up tomorrow or not? What should I do?"

"Come on over in the morning, and we'll drink coffee. If she comes, she comes, and if she doesn't, well, we'll cross that bridge when we come to it."

Ellanor got up. "I'm going home and see what if anything is on TV. See you all later. I wouldn't count on Blair Don coming, but if she does, good for her. Lorraine get married? Really, Mae. Night, all. See you tomorrow."

"Night," they answered and watched Ellanor stroll home. They all watched as the blue jays across the street dive-bombed two neighborhood gray cats, who had hunkered deep into the grass to avoid the enraged birds. The cats' harrowing escape was accompanied by an evening symphony of chirps, songs, and croaks that filled the air. A cool breeze succeeded in pushing away the remaining heat of the day. The Japanese maple's red leaves swayed in the light wind. Booty and Mae glided back and forth in the noisy swing while Eli aimlessly watched the cats, each in their own thoughts.

★ ★ ★ ★ ★

The next morning, Eli sat in the kitchen with Lena and Mae, drinking coffee. Instead of his usual Bermuda shorts, he decided to wear blue jeans, just in case she actually did come. He had on a navy Polo shirt that he didn't bother to tuck in and loafers without socks. He started to take a jacket and then decided against it. As the time crawled closer to ten o'clock, conversation spurted before coming to a halt. Everyone strained to listen while trying to act like they weren't. All eyes jumped to each other when they thought they heard a car. No, it wasn't a car. Was that a car? Lena had made donuts that morning, which were absolutely delicious, although no one tasted much. Mae got so nervous, she kept grabbing a donut. She quickly nabbed one, dunked it in her coffee, and ate it. If she kept this up, she was going to have to unbutton the top button of her skirt so she could breathe, but this was no time to think about that now.

All eyes got bigger when they were sure they heard a car drive into the driveway and stop. It was exactly ten o'clock. Mae leapt up and zoomed to look out the kitchen door. She thought if it were Booty, she'd kill him for coming right now. Lena hopped up alongside Mae, but Eli beat them both to the door. Herschel started barking, which was a good sign. It meant that someone was here—and it wasn't Booty. He didn't bark at Booty. This was someone he didn't know. Eli walked out the storm door to Blair Don, who was sitting in her car. She had just turned it off and was getting ready to come inside to get him.

She still drove the brownish-gold Lexus sedan she had bought while married and living in Dallas. The car was full of gas and ready to go. As she expected, her mother had barged into her apartment early that morning in a full-blown harangue about her not going. Her mother screamed, threatened, demanded, and then resorted to screaming again. Blair Don had already showered and dressed and was getting ready to flee before her mother could catch her. Unfortunately, she wasn't fast enough, because Precious flew in the door before she had a chance to fly out. Damn. She wore blue jeans with a light-blue linen shirt and embroidered espadrilles that tied around her ankles.

She grabbed her summer purse just as her mother barged in and was searching for the car keys.

"You are *not* going!"

"Oh, for God's sake. Must we do this?"

"I'm telling you, you are not going out with that boy."

"He isn't a boy."

"He is to me, and I am your mother, and I'm saying no!"

"Mother, there is no need to scream."

"There is too! What do you know about this boy? You don't know anything about him. Who is he, other than an Oriental of all things? How could you go out with someone Oriental? Really, Blair Don, I wonder about you sometimes. I really do. Going out with an Oriental? What has happened to you? You don't care what you do to our family, do you?"

"I'm not 'going out' with him. I'm simply taking him to show him the area, that's all. It isn't a big deal."

"You don't know one thing about him, and you're getting in a car with him?"

"Oh, for God's sake."

"You'll always be my little girl with no sense at all, and I have to watch out for you."

"I'm an adult, and I'm not doing this to you."

"Oh, yes you are. What are people going to think? You going out with an Oriental. Really! I truly do wonder about you sometimes. What do you know about this man? He could be some Oriental white trash that eats dogs. I've heard the Chinese eat dogs. You wouldn't know."

Blair Don found her keys and grabbed a pair of cowboy boots with a pair of white socks stuffed inside one boot.

"Where are you going with those boots? Are you taking that boy out to the ranch? You better not. I don't want Charge and Henry and them to see him. What will they think? You and an Oriental! I suppose it could be worse, but not much."

"If I go to the ranch, they won't think anything. They're not like you, Mother. They don't care."

"Just what do you mean not like me? What do you mean by that?"

"I'm not doing this with you, Mother."

"I'm going to call your uncle Charge and tell him to not let you and that boy on the ranch. They better not."

"Or what, Mother? You sold Daddy's part back to them after he died."

She walked out the door with her mother following her down the stairs.

"Bye, Mother."

Precious shook her finger. "I am ashamed of you, Blair Don. I really am. How could you do this to me? Going out with some Oriental trash that you don't even know. What about Bobby? What about him? What is he going to think? What if someone sees you all and tells him?"

"I've told you, I don't care what Bobby thinks. I don't like Bobby. I have never liked Bobby. He's a conceited jerk, just like his father. *You* go out with him if you like him so much."

"Blair Don! Really! I don't know how you can say such a thing about such a nice boy. I just hope he doesn't hear about this little escapade of yours, that's all I hope for your sake. This could ruin your reputation, and then who are you going to get to marry you?"

By this point, Blair Don opened the door of her car, almost leaping in and starting the engine. "Good-bye, Mother."

"Shame on you, Blair Don! I'm so disappointed in you, I could cry. How could you do this to me? You hate me."

But Blair had rolled up the window and blasted up the radio and air conditioning while speeding out of the driveway and up the street. It was too early to pick up Eli, so she decided to get gas and calm down. She drove out to the truck stop filling station and diner outside of Cedar Springs on the highway to Athens. After filling up and getting coffee, she pulled over to the side and stopped. She leaned her head back against the seat and sipped the hot coffee, trying to forget the morning.

After she stopped her car under the portico, she saw Eli, followed by Mae and Lena, coming out the back door. She started the car and drove to the back gate to meet them. She sighed with relief and smiled.

Eli opened the front door of the car. "Hi."

"Hi. Do you have a pair of boots? I thought we'd go out to the ranch and ride."

"No."

Mae and Lena had made it to the car. "Hi, Blair Don," said Mae, hearing what Blair Don had just said. "No need to worry. Booty has more boots that you can shake a stick at."

"You think I can wear Booty's boots? He's bigger than I am."

"Sure. We'll get a bunch of socks and you'll be fine. Come on in, and we'll get you something."

"Come on in, Blair Don. I made donuts this morning, and you need to have some before Mae finishes them off."

Blair turned off the car and followed everyone into the house. While she had coffee and a wonderful fresh donut, Eli and Mae were quickly going through boots upstairs. They came into the kitchen with Eli holding a pair of brown lizard cowboy boots and several pairs of socks.

"Mae, are you sure Booty isn't going to mind me wearing these boots? They're custom made. I wouldn't want anything to happen to them, and they'll get dirty."

"Honey, they're called boots. That's what they're for. Don't you worry about a thing. You saw he has plenty more boots, for goodness sake."

Blair Don got up from the table, and they all walked to the back door and out to the car.

"This looks like real fun, you all going out to the ranch and riding. You be sure to tell Charge, Henry, and everyone hello for me," Mae said.

Eli threw the boots into the back as they got in the car.

"See you later," said Blair Don as she rolled up the window.

Lena and Mae waved at them as they drove out and then returned to the house with Herschel following them.

They sped past Blair's house. Precious was in the front yard, pretending to pull weeds, but watching everything. Her eyes followed the car from Mae's until it turned the corner and was out of sight. She smacked her lips in disgust and swore under her breath. "God damn her. She's gonna be sorry."

They drove some miles outside of Cedar Springs on the highway going another direction from Athens. It was a lovely morning.

Eli said, "Blair Don—"

"Oh please call me Blair. Only the people in Cedar Springs call me Blair Don. I can always tell when there is someone from Cedar Springs, because I'll hear *Blair Don*."

"I like Blair better," Eli answered. "So, where is the ranch?"

"My father's family has a ranch outside of town. Believe it or not, my mother actually lived there until my father died. Fortunately for her, he died when I was a baby. Unfortunately for him and for me, he died when I was a baby. There's a family compound where some live. I like them. I've always liked them. My cousins are around my age. Some live here. Some live in Dallas, which was fun when I lived there. Most of us went to the University of Oklahoma. It's almost a family requirement to go to school there. Most of us live in Oklahoma. I called my uncle Charge and told him we were coming. I asked if it was all right, and he was thrilled. I used to go out and ride horses with my cousins. I haven't been out there in a while."

The ranch was huge and located next to what are called "mountains" in Oklahoma and "hills" anyplace else that has real mountains. At one point in prehistoric times, they were mountains, but now with age and erosion, they were hills. There was a lake on the ranch, and it made for pretty riding. Eli had not been on a horse in years. When he did ride, it was with an English saddle and bridle. He had never ridden Western. It was a new adventure.

Blair showed him the ranch. She showed him the place in the trees where her father died while walking to get the truck, having sent his horse back to the barn. He tripped over a tree limb, but they figured he was dead by the time he hit the ground because of a massive heart attack. It was terrible, especially since there was no history of heart disease in the family and he was always so healthy without any health problems.

She showed him a pasture with the biggest bull Eli had ever seen. It was the size of a boxcar.

"My God," said Eli, "he's huge."

Blair smiled. "They showed him. He's a major prizewinner and worth so much you wouldn't believe it. He's been vacationing in New Mexico at a place where they gather semen and freeze it. He's returned to be with his current harem in the pasture."

"Not a bad life," said Eli.

Her smile was beautiful, as was she. "Come on," she answered and rode off in another direction.

After returning the horses, they visited for a while with her uncles Charge and Henry and a couple of cousins. Both of their faces were sunburned. They were hot and dusty. Booty's boots were really dirty. Eli was having a wonderful time.

Blair started the car. "You hungry?"

"Sure."

"How about some barbecue? It's late for lunch, but these places are open all the time."

"Great."

"There's a lake outside of town, Lake Trapp," said Blair as she drove toward there. "It's man-made—for all I know, all of the lakes in Oklahoma are. There's a lodge and cabins. I heard they've redone the lodge. God knows they needed to. We're not going there. I'm taking you to some of the best barbecue you'll ever have in your life. I just hope we can find a place. The problem is that just as soon as you know a place, they blow it up for the insurance. They rebuild, but you have to find the new place."

Sure enough, they drove to a burnt-out joint and had to drive around for a while before they spotted another wood joint with a red neon sign flashing Bar-B-Q. Old weathered redwood picnic tables were over at the side under big shade trees. When the owners made their quick move, they took everything moveable with them, including the picnic tables. Smoke from the smoker in the back puffed into the blue sky.

Blair turned off the car. A few pickup trucks and an old Buick sedan with a big dent on one side were in the dirt parking lot. Eli followed Blair inside a wooden building. It was dark entering from the bright sunlight. On one side, a few people were gathered around a long bar, drinking beer. The bartender leaned on the bar talking to one of the men with a cigarette hanging out of his mouth. He looked up when they walked in, watched for a moment, and then returned to his conversation. Metal tables with greasy plastic red-checked tablecloths with metal or wood chairs filled the remaining area. Fans whirling overhead competed with the rumbling from a window air conditioner. The place looked as though it had never been cleaned, including the windows, which you could barely see through. It had the feel of being a tough joint. An old jukebox pushed against one wall was silent until a cowboy strolled over and dropped in some change, and out came a woman's plaintive voice in an old country-western song.

Blair led him over to one of the tables for four next to a window, and they sat down.

Eli looked around, trying not to show his amazement. He was taken aback by the smell of cigarette smoke. It had been a long time since he smelled smoke in a restaurant. New York didn't allow smoking.

Blair looked at him and smiled. Some of her hair was wet from the heat and plastered to her face. "What?" she asked.

Eli looked back at her, smiling. "I didn't know there were places actually like this. It looks like a movie set."

"I didn't think you'd seen a place like this."

"I haven't."

A waitress, probably forty-something, but it was difficult to tell because her face was so hardened and lined, strolled up. She had on jeans, a checked shirt that was rolled up and tied at her waist, and cowboy boots.

"Hi."

Blair answered, "Hi."

"How you all doin'? Hot enough for you?"

Blair nodded. "Hot enough to fry an egg."

"Ain't that the truth. What will you all be havin'?"

Eli looked at Blair. He didn't have the slightest idea what to order, which she knew. "How about slabs of you all's ribs."

"French fries or beans?"

Blair looked at Eli. "It's up to you," he replied.

"How about french fries and two Coors."

"Sure," she said and strolled away.

"My God," said Eli.

"You're right—and just wait until you taste their ribs. You are going to be surprised."

The waitress returned carrying a metal tray with a picture of a bottle of Bud on it. "Here you go." She handed them two tall bottles of ice-cold Coors beer and then placed two plastic bottles containing sauce on the table. "The redder bottle is hot."

"Okay," said Blair. "Thanks."

"How hot is hot?" asked Eli.

"Hot. You probably better stick to mild. It's the other bottle."

Laughter burst out from the bar and then quieted down again.

Blair leaned back in the chair and took a good, long drink of the cold beer. "Oh my God, that tastes good."

"It certainly does."

By the time the waitress returned with the ribs and french fries, their beers were empty.

"Here you go, you all." She put the plates in front of them and then pulled out a bottle of ketchup from the pocket in her apron. She looked at the empty bottles and took them.

"Can we have two more, please?" Eli said.

The waitress looked at him, surprised. "Sure. Be right back."

"What did I say wrong?" Eli asked Blair after she was hopefully out of hearing.

"You were so polite. I'm sure she isn't addressed that way too much. Here." She handed him the mild bottle of barbecue sauce. "Try that. If it's too mild, then grab the red bottle."

Eli squirted it all over the ribs. "I think it will be fine."

Blair covered her ribs in the hot sauce before the waitress returned with two more beers, put them down, and then strolled away.

"These potatoes taste like they're homemade, not frozen," said Eli with barbecue sauce all over his mouth.

"They are homemade. Everything is made and cooked right here."

The waitress returned with two small plates, each holding a large biscuit and a big pat of butter. She told them, "They're hot, fresh out of the oven."

"Great," Eli said with a smile, looking up at her.

She took one look at him and grabbed the metal napkin holder, teeming with napkins. "Here, I just filled this one." She reached over both of them and grabbed the half-empty holder and took it with her.

"I am a mess," said Eli.

"You certainly are," answered Blair. She had some barbecue sauce on her mouth and a little on her face, but nothing like Eli, who had smeared it across his face. Some sauce dripped down his Polo shirt.

"You're right. I have never tasted anything like this in my life. Even the barbecue Booty brings back from Athens isn't as good as this, and I thought *that* was the best I'd ever tasted." He noticed the sauce forming into a dark circle on his shirt. "Oh my God—I am a mess." He tried to wipe it off only to smear it more.

"They should give out bibs."

"Right," answered Blair. "I can just see these tough old cowboys tying bibs around their necks." Her eyes were bright and smiling.

Eli looked at her and laughed. "I think I need to get out a little more. These are delicious. Oh! I dripped it on me again." He shrugged. "Oh well."

When the waitress first placed the slab of ribs and mound of fried potatoes on his plate, Eli thought he would never be able to finish so much food. He and Blair leaned back in their metal chairs. The ribs were all eaten. Blair had some potatoes left, where Eli's plate had nothing but licked-clean rib bones. In the course of lunch, they had downed another beer.

The waitress cleared the plates and stood at the table. "How about dessert for you all?"

"Oh my God," Eli moaned. "Are you kidding?"

"Peach cobbler?" said the waitress.

"Do we dare?" asked Blair. "I know it's delicious."

"It is," assured the waitress. "Made just a while ago with fresh peaches. Or we have watermelon, nice and chilled."

Blair and Eli looked at each other and almost at the same time said, "Peach cobbler."

"And some water," Eli said after the waitress, who nodded. He looked down at his shirt. "What a mess."

Blair smiled. "You've got sauce all down you."

Eli continued to survey his shirt. "Well, at least I don't have it in my teeth like you do."

It seemed like they laughed all the way through lunch, as if they'd known each other for years. Later, Blair drove them to a place at Lake Trapp full of old shade trees. There was a small beach where they rolled up their jeans and waded in the cool water. Eli tried to wash off his shirt as best he could but only drenched it. The wet against his hot skin felt good as they lay under the shade of the trees on a big blanket Blair had gotten out of the trunk. They spent the rest of the afternoon there into the evening.

Water skiers glided over the glass-smooth lake. Screams of children jumping into the water off of the many docks dotted around the lake carried through the air, though it was doubtful Blair and Eli were listening.

Chapter 4

The Japanese maples' red leaves stood almost still waiting for the breeze to pick up. The slightest hint of cool air, a promise of oncoming fall, tickled under the heat of late summer. The season's clock ticked toward change as the sun crept down earlier each evening. Late-afternoon light wrenched the last bit of brightness from the summer-weary red geraniums overflowing in the ceramic pots on the front porch. A red hibiscus held court for hummingbirds, while other birds resumed life from their respite, avoiding the breathlessly hot day. Without anyone noticing quite when it happened, the evening star twinkled in the bright-blue sky. Cardinals enjoyed an evening bath in the roof gutter's water, as blue jays flew between trees and doves busily pecked the ground. Every so often, a fat toad leapt across the grass while the dusk, rich with deep reds and pinks, pushed away the bright-blue sky to become only a memory. Evening passed into night to the boisterous accompaniment of a chorus of katydids.

Routine sprang into existence with such familiarity that they felt like they had always been there. People seemed not to notice something new had entered their lives. Ellanor joining Mae and Booty on the front porch wasn't new, but Lorraine living at Precious's certainly was, as was Blair joining Eli surprised everyone except Mae.

Herschel, as usual, snored loudly under the old, squeaking swing. Almost every night, Blair and Eli joined Mae and Booty for dinner. They sat on the front porch, slowly digesting Mae's fried chicken, mashed potatoes with cream gravy, freshly baked biscuits, fresh green beans, and chocolate pie topped with meringue. Eli and Blair had taken the wicker couch against the house. Their feet flopped upon the wicker coffee table, and tall glasses of iced tea sat on small tables at each end of the couch. Eli's arm was casually draped around Blair. His head leaned back upon the yellow chintz cushion with his mouth open, snoozing. Blair's black hair was tossed about the top of his shoulder, where she rested her head and watched nothing much in particular.

In the midst of the comfortable silence, Ellanor strolled over, poured a glass of iced tea, and took a seat in his usual big, old wicker chair. He propped up his feet on the porch railing and quietly sipped the tea.

Booty looked around the yard as the swing loudly moaned back and forth. "There used to be fireflies."

Mae looked around the yard too. "There were. Where did they go? Seemed like the yard was full of them, but now I don't see a one."

"Doesn't seem like there are too many chiggers," Ellanor said. "You used to not be able to sit out here after dark because of them. I always thought you should screen in this porch, Mae, because of the damn things. Ran us inside. With any luck at all, they'll go extinct."

"I remember running after fireflies," said Blair in a lazy voice. "Used to put them in mayonnaise jars with holes pushed in the top and watch them flying around flashing their lights. I'd forgotten about the fireflies."

Mae looked at the yard, and so quietly that you would have had to strain to hear her, said, "Eons ago—that's what it feels like. The porch always had people visiting. So many of them are gone now."

Booty's arm was around Mae, and he softly patted her. "Yes, many are gone."

Ellanor took a long drink of iced tea and placed the glass back on the side table. "I'm glad the damn chiggers are mostly gone. To hell with the damn things. It's getting dark. Mae, I'm going to light the citronella candles. And speaking of mosquitoes ... I hate the damn things. Why can't they go extinct? Who'd miss them?"

"Who was talking about mosquitoes?" Mae asked.

"Probably whoever eats them in the food chain would miss them," Blair replied.

"Surely there is something else they can eat. Who lives on a diet of mosquitoes?" Ellanor answered.

"I had a dog that could catch them in midair," Blair said.

"How fascinating," Ellanor muttered.

Mae leaned her head back, looking past the porch roof. Her curly white hair flitted in the breeze. "Ellanor, you know about the location of stars in the sky. Why is it I don't see one firefly? They were so nice to watch. Anyway, Ellanor, there was a summer constellation I wanted to ask you about. Oh look, there's a shooting star! Too late. It's already gone. Now what was going to ask you? Oh, well, it couldn't have been that important."

Quiet descended again on them. The citronella candles created puddles of light around the front porch.

Blair smiled as she looked at Eli. "He's asleep."

Ellanor turned around and glanced at Eli. "Tomorrow is the big day. School starts."

"Yes, it does," Mae replied. "He's been up there all week, getting ready for classes, and who knows what else. He told me Lucille was a bigot, which is news to no one. Evidently she's been rude again as usual to Mary McKeen and Prudence Carpenter. Lucille told Eli, 'Unfortunately, the school allows ho-mo-sex-uals—and that's the way she said it to him, separating the words and scrunching up her nose like a bad smell. Really, Booty, the board needs to do something about Lucille. She's intolerable."

"She's a bitch," Eli said, his head still back against the pillow and his eyes closed. "I wish you could have heard the way she spit out *ho-mo-sex-uals* like she could barely get the word out. What a horror that woman is. I heard her calling me 'that Oriental.' I told her, 'Lucille, that's not my name.' And what's with her sister? Jesus! I couldn't figure out what she was doing at first. Who goes around whispering all of the time?"

"Oh, you mean *that* sister. Whisper Woman," Ellanor said. "What's she doing up at Lincoln fluttering around? Tell her to go back to her cave and hang upside down."

Eli sat up and looked at Ellanor. "I thought Lucille was kidding when she introduced me to her. Her name really is Whisper Woman?"

"No," Booty said, "Her name is Amanda."

"Is it?" interrupted Blair. "I'd forgotten that … if I ever knew it. All I've ever heard her called is Whisper Woman."

Eli continued as if he had not been interrupted. "Maybe if she was an American Indian, I could believe it."

"When was it?" Blair chewed her bottom lip as she thought. "I don't know how old I was when I first encountered Whisper Woman. It had to be at somebody's funeral with my mother. I remember standing in the old room they used for receptions and things at the church—the old one before they tore it down and built the new wing. It must have been summer, because I remember how hot it was. Didn't that big old room have air conditioning? Anyway, I remember watching this woman busy rearranging all the flowers and sprays. I thought she was the florist."

Booty interrupted again. "Whisper Woman is wont to do that. She doesn't seem to be able to leave flowers alone at funerals. I don't know why she does that, but she always has. What I thought was strange is why doesn't she do that at weddings? Why does she rearrange flowers only at funerals?"

"Because someone would kill her, doing that at a wedding," Mae replied. "At a funeral, the person is dead, so what do they care? The family is usually so upset, they can't be bothered with her. Although I do remember one time … Some people take their funeral flowers very seriously."

"So," Blair continued, "I said to my mother something like 'That lady can't decide what to do about those flowers.' I remember my mother saying, 'Damn Whisper Woman, why can't she leave anything alone?' I thought my mother was going to go to hell swearing in church, even if it was only the reception room. And wondering if that really was her name. Mother got in a real snit and dragged me over to her. Probably it was the flowers she sent that Whisper Woman was moving. I remember Whisper Woman whispering, and I thought it was because we were in a church. I didn't realize she did it all of the time until later. So her real name is Amanda. Why doesn't she want to be called that? It's such a pretty name! Much better than Whisper Woman."

Mae said, "I'll tell you why the crazy women whispers."

Ellanor interrupted. "How do you know why she whispers? Who told you?"

Mae shot Ellanor a look. "Really, Ellanor, sometimes you can be such an ass!"

"Why? What did I say?" asked Ellanor, quite offended.

"My mother told me," Mae said. "That's how I know."

Booty blurted, "Since when was your mother friends with Mrs. Pawn? Neither of them left their bedroom, as far as I knew."

"Booty," Mae said, "everyone gets themselves together to go to the beauty parlor. You know that. Anyway, someone asked—"

"I did," interrupted Eli.

"Oh, that's right, it was you. Eli asked how Whisper Woman got called that, and I just happen to know."

"I bet my mother knows too," Blair said.

"Well, yes. I'm sure she does," Mae answered. "But thank God your mother isn't here. The point is we were at the University of Oklahoma. In our sorority, some of the girls from Oklahoma City and probably Tulsa too—I've forgotten—who were debutantes were talking about their dresses and parties and such. Well, Whisper Woman wanted to be a deb so bad she could taste it, and so did her mother, except there weren't debutantes in Cedar Springs or Athens. Her mother got it into her head that even though her daughter couldn't be a deb, she could by God act like one, and Mrs. Pawn, who always had a little trouble discerning reality, decided proper Southern girls don't talk, they *whisper*. So Whisper Woman started whispering all the time, and someone started calling her 'Whisper Woman,' and it stuck. I've always said be careful about using nicknames, because they seem to always stick. It's like some seventy-something-year-old man being called Junior. I mean his father has been dead for a hundred years and he's still called Junior?"

"I'm called Booty," Booty said. "That's a nickname. You don't like it, Mae? You never told me. I think it is a little late to be called Julius, since no one would know who that was … including me."

"Oh, honey," Mae said. "Oh, no! I didn't mean you. Booty is a wonderful name, and I love it just like I love you. You are and always will be Booty. No, no, no, I did not meant that at all. Who I was thinking about was Punky. He'll be called Punky until the day he dies. I don't even remember how we started calling him Punky in the first place or what is real name is, now that I think about it."

"Harold," Booty answered. "His real name is Harold."

"Is it?" Mae said. "Well, good Lord! He's Harold Jr.—that makes sense."

"I do," said Ellanor.

Mae looked at Ellanor. "You do what?"

"I remember how he got called Punky. His father called him that," Ellanor said. "And before you ask how I know, I distinctly remember his father calling him that."

"Well, that's settled," Mae said.

"You don't have to be snide," snapped Ellanor.

"I wasn't being snide," Mae said.

"I thought you wanted to know," Ellanor said.

"I did want to know," Mae answered.

Eli interrupted, "I don't think of Oklahoma as a southern state."

Booty looked at Eli. "You would if you were black. Did you know there was a Confederate Army nursing home in Athens? Now, it's a VA nursing home. When we were growing up, Athens had three different school systems: white, black, and the Indians went to an Indian seminary outside of town. That's why I went to boarding school at a very young age. No one wants to be discriminated against, and no one should be."

Ellanor interrupted. "I'll tell you what I've always wanted to do, and that is go up to Whisper Woman and yell 'Speak up, God damn it! God gave you a voice, now use it, for Christ's sake!' If I had to live with her, I'd kill her. I really would—and I'd enjoy it too."

"Really, Ellanor," Mae said. "Didn't anyone ever tell you that if you can't say something nice, don't say anything at all?"

"I don't give a damn. Her whispering is unnerving. She should be shot. That would be the merciful thing to do for her and everyone who has to listen to her."

"How very generous of you," Mae said. "Eli, did Lucille give you a list of your students? Who are they? How many are in the classroom? It can't be too many. There aren't that many kids anymore in Cedar Springs. We'll see who we know—the parents. I don't know too many kids anymore. They've all grown up. I remember Blair Don growing up. Why, I can see you right now as a little girl, just as clear as my hand in front of my face."

"Blair," Eli corrected.

"Blair," Mae answered.

Blair said, "Eli has the pastor's kids."

"Oh, God," moaned Ellanor. "I hope they're not like him, or you will wish they whispered."

"Which ones?" asked Mae. "Seems like he has a whole gaggle of kids."

"These are the youngest, the twins," Blair said. "I saw Helen, their mother, at the grocery store in Athens. We ended up talking for I don't know how long. She was just sick her youngest ones were in their last year at Lincoln and would be leaving to go over to Athens to school. You'd think it was the end of the world by the way she talked about them *leaving.* I told her they're not leaving; they're not going anyplace. They're eleven years old. She used the usual answer, you know, 'You don't know what it is like because you don't have any kids.' She's right, but still, the kids haven't gone anywhere yet. They have a whole year to go in the sixth grade here at Lincoln."

"Wonder if there are twins in the family?" Mae said.

"So they're twins," Booty said. "What are they?"

"A girl and a boy," answered Blair. "Betty Ann, who is named after Helen's sister Betty Jane, and Hiram, who I guess is named after someone in the Bible. I don't know."

"You mean Precious didn't trot you off to Sunday school?" asked Ellanor.

"Sunday morning, I went out to the ranch and rode horses with my cousins."

Eli spoke, still resting with his eyes closed. "If Betty Ann is named after Betty Jane, then why isn't her name Betty Jane?"

Mae spoke up. "My dear, you are trying to make logic out of an illogical source. It won't happen."

Booty asked, "Eli, have you met any of the kids yet? How many do you have?"

Eli leaned his head back against the house with his eyes closed. "No, I haven't met any of them. Nine. Blair knows who they are."

"Who are the rest?" asked Booty.

"He's got some of the Herzstein clan," said Blair.

"Now that really is a cast of thousands," interrupted Mae. "All those sons got married—some who knows how many times—and had kids. That compound out there on their ranch must look like a tiny town."

Blair continued, "Eli has some of the cousins, Joe Tom, Clare, and A.J."

"Sweet," interrupted Mae. "A.J. must be named after his grandfather, Albert John Herzstein, but everybody called him A.J. Honey. That man made a ton of money, and he needed to, having all those kids. Poor man! Terrible alcoholic with one of those W.C. Fields noses, great big and bulbous, except I remember his was sort of blue. He died drunk in a motel room all by himself with both his legs cut off. How lonely and sad. Who's left, Blair?"

"He has Miriam McKeen and Lynette Sue Harper."

Eli interrupted, "Ah, the daughter of my fellow sixth-grade teacher, the dreaded Mary McKeen, who Lucille so thoughtfully warned me about. I don't know how Mary and Prudence have put up with her all the years. I couldn't do it. I've been with them this week. They are such nice women and they're funny. I guess you need a sense of humor to put up with Lucille. Either that or be deaf. They certainly have been helpful to me. I didn't know what I needed until they told me."

"According to Helen Pastor," said Blair, "Betty Ann can't stand Lynette Sue. Helen told me that Miriam and Lynette Sue are considered the stars of the school. Lucille has them dancing at every school program. I suspect there might be a little jealousy because Betty Ann sings and Helen doesn't think she is appreciated enough. I don't know. I haven't gone to a Lincoln School assembly or whatever they call it now since I was at Lincoln."

"You will," Eli interrupted. "If I have to go, you have to go."

She kissed him and said, "We'll see. To complete Eli's class, he has Heppy and Isabelle White."

"White?" asked Mae.

Ellanor sat straight up and looked at Blair. "Who did you say? Who are these White kids? Surely they aren't—"

Blair interrupted, "Oh, yes they are."

"But there aren't any children in that family that I know of!" Ellanor said. "They can't be the same Whites. They can't be. There aren't any children. Everyone is too old. As I remember it, my mother's brother Elmer only had Elmer Jr."

"Who are the children?" asked Mae. "I didn't know there were any children and certainly not young ones. Are you sure it is the same White family? There are other Whites around. It can't be the same family. There can't be kids in the sixth grade! My God, Lee Tom and Elmer Jr. are around our age someplace. If they have kids in the sixth grade, it's a miracle."

"This isn't possible," said Ellanor, astounded. "It isn't! Who are these children, because I'll tell you who they are not. Like Mae said—and it's true—the area is full of people named White. It's not an unusual name."

Booty entered the conversation. "Ellanor, do you remember or did you even know that Lee Tom and Elmer had a son? His name was Ellie."

Mae thought about this. "Hmm … Ellie White? Did I know an Ellie White? I don't remember if I did. How old is he?"

"I knew him a little at school. At least, I remember him," Blair said. "He was, I think, about five years older than I was. Ellanor, you never knew him?"

"Of course not," snapped Ellanor. "When my mother got out of that horrible family, she left them completely. Seems to me the only time I ever met her brother Elmer was at the hardware store, when he'd come in to get something. Father introduced us. He told me not to tell Mother, and I never did. I don't know if Lorraine ever met him, since he wasn't at the store much."

"These are Ellie's kids in Eli's class?" asked Mae. "Who is the mother? Who did he marry? Do we know her?"

"She's dead. Seems to me her name was Val," answered Blair. "Dead along with Ellie."

"I never met him alive," Ellanor said, "and now he's dead. He certainly must have been awfully young when he died."

Mae interrupted. "He must have been awfully young when he got married."

"They were in their early twenties when they died," answered Blair. "Don't you all remember that terrible motorcycle accident on the way to the lake?"

"Which one?" asked Mae. "People are always getting killed going to or coming from the lake, usually drunk as skunks. That back-way road is too curvy. I've always said so. And if you go by way of the highway, you have to cross the railroad tracks, and I always think a train is coming because there aren't any lights or anything. Both ways are dangerous. Don't you remember someone drove right into the train once? And then there was that poor boy who was drunk who walked straight into a train! I'm sure it nearly killed his parents. I remember hearing talk about maybe the boy was a suicide, but we'll never know. Seems to me both those accidents happened at night. I bet they did."

Booty continued, "Mae, it was years ago when that happened."

Mae snorted, "I don't care. It could happen again."

Blair persisted in trying to get them to remember the particular wreck in which Ellie White and his wife Val died. "Come on, you all! Don't you remember a couple hitting a tree and dying? They left a little baby and a two-year-old. I'll never forget it because Ellie was the first person around my age that I knew who died. Well, there was that boy who died of a brain tumor, but he was sick anyway. Everybody knew he was going to die, so that doesn't really count as shocking. Oh, and then there was that boy who got drunk and had a car accident. I'm going to say he was sixteen or so. At least he didn't take anybody with him like Ellie White did. It was terrible. I remember it was all over the paper at the time with pictures—not of them, of course, just the twisted motorcycle. One look at that motorcycle and you knew no one was going to walk away from it. When I say they were smashed against a tree, they were *smashed* against a tree."

"Who was his wife?" Mae asked.

"I didn't know her," Blair answered. "She was from some little town around here. He was kind of thuggy, so I never really knew him. Somehow, the Whites got the kids. I don't know the story on how that happened. I thought usually the mother's family ends up with the kids."

Ellanor interrupted. "Now, are you sure you're talking about Elmer Jr. and Lee Tom?"

Blair nodded. "Yes. I looked at the list of kids in Eli's class, and it lists their parents. Mr. and Mrs. Elmer White, Jr. are listed as parents."

"Jesus Christ!" Ellanor said.

"Oh my God," Mae moaned.

"Well, I'll be damned!" Booty exclaimed. "I hope you never have to meet Lee Tom or Elmer Jr."

"Jesus Christ," Ellanor said again.

"Isn't that the truth," Mae agreed.

"Jesus Christ," said Ellanor again, shaking his head. "Amazing. I'll never have to see them, thank God. You might, Eli, if they come in for some teacher-parent thing. I'm never telling Lorraine this. With any luck at all, they won't come in for the teacher-parent thing. My parents never did, so it is a possibility they won't either. If they do, just ignore them, Eli. That's all you can do. Just ignore them. Pretend they don't exist. That's the only thing to do."

"Why?" asked Eli. "And how can I ignore them if they are sitting across the desk at a parent-teacher conference? It's a little difficult to ignore someone sitting right in front of you. I'm the teacher. I can't ignore them. Why do you want me to anyway?"

Ellanor became very serious. "Just do. Pretend they don't exist. If you have to meet with them, make it quick, and don't tell them you know either Lorraine or me."

"I still don't get why," said Eli.

"I'm sorry to say this, Ellanor, but Mother calls them white trash," said Blair.

"Honey," Mae said, "your mother thinks everybody but her little group and old Athens society is white trash."

"I'm still not getting it!" said Eli. "What is the deal with the kids? I understand that they live with their grandparents. So what?"

Mae looked at Eli and said, with seriousness in her voice, "Honey, like we said, Lorraine and Ellanor's mother, Billie Rae, and Elmer were brother and sister. Now Billie Rae was the kindest, sweetest thing that ever happened, and the loneliest. She happened to be a little bit crazy, but then, who isn't? She and my mother were good friends."

Ellanor interrupted. "My mother was crazy."

"Yes, she was," Mae agreed, "but she was also very sweet, and anyway, nobody's perfect."

"I still don't get it!" insisted Eli.

Booty said, "You don't have to. Believe me, everything is ancient history and left well enough alone. I'm sure those White children are very nice and will fit right into your class just like everybody else."

★ ★ ★ ★ ★

103

Eli stood staring at a bunch of children who stared back at him. One thing was obvious after calling the roll and starting to put names with pupils: Heppy and Isabelle White were not like anybody else. All of the rest of the kids were well dressed and clean. Heppy and Isabelle had chosen back-row seats, where they hid. They didn't really look dirty, but they didn't look clean either. Heppy was tall and terribly thin and looked like he was about to throw up from fear. He failed the sixth grade twice and was repeating it for the third time. He was thirteen years old, and his evolution from childhood to teenager was evident in his face, a battlefield with outbursts of acne.

Lynette Sue Harper was blonde, cute, and perky, with an upturned nose. Her curly hair bounced around her sparkling bright-blue eyes and gleaming white, perfect teeth. She smiled all the time. Betty Ann Pastor shot her looks that could have killed, especially since Lynette Sue was developing out of childhood into young womanhood, while Betty Ann's chest remained steadfastly flat. Even though Betty Ann was secretly mad at God because she had not started to develop, she was beholden to Him. After all, he had plagued her brother Hiram with freckles all over his face to go with their dark-red hair and spared her that spotted fate.

Miriam McKeen was stately with light-blonde hair. She was tall and thin with a square jaw. The Herzstein cousins shared brown eyes and light-olive complexions. The boys had dark, rich, brown hair, whereas Clare's hair was a deep auburn. Joe Tom was turning from a darling little boy into a handsome young man. Already the girls chased him, but to no avail, Lynette Sue had claimed him as hers in the third grade. She told all the girls that she was going to marry Joe Tom and devoted great amounts of time worrying about names for their five children.

Through the rumble of the air conditioner, Eli caught sounds of a dog barking somewhere. A crow loudly fussed at something, accompanied by a coughing lawnmower. He stood in his classroom glancing outside one of the long windows at the sway of the leaves on an old oak tree. Eli had started walking over to Lincoln while preparing for classes and already had gotten into the habit. He enjoyed the walk over aged cement sidewalks that were cracked and buckled and shaded on both sides of the streets by old elm trees. Miss Marie greeted him from the front porch of her stone house, as did Mrs. Harrell down the block. She was always busy working in her yard. Miss Marie was obese to the point of filling up the entire swing seat, where she held daily court while reading the paper or a book. When Eli walked by, she'd stop, look up, and say hello.

Mary McKeen, the other sixth-grade teacher, suggested having the children write about their summer vacation, which is exactly what Eli did. The children were busily writing as he mused about his first morning as a schoolteacher. Somehow just the thought of him being a sixth-grade teacher, of all things, made him want to burst out laughing. It seemed incredibly absurd. Only months ago, he was living in New York City, working at the family's Wall Street investment bank, wearing exquisitely tailored suits. Now he was sitting at a well-used desk in a navy blazer and slacks in Cedar Springs, Oklahoma. Amazing—absolutely amazing. The best part was the discovery of Blair Mason, who stayed at his cottage behind the big house more than she did her own apartment. Eli smiled at the very thought of her.

Blair got him off for his first day at school. She was very loving and excited for him. When he walked down the driveway, Mae was already on the front porch to wish him well. Eli loved them both. They already were such a part of his life. And that surprised him too. He didn't think he truly loved much of anybody in his life—terrible crushes yes, and maybe thinking he was madly in love. What he felt about Blair he had never felt in his life, and he had never experienced such motherly compassion as he had with Mae. Certainly not from his own mother, who had divorced his father. After presenting him with an infant Japanese heir, she returned to live in Japan, where she remarried. They never heard from her again. His Greenwich, Connecticut-born blonde stepmother wasn't interested in him. She had her own brood with his father to rear.

The noise of children talking shook him back from musing. He looked quickly at the class. They had finished their assignment and were visiting with each other.

"Okay," Eli said in an official voice, "obviously you've finished, so let's hear how you spent the summer. Who would like to start?"

Betty Ann Pastor's hand shot up.

"Betty Ann," Eli said, "read to us about your summer."

"Okay," she answered, "Hiram and me—"

Eli interrupted her. "Hiram and I."

"Okay. Hiram and *I* had a real good summer, didn't we, Hiram?" She shot him a look like he'd better agree.

Hiram froze. He was scared to death of his sister. She was bigger, and to make matters worse, she was a bully. If and when the day ever came that he would be bigger than she was, he had his revenge all planned out. He'd get her behind the holly bushes at the back of the church and show her what it felt like to be beaten up. He honestly believed if he hated anyone in this world, it was Betty Ann. She blamed him for everything, and their mother always took Betty Ann's side—always. It was truly awful. He was little, skinny, and had freckles all over. There was nothing he could do about any of those things. He fantasized about ways to kill her that were always wonderfully slow and painful. This made him happy.

"Hiram!" Betty Ann commanded. "Didn't we?"

"Yes," he muttered and nodded to make sure she knew he agreed.

"Well," Betty Ann continued, smacking her lips, "Hiram and I had a good time this summer. We went to Bible camp with our sister, Yolanda. It was very pretty. There was a waterfall, and we swam in the lake. Hiram got an ear infection. Didn't you, Hiram? I knew he would. He always gets sick."

Hiram wanted to disappear at his desk. He said nothing.

"We stayed in cabins with bunk beds, and I said I wouldn't sleep on top. I wouldn't either. You could fall off and die. So this girl from Springer, who I didn't like, did, and there wasn't any air conditioning. It was hot. Why wasn't anything air-conditioned? I didn't like the toilets either. They were old and yucky, and you had to walk to them, just like you had to walk to take a shower. I didn't take a shower the whole time I was there except when my counselor said that I smelled and all the girls in my cabin agreed, which I thought was rude. So I took one shower. Who wants to take a shower with no hot water? I swam in the lake every day. That counted as a bath, and I told them so.

"Two of the girls in my cabin had been to the Bible camp before, and they said it was real fun to go spy on the older kids, because there was a place they went to make out. They knew where it was. I told those girls that we weren't supposed to leave the cabin and we shouldn't go, except they all wanted to go. So I went too, but I told them we weren't supposed to and we could get into trouble. The girls who had been at camp before said it was okay and to come on. We sneaked through some of the woods to this big room with screens on the windows like a big-screened porch, and guess who we saw? My sister, Yolanda; there she was with her boyfriend, Roger, and it was horrible. They were *naked as jaybirds,* and they were doing it. I know because I watched them for a long time. I'm surprised they didn't wake the whole camp, they made so much noise. Shame on them. I thought lightning would strike them dead, because they are not married, and my mother said never to do it until we were married. It's a sin, and we'll go to hell. Yolanda and Roger are going to hell and I'm going to tell my mother."

At that point, Lynette Sue let out an ear-splitting scream. "No! That's not true!"

Eli was struggling to believe that he actually heard what he just heard.

The girls in the class gasped, except for Isabelle, who sat like a stone. The boys winked and did thumbs up to each other, except Heppy, who didn't have any friends.

Betty Ann looked over at Lynette Sue with her arms folded. She said, "It is too true! I saw. Yolanda and Roger have been watching too many movies, because I didn't know human beings could do that."

Lynette Sue's eyes bulged with fury. "That's a lie, Betty Ann, and you know it!"

Smugly, Betty Ann answered, "No, it's not."

Miriam couldn't help herself. She burst out laughing, followed by Clare. Lynette Sue whipped around, pointing and glaring at Miriam. She screamed, "This is *not* funny!"

Hiram begged to disagree, although he would never have said that out loud. Tears wanted to roll down his face in joy. He did not know any of this until now. It was truly a miracle. When Yolanda found out who told (and she would), she would kill Betty Ann. *Thank you, Jesus!*

"I saw what I saw, and I saw Yolanda and Roger buck naked, at it," said Betty Ann with her arms folded. "If the camp hadn't taken all of our electronic stuff when we checked in, I would have pictures to show you and the Internet. Yolanda is not going to be Mommy's favorite anymore."

Lynette Sue turned white with rage. "I am going to kill you. I thought I was too nice to hurt anyone, but I'll make an exception with you. Yolanda, just like me, has been a cheerleader since we could be cheerleaders. She is head cheerleader at Athens High School. She is perfect, and I want to be just like her."

Eli had to do something. What, though? That was the question. He could always run out of the classroom and quit. He would have to leave town, which meant leaving Blair. He was afraid Lynette Sue was about to do something like beat up Betty Ann, which would be terrible, especially on his first day. Oh God, this was maybe the worst day of his life. Eli did the only thing he could do without actually leaving school. He ran across the hall to Mary McKeen's class for much-needed help. As he ran out, he heard screaming and laughing.

When he got Mary into the hall to tell her what happened, all she could do was laugh. She thanked him for making her day and returned to class. When Eli returned to class, Lynette Sue was over Betty Ann at her desk, screaming at her at the top of her lungs.

Eli clapped his hands, trying to get their attention. "That's enough!"

Lynette Sue was too involved to hear him. Betty Ann looked scared. She believed that Lynette Sue was going to beat her up. She always beat Hiram up. No one dared try that with her, but Lynette Sue was mad enough.

"Okay, that's it," Eli said to take control. "Miriam—you and Clare take Lynette Sue to the bathroom. She needs to calm down. Put a cold, wet towel on her head or something."

They looked at him and then slowly got up.

Lynette Sue dramatically put her hand to her head. "I feel faint."

Her boyfriend, Joe Tom, suddenly got concerned and started to get up. "Can I help?"

"No! Sit down. Now!" Eli said. "Girls, take her to the bathroom."

"Maybe I need to take some deep breaths," Lynette Sue said. Her voice shook dramatically as she spoke. "I'm in shock. I know I am. This is the worst day of my life, and it's all your fault, Betty Ann. You have given me the worst day of my life. I'll never get over it. Never."

Lynette Sue moaned as Miriam and Clare led her out of the classroom. Eli looked at Betty Ann. "Betty Ann, you are done with your story."

"No, I'm not."

"Yes, you are. Did anyone go to Disneyland or someplace or anyplace but Bible camp?"

★ ★ ★ ★ ★

That evening, all Eli could do was lie on the bed and moan. Blair found him lying there after she left Booty's. He had not taken off his navy blazer or shoes or let go of the briefcase. She called Mae and told her dinner was off, explaining that she would talk to her later. After she got him comfortable in bed with a cold compress on his head, she asked what happened.

"I took four headache pills," replied Eli.

"Four? I think you should take only two."

"My head aches."

"Eli, what happened at school today?" she asked as calmly as possible. Based on Eli's reaction, Blair worried that some awful tragedy had happened at school today. She had not heard anything, but surely, someone would have called her if something terrible had happened. She tried to remain calm. "Eli?"

"What?"

"Quit moaning and tell me what happened. Did it happen at school?"

"Yes," he moaned. "I have to quit."

Oh, God, she thought, *what happened?* "Eli, this is enough. You must tell me what happened right now."

Eli could not miss Blair's command. He told her about Betty Ann and her essay on what she did this summer.

When he finished, Blair laughed with relief. "Oh, thank God."

"Oh, thank God what?" asked Eli.

"I thought someone died, the way you were acting. Yolanda's parents are going to have a fit. Poor Helen! It will kill her. The town's pastor's daughter caught screwing at Bible camp? By her sister of all people? I love it."

"I can't teach school. I didn't know eleven-year-olds knew things like that. I don't know what eleven-year-olds know. I don't know any eleven-year-olds. I can't go back there tomorrow."

"Why not?"

"I've made a terrible mistake. This is over my head. I didn't know what to do. When I asked Mary McKeen, all she did was laugh. She didn't help at all. I was stranded. Alone. Lynette Sue was threatening to kill Betty Ann, and she was mad enough to maybe try. Oh God, these children are dangerous! I don't feel well. How can I go back there? I can't. This is horrible."

"Horrible for whom? Seems to me it is a whole lot more horrible for Yolanda. She's the one who has to live with it, not you. This is not about you."

"Yes, it is. I'm the teacher."

"Why would Betty Ann tell that?" Blair wondered.

"Why? I don't know why! Why couldn't she have just broken her leg at camp or something normal? Don't kids climb trees anymore?"

"Did you climb trees?"

"No, certainly not! I would never do that, but you know … Why would she do this to me on my first day?"

"This is not about you."

"Oh God! Betty Ann is an idiot. Could she be that dumb? I don't know. It was my first day, and this happened! How can I teach school?"

"You didn't know what Betty Ann was going to say. Like I told you, if you would listen, this is a small community. I've seen Yolanda's picture in the Athens paper for years. She is Miss Goodie-Goodie. Having this happen—and good gossip spreads like wildfire around here—Yolanda is looking a little like Miss Do-What-I-Say-and-Not-What-I-Do. You need to understand that even though times have changed, they have not changed much *here*. This has nothing to do with you, and it certainly isn't your fault. How can it be your fault? Of course you can teach school. This is just the first day."

"This is a disaster. I'm not going back."

"Of course you are. Don't be silly! You'll be fine. Blanquitta left you all sorts of notes plus her teaching plans. You're going to be a great teacher. All you have to do is just do it. What else would you do? What would happen to the sixth grade if you quit? Who would teach it? No, Eli, you said you would do it, and you will."

"I can't," Eli moaned.

She smiled at him. "Yes, you can."

"How do you know?" Eli said.

"Because I think it's time we thought about something else."

And they did. Eli forgot all about Betty Ann and his decision to quit as he walked to school the next day. All he could think about was Blair and how he couldn't wait to hurry home to her after school today.

★ ★ ★ ★ ★

Suddenly it was October. Eli felt that September had just arrived, and now it was October. With the coming of fall, the annual pilgrimage began in Oklahoma. Living on the East Coast all of his life and attending school there, Eli enjoyed fall weekends of football, but this was entirely different. This was serious. People drove to their various alma maters (or wherever their favorite teams were playing) to watch the quest to win, and if at all possible, be the number-one football team in America. The world according to football fans stopped when their team played. Precious was an enormous University of Oklahoma football fan. Every fall throughout the football season and into the new year, a huge neon red-and-white OU sign glowed on top of her house. Cars drove by just to pay homage to it. Blair tried to prepare Eli for it. She said it was big and neon and red and white. Every year, she begged her mother to please not put it up, but to no avail. Precious loved it. She had it made especially for the top of her roof. Eli had no idea how big it was until he saw it and nearly ran into a tree staring at it as he walked to school. All he could tell Blair was that it was breathtaking, which it most certainly was. It was also garish and huge.

Mae, Booty, and Ellanor wondered what in the world Lorraine thought about it, now that he was living with Precious. Before he vanished into her arms and the house, they all had great laughs about Precious's OU neon letters. The only people who saw him now were Ellanor and

111

Lorraine's cousin, who lived with them, and Precious's friend, Geneva. Once Lorraine moved everything he wanted up the block to live with Precious, he had little to no contact with Mae, Booty, or his brother. The three of them worried about that stupid fool actually marrying her.

One morning at breakfast, Geneva told Ellanor they were getting married. Ellanor immediately ran over to Mae's and told her and Lena, who then ran over to Booty's to tell him that Precious and Lorraine were getting married. After Ellanor gave Mae the news, he went home and took to his bed with the vapors, until the next day, when Mae made him get up and come have dinner with them.

Blair had no idea until Lena rushed into Booty's house and told them. She now lived with Eli and rarely returned to her apartment, except to get clothes or something. Even then, she didn't stay. She timed going there when she knew her mother was not at home. The last thing Blair wanted to do was to run into her mother. Precious called her every day and even went so far as to write her letters delivered to Booty's house. Precious hated Eli and was bound and determined to break them up. She would do whatever it took to make Blair return to her senses. She had plans for Blair, and they certainly were not with some Oriental whose family (and more importantly, finances) she did not know. He wasn't even from Oklahoma. He didn't graduate from the University of Oklahoma. He went to that school full of Communists—Harvard. Blair argued that there aren't any Communists anymore, but to no avail. Precious insisted that she knew what she was talking about. Anyway, who knows who his family is? Does his family have a dime to their name? She doubted it very seriously; in fact, she highly suspected that this Oriental boy was only after all the money Blair Don was going to inherit after Precious married Lorraine. This boy was socially beneath Blair Don and a nobody, period. She didn't raise Blair Don to live on a schoolteacher's salary. She raised Blair Don for better things in life. Who would be her friends if she married Oriental white trash? At that point, if Blair were on the phone, her mother would burst into tears. This made Blair both mad and guilty that she made her mother cry.

Precious was fit to be tied. She was determined to stop this crazy thing Blair Don was doing. This was not going to happen. Precious and Maeva

(Bobby Wrightsberg's mother) decided their children were a perfect match in every way—socially and financially. It was high time for them to marry.

Eli knew that Blair's mother greatly upset her, plus Precious called way too much. He didn't know about the letter writing, because Blair threw them away at Booty's after she read them. Most importantly, he didn't know what to do. Precious was, after all, Blair's mother. People usually get mad if you say ugly things about their mother. He really wanted to tell Precious that she was not to call Blair at his house (except in emergencies), but he was afraid to. He didn't know how Blair would take that ultimatum. As it happens, it would have been fine. Blair didn't want her to call either. He could see how much the calls upset Blair, which in turn upset him. He could not understand why her mother was so against him. When Blair told Eli that her mother was trying to break them up, he was astounded. He didn't know people did that in this day and age. Why would her mother want to take away Blair's happiness? Blair was happy as he was, and Eli knew it. He felt her happiness along with his. Yet her mother was trying to take that away. Why? It didn't make any sense at all.

One night in bed, she told him, "Eli, listen to me. My mother is doing her best to break us up. The worst part is that she knows how to wear me down. She's done it before."

Eli wasn't listening. He was much more interested in her than Precious.

"Eli, you're not listening."

"No, I'm not."

"Well, you better listen to *this,* because she told me today that she wants Bobby and me to get married."

That did get Eli's attention. "Bobby? Who is Bobby?"

"Eli, you know very well who Bobby is. Bobby Wrightsberg."

"Bob Wrightsberg? Bob Wrightsberg of all people? Why would any mother want her daughter to marry him? I don't believe it."

"Believe it. My mother has this plan for Bobby and me to marry."

Eli burst out laughing. "That is the craziest thing I have ever heard. Bob Wrightsberg! This guy is a real ass, and God, he is dumb! How did he ever get through law school or any school, for that matter? I told Booty so. He asked me what I thought of Bob, and I told him exactly what I thought of the new principal. My strong guess is he will not get hired to be the principal after this year. I told Booty he was a sleaze and not to trust him. Booty agreed and said he would be the last person he would trust. It seems Bob's mother put a lot of pressure on the Lincoln School Board to give him a chance. After a considerable donation to the Lincoln School Trust by his mother, the board provisionally hired him. He's on probation this year, and they'll decide next year, although the truth is—from what I gleaned from Booty—that Bob is not going to be rehired as the principal of Lincoln School. Your mother wants you to marry that jerk? I don't believe it."

Blair sighed and gave up. So much for talking. She'd try another time.

Eli followed Blanquitta's lesson plans meticulously, which were easy compared with learning how to be with and teach sixth graders. Which was more difficult—working with the powerful CEOs of companies around the world or sixth graders at Lincoln School? He decided that it was a little easier to get a CEO to listen. But only a little. Both situations took an extreme amount of patience, which Eli was slowly and painstakingly developing. If only he could gag Betty Ann. Ignoring her was impossible.

Precious was still a problem. She called Blair too much, and the calls always upset her. Like Betty Ann, getting her to shut up was just not an option. The first thing Blair did when she got home—and Eli's house was home to both of them—was turn off her cell phone. She admitted to Eli that her mother called her at work so often that Booty took the phone out of Blair's hand and told Precious to stop calling. He told her to stop interrupting Blair's workday. Blair profusely thanked Booty, hoping that her mother would listen, while knowing that she wouldn't.

Precious was having her own love affair with Lorraine, who moved in with her, to everyone else's horror. Mae, Booty, and Ellanor knew that Lorraine had lost his mind. They assured each other that this little affair would run its course. When it did, Lorraine would come to his senses and return home. Ellanor went so far as to promise him another Irish wolfhound if he would come home.

Eli wasn't thinking about Precious and her tantrums as he walked home from school late that afternoon. His thoughts were only on Blair and the wonderful day he had at school. Everything went well. He enjoyed lunch at school with Mary and Prudence. Without thinking about it, they had formed their own little group, since they were considered outcasts.

The test he gave had gone well. No one argued with him; of course, Betty Ann was out sick. Eli's mind turned to the White children. He didn't quite know what to do about them. Something was happening at their home, but he couldn't put his finger upon what it was. He was too inexperienced with children. He decided that he would talk to Mary and Prudence tomorrow at lunch and ask them what to do. If something wasn't done, it was obvious that Heppy was going to fail the sixth grade again. Eli was determined not to let that happen. Yet there was something badly wrong that was deeply affecting the boy. If possible, he was getting skinnier and paler than he already was. Did he see bruising on the boy? Was that it? Something terrible was happening to him. What? Eli was determined to find out.

Chapter 5

Eli glanced out one of the schoolroom windows at the blue sky dotted with white clouds. It was a beautiful day.

The classroom sat empty for the hour when the kids were at chorus or art class. Lucille taught chorus three days a week. The other two days, the kids went to art class. During the hour they were gone, he usually worked, but not today. His feet were propped up on the desk. All he had to do was swivel his chair a little to gaze out the windows. Since the hideously loud rumble of the air conditioner was silenced for the winter, he could open the windows, letting in cool air. He closed his eyes, breathed in the freshness of the air, and smiled. Leaves fluttered to the ground, covering the dying green grass. Eli felt happy. Maybe for the first time in his life, he was happy, and he savored the feeling, wanting to hold on to it forever.

At the same time Eli sat dreaming, Blair was trying to concentrate on work. Truth is, she didn't care about work. She thought she cared and was interested in Booty's oil business and the Foundation. She had been interested until now … and now, she didn't care, which surprised her.

Booty was over in Athens at the Crutchfield Oil building. When he left, he told her she could leave whenever she wanted, as there wasn't anything terribly pressing for today. She knew that, yet she enjoyed being at work, and Eli was still at school, so she might as well stay. While Booty was gone, it gave her an opportunity to catch up on things, until she took a break to gaze out the window.

She felt happy and, to her surprise, content. Blair wondered if she had ever actually felt content before and didn't know. What a fun time she was having. She didn't know she could have so much fun. She also didn't know before how much she liked Booty and Mae. They had always been on the periphery of her life. They were her mother's age but not friends with her mother. She only knew them to say hello to and nothing more. Booty was her employer, and that was about it. When she accepted the job, her mother had mixed emotions. Blair worked close by, which was good. She worked for a black man, that was bad, except this particular black man was extremely prominent and rich, which was acceptable. He also didn't have any children, which was good according to Precious, since he might leave Blair Don something in his will. That was typical of the way her mother thought. Blair shook her head to clear away thoughts of her mother and looked around her desk, deciding what to do next.

Out of the side of her eye, she caught movement and turned to look. "Damn it."

Precious stormed across the lawn. She was on her way to Booty's to talk to Blair, and she walked like she was on a mission. Blair wondered if she could make it to the door in time to lock it. "Damn it!" She kept the door unlocked for Eli to come in after school and visit. If he saw she and Booty were busy, he would just say hello and leave. Booty didn't care. Sometimes the three of them ended up sitting around her desk talking. It was wonderful when he dropped by, even for a moment. Blair smiled, thinking about Eli, and for a moment forgot about seeing her mother. She knew her mother watched Booty's house like a hawk. Lorraine must not be there, because Precious would never come charging over with Lorraine watching. Lorraine could not know Precious had badgered Blair about Eli. Lorraine liked Eli and wouldn't hear anything said against him. Precious learned that early on in her project to marry him. Blair caught sight of her again. Precious headed to the house like a bull charging with intent to kill or at the very least do harm. She had a look of determination that was clear. "Damn." She heard the heavy wood front door open. "Damn." All the day's delight vanished. Her stomach tightened. "Damn."

"Blair Don." Her mother's voice was raspy like the heavy smoker she was for years until the doctor demanded she quit. Mixed with the rasp from the smoking was a whiskey voice. Even though she was a small, thin woman, she was wiry and tough; a woman who demanded things done her way—no exceptions.

Blair's stomach tightened. "Yes, Mother?" She did her best to keep her voice without emotion.

"You know that Lorraine asked me to marry him." Precious sat in one of the chairs in front of Blair's desk.

"Of course."

"You don't sound very happy for me. Why aren't you happy for me? I've been alone for so many years, and now I'll have a companion for the rest of my life. Geneva said that Ellanor got mad because we took his mother's big diamond ring and her wedding band out of the safety deposit box."

"I heard."

"Geneva said the stupid fool has taken to his bed again."

Blair knew this was only an excuse for her mother's visit. She waited with growing anxiety for her to get to the real subject, which was Blair and Eli.

Precious looked around at the large room that was Blair's office. "That's not a real Picasso, is it?"

"It is."

Precious continued to look at the picture. "I don't remember seeing it before. It hasn't always been in here, has it?"

"Yes," answered Blair.

Precious smacked her lips and crossed her legs, smoothing the top leg of her slacks. "I wouldn't know. The only reason I'm here is to see my only child, since she won't come visit her mother now that she's living in sin with that Oriental!"

Blair bit her tongue. Don't argue with her. Just get rid of her as quickly as possible.

Precious smacked her lips again. "I doubt if you noticed I had gone out of town last week for a couple of days." Precious waited for a response. When she didn't get one, she continued, "I didn't think you cared. Lorraine and I went to Dallas. The rings are being reset and changed a little. They're going to be gorgeous. The best jeweler in Dallas is doing it. One day after I die, they will be yours. You know, Blair Don, the reason I'm marrying Lorraine is for you. I want you to have a wonderful inheritance, and since neither Lorraine nor Ellanor have children, you are it. Just be nice to Lorraine. Who knows? He may adopt you."

Blair felt anger rushing up to her face.

Precious's hand smoothed out her slacks as she said, "You could be a little grateful. Anyway, that's not why I'm here."

Here it comes. Blair glanced out the window, took a deep breath, and then returned to look at her mother.

"When is Booty coming back?"

"I don't know," answered Blair.

"He didn't say? He didn't tell you?" Precious demanded.

"He didn't know when he would return. He'll be at Crutchfield Oil all day today."

"Oh," smacked her mother while uncrossing and crossing her legs. "While I'm here, I need to talk to you, since you don't come home—"

Blair interrupted her. "Mother, I have work to do."

"Oh, so you're trying to get rid of me now. I see. I'm sure you are very busy, but I need to talk to you. I was having lunch with Maeva the other day at the Athens Country Club."

Blair waited. She knew something to do with Eli was coming, and she waited. It was the longest wait.

"We had the nicest visit. Maeva is the sweetest thing in the world. And the food at the country club is better. Must have a new chef, because it was edible. So anyway, Maeva and I were talking. She really has magnificent jewelry. We decided you and Bobby make the most beautiful couple. You all should be together. You really should. Think what it would do for our families. It would bring them together, and we'd have the best time. I don't know why you want to be with that Oriental boy. I've raised you better than to end up with white trash. You know that, and Bobby is so nice just like his mother."

"Mother," said Blair.

"Now I knew you'd say that and use that tone of voice with me, but Blair Don, I am doing this for you. This is for your own good. It is for your future. Where did I fail? An Oriental, of all things! For all you know, his family just walked out of the rice paddies. I don't know what you think you're doing! This is your life, and for the rest of your life! You're not using good sense. You're not using any sense at all with that Oriental boy. Here is Bobby Wrightsberg, back in Cedar Springs, and you're wasting your time with that boy. I really don't understand you, Blair Don. I really don't. I don't know how in the world you can sleep at night, doing this to me! I just don't understand how you could do this to your mother!"

Blair remained silent.

"Here's what I want, and so does Maeva. We both want you all to get married."

"No."

"Now, Blair Don, don't you use that tone of voice with me. I am your mother. You obviously don't know what is best for you. Bobby Wrightsberg is a nice boy from a good family. After his mother dies—God forbid anything happens to Maeva—but after she dies, he is going to inherit millions, and I mean millions. Maeva said that he is already getting some money now from his father's trust, so you all could be living very well right now. Maeva said so. She said that she'd be more than happy to give you that lovely family home. She'd love to move into something smaller. She wouldn't mind at all, not one bit. There you'd be the lady of the manor in that lovely home. I can't think of anything better for you. Maeva said the same thing about Bobby. She always expected you all to get married."

Blair was furious and did her best not to sound it. "I don't know why Maeva expected us to get married. Bobby Wrightsberg never has been my boyfriend and never will be. Bobby Wrightsberg? Mother! You want me to marry him? He couldn't be faithful if you put a gun to his head. I heard his ex-wife divorced him because he beat her up horribly. That's what you want for me?"

"Listen," smacked Precious, "you do not know that he hit that ex-wife. Maeva told me that that ex-wife was awful and never nice to Maeva. I don't believe that about Bobby for one minute. Maeva told me that woman was just after Bobby's money."

Blair's insides seethed. "He's so nice that the reason he lost his job was he got caught doing cocaine in bed and screwing the wife of the partner he worked for. And that's who caught them."

"Blair Don, don't use that word—screwed. It's so vulgar. He was in bed with that woman, and whatever else he is said to have done, you don't know that."

"Of course I know. Everyone in Oklahoma City knows. How do you think I found out? It was common knowledge. He got fired. He's lucky he didn't get disbarred. The idiot would choose to have an affair with the wife of one of the most powerful lawyers in the state of Oklahoma. He's lucky to have a job at all. The only reason he's the principal of Lincoln Grade School is because of all the money Maeva gave the Lincoln School Trust, and that just bought her a one-year contract. The only reason that job was available is because Lucille ran the last principal off, and the school needed someone. He is on one-year probation. And he's an alcoholic. *This* is who you want me to marry?"

Precious stiffened up. "That's not funny, Blair Don! Maeva told me all that stuff in Oklahoma City is ugly gossip. I'm sure that lawyer's wife made him do it. Bobby's a good boy, and he is certainly not an alcoholic. I don't know who told you that! Who told you Bobby was an alcoholic? You should be proud to be married into that nice family. Honestly, Blair Don, I wonder what has happened to you. I just don't know. Being with that Oriental has not done you one bit of good. I can tell you that, not one bit. That's what happens when you hang around white trash. And don't say I didn't tell you so."

Blair squeezed her fingernail into the palm of her hand to get her mind off the real pain she was feeling.

Precious got up out of the chair, marched over to Blair's desk, leaned on it, and glared at her. She pointed her finger in Blair's face. Her eyes flamed with anger as Blair struggled not to lose it and start screaming.

Precious spat as she talked. Her grip on the desk was so tight it turned her fingers white. "Now you listen to me and you listen good. Don't you buck me on this. Do you hear me? Because you better hear me and hear me good. I know you had an abortion when you were almost sixteen."

Blair gasped. This shocked her. She did not know her mother knew her big secret, and yet deep down inside, she had known all the time that her mother knew. She had not quite turned sixteen. It was the summer before her junior year in high school. Her aunt Bunny Lou took her kids and

Blair to spend the summer at their house on Lake Texhoma. Blair's heart smiled at the memory. What a wonderful summer she and her cousin had with the two boys from Oklahoma City. Blair was so in love with a darling boy with brown eyes and brown hair. In the midst of her mother's tirade, his memory and their magical summer touched her soul. She yearned to cry, but knew she couldn't let her mother see. Theirs was such a passionate teenage love, and there's nothing like being madly in love as a teenager— that is, until she discovered she was pregnant.

Blair could always talk to her aunt Bunny Lou, who made all the arrangements. The next thing she knew, she and her cousin, who went as a companion, were on a plane flying to Houston. A doctor there took care of everything, and then she and her cousin were back at the lake. Blair never saw the boy again. Her heart was broken. She cried herself to sleep for the longest time. Just remembering him now created a heavy lump in her throat. She wondered what happened to him. The break in her heart never fully healed. His memory crept to the shadows of her past, where it remained untouched.

So Bunny Lou *did* betray her. Blair wasn't terribly surprised. She thought she might have; yet when her mother didn't say anything, she hoped that Bunny Lou had kept her secret.

"Now we don't want to cause trouble, do we? I would hate to have to tell everyone at the beauty parlor how I had to unburden myself of the terrible thing my daughter did to me. I know times have changed, but not here. This would be just as terrible a scandal today as it would have been then. We have long memories in this town. What would it do to the fine Blair family name we cherish? What would it do to me? You know I would never get over a scandal like that. It might kill me. Is that what you want? Do you want to ruin us both forever? Because it would. You know this town. You know how people talk. You know what women say. They would crucify you and then me because I'm your mother."

"Times have changed," Blair insisted as her heart sank. She knew she had lost. Her mother had her. She knew it, and she knew her mother knew it.

Precious smiled. "Times may have changed for other places, but not here. Dooley Pastor runs a tight little church. He constantly preaches against abortion. We're a town where everybody knows everybody else and has for generations. Think what it would do to me! I couldn't raise my head at the Athens Country Club. Lorraine might not even marry me. Bad reputations ruin people. They are a stain that doesn't go away. I am your mother, and what you do reflects on me."

Blair simply looked at her mother. Times didn't change in Cedar Springs—people simply got older and died. People didn't forgive. Scandals transcended generations and continued to be the fodder for gossip long after the people involved were dead. Blair thought about Booty and Mae. They would always be ostracized. Booty was black and Mae was white, and they married, but that wasn't the only reason. No. The real reason was that W.D. Hoover made it possible for Able Crutchfield and his family to live in a white neighborhood. Neither W.D. nor his wife, Rose, nor members of the families were ever forgiven for integrating Cedar Springs.

Blair looked at Precious. Her mother had known about the abortion all these years and waited, holding the information until she needed it. She didn't need to use it when she broke up Blair's first marriage. She wore Blair down simply by calling and writing constantly day after day. Blair was too young and weak to stand up to her. Now Blair was older and stronger. Her mother knew she was not going to win wearing her down by harangues. No, it had to be something else. This was that something else— her teenage abortion. Blair had to hand it to her mother. It was smart and the only way to succeed. Precious knew that Blair would succumb rather than expose her mother to scandal, for scandal with its social ramifications was the thing her mother feared the most. Precious's life centered around society and always had. Precious counted on Blair not doing that to her— and she was right. Blair couldn't and wouldn't.

Her fingers relaxed upon the desk. Blair Don was going to do as she wanted. Precious saw it in Blair's eyes. All the color drained from Blair's face. She looked like she was about to be sick.

A smile crossed her face. Precious smacked her lips in victory. "Go back to Mae's grandmother's cottage and get your things. You move back home right now. I'll call Maeva and tell her to have Bobby call you. Don't be so mad. Believe me, you will thank me. I have saved you from a horrible fate with that Oriental. In a little while, you won't even remember his name. You're going to have a happy life. You'll see. Now get going."

Precious turned and walked out of the office, a bounce to her step. Blair heard the heavy front door slam. She sat at her desk frozen, staring out the window, as tears ran down her face. A wind picked up and started rattling what was left of the leaves on the trees.

★ ★ ★ ★ ★

When Eli came home late that afternoon, he noticed Booty's house/ office was dark. He knew Booty was in Athens all day and returning with barbecue. They were all having dinner. Eli figured Blair finished early and went back to the cottage. He stepped up his pace and hurried. As he opened the gate to the backyard, Herschel barked from inside the house. Eli rushed to the cottage and threw open the door. His excitement turned to curiosity. The cottage was dark. He walked into the living room.

"Blair?" When there wasn't an answer, he called again. "Blair, I'm home."

Eli hurried into the bedroom. It was empty and dark. "Oh, she's at Mae's," he said out loud and relaxed. He put down his briefcase, took off his blazer, and opened the closet to change clothes. Except for his clothes, the closet was empty. Eli stood dumbly, staring at the closet, trying to understand. Quickly he ran over to the chest of drawers and then rushed to the bathroom. Gone—everything was gone. Slowly he sank onto the bed and stared around the room. He could not believe it. Blair was gone. Suddenly the emptiness of the room filled him with horror.

What happened? Why didn't she say something? He stared around the empty room, trying to grasp what happened. He could not fathom it. They talked to each other about everything, or so he thought. She wouldn't just vanish. Yet that is exactly what she did. Eli kept looking around the room, hoping that he was wrong; hoping she would suddenly come in and explain. Why? The cottage remained quiet, dark, and empty. Blair had left him without a word, without a note, without a warning. She left him. Why? As evening became night, Eli remained paralyzed, sitting on the bed, and wept.

At the same time Eli wept, so did Blair. She sat in a chair in her living room, hating herself. She slowly carried her stuff up the stairs to the apartment and dropped everything in the bedroom. Her knees felt weak as she sank to the floor sobbing. She would never get over betraying Eli and herself, their happiness, and their future. She made a cowardly choice and for what? For her mother. She might as well die.

The door to her apartment slammed shut as her mother came in. "Blair Don," said Precious, "I have something to tell you. Where are you?"

The moment she heard her mother's voice, Blair scrambled to her feet, wiping her eyes and trying to get rid of the smeared mascara.

"Blair Don!"

Blair walked around the bedroom door into the living room and stood there.

"Well, there you are. My God, you look awful. Thank God you are not meeting Bobby tonight, because you would scare him to death. Maeva couldn't be more pleased. So am I, and you'll thank me someday. Your mother saved you from a fate worse than death. You all are going to be so happy. We'll have to wait until after Lorraine and I are married. We don't want to put too much on Lorraine all at once having to pay for our wedding in Hawaii. Did I tell you we are getting married in Hawaii and taking some people with us? Including you, of course. We'll have so much fun. No, we'll wait until after all that before telling Lorraine that he is going to pay for a fabulous wedding for you and Bobby. He won't mind. He'll do anything for me.

"Now don't you look at me that way, Blair Don," scolded her mother. "Here I am opening up the world to you, and you just stand there glaring at me. I don't understand it. I really don't. I have saved your life, and this is the thanks I get. Oh well, I might have known you have never appreciated anything I've done for you. No wonder all you could get was that Oriental. Who wants a sour old woman? I don't know how you could have been around Mae and Booty. It is one thing to work for him and quite another to have dinner with him. I am ashamed of you, but it is all over now, thank God. It's gone and forgotten as far as I am concerned.

"Okay, then I'll leave you to your unpacking. Be happy now. You certainly should be. Don't rub your eyes, or you'll make more lines, and you don't want that. You have to stay pretty." Precious turned and walked out the door. "Oh, look. Lorraine just drove in the driveway."

Blair's body felt lifeless, and she sank back to the floor weeping.

Mae saw the whole thing. She had been snapping green beans, sitting at the kitchen table when Herschel started barking. She got up to see why, and there was Blair running across the grass to the cottage. Something had happened. Herschel pawed the door to run down to the cottage and greet her. He looked back at Mae and barked.

"Herschel," she commanded, "come here."

The dog looked at her questioningly. He always ran down to greet Eli and Blair. He barked again, looking at Mae to let her know he wanted out to go down to the cottage.

"No, Herschel, not today. Not today. Come sit next to me." Mae stood beside the kitchen window so she could not be seen. The big white dog looked at her and obeyed. He sat so tall that she easily patted his head while he leaned against her.

"What's happened, Herschel? Something has happened. I know it. I'm afraid. I really am. I've been afraid about this, but I thought maybe I'd be wrong. I hoped so, but now I don't know."

Blair had moved her car to the third garage behind the big house. Mae watched her as she rushed out of the cottage and backed her car up to the gate. She left the door open and rushed into the house, carrying out bunches of clothes and bags, throwing them into the car. Blair wondered if Mae was watching. She saw her car in the garage when she went to get hers, so she knew Mae was home. *Just as well if she is. Let her tell Eli.*

But Mae was not going to do that, no. This was between Blair and Eli. She watched Blair finish shoving everything into the car and speed away. She made herself stay in the house, rather than go to the cottage or look to see if Blair's car was back in the Blair family's driveway. She figured it was. Mae was more disappointed than mad at Blair. She hoped she would be a stronger person. Booty told her how Precious called all the time at work, to the point where he tried to stop it and failed. Booty told her how upset Blair was getting, especially after talking to her mother. Mae knew the pressure. Even her mother, who knew Booty since he was born and loved him, did not want Mae to marry him.

She slowly walked over and grabbed the phone. Mae had to sit down. "Booty."

The instant Booty heard Mae's voice, he knew something was wrong. "What happened?"

"Blair left Eli, and he doesn't know it. I'm sure he doesn't. He was so happy when he left for school. She seemed happy too, now that I think about it. By this afternoon, everything had changed, because Blair moved all of her things out, and I would be willing to bet she's back at her apartment."

"Oh, my God."

"Yes. It's very sad. I don't know what it will do to Eli. It will break his heart, but what he will do—I don't know. If he up and leaves I wouldn't blame him."

"It was Precious," said Booty.

"Of course it was Precious! But Blair agreed. Precious didn't come over and move her out. She did that all on her own."

"I thought Blair was serious about Eli. I don't understand why she would do this to him."

"Oh, Booty, you know what it's like here. I hoped Blair would be stronger."

"She's made a terrible mistake."

"Yes she has, dear. Terrible."

"What do you want me to do about dinner? Do you still want me to bring home barbecue?"

"I don't care; I'm not very hungry. We won't be seeing Eli tonight. I don't know what to do."

"Mae, you're the one who always knows what to do."

"Not this time I don't."

It took a couple of nights before Eli could get himself together enough to join Mae and Booty for dinner. Blair was not mentioned. What was there to say? Mae told Ellanor not to mention Blair, and he didn't. They sat on the front porch, bundled up since the nights were turning chilly. The birds' summer chatter accompanied by the songs of the insects and frogs were gone. It was silent. Booty, Mae, Ellanor, and Eli sat on the porch, immersed in their own thoughts.

Chapter 6

Cold breaths nudged Indian summer away for another year. Even Mae had to admit it was getting too chilly to sit outside. She, Eli, Booty, and Ellanor moved into the den after dinner. With the shorter days, it was dark by the time they got there. Booty made a fire, and they burrowed in for the winter.

Mae was amazed that Eli chose to stay. With Blair's abrupt departure, she had been afraid he would leave Cedar Springs—and she wouldn't have blamed him one bit. However, Eli continued his routine, and life seemingly went on. Mae forbade Ellanor and Booty from mentioning Blair. "We are not going to rub salt in the wound," she said. "He's had quite enough hurt already, and nobody is going to add to it by bringing up Blair. Do you all hear me?"

That's why she had gotten so mad at Ellanor. Why didn't he have the sense to keep his mouth shut? The stupid fool!

They sat in the den, digesting a dinner of Mae's chicken-fried steak, mashed potatoes, cream gravy, Le Sueur peas, and coconut cream pie. Eli learned that if it was a meat, it could be fried along with everything else. He wanted to enjoy himself with his friends, but his heart wasn't in it. He didn't think he would ever get over Blair. Maybe the best he could hope for was that someday her memory would fade a little, but right now the wound was festering, fresh and open.

Every day, he passed by Booty's house, by the office where Blair worked, and then walked by her house. It was awful. He did his best not to sneak a glance, and mostly he succeeded. He pretended Blair was not there, but that didn't work, because he knew she was. He didn't mention her to Mae or Booty, and thank God they didn't bring her name up. What was there to say? Nothing. He was humiliated and hurt she had left him without so much as a good-bye. He had truly believed she loved him. He certainly knew he loved her like he had never loved before. How could he have been so wrong about her feelings? He would get over her—if he lived long enough.

Every day, Blair tried not to look for Eli, knowing he passed by twice a day. She hated herself for being so weak and ruining her life, because Eli was her love. She knew it, and he always would be. She thought she loved her ex-husband, and she had. After moving back to Cedar Springs, Blair resigned herself to her life being over and never meeting anyone again. No one was more surprised than she when Eli entered her life. It was wonderful, a miracle, and now it was gone.

She was wrong in having hoped that leaving Eli would shut her mother up. Her mother got what she wanted, or so Blair thought. Blair should have known her mother wanted more. Now she constantly nagged Blair about going out with Bobby. Just the thought of Bobby gave Blair shivers. He was like a bad smell that wouldn't go away and permeated everything. Blair's only hope was that she and Bobby had known each other all of their lives and never liked each other. She knew Bobby didn't want to go out with her as much as she didn't want to go out with him, and that was her saving grace. Except she was wrong about that too. He did something he rarely if ever did. He told the truth when he called, he said his mother bribed him with lots of money. He kept calling because he wouldn't get the money until Blair agreed to go out with him, and that made him persistent.

Precious knew bribes wouldn't work with Blair Don. She played the big abortion card to get her away from that Oriental, so that was done. The only route left was constant nagging, crying, throwing in guilt that this was going to kill her, and screaming often and loudly. When Precious got particularly angry with Blair for not doing what she wanted, she slapped her face. Worst part is, Precious got so mad that she couldn't stop slapping Blair, but it was Blair's fault for not doing what she said and not listening. Precious knew in the end she would get her way. It had always worked before. No reason it wouldn't work now. The worst part was that Blair didn't seem to care, but Precious felt sure she would win. She always did.

As Ellanor, Booty, Eli, and Mae sat watching the fire dance, Ellanor hopped up and said, "Let's have a drink."

This should have been a clue for Mae, but it wasn't. "Good idea," she said. "It's rather a bleak night."

"Fine and dandy," said Ellanor as he proceeded to be bartender, mixing and serving everyone drinks.

"This is nice and cozy, Ellanor," said Mae. "And strong. My God! Did you pour in a whole bottle of Jack Daniel's?"

"So here's what I was thinking," said Ellanor.

"What?" asked Booty.

"Why?" asked Mae. "Ellanor—you know thinking is not good for you."

"Since Thanksgiving is coming up, I thought we could all go to Hawaii for Thanksgiving."

"What?" they all replied almost at the same time.

"For two weeks."

"Why Hawaii?" asked Eli. Eli had heard Precious and Lorraine were getting married in Hawaii. Everyone in town knew that.

"Why not?" said Ellanor. "Then I could be with you all and still go to Lorraine's wedding. Makes sense to me."

Both Eli and Mae sat up and stared at Ellanor.

"What are you saying?" asked Booty. "We're not invited to their wedding, so why would we want to go?"

"No, of course, you're not invited to their wedding. I am, and so is Geneva. She is all excited. She's never been to Hawaii."

"Neither have you," said Mae.

"I've been to New York, and Booty and I spent a summer in Europe after our junior year in college. Remember that, Booty?"

"Certainly. We didn't even try to see my parents while we were there. I think that's why we avoided Switzerland except to travel through, and that doesn't count as visiting."

"You didn't stop to see your parents?" asked Eli. "Did they live in Switzerland?"

"They lived in Switzerland, and now they are dead in Switzerland. No—no need to stop. Ellanor and I had a great trip, so why ruin it?"

"Absolutely! Couldn't agree more." Ellanor nodded. "I'd like to go back sometime."

"No," said Mae, "Hawaii is out."

"No," said Eli.

"No?" said Ellanor. "Why? It's pretty. You could go to a different island, and I could fly over for the wedding and return and be with you all."

"No!" said Mae. "I don't want to be in the same part of the world with them."

Eli did something he had not planned to do. He blurted out her name. "Blair—isn't Blair going to Hawaii for the wedding?"

Ellanor looked at Eli like he was crazy. "Of course she is. So what? She won't bother us. We can stay at a different hotel on another island, and I'll just go over to wherever they're getting married and come right back after the ceremony. Why would I want to be with Geneva, who I see every day; Maeva, who I can't stand and never could; and Bobby, who I don't know and don't want to know? I don't know why you think I would want to be with them! I can't stand them. I'll be fine if you all go. Then I won't have to be with them."

"God damn it, Ellanor!" said Mae. "Sweeten my drink, and then I'm going to strangle you."

"Why?" Ellanor said as he got up to refresh Mae's drink. "Can I get anyone else another while I'm up?"

"Yes," answered Booty and Eli almost together.

"Jesus Christ, Ellanor," said Booty, "what are you thinking? Why would you think we all, including Eli, would want to go?"

"Because I have to go; at least, Lorraine and Geneva say I have to go. You all can go too. Wouldn't that be fun?"

"No!" said Eli. "Why would I want to go where Blair and her future husband are going?"

"What future husband?" asked Ellanor. "There's only one wedding, and it is my crazy brother and that harpy."

"Blair and her future husband?" said Mae. "Never. Blair would never marry that scoundrel."

"She told me that her mother wanted her to marry Bob … and I thought she was joking," mumbled Eli.

"It is a bad joke," said Booty.

"That's rather an old-fashioned word to use, Mae," said Ellanor. "Scoundrel. How charming! How about rogue? He's a rogue. It has a lovely ring to it. Rogue."

"Bobby doesn't have the class to be a rogue," said Booty.

"He's a fucking son of a bitch," interrupted Eli. "And if you think I am going to the same place or even near the same place except on another island as he and Blair are going, you are crazy. No! I'm not going, and that's it."

"Ellanor," said Mae, "you are crazy, but then again I always thought you were a little bit crazy."

"My mother was crazy. Lorraine is on the eccentric side, and I'm just fine, thank you very much. I don't know how you could possibly put me with those two, although my mother was sweet and Lorraine has never been sweet a day in his life. In fact, I don't like Lorraine. Never have; that's why you all have to go with me."

"No!" said Eli.

"Why not?"

Booty said, "Ellanor, you really don't get it, do you?"

"Get what? What is there to get? All I did was offer the lovely idea of Thanksgiving in Hawaii. Most people would jump at the idea. Seems like a good idea to me. Just think sunset over the ocean. I've come up with a great idea, if I do say so myself."

"Well, it isn't," said Mae. "God damn it, Ellanor, fix me another drink and shut up. I wish we could unplug you."

"If that's the way you want to be. All I was suggesting was—"

Ellanor didn't finish his sentence because Eli interrupted. "Ellanor, did it ever occur to you that maybe, just maybe, I don't want to see Blair?"

"No. I thought you might want to go to Hawaii. The pictures all look pretty. Palm trees swaying in the gentle tropical breezes. What is there not to like?"

"Shut up," said Mae.

"Okay, but if you all don't go, I'm not going. I don't want to go alone. Then I just won't go."

"Fine," growled Eli.

"Fine," snapped Mae.

"Don't go," Booty agreed.

"Fine," said Ellanor.

"Shut up," Mae insisted.

"I don't like Lorraine anyway," said Ellanor. "Or Precious. I can't stand Precious. Never could. Okay, fine. I won't go either. Good. I feel better. I didn't want to go in the first place."

"Fix me another drink," demanded Eli.

★ ★ ★ ★ ★

Lynette Sue Harper sat at her desk smiling. Before school started, she, Miriam, and Clare stood outside on the playground as she bored them to death talking in great detail about her future plans with Clare's cousin, Joe Tom. She planned to be a cheerleader until she and Joe Tom graduated from high school. She and Joe Tom would go to the University of Oklahoma, where they would pledge the appropriate fraternity and sorority. She had to get initiated into the sorority so her daughters would be legacies, and then she and Joe Tom could immediately marry and start producing little Herzsteins. She couldn't stop giggling at the thought. Lynette Sue went on to announce how hard she worked on the children's names and their monograms, always such a task. At that point, Miriam considered screaming but instead turned and left, followed by Clare.

Lynette Sue was shocked at this sudden departure. "Hey, wait a minute! Where are you all going?"

"Class," answered Miriam.

"Why? The bell hasn't rung. Oh, okay, I'll go too," said Lynette Sue, hurrying after them into Lincoln School.

Lynette Sue smiled and bounced all the way into class. She was very happy, especially about making Miriam jealous and envious. She was just sure as sure can be that Miriam was both. How could she not be? And so was Clare, even though Joe Tom was her first cousin. Who wouldn't be jealous and envious of her?

Clare sat at her desk, giddy with the thought that she was going to tell Joe Tom about Lynette Sue's future plans, including the monograms. She couldn't wait. Lynette Sue was such a conceited bitch and treated Clare as if she barely existed, since she had never been a cheerleader and was smart. Lynette Sue pointed out to Clare all too often how boys didn't like smart girls, and she was developing breasts and Clare wasn't. Clare plotted how she would get her revenge. She needed to talk to Miriam after school. Clare had a piece of information that she knew would crush Lynette Sue, and she couldn't wait to use it. Lynette Sue assumed Joe Tom was going to Athens Middle School and then on to Athens High School with her, and she assumed wrong, much to Clare's delight. What Lynette Sue didn't know was that Clare, her cousin A.J., Joe Tom, and Miriam were not going to Athens Middle School. They were going to the private Episcopal school, and Clare couldn't wait to tell her.

Miriam saw that Clare was trying to get her attention and mouthed, "What?"

The rest of the class quietly talked among themselves, except Heppy and Isabelle White, who sat like stones in back-row desks. Eli wasn't paying attention to the class, so he let them talk for a minute. He had to think as he looked at Isabelle and Heppy. He had finally gotten the information and proof he needed. Heppy and Isabelle had missed too many days of school. When they returned, it was obvious something terrible had happened to them. When Eli saw them, he jumped at the opportunity; he was ready. Eli had talked to Booty, who introduced him to his attorney, Oliver Stein, who introduced both of them to a woman in Oklahoma City who handled abused children cases. Eli was going to leave Cedar Springs but not until he had made sure Heppy and Isabelle were out of that house and safe. He had never undertaken anything like this. Then again, he had never been around children or in a situation like this. Before he left town, he was going to do something good. He was going to save those kids, and now he had the answer as to how.

There were bruises on Heppy's face. Isabelle was shaking. Both were pale, and their eyes looked haunted and terrified. Neither had a drop of color in their cheeks, and both were skinny. That morning, it was clear that neither could concentrate. Eli knew this was the morning for action, so when the morning recess bell sounded, Eli rushed down to the principal's office. Bob, as usual, had called in sick, and his office was vacant. For once, Lucille was actually helpful—probably because she had been told in no uncertain terms what was expected of her by Booty and because child abuse would not look good for her school. That was not allowed to happen at her school. Nothing could tarnish Lincoln's reputation. Lucille didn't give a damn about the children. She repeatedly said that the Whites were white trash. If she could have prevented it, Heppy and Isabelle would not have been allowed at Lincoln, but then this was the only school close in the area. So what could Lucille do about Heppy and Isabelle and the other white trash (a term that included black and Hispanic children too) allowed there? She couldn't do anything except pretend they were not there.

Eli leaned on Lucille's desk, trying to get a word in edgewise.

As her smile parted, showing the tiny teeth, Lucille smacked her lips and said, "I do not for the life of me understand why you want to tarnish Lincoln's fine reputation by starting gossip about those white-trash Whites. Let sleeping dogs lie, for the Lord's sake. What do you expect of those children with Elmer Jr. and Lee Tom? Drunks, the whole family. If Elmer Jr. hadn't inherited that old dirt farm outside of town, they'd be living in the street. My mother said the luckiest thing that ever happened to Billie Rae White in her life was having Walter Tree fall madly in love with her. My mother told me all about it. She said that the town was horrified at a member of the fine, rich Tree family marrying a White. My mother just knew the whole family practically died of shame with him marrying her. She said she would have. It was a scandal. Of course, my mother said that everybody thought Walter would never get married, and then he up and marries the bottom of the barrel."

"Lucille, I am going in to Bob's office to make a call. Do not interrupt me."

Lucille patted her hair and smiled at Eli. "Well, you don't have to be so rude. Why would I want to interrupt you?"

Fifteen minutes later Eli opened the door and hurried out of the principal's office. "I have to get back to my classroom."

"You certainly do. If you had been any longer, I thought I was going to have to go down there and take over your class. I have a school to run."

After Booty hung up with Eli, he immediately called his attorney in Athens. From previous conversations with Booty, Oscar Stein already knew about the children and had made the appropriate calls. A meeting was hastily arranged for that afternoon in the empty principal's office at Lincoln. It had to be during recess so that it would not be noticeable that Heppy and Isabelle attended the meeting. Eli counted on none of the children noticing the White children were not on the playground.

The day dragged on, and Eli waited impatiently for recess. Heppy scared him; Eli was truly afraid Heppy would commit suicide. Eli knew depression. He had certainly experienced it as a child with his father and stepmother and their family. He wasn't wanted there and was in the way of their family. Eli knew he did not have a home. Many a time he cried himself to sleep. If he had thought about killing himself to get away from them, the hopelessness, and the loneliness, Eli was certain Heppy was thinking that too. At least Eli knew he was going to boarding school the minute he was of age to be accepted, because his stepmother told him so. He wanted to get away. For Heppy, going away to school was not a possible out, and that is what scared Eli. The hopelessness in Heppy's eyes gave urgency to the plans. It was obvious that Heppy was worn down and worn out. Black circles made his eyes look hollow. He nervously chewed the inside of his lips constantly. Eli recognized childhood pain; he knew it. He saw it in Heppy, and that's what scared him.

Eli longed to call Blair, for it was she who told him to talk to Booty. He talked to her about the White children, and she told him what to do and how to recognize the signs of child abuse. She suggested bringing in Geneva because the children were related to the Tree family. Geneva immediately offered for the children to live with her and Ellanor. She had always wanted children—yearned to have them—but since she never married, that was impossible. Having the children live there would be a dream come true for her. Ellanor felt differently, though. He offered to pay for anything. He refused to live with children. If only Eli could talk to Blair. If only Blair had not left him. She would be here and could help guide him with this. Eli took a deep breath. No. He had to do this, and he hoped to God he could do it and get those kids out. Then he could leave Cedar Springs and get away from Blair.

Eli talked to Mae, asking her what to do, especially about Ellanor, who was being such an ass. Mae told him to go ahead as if Ellanor agreed, because in the end, she felt sure he would. Eli didn't know whether Mae actually believed that, but it made him feel better. He decided to believe it too. Ellanor would accept the children after all—he had to. What would happen to them if he didn't open his home? He had a big enough house for everybody. They proceeded as if the children would go to the Tree family home. Certainly everyone did, except Ellanor.

Eli forced his attention back to the classroom. The children were talking among themselves and squirming. He had borrowed a *National Geographic* from Booty and Mae's on the evolution of man. Mae warned him not to do it, not to talk about that. He had Blanquitta's lesson plans, and nothing contained a hint about evolution, which Eli found odd. He told Mae not to be silly. He had never heard of such a ridiculous argument and took the magazine to school with him that morning.

Eli unfolded the large map-sized picture from *National Geographic* showing man's evolution and taped it on the blackboard at the front of the class so all could see. Silence descended over the classroom as the kids saw the map. Eli smiled, proud that he silenced the class with the picture. He glanced about the class. Some of the kids smiled, which confused Eli as to why they had laughing smiles. Lynette Sue looked dumbfounded, as if she had never seen the picture before, which she hadn't. Betty Ann's mouth dropped open, and her face flushed with anger.

"This is from the *National Geographic* magazine. What does this picture represent?" Eli innocently asked.

Miriam's hand shot up. "The evolution of man."

"That's right. A new discovery of ancient bones has been made, dating the hominid earlier than originally thought. This makes the precursor to *Homo sapiens,* as we know the species today, older than we thought. It's—"

"No! You can't say that!" interrupted Betty Ann.

"What?" asked Eli.

Betty Ann pointed wildly to the picture. "That!"

"What? That?" Eli asked again. He couldn't figure out what upset her.

"That picture." Betty Ann continued to point.

Eli turned and looked at the picture and then back at Betty Ann. "Why not?"

Betty Ann's face was bright red. "Because you can't show that."

"Yes, I can," answered Eli.

Betty Ann's hands were clenched into tight fists. "I am no monkey."

"That is not a monkey," he said. "It is an ape. There is a clear difference between a monkey and an ape. You can see that."

"Looks like a monkey to me," said Betty Ann.

"No, it doesn't," said Eli.

"I'm no ape," announced Betty Ann.

Hiram was dying to tell her that apes were probably nice, which Betty Ann had never been in her life. He knew better, having been beaten up so many times in the holly bushes behind the church, but he thought it.

"I've never heard such a thing. What is it?" said Lynette Sue, confounded by this information. "It can't be."

"Ninety-six percent of our DNA we share with chimpanzees," Eli continued. "Obviously, there are differences in the skeleton. For example, we're bipedal without the elongated arms and knuckles helping us along. We stood upright and walked looking straight ahead out of Africa."

"What?" asked Lynette Sue.

Clare and Miriam loved this, as they couldn't stand the self-righteous, holier-than-thou Betty Ann and Lynette Sue, who they considered dumb as mud. They looked at each other, trying not to giggle.

"No, we did not. No, sir! I was not born in Africa. I was born right here. Just ask my mother." Betty Ann was not to be dissuaded. "I didn't come from any Africa."

"Your ancestors did, as did all our ancestors," replied Eli.

"No, they didn't," declared Betty Ann, glaring at Eli.

"Yes, they did."

"There aren't any black people in my family or Indians or Jews. They're not allowed in my family, or my grandfather would shoot them," said Lynette Sue. "We're not from Africa. We're from Kansas."

Clare couldn't stand it and blurted out, "Joe Tom's grandfather was Jewish. Does that mean you can't go with Joe Tom?"

Lynette Sue turned even whiter and quickly turned to Joe Tom. "I didn't mean you."

Eli ignored Lynette Sue and Clare. He was much more interested in what Betty Ann was saying. "I need to understand this. Are you really telling me that you do not believe in evolution?" And he thought to himself, *my God, Mae wasn't kidding.* The Scopes trial was long over, or so he had thought.

Lynette Sue turned around to the class and announced, "There are *no* black people or Indians or anyone else in my family, so don't you all get the wrong idea. We are not from Africa. We came from Kansas, and I think my grandmother's family came from Kentucky."

"Hush, Lynette Sue," said Eli. "Your ancestors walked out of Africa, as all our ancestors did. That's where our species originated. There is speculation from DNA studies that the mitochondrial DNA—by the way, does anyone know what mitochondrial means?"

A.J.'s hand shot up. "The mother's DNA."

"Yes, that's right, and research is working to trace back to a female or possibly a small group of females being called Eve."

"What?" said Lynette Sue. "You're not talking about *our* Eve. *Our* Eve did not live in Africa. She and Adam lived in the Garden of Eden. Everyone knows that. Don't you read the Bible? I don't know what you are talking about! That's not Eve. You're not talking about our Eve." She looked at Joe Tom and bleated, "What is he talking about? He can't talk about our Eve like that."

A.J. Herzstein couldn't stand Lynette Sue, who was consistently rude to him. She thought he was a nerd and didn't deserve her attention. The only reason she acknowledged his existence was because he was Joe Tom's first cousin. He knew he was a nerd, and her meanness made him feel worse about himself. He couldn't help himself. He blurted, "Mr. Take is talking about our evolution. How we got to be who we are as a species. The species you see walking around today. Do you even know what a species is?" A.J. felt better after saying that.

Eli said, "Thank you, A.J., but I'll take care of this."

Betty Ann gasped. "Blasphemy! This is the most horrible thing I have ever heard since I heard how babies are made, and I am never going to do that. Yuck! My daddy preaches about the truth of Creationism and how evolution shouldn't be taught because it is a lie. My daddy would whip our butts off if he ever heard any of us use that word. Oh, dear Jesus! Look what you made me say! I said that E word. I am going to hell, and it is all your fault. Oh, dear Jesus."

"You're kidding." Eli couldn't help himself. It just came out. "People actually believe in Creationism?"

A.J. said, "It's obvious you weren't brought up around here."

Clare couldn't help herself and laughed. Eli glared at her.

"Excuse me," she said. "I've been hoping for this."

Betty Ann looked like she was about to explode, she was so mad. "I can't believe it! I am hearing blasphemy in Lincoln School. Just wait 'til my daddy hears about this. You're going to get fired. What are you, an Arab?"

"What?" said Eli. "An Arab? Do you think I look like I am from the Middle East? Do you grasp where Japan is located?"

"Wait a minute!" demanded Lynette Sue, who was close to tears. "I don't get what you're saying."

Miriam said, "Japan is located in the Far East. Do you know where China is located?"

Eli looked at Miriam.

"That's obvious," announced A.J. "Lynette Sue never heard anyone talk about evolution."

"Not at *my* church or school or anywhere!" Lynette Sue said to A.J.

"That's what I said," he answered.

Lynette Sue was nearly in tears. "This is wrong—all wrong and against Jesus my Lord and personal Savior. The Bible tells us that God made us in His image. God was no monkey. I don't know how you can say that! I'm going to tell my parents that you said God looked like a monkey and where you said we came from. We came from Kansas. You have blasphemed, and you are going to hell. When our pastor finds out what you have done—"

"And he will," interrupted Betty Ann. "Because he's my daddy, and I'm going to tell him the minute I get home. He's Hiram's daddy too, and Hiram's going to tell our daddy too. Aren't you, Hiram?"

"Yes," continued Lynette Sue, "Pastor Pastor will blast you straight to hell. You're going to be run out of town. My parents were worried about you because you are foreign and live with those people, and Daddy and Mama were right. Last Sunday, Pastor Pastor preached a wonderful sermon how the Statue of Liberty was a foreign gift from France from the Masons and is an *idol!* There is an idol right there, and having that statue there is idolatry, and it should be torn down. The Statue of Liberty should be torn down, and so should that picture! Praise Jesus!" Lynette Sue turned red in the face. Her bottom lip trembled. "This may be the worst day in my life."

Betty Ann preached, "The Bible tells us how the earth was made. The Bible never says I came from any monkey. I came from Adam and Eve in Eden, and that picture is a lie!"

"Mr. Take said science is suggesting from mitochondrial—that means mother's DNA—evidence that there is the possibility of an original Eve in Africa," said A.J. "Unless the garden of Eden is located in Africa."

"*It is not!*" screamed Betty Ann.

"Ape, not monkey," said Eli. "The picture represents man's evolution in a clever way, and I am not taking it down. What I don't understand is why anyone in this age of mass communication and information can deny physical data."

"The Bible is the truth," explained Betty Ann. "The Bible says we came from Adam and Eve, and they weren't monkeys, and the earth is seven thousand years old, and that's the truth."

Eli looked at Betty Ann. "That is an ape, not a monkey, and the earth is four to four and one-half billion years old. There were thriving civilizations seven thousand years ago."

Betty Ann turned up her nose. "No, it isn't. You are just flat-out wrong."

"What about fossils?" asked Miriam.

"Yes. What about fossils?" Eli picked up Miriam's idea.

Betty Ann glared with fury. "Fossils came ready-made with the earth."

"As what? Party favors?" joked Clare.

"When God made the earth, God made fossils in the earth," replied Betty Ann. "Isn't that true, Lynette Sue?"

"Yes," Lynette Sue firmly answered. "What's a fossil?"

"My grandmother," said Clare.

A.J. and Joe Tom giggled and nodded. A.J., whose voice had not started to change along with anything else in his body, blurted out, "My grandmother looks just like a sea turtle—bald and no teeth."

"I like dinosaurs," Joe Tom said.

"And they lived a whole lot more than seven thousand years ago," said A.J. "How do you explain that?"

"I like dinosaurs too, Joe Tom." Lynette Sue's blonde ponytail bobbed rapidly, showing how much she agreed. Then her head whipped around to A.J. and she hissed, "When God made the earth, He made dinosaurs at the same time he made us."

"What?" said Eli. "I've never heard anything like this in my life. Dinosaurs and the budding of pre-humans were millions years apart. How can you say that?"

"Because it is *true!*" said Lynette Sue.

"Yes, it is! The Bible only speaks *the truth!* Praise Jesus!" yelled Betty Ann.

Eli was astounded by this conversation. It certainly took his mind off Heppy and Isabelle.

Miriam looked at Lynette Sue. "Do you know what a dinosaur is?"

Lynette Sue glared back at Miriam. "Everyone knows what dinosaurs are. I've seen them on TV. Yes, I've seen dinosaurs. I know what a dinosaur is."

"Dinosaurs and us were here together," said Betty Ann. "And the earth is seven thousand years old because that's what the Bible says—"

Miriam glared at Betty Ann. "My mother said that the dumbing down of America worked."

Betty Ann glared back at Miriam. "I don't know what you mean by that."

Eli simply looked at Betty Ann and shook his head. The conversation depressed him.

★ ★ ★ ★ ★

The few remaining leaves on the old oak trees and their soothing rustle were gone. The lifeless, brown leaves had drifted to the cold, hard ground, and only the wind remained to whine through the barren limbs.

The day had gotten chillier. Mae hurried over to Booty's to get him. A cold wind came up and whipped her face to a bright red. She and Booty were driving over to Athens to have lunch with Oliver Stein before the meeting that afternoon at Lincoln School.

The minute Mae entered Booty's office, warm air took away the chill. Blair was at her desk, working at the computer. Mae hoped she would not have to wait for Booty. She felt uncomfortable around Blair. She didn't know what to say.

"Hi, Blair. How are you?" Mae forced her voice to sound light and happy as usual.

"I'm fine, Mae. How are you?" answered Blair, smiling and forcing her voice to sound normal.

"Oh, I'm just fine, honey. Is Booty ready to go?"

"He was just getting ready to go when the Athens office called and he told me to tell you he had to take the call. I'm sure he'll be off the phone as soon as he can."

Mae looked around the office, trying to decide where to sit. The furthest away from Blair was a couch against the wall. It was comfortable, and she could look out the long windows, which gave her something to do while waiting.

"Can I get you some coffee?" asked Blair. "I just made some."

"Oh no, honey. I'm just fine. I've had so much coffee I'm about to float away as it is."

"Okay," answered Blair. She immediately returned to typing.

Mae sat back against the couch cushions and felt uncomfortable. She considered leaving and telling Blair to call her when Booty was off the phone, except Booty would probably get off the phone the minute she walked out the door. It was chilly outside, and walking back and forth between the houses wasn't very appealing. She fidgeted because she couldn't decide what to do. Why didn't she call first to see whether Booty was ready to leave? Why didn't she think of that? Why was she there in the first place? She wanted to be there for Eli—that's why she asked Booty if she could come too—and she wanted to know what happened. Booty knew what time she was coming, and like Blair said, he was getting ready to go. Whatever the office wanted, it sure better be important. She told herself to remember to tell Booty to leave magazines for people waiting, except people didn't wait very much at this office. This office handled the Crutchfield Foundation.

An uncomfortable silence hovered between Mae and Blair. Both thought they should make some sort of conversation, and neither could think of one thing to say. Eli hung heavily in the air between them. Blair

143

pretended to work, and Mae pretended to be fascinated with something just outside the window. It felt like an eternity passed before Booty finally walked out of his office.

"I'm sorry to have kept you waiting. The call took longer than I expected. Ready to go?"

Mae jumped from the couch and headed toward the door. "Bye, Blair, nice to see you."

"Bye, Mae. It was nice to see you too."

"I don't know when or if I'll be back today," said Booty. "Bye."

"Bye. Good luck, you all. Ellanor is meeting you at Oscar's office. I saw his car drive by, so he's on his way. He'll probably be there when you get there," said Blair. She knew what was happening this afternoon and wished she could be there too. Blair's heart sank as she heard the front door slam shut. She had done it. She burned that bridge by doing a terrible, cowardly thing to Eli. She had left him without even saying good-bye by slipping away while he was at school, leaving him to find her gone. It was an awful thing to do, and it made her sick to be such a weakling that she could not face him to tell him the truth. She was never going to forgive herself. How could she have hurt him, of all people? Tears streamed down her face while she typed.

★ ★ ★ ★ ★

Oliver Stein sat in the principal's chair at Lincoln School, overlooking the room of waiting adults. His thick, curly hair falling about his head was the only hint suggesting unruliness about this otherwise orderly man. He was impeccably tailored in an expensive blue pinstripe suit and wore horn-rimmed glasses. Oliver's reputation was well known throughout the state as someone with whom one messes at their peril.

The recess bell clanged loud and clear down the halls. Geneva jumped when she heard the bell sound. This had to be the most nervous she had been in her whole life. Geneva was terrified because this was a life-changing day if it went the way she hoped. She wasn't scared because of Ellanor's threat to move out if the children moved in. She didn't care about that. Ellanor was a pain in the ass. No, it wasn't that. Her dream might come true. All her life, she wanted to be a mother, and now, out of the blue, two children were maybe coming into her life. She didn't think she could breathe.

Mae felt nervous and didn't know why. *Her* life was not going to change. She looked around the room. Booty's face was frozen, and he sat up very straight. Geneva could barely sit still and fidgeted while pretending to look out the long school windows. She was white as a sheet and clutched her purse in a death grip on her generous lap. Mae hoped Geneva didn't faint. Geneva was not the fainting type, but if ever there was the day for her to faint, today was it. Ellanor refused to come. He signed all of the necessary papers and then left from Oliver's office in Athens, returning home. Ellanor drove home in a rage. His life was ruined. He had spent his adult life in a nice, safe routine, and shortly it would be gone. He was taking Eli out to dinner in Athens because he had to talk to him. This was the worst day of his life, and he hated Geneva for doing it to him. His hands shook with anger, gripping the steering wheel as he zoomed back to his house from Athens.

A good-looking African-American woman dressed in a black Armani suit joined the group, waiting for the White children in Bob Wrightsberg's office. Norell Hopkins was senior partner in family law at a prestigious and politically well-connected Oklahoma City law firm. She and Oliver Stein graduated from the University of Oklahoma law school together, were on law review together, and remained good friends. He called her immediately after hearing about the White children. She was hired by Ellanor at Oliver's request to take care of everything. She sat at Oliver's side, facing everyone.

Eli walked into the office with Heppy and Isabelle White. The children looked as terrified as Geneva felt. Their eyes darted around the room, trying to figure out who the unfamiliar people were. Lucille standing at the door of the principal's office and Eli were the only two they knew. Heppy wished he had gone to the bathroom before going with Mr. Take. Isabelle looked like she wanted to cry. Her bottom lip trembled.

Oliver and Norell looked up from the desk. Geneva, Booty, and Mae turned around in their chairs and tried not to stare. What they saw were two poorly dressed, skinny children with ashen skin and dirty hair. Under both children's hollow eyes were deep, black circles. Mae's hand went to her heart upon seeing the children. Geneva's hand rushed to cover her open mouth. Both women were shocked at the bad state of the two children. The children looked unhealthy, with colorless cheeks. Red blotches of acne dotted Heppy's face. Both women's minds shouted, *where was Social Services and why weren't they called in before now?* It was obvious that there was something terribly wrong happening to the children. Eli told Mae and Booty that Prudence and Mary had said how over the children's school years, their teachers did report abuse. Lucille would not hear anything about it, and neither would the last principal. Mae wanted to let Lucille Pawn know exactly what she thought about that, but now obviously was not the time. Mae had never liked Lucille, and now she really did not like her. Lucille was always such an insensitive, self-serving jackass. Mae also decided to make damn sure there were no other children at Lincoln in distress, and if so to take care of them. She planned to have a little conversation with Booty later. Mae did her best to calm down and be attentive to the children right now.

"Thank you, Lucille," said Oliver. "You can close the door as you leave."

Lucille glared at Oliver, since she had planned to stay and find out what was happening. This was her school, and she wanted to know everything that happened in her fiefdom. She considered it her right and consequently was shocked when Oliver told her to leave. She sputtered, "I thought I was to—"

Oliver did not let her finish her sentence, which really made her furious. "Thank you, Lucille. We'll call you if we need you. Please close the door on your way out."

Lucille had known Oliver for years and was not to be dismissed so easily—not by Oliver Stein or anyone else. She looked around the room. All eyes looked back at her. "Oliver—"

Again Lucille was thwarted by Oliver's interruption. "Thank you, Lucille."

"But Oliver!" She needed to know who the black woman was sitting near Oliver. She did not allow just anybody in her school. Lucille puffed up and was determined to plow through Oliver's interruptions.

Except it was not Oliver who interrupted her this time; it was Eli Take. "Lucille, we need to get going. We don't have much time. Please."

Lucille pursed her lips and glared at Eli. The nerve of that little Oriental twerp interrupting her, who had been at Lincoln School longer than he had been alive. She was not going to take anything off this newcomer to Cedar Springs. He did not know who was who around here, and she was just about to tell him.

Booty gracefully slid out of his chair and walked over to Lucille. He took her by the elbow and escorted her out of the door. "Thank you, Lucille. We'll let you know if we need anything." He closed the door of the office and returned to his chair.

Lucille stood in front of the closed principal's office door fuming. There was nothing she could do, and that made her even madder. Booty was the president of the school board. He organized and heavily financed the trust that ran the school. If anyone had more power regarding Lincoln School than she, it was Booty Crutchfield, and that really made her mad. Booty was black, and he had the audacity to take her by the arm. He touched her. Lucille had never been touched by a black man in her life, and she did not like it one bit—not one bit. She yanked the bun on top of her head tighter in fury and brushed away where his hand had touched her arm.

When she grew up after finishing Lincoln Grade School, the schools in Athens were segregated. The only positions blacks held were as the help, even though that damn Able Crutchfield and W.D. Hoover ruined Lincoln School by integrating it, and Crutchfield Oil Company hired anyone they pleased, regardless of color or anything else. Athens schools held firm until the law forced them to integrate. Lucille smacked her thin lips and stuck her nose in the air as she marched back to her desk in a huff. She pitied poor Precious, whose street housed Crutchfield Foundation and a black man living with a white woman and an Oriental, and now possibly white trash in the form of the two snot-nose White children. When Geneva told Lucille in the strictest confidence that maybe the White kids were going to live with her, Lucille nearly fainted. What was this world coming to? Where did the good old times go, when people knew their place and didn't get uppity? Lucille shook her head sadly and sneaked back to the office door to try to listen.

The purposeful way Norell Hopkins set the room up made the children feel as comfortable as possible by talking only to Norell and Oliver, with Eli sitting closely behind them to help them feel safe. Booty, Mae, and Geneva sat further back and away from the children in a semicircle behind them. Upon entering the principal's office, Eli led them immediately to the chairs placed in front of Norell and Oliver. They had told him about the seating arrangement. He took his seat directly behind the children. Heppy and Isabelle stared straight ahead, scared to death. They had no idea why they were there. Neither had ever seen the inside of the principal's office, but they knew that being in the principal's office did not bode well. There was a reason kids were sent to the principal's office, and it wasn't good. Their minds raced to what they could have done and why they were there. They did their best to be invisible and never cause trouble. Now they found themselves sitting in the forbidden office with strange people except for Mr. Take. Something was happening, and whatever it was, it was very serious. Isabelle bit and chewed her lip. She wanted to cry, she was so scared. Heppy did not think he had taken a breath since Mr. Take walked them toward the office and they actually went inside to the principal's own office. He knew the people sitting there could surely see his heart pounding in his chest. It beat so hard, it must be making his shirt go in and out. He hoped not. He had to be brave for Isabelle. She couldn't see how scared he was, even though she knew.

Once Lucille was out of the room, Booty, Mae, and Geneva did their best to relax or at least appear relaxed.

Norell and Oliver certainly seemed relaxed and firmly in control of the meeting.

Oliver spoke first. "I'd like to introduce myself. I'm Oliver Stein. I'm your cousin Ellanor Tree's lawyer. He could not attend today and apologizes." Oliver added that because he'd told Ellanor that he should attend, and Ellanor said that wild horses couldn't make him go. Mae, Booty, and Geneva also knew that Oliver made that up because they knew Ellanor. "This is Mrs. Norell Hopkins. Mrs. Hopkins is also a lawyer and from Oklahoma City."

Norell looked at both children and spoke quietly and with kindness in her voice. "I'm glad to meet you both."

Oliver continued, "Behind you are Geneva McLish, who is your cousin, Mae and Booty Crutchfield, who are old friends of your cousin, Ellanor Tree, and are here representing him." Oliver lied, which all in the room except the children knew, because the truth was Booty and Mae had no legal reason to be there. They were not there for Ellanor. They were there because they wanted to be there. No one was going to tell Booty and Mae Crutchfield not to attend, especially Oliver, who was also their lawyer. His firm represented Crutchfield Oil Company and the Foundation, which supported Lincoln School.

Both of the children's hearts pounded so badly that they thought they were going to throw up from fear. Heppy rubbed his palms, which were soaked in sweat. He wanted to die. He did not want to be in this room with these strange people. Neither did he want to be at home. He had no place to run, which really made him sick with nerves. His mouth was so dry that if questioned, Heppy did not think he could talk to answer. The only way out he could think of was dying.

One lone tear escaped and fell down Isabelle's pale cheek. She shook. She hoped it wasn't obvious, which unfortunately it was to those sitting close to the children: Eli, Norell, and Oliver. Isabelle held her own hands, trying to give herself comfort. Her hair felt dirty. She *was* dirty, and it made her feel horrible. Isabelle had cried almost all night because Heppy got beaten so badly. He told her how much he did not want to live, and it scared her. She squeezed her hands and tried her best to calm down just a little, so she could breathe. Her mind raced as to what they could have done to get them into this room with these people. It must have been pretty bad, except she could not think of one thing. Suddenly the thought that something must have happened to her grandparents flashed through her mind. That had to be it, and Isabelle felt relieved.

There was something about Oliver Stein and Norell Hopkins's manner and voice that relaxed them. Most importantly, there was something about them that told Heppy and Isabelle they could be trusted, and it made them feel safe. As they talked, the children forgot about the adults sitting behind them in a semicircle. They didn't mind when the recess bell sounded and

Eli Take touched both their shoulders and quietly left the room to return to the classroom. There was something curiously magical about the meeting, because all the children remembered was that the room seemed dark except for the daylight coming through the long windows and a light around them that also encircled Oliver Stein and Norell Hopkins. "It was weird," they told each other later, and they felt so much better.

Oliver rested forward on the desk with his hands folded in front of him. It felt like they were the only people in the world, and he talked to them. "Mrs. Hopkins and I want to ask you some questions. What you say to us is in the strictest confidence. Everyone in this room understands that nothing said here will be repeated. I want to assure you that you have nothing to fear. We are here to help you. We ask you to tell us the truth. Your grandparents will never—and let me repeat *never*—know what is said at this meeting.

"As you can see, I am taping this conversation only for our information. If we need to use it in a legal situation, we would let you know beforehand exactly what is being used and to whom and why. Nothing will be done without your knowledge. Mrs. Hopkins and I are also taking notes, again for our information."

At first, both children looked glassy-eyed and confused. They did not know what was happening, and it scared them. Heppy tried to breathe but could only gasp shallow breaths. Isabelle's hidden hope that this meeting was to tell them something had happened to their grandparents evaporated. She had no idea why they were here. Her only hope was that Mr. Stein was telling the truth and her grandparents would never discover this meeting took place. Isabelle's eyes flashed back and forth from Norell to Oliver, waiting with real fear and dread for someone to tell them what was going on here. Her stomach felt like it was doing flips inside her body, and she felt sick. She and Heppy sat there as if waiting for the executioner.

"I'm going to turn the meeting over to Mrs. Hopkins," said Oliver.

"Thank you," replied Mrs. Hopkins in a kind, soft voice. Her beauty and the softness in her voice helped to relax the children. They felt safe with her, and their instincts knew she was not there to harm them.

"I want to talk to you about your life with your grandparents," Norell said.

Both children froze when she said that. They had never discussed their grandparents with anyone, much less people they did not know. Both immediately understood why Mr. Stein stressed the confidentiality of the meeting. They wanted to know about their grandparents. But *what* did they want to know?

Norell continued, "We know your parents died in a motorcycle accident when you were two, Heppy, and you were a baby, Isabelle. You've lived with your father's parents since their sudden death. Do you know why you did not go to your mother's parents? I understand that she was living with her sister and her sister's husband and their five children before meeting and marrying your father. Do you know or remember anything about your mother's family?"

"Our grandparents told us," said Heppy slowly.

"What did they tell you?" asked Norell.

Isabelle jumped in, wanting to save Heppy from talking, which she knew he did not want to do. Heppy never liked to talk. "Our grandmother told us that our mother's side didn't want us, and that's why they have us. She told us how they wanted to give us to our mother's people and couldn't find them to give us to. She said that the minute the motorcycle accident happened, our mother's sister and her husband and five kids vanished and haven't been heard from since, and no one is sure where in Texas our mother and her sister came from, so Grandmother doesn't know where to send us, or she would. She said that Heppy and I have been a terrible burden on them, and they don't want us. Maybe we'll get sent to an orphanage. That's what she says."

"Do you know what your mother's maiden name was?"

"No, ma'am," said Heppy.

Isabelle jumped in. "Our grandmother told us that she threw everything out right after our parents died. She told us that she wanted to get everything about that whole marriage out of the house and gone because it gave her bad memories. She told our father not to marry our mother, but he wouldn't listen, and now she's stuck with us."

"Tell us about your school day," urged Norell.

Both children suddenly looked at each other with real fear in their eyes. They did not know what to do or say.

"Heppy," said Norell.

He obviously jumped. "What?"

"What's your school day like? Do you and Isabelle have your own rooms?"

"No," said Isabelle, "we share a room. It's easier to clean that way. Besides, the other bedroom was our father's, and Grandmother won't let anyone touch it. We better not get caught opening up the door to look in."

"But you have looked inside?"

"Yes. We peeked a few times. We just wanted to see, that's all. We never touched anything," said Isabelle.

Heppy said, "Grandmother said that she wanted to keep it exactly like it was."

"And we go to school, and that's pretty much it," continued Heppy. "That's our day."

Norell asked Isabelle, "Do you agree that is your day?"

Isabelle shot a look at Heppy and then back to Norell. "Yes, ma'am. That's pretty much it. Can we go now?"

"Do your grandparents drink?"

"Drink what?" asked Heppy.

"Alcohol," said Norell. "Do they drink alcohol?"

Isabelle asked, "You mean like liquor?"

"Yes," Norell answered.

Both children looked at each other, not knowing what to say.

"Do they drink liquor?" Norell asked.

Heppy said, "I guess."

Norell looked at Isabelle. "Isabelle, what do you think? Do they drink liquor?"

Isabelle's heart pounded in her chest. *Why did they want to know about the liquor?* What should she say? She didn't want to get her grandparents in trouble.

Norell saw the struggle in Isabelle's eyes as to what to say. "Don't be frightened. All we want to know is do your grandparents drink liquor?"

Heppy looked at Isabelle. She took a deep breath. "Yes. Grandmother has a bottle of Old Crow under the sink in the kitchen. Our grandfather doesn't think that we know he hides a case of bourbon in the barn in an empty horse stall."

Heppy interrupted. "He doesn't know we've seen him sitting in a lawn chair in the barn with a bottle of Old Crow. He always has a bottle of Old Crow with him in the barn. That's why we think he is in the barn so much, but maybe it's to get away from our grandmother."

As dangerous and scary as it was for Isabelle and Heppy to talk, inside them there was a great sense of relief. Whether it got back to their grandparents or not, it still was a relief, even if they got beaten for it.

Norell continued questioning. "Would you say that they drank every day?"

Both children looked at Norell.

"Sure," answered Isabelle.

"How do you know?" asked Norell.

"Because we see them," said Heppy. "Grandmother pours Old Crow in her coffee cup all the time, even when she has coffee in her cup. I've seen our grandfather come in the house, and about the first thing he does is go to the cupboard under the sink. He takes out the fifth and drinks it."

Norell took a chance. "Do they beat you? When do they beat you? I mean how often?"

Heppy was matter-of-fact about it. "Oh, about every night. They get fussing at dinner. After we clean up, we're sent to our room. You can hear them coming down the hall, and we know what's going to happen. They're going to come into our room screaming, grab me, take off my clothes except my underwear, and spread me across the bed. Everything is really loud. I don't know what makes them so mad. Grandmother is really mad. She holds my hands down on the bed. Grandfather takes off his belt and whips me for a long time. Isabelle hides under the bed. I run to the closet or under my bed. They always find me. Sometimes they forget about Isabelle. They drag her out from under the bed just like they do me and do the same thing. It's pretty bad."

Norell had a feeling to continue pressing. "Is that the only time? At night after dinner?"

"Oh no," said Isabelle. "Grandmother seems to wait at the back door when we get out of the truck and come in the house, because we go inside and she's right there by the door. She's really mad—"

Heppy interrupted. "And I don't know why, because we just came home from school. We haven't had time to do anything wrong—yet."

Isabelle nodded in agreement, "But she's still mad all the same, because she starts yelling and slapping our faces with both hands. She'll slap me and then Heppy then back to me until we can get ourselves out the back door and away from the house."

"Where do you go?" asked Norell.

"Not to the barn," said Heppy. "Our grandfather is in there, sitting in the lawn chair. We think he's drunk."

Isabelle shrugged. "We just kind of walk around, up and down the road mostly. We don't go back to the house until we have to, or Grandmother will get really mad. If we stay out too long, she gets mad."

"Can you study?" asks Norell.

Heppy shook his head.

Isabelle answered, "Sometimes."

Norell looked at Heppy. "Heppy, can you study?"

He shrugged. "I don't know. It's not very quiet, and you never know when they're going to come in our room."

"How are weekends and school vacations?" Norell wondered.

"The same as school," answered Heppy. "They're mad a lot."

"I see," answered Norell and glanced at her watch. She leaned back into her chair and took a moment, looking at the children.

"It's not so bad," said Heppy.

Isabelle glared at him but said nothing.

Norell asked Isabelle, "Is it not so bad?"

Isabelle's entire demeanor changed. She looked straight into Norell's eyes as if only she and Norell were in the room. "Please. You've got to listen to me. Please get Heppy out of there. Please," Suddenly her head turned to Heppy as tears sprang out of her eyes and ran down her thin cheeks. "Heppy, you've got to get out. You do. You know you do."

Isabelle returned to Norell. "Please. Help him. He needs help. Please."

Heppy looked shocked by what she said. "Isabelle! You can't say that!"

His eyes pleaded with Norell. "Forget what my sister just said. She didn't mean it."

"Yes, Heppy, I did. I did mean it. You've got to get out." Isabelle's child's voice wailed, which caused chills to run through everyone sitting in the room. "Help him," she pleaded.

Norell realized it was time to let them know action was being taken. "Here is what we are going to do. Both you and Heppy are leaving your grandparents. Your cousin Geneva wants you to come live with her and your cousin Ellanor."

Isabelle shook her head hard. "Oh, I don't think they'll let us do that."

Norell's voice was strong. "I think we can work this out so your grandparents will agree. In the meantime, let's not mention anything to your grandparents."

Isabelle almost jumped out of her chair. "We'd never do that. They'd kill us. They hate us. They tell us so, and it's true."

"We won't talk to them until the time is right," assured Norell. "We have some legal matters to attend to, and then we'll let you know. This is our secret for everyone in this room."

Isabelle sat in the chair shaking. She never thought this meeting was about them moving away from their grandparents. She wondered if it were true. *Can that happen?*

Heppy was extremely skeptical about this. He didn't believe it. It was too good to be true. "Where do our cousins live? Are we going to be moving far away?" Moving far away was possibly the only way they could get away from their grandparents.

Even though Geneva was sitting in the room, Norell controlled all the conversation. Mae, Booty, and Geneva were told prior to the children arriving not to say one word unless specifically asked to respond.

"Oh, no," said Norell. "Your cousins live right here in Cedar Springs, on the first street from Main Street. They live across from the baseball field and the park. Have you been to the park or the baseball field?"

Isabelle looked confused. "We've been to Grovner's grocery store. We usually wait in the truck. I've seen the park."

"Okay," said Norell. "You've seen the houses across from the park? You know there are houses across from the park?"

"Yes," Isabelle answered as Heppy nodded. "On that other street."

"There's a big pink house on that block. I don't know whether you have noticed it or not. Have you?"

Isabelle and Heppy looked at each other. They didn't know. "Maybe," answered Isabelle.

"The big pink house is where your cousins live. You'll be right here in Cedar Springs, across from the park and baseball field."

Isabelle's blood ran cold when she heard they would be in Cedar Springs. Their grandparents would never let them live in town. If they did stay in Cedar Springs, their grandparents might come over and take them back. As much as she knew their grandparents hated them, Isabelle could not imagine them letting someone take the children—although maybe they would. Grandmother threatened to send them to an orphanage all the time. Maybe she would agree. The children would be out of the house, which would make her happy, since she talked about getting rid of them so often. Isabelle dared not hope.

"Really?" asked Heppy.

"Yes, really," assured Norell. "That is where you will live."

"When?" asked Heppy, afraid to get excited. As quickly as the flutter of excitement shook his insides, all hope vanished. Heppy could not see his grandparents allowing the cousins to take them. No. He could not see that at all.

"As soon as we can get all the legal things cleared, we'll let you know. Hopefully before Christmas, but I can't promise."

Isabelle's hand rushed to cover her mouth. "Are we going to have to go to court and sit in the box? We can't do that."

"There will not be any court. Don't worry about that. You won't have to go to court, and your grandparents will not know what you have said."

Norell prayed that was true and that this could be done without going to court. She hoped so, for the children's sake. She and Oliver and her firm and his were going to do their best to make sure that was not going to happen. She had a lot of political contacts, and she knew how to use them. Ellanor told them to spare no expense, and she was taking him at his word. It was strange to her that he had no interest in actually living with the children, and yet he wanted the best for them. Ellanor was a strange man, but then Ellanor was not her focus. It was the children and getting them out of that house and away from their grandparents. Norell felt confident that she could do that. She was fully prepared to pay the Whites off if it came to that, but it may not. A lot of work had already been done, and she felt encouraged. She knew from experience not to get too encouraged because things seem to happen. *Still … we'll see.*

Norell looked at her watch again. "The last bell of the day is about to ring."

Everyone in the room was surprised. They had no idea how much time had flown by. "We have to get you ready to leave school. Won't your grandfather be waiting?"

Both children nodded.

Heppy said, "He'll probably be here. He may be a little late. You can't ever tell, but he'll be here sooner or later."

"Okay." Norell nodded. "Remember, this is our secret. You understand?"

Both children nodded. They certainly understood that.

"If anything happens that's really bad, you tell Mr. Take. Tell him without having other students hear, but tell him. He'll let us know, and we'll do something. In the meantime, we are all working hard for you, and we'll get you out as soon as we can." Norell got up and helped the children up. Oliver was out of his chair and at the office door before anyone realized it, he moved so quickly and smoothly.

Oliver threw open the principal's door. Lucille nearly jumped out of her skin, she was so surprised.

"Oh, Lucille," said Oliver with real condescension in his voice. He wasn't at all surprised to see her eavesdropping. He figured it of her, the nosey bitch.

He turned to those in the room. "Just a moment." He quietly closed the door and grabbed Lucille's arm.

"If this gets out, I am going to know who it was, and Lucille, I will get very—and I mean *very*—mad at you."

She stiffened up. "How dare you think—"

"I don't *think*, Lucille. I know. You better not say one word and ruin this for those children."

"Or what will happen, Oliver? Are you threatening me?"

"Yes."

An icy chill ran through her body. Oliver meant it. He was a powerful man. He was not someone she wanted as an enemy, not Oliver. He had a reputation, and he lived up to every word of it. He was someone never to be underrated or messed with at all. Oliver showed no mercy, ever.

"You don't have to be rude about it," said Lucille, trying to regain her dignity, since no one threatened her and got away with it—except Oliver. His law firm controlled her family's trust, and she relied upon that money to live. Oliver never joked. She needed Oliver and his firm, and he knew it.

"Yes, I do," he answered too quietly. "I want you to understand that you say absolutely nothing at all without exception, and that includes Whisper Woman."

Lucille swore to herself. She couldn't wait to get home and tell Whisper Woman. Damn him. She'd give anything to get that trust away from Oliver so she could get him. She couldn't. Her grandfather set the trust up, right before he died, with Oliver's father at their firm. It was there and she could not do one thing about it, despite how much she wanted to. She glared at Oliver like she wanted to kill him, which she did.

"Here is what I want you to do, Lucille," commanded Oliver. "You are going into the office and get the children. You will smile at them and say that you are here to take them back to their classroom. Are you still doing your Christmas Extravaganza?"

"Yes, I—"

"Fine," Oliver interrupted. "You'll say to Eli when you get to class how sorry you are that time got away from you. You wanted Heppy and Isabelle to see their special parts. You got involved and forgot about the time."

"Use those dirty kids in my Extravaganza—never!"

"This time you are."

"No one will ever believe it."

"Say it, and let the kids wonder."

"No one will ever believe I would use them."

"You say what I tell you to say."

"Okay, but no one will believe it."

Oliver opened the door. "Are you kids ready to go back to your classroom? Miss Pawn is here to escort you."

The kids were terrified of Lucille Pawn and slowly got out of their seats. Norell walked them to the door. They passed Booty, Mae, and Geneva, who tried their very best not to stare or say anything. The women smiled at the children as they passed by.

Norell looked down at the kids. "Don't worry. Everything is going to be all right. I promise you." She knelt down and hugged the children, who held on to her.

Lucille said, "The bell is about to ring. I'll just have time to get them back to class. You all have coats, don't you?"

Both children nodded.

"Okay then, let's get going." Lucille took their shoulders and guided them out of the room and into the hall.

Norell turned around to the people sitting and staring at her in the room. She had tears in her eyes.

Chapter 7

Thanksgiving vacation allowed Eli a much needed break. Mae, Booty, and Eli had thought to go to Dallas for Thanksgiving, just to get away. Then, as plans are wont to do, it got to be too much trouble. Mae fixed Thanksgiving dinner and brought out the china and silver to make it special. Ellanor was there as usual. For the first time in their memories, Lorraine wasn't.

Lorraine was in Hawaii, getting married to Precious. They had left for Hawaii the week before Thanksgiving. Blair flew over with her two aunts (whose husbands refused to go), followed by Geneva, Maeva, and Bob on a later flight. Blair made sure to arrange separate flights. It was enough to suffer Bobby Wrightsberg in Hawaii. She certainly didn't need to share the long flight with him and his mother.

It was obvious to Booty that Blair was deteriorating. She could do her work—it wasn't that. She was getting too thin, and her skin looked sallow. Booty told Mae that she stooped over when she walked, like an old woman with a widow's hump.

One day before her trip to Hawaii, Booty pulled up a chair in front of Blair's desk with coffee for both.

"Now, Blair," Booty said, trying to sound casual, "I'm wondering how you are."

She took a sip of coffee and smiled at him. Blair knew exactly what Booty was doing. It both touched her and at the same time annoyed her. "I'm fine, Booty."

"Are you?"

"I appreciate your concern, but really and truly, I'm fine."

Booty looked at her and smiled. He could not push her, but he had to try. "Are you looking forward to going to Hawaii?"

"Who wouldn't want to spend Thanksgiving in Hawaii?"

"I wouldn't, not with that group," said Booty.

Blair looked at Booty and shook her head. "No, neither would I. It's my mother's wedding. I have to go."

"And Lorraine's," added Booty.

"Yes, it's Lorraine's wedding too. Poor Lorraine."

"Yes."

They sat in silence, drinking coffee until Booty got up and returned to his office. There was nothing more to say. They both knew that.

★ ★ ★ ★ ★

After the last bell of the day sounded, Thanksgiving vacation officially started. Eli walked down the nearly empty halls. A few teachers were left, hurrying to finish and jolt out of the school to start their vacations. Eli slowly walked home. Usually he greeted Mrs. Harrell and Miss Marie on his walks to and from school. Not today; it was quiet. Mrs. Harrell and her dog had left to visit one of her daughters and her family for Thanksgiving. Miss Marie retreated into her house when the weather got cold, and he had not seen her.

He got to Blair's house and stopped. The house stood dark and empty. The occupants were in Hawaii. It looked hollow, lifeless, and cold. Eli remained there for the longest time. He felt equally hollow and lonely. He ached for Blair, and he was mad. *Damn it,* thought Eli. *Why did she do that? Why did she just up and vanish like that?* Didn't it ever occur to her that it might hurt him? What a selfish bitch! How could she have done that? He would never have done that to her. His heart ached, and he wanted to cry but refused to let himself. He was not going to stand there in the cold, staring at her house, and cry. He would wait until he got back to the cottage, where it would be warm. What did he do? What could he have done? And the sad answer came—nothing. Nothing! There was nothing he could have done. She packed up and left, and that was what happened. Did she hate him that much? Must have, because that is what she did without so much as a good-bye note. He sighed and looked at the back of the house at Blair's apartment. What had he done to make her want to leave? Nothing. Nothing that he could think of.

Eli's chin quivered. No, he was not going to cry. This was all Blair's fault, and he was not going to cry. Later maybe he would, but not now in front of her house. He sighed a long, slow sigh of pain. All he could do now was get the hell out of this town ASAP, but not until Heppy and Isabelle White were taken care of and out of their house. He promised himself he would do that. No one noticed when he was a child and lived in deep depression, teetering back and forth with suicidal thoughts, and he was not going to let that happen to Heppy. That was not going to happen again if he could help it. That is no way for a kid to grow up. *Just focus on the kids. Don't think about Blair. Just think about the kids.* Once they were out of that house, then he could leave. Watch how fast he was out of here. Then it would all be over. He never wanted to see Cedar Springs again or the whole state of Oklahoma, for that matter. Maybe even the whole Southwest. He would miss Mae and Booty, but that's the way it was. If they wanted to see him, they would have to go where he was living, because he would never return, not even for their funerals. Never. He stared at Blair's house until the cold forced him away.

Herschel bounded up to him in the backyard as he opened the gate. Mae opened the back door. She had watched him standing in front of the Blair house for the longest time. His sadness wrenched her heart. She wondered if she could ever forgive Blair Don for hurting Eli. Mae shook her head and thought, *not anytime soon.* She knew Thanksgiving would be hard for him, which was why she fixed his favorite dinner tonight. Maybe it would cheer him up a little to start the holiday. He loved her fried chicken with all the fixings and chocolate pie for dessert. She wanted to do something for him. Mae yearned to make Eli happy. If she couldn't make him happy then maybe she could help him not to be so sad. Anything. She hoped his favorite dinner might help a little. She would do anything for Eli, and all that occurred to her was cooking.

Eli saw Mae open the back door. He knew she was going to say something or invite him over for dinner, and he did not want to go. He did not want to talk to anyone or be civil. All he wanted was to be left alone and go to the cottage.

Mae saw Eli hunched over, trying to avoid her, almost running toward the cottage. It was obvious that he was not interested in talking, but this was no time to worry about that. She had to do something—fast. There was no time for pleasantries. She had to get him and talk to him now, because once he got inside the cottage, he would stay there until school resumed on Monday. "Hey, Eli! I fixed fried chicken, cream gravy and mashed potatoes, and a chocolate pie. The pie is still warm. We can sit in the den. Booty is in Athens. It will be a while 'til we have dinner. Nothing's wrong with a little afternoon snack of warm chocolate pie and Jack Daniel's. The fire is going. Come on in. Won't hurt."

Damn it, thought Eli. *She is doing this on purpose, trying to cheer me up, and there is no way I am going to be cheered up. Why can't she leave me alone?* All he wanted to do was to be left alone. At least, that's what Eli thought as he turned and walked toward the brightly lit house.

Mae led him into the den and put him in a comfortable chair with a pillow at his back. He plopped his feet on the ottoman and leaned back into the deep, rich, brown leather armchair. Mae fussed over him, bringing him a nice, strong drink before she scurried to the kitchen, returning with an oozing, warm piece of chocolate pie. After giving it to Eli, Mae fixed herself a drink and joined him as they both watched the fire.

They sat in silence for the longest time. Without asking, Mae freshened up their drinks and asked, "How would you like to hear a story about the Blair family?"

To Eli's surprise, he felt better. He smiled. He loved Mae's stories.

Mae continued without waiting for an answer. "Booty regretfully missed this because he was at boarding school in the East. He would have loved it. What a shame. Oh my, was it cold! It was early in the morning and cold. You could see your breath in the car until it warmed up. I was fourteen, maybe fifteen. I didn't have my driver's license yet, and my mother was still driving me over to Athens to school. We had to leave at the crack of dawn to meet the other kids at the school so I could join them, then drive on over to Durant for a piano contest. It was just barely getting light, and the houses were still dark. My mother, who drove like a snail, was driving down the block when suddenly she grabbed me and screamed. It scared me half to death because she screamed so loud. I thought, *what in the world?* 'Don't you look, Mae! You hear me? You hide your eyes! Close them! Both of them! Right now!' Well, I mean, what are you going to do when your mother tells you not to look? Of course you look! You have to. At first I couldn't see what she was screaming about. I didn't see anything, and then I saw Judge Blair. I thought, what is Judge Blair doing outside asleep over their crepe myrtle bush? That's an odd place to sleep. Why was Precious's daddy draped over the crepe myrtle bush in the front yard in his bathrobe? Why wasn't he in bed like everybody else?

"I said, 'Mama, what is Judge Blair doing outside in his bathrobe, asleep over the crepe myrtle bush?'

"My mother jammed on the brakes and grabbed my arm and shook it. She yelled, 'I told you not to look!'

"Didn't make any sense to me. 'Why's the judge asleep over the crepe myrtle bush? How come he isn't in bed?' I couldn't understand why my mother was so mad at me. I hadn't done anything. She gunned that car and drove like a bat out of hell all the way over to Athens. We were the first ones to get to the school. She shoved me out of that car and told me to sit on the steps and wait for the other cars. It was cold, and she left me standing there as she burned rubber leaving. I couldn't believe it. My mother would never have done that, and she never sped. I couldn't figure out what happened. Thank God the people took me back home from Durant, or I would still be waiting at the school. I saw white flowers on the Blairs' front door. They used to always put white flowers on the front door of a house when people died. So I figured someone died and wondered who. Cars were parked up and down the block, and people were coming and going. My mother was standing in the living room, looking up the block at the Blair house when I walked in the door. I asked, 'Who died?' My mother said it was the judge. She snorted and said that the family is saying he had a stroke. She said the judge no more had a stroke than she did. Mama told me the old fool got drunk and more than likely wandered out the door to the front yard and passed out over the crepe myrtle bush and froze to death. Served him right. The whole family was mean as snakes. Everybody knew he was a drunk. I remember my mother telling me that she heard Precious's mother was mad as a wet hen. She was furious he had the nerve to die in the front yard for everyone to see. She didn't care if he died, but to pick the front yard was just a downright thoughtless thing to do to her.

"At least my father had the common decency to get drunk and die in the garage after he slammed the garage door on his head. My mother said that she always appreciated that. No one can see the garage from the street very well, and you sure couldn't see someone lying on the ground. Well, it was Christmas, and we had been to a party. He dropped Mama and me off under the portico, and we went on in the house and to bed. I was home from college, and there was a big party that my parents took me to with them. I'll never forget it. Other than the fact that my father killed himself with the garage door, it was a lovely party. You probably don't know that before garage door openers, you had to pull the garage door open and then close it by pulling a rope. There wasn't any automatic stopping the door. It got a momentum going and slammed down shut. Anyway, it was a beautiful party. The hostess had a big bowl out full of blow-your-head-off strong punch, and you drank it through these long straws. I loved it.

"We didn't quite realize how drunk my father was when were leaving the party until he put the car in reverse instead of drive and nearly drove through the big bay window. I remember seeing people's faces staring at us, probably thinking we were coming right for them, which we were. My mother was mad because she thought my father was going to hit one of their brand-new brass pineapples at the front of the house. They had just got them in New Orleans. He had a lot of trouble getting out of their yard. Drove mostly over the whole damn thing and then ran right in a bar ditch, but he finally got the car out of that. After the funeral, my mother had to pay to resod their entire front yard. I didn't know he wasn't in the house, and my mother figured he just passed out on the couch downstairs. Neither one of us had the faintest idea he was out there and wouldn't have, except the maid saw him when she got to work. She got us up. She was more upset than we were, of course. I did have a hangover that I thought I'd have to be hospitalized for, so I wasn't feeling particularly well enough to look at him the way he was. My mother just turned and went in to have a cup of coffee. We told everybody he had a heart attack, and nobody was the wiser."

★ ★ ★ ★ ★

The last bell of the day rang, and Eli looked around his empty classroom. The kids had been gone for the last hour. Preparations were well underway for Lucille's big Christmas program. Mary and Prudence told him all about it. This was Lucille's reason for living. Lucille loved it. Mary and Prudence said that it was a new form of torture. Personally they said that they'd rather be taken outside in the backyard and shot before enduring another Christmas Extravaganza. All of the teachers were commanded to attend. Now Eli was to join the suffering masses, and that pleased them to no end.

With the solstice approaching, the days got shorter. It was nearing dusk as he strolled down the hall, heading to the front door, children's voices singing Christmas carols in the auditorium caught his attention. He stood for a moment and listened. It was sweet. Eli looked up and down the decorated halls. Mae and Booty had gone to school here. Mae told him that her grandparents graduated from Lincoln. Then it was a high school. They have family history here, and it touched him. He didn't have history anyplace. At one point, he hoped to have a history here, but not now. Now it was too late.

Eli slowly buttoned up his black overcoat and walked out the metal doors, which slammed behind him. It was cold, and he tightened the scarf around his neck and then put on his black leather gloves. Yellow lights from the classrooms where the teachers were still working glowed through the coming dusk. He breathed in the fresh, cold air and strolled home. Clumps of bright-green mistletoe offered respite of color in the otherwise gray, barren trees lining the sidewalks. A crescent moon waited in the sky for night to fully reveal itself. Eli followed his daily path on the uneven sidewalks full of dead, brown leaves. He always looked over to Mrs. Harrell's and then Miss Marie's houses. It was too cold for them to be outside. Sometimes they were at their windows and would wave. All the houses had some sort of Christmas decorations celebrating the season. Lights twinkled from trees and bushes, giving the street a festive air.

166

When Eli turned the corner, it seemed Precious had added something more to the house's decorations. He knew the huge red-and-white neon OU sign would grace the top of her house until New Year's. Today, Precious had added two Santas, one on each side of the OU, waving. It was truly hideous, and Eli smiled. Little twinkling white lights encircled tree trunks, snaking up around the barren limbs, lighting every tree in the yard. Around the yard were tumbleweeds that were sprayed silver with glitter. Christmas trees were in the downstairs windows. Eli thought surely Precious was finished. There wasn't any room left. As he continued walking, Eli smiled looking at the small colored lights wound around the columns on Booty's southern colonial mansion/office. It was pretty. Eli got to Mae's house, where there was a wreath with little white lights on the front door and small white lights twinkling through the dark-green holly bushes in front of the house. Then there was the house where Ellanor and Geneva lived. In anticipation, prayer, and hope that the children would actually be there for Christmas, Geneva truly went overboard on the decorations. She hired a landscaper from Athens to come over to Cedar Springs and "do the yard up proud," which the landscaper did, to Ellanor's horror. Every year, Geneva decorated the house, but nothing in the scale of this production. Ellanor felt sure that all the lights could be seen from outer space.

Ellanor had invited Eli to dinner after the Thanksgiving holiday over in Athens. He called Eli following the meeting with Oliver the day he gave Geneva legal authority and signed all the necessary papers. The same day the children met Oliver, Norell, Geneva, Mae, and Booty in the principal's office, that's when Ellanor decided. He was furious all the way back to Cedar Springs after meeting with Oliver. When he got home, he went straight to the computer and got busy. Until then, he had always liked Geneva. She had lived with his family since she was thirteen, when her parents died after they hit a sandbar out at Lake Trapp. He had not minded Geneva one bit. He thought she and her girlfriends (now lady friends) were silly, but that was about it. Ellanor thought their lives were very comfortable; no reason to change anything at all. And now Geneva had ruined his life, and he had to do something about it. Ellanor was mad.

He hated change, and it was being thrust upon him, like it or not, and that made him madder.

Ellanor liked Eli. He was glad he had appeared in Cedar Springs and enjoyed his company. This bringing in the White children to invade his house was a little much and quite another matter. Why did they have to have ties to his family? Why couldn't Eli have found some pitiful children that belonged to some other family? Any other family but his would have been fine. It was Mae's fault. It was her idea for him to teach at Lincoln. This turn of events was not making Ellanor happy at all. In fact, he was quite unhappy and mad and worried, and he didn't like living that way. His whole routine was ruined, and it was all of their fault, especially Geneva's, who insisted those kids live here in his house. Terrible. The whole thing was terrible.

Eli rode over to Athens with Ellanor, wondering why he insisted that it was only the two of them. Mae and Booty were expressly not invited, and Eli wondered why. They always went to dinner together. He had never gone to dinner with just Ellanor and could not imagine why Ellanor was so insistent. He said that he wanted to talk to Eli. About what? Ellanor didn't have anything to talk to Eli about. It didn't make any sense to him, but Mae said to go, and he did. Mae said that it must be something important, and she wanted to know what it was that they couldn't come too.

After a surprisingly excellent dinner at what was considered the best restaurant in Athens and certainly the most expensive, Eli relaxed in a comfortable chair, enjoying a cognac with his coffee. This was nice. He enjoyed Ellanor's company. It had been a good idea for them to have dinner together so Eli could get to know him better. Eli congratulated Ellanor's good idea and let the waiter pour more coffee.

Ellanor waited as the coffee was poured and then said, "Eli, I was wondering."

"Wondering what?"

"You know I said I was leaving my house if the children move in. I've said so time and time again, but no one seemed to take me seriously. I mean it."

"Okay."

"Okay? That's all you have to say is okay when I say I am leaving? Don't you want to know where I am going?"

"To Mae and Booty's until you quit being mad. You could have a house built in back of your property. There's plenty of space. I like my cottage behind Mae and Booty's."

"Hmm," said Ellanor. "I hadn't thought about that. It's not a bad idea, but I didn't think about it earlier. Now I've thought about something else."

That got Eli's curiosity. "What?"

"I'm moving to New York and will live in your apartment."

At first Eli wasn't sure he heard Ellanor correctly. "Did you say my apartment?"

"Yes."

"My apartment in New York City?"

"Yes, of course. Where else would it be?"

"You can't just move to New York City and live in my apartment."

"Why not? You told me it was empty. You said that you couldn't ever get rid of it because you will never be able to get a two-bedroom with two baths in that location for that price again. So there you go."

"Have you ever been to New York?"

"Yes. Years ago."

"You don't know anything about living in a city, much less New York City. You have no idea what you are talking about."

"Yes, I do."

"No, you don't."

"Yes, I do."

"No, you don't."

"No one knows until they do it, do they? So I am moving to New York."

"Ellanor, this is crazy! Move to Athens or Oklahoma City or Dallas. See how you like it."

"No. I don't want to."

"Ellanor, you haven't the slightest idea what you are talking about."

"Yes, I do too. I've been studying New York. You told me where your apartment was, and I've studied the area. I know where the closest grocery store is and the bus lines and the subway. I've read the *New York Times* for years."

"Ellanor, reading the *New York Times* has nothing to do with it."

"Yes, it does. I know what's going on, and I want to go. Soon."

"Ellanor, this is crazy! You have no idea what it is like living in the city."

"So what?"

"And to tell the truth, you're too old."

"No, I'm not."

"Yes, you are, to move someplace where you don't know anyone, where you don't know the first thing about living there and you are alone. No. This is a bad idea. What if something happens? Who would you call? You don't know anyone, and we are too far away to get there quickly."

"I find that insulting. One is never too old. I want an adventure, and this is a perfect one. What you don't understand—actually you *can't* understand—is that I haven't had a real adventure since I was in college and Booty and I spent the summer in Europe. It was wonderful. I didn't want to come home, but of course I did and never had an adventure like that again. The only way I gauge time passing is the rotation in the winter and summer constellations and watching them move through the night sky. When Orion appeared this year, I knew fall arrived and that I had lived to greet another season of life. I mean I know Mae and all of us have aged. She's gotten fat. Oh my God, don't tell her I said that. Plump, she's gotten plump, and her hair is white, and Booty, Lorraine, and I are gray. At least we all still have our hair. There's that to be thankful for. When you see people every day, you can't see them or yourself aging, and then suddenly we have gray or white hair, and we are our grandparents' age. People start dying because we are next in the line of succession, since our parents are gone. We are it. We're there, and I haven't had another adventure. Let Geneva have the kids, if that actually happens. I don't care, because I don't want to live here. I am going. Besides, I won't be alone. You told me about the mother of a boarding-school friend who lives in New York City. Why can't you introduce me to her? Then I would know someone in New York."

"What?"

"Don't you remember? You told me about how you know the mother of your friend. She's a concierge at a five-star hotel. You told me about her. Said she was divorced and how nice she was to you. How you stayed in touch with her, and sometimes when her son and his wife were in town, you would all have dinner. You can call her and ask her if you could give her number to me. Surely she would take pity on a lost Okie."

"You mean Christine Klassen? I don't remember talking about Christine."

"If that's her name, yes, that is who I mean and I remember."

"Surely I was talking about my friend and not his mother."

"I remember you talking about his mother and thought at the time I'd like to meet her."

"I can't believe this. You want to move to New York, live in my apartment, and have me fix you up with one of my friends' mother?

"Yes."

"Ellanor, this is crazy! No. I'm not going to do it."

"Why not?"

"Because you can't. When I leave Cedar Springs, what if I want to go back to New York? Where will I live if you have my apartment?"

"Are you returning to New York?" asked Ellanor. "And when are you leaving? This will kill Mae. She loves you, but I can understand after the stunt Blair Don pulled, who wouldn't want to leave? Stupid girl! But then, her mother is dumb as a rock and meaner than anything. Precious doesn't have a lick of sense, and my idiot brother married her. Well, I can tell you one thing, I have made damn sure that she can't touch the Tree Family Trust that Geneva, Lorraine, and I share. Among other legal details I settled with Oliver, I made damn sure that Precious can't get her greedy little hands on a dime. I could kill Lorraine for marrying her. Why? Lorraine has always been odd, to put it mildly, but this is a new low, even for him. He will regret it. You mark my words and see if I care, because I will be long gone, and he will be sorry he moved out on me."

"Ellanor, I was talking about my apartment. I don't know that I might want to just go back to New York and to hell with it, work at the bank, and that means moving to Japan for who knows how long. If it is up to my stepmother, I'll be there forever. Even if I end up in Japan—"

Ellanor interrupted. "Japan? Why would you move to Japan? Who is talking about moving to Japan? Not me. I'm most definitely talking about New York City. If you feel the urge to trek on over to Japan, be my guest, but count me out. I'm not going. It's too far, and I could never get the language. Why don't they use articles when they speak English? I always shout *the* at the TV when I hear them speaking English. *The!* How hard is it? You don't do that. Your English is just fine."

Eli looked at him. "Ellanor, I wasn't talking about you going to Japan. I was talking about me. And, of course, my English is just fine. For Christ's sake, how many times do I have to tell people here that I'm an American? I was born here. Jesus!"

"Well, I am not going with you to Japan, and that is that."

"Ellanor, forget Japan. The point is, it's my apartment."

"We'll share. You said there are two bedrooms and two baths. It will be fine."

"I don't want to live with you."

"It wouldn't be forever. One of us would move. I don't see why you are so upset. Besides, you just said that you were going to move to Japan, so your apartment would be empty. Wouldn't it?"

"Ellanor, you can't do this!"

"Yes, I can. Why not?"

Eli thought he was going to start screaming out of frustration. "No!"

"Why are you doing this to me?"

"I'm not doing anything to you. Ellanor, this is a terrible idea!"

"Why?"

"It just is, that's why."

"Really, Eli, I don't understand you. Didn't you tell me the apartment was empty?"

"Yes," Eli moaned.

"Didn't you tell me it was a two-bedroom, which means if you want to return there's a bedroom for each of us?"

"I didn't mean it that way."

"It's two bedrooms, isn't it?" asked Ellanor.

"Yes." He was trapped, and he knew it. Ellanor trapped him, and he was too tired to keep arguing.

"So why not?" asked Ellanor. "I think it's a good idea. There's no reason not to. Will you call your friend's mother, Christine, and introduce me so I can call her? Is she attractive?"

"She's my friend's mother."

"I could at least ask. Doesn't hurt if she's attractive."

"She's attractive."

"Good."

Eli glared at Ellanor. "You've got a lot of nerve!"

"Not really," replied Ellanor. "It answers all of our problems."

"Not my problems."

"My problems," said Ellanor.

The waiter walked by, and Ellanor looked up at him. "Check please."

★ ★ ★ ★ ★

One pleasant morning, as Eli walked to school, he was thinking for once not about Blair, but how suddenly mild the temperature had turned in December. He glanced over, and there was Blair. What was she doing striding across the dew-laden lawn to work? Usually she was already there or arrived after he walked past. They had never crossed paths. Then, to his shock and surprise, he was rushing across the lawn to catch her.

"Blair."

"You're going to be late for school," she answered quickly.

"I don't care. What were you doing? That's what I can't stand—I want to know what you were doing. And why? Why would you? Why? No note! No good-bye! Nothing! You slip away and leave me without even a word—no explanation. Nothing! You vanish from my life. You left me. And I heard for Bob Wrightsberg, of all people. Bob Wrightsberg!" All the anger that had been festering, churning, and boiling inside him spewed out. He was shaking, he was so mad.

Blair put her hand on his. "Eli, I am so sorry. Don't you think I think about that every day? What I did to you? It was horrible! I was such a coward. I can't forgive myself."

"Well, stand in line, because I can't forgive you either. How could you do that to me? How could you have done that? I believed you. That's what gets me. I was fool enough to actually believe you when you said that you loved me. What a fool I was! And to think I wanted to marry you! How could I have been so stupid and blind?"

Pain flooded Eli's body. He was furious, and all the pent-up fury and humiliation spewed from his mouth. They stood on the dewy, dead winter grass. Blair didn't argue. She just stood listening as tears ran down her face. He was right. She deserved this. There wasn't an argument. She felt dead inside.

Blair whispered, choking back the tears, "You never told me you wanted to marry me."

Eli grabbed her shoulders and glared into her eyes. He screamed, "You *idiot!* How dare you tell me that you didn't know? How could you not know? I told you! I told how much I loved you. Doesn't that mean anything? You knew I wanted to marry you! You knew it, and you left me."

Tears streamed down Blair's face. "I didn't know it. I didn't. You never said. How could I know if you never said? How?"

Eli hissed, "Bullshit! You knew. I wouldn't have told you I loved you. I wouldn't have talked about plans. I wouldn't make plans with someone I didn't want to share my life with. I wouldn't do that."

Blair felt sick. "I can't know what you don't tell me. I wanted our plans. I wanted everything with you. I wanted a future with you."

Eli looked coldly at her. "I don't believe you. If you wanted that, then why did you run away? You don't leave something you love and want!"

"My mother—"

Eli interrupted her. "Oh, please. No. I won't hear that. As heartless and mean as Precious is, she didn't walk out on me. You did."

Blair's knees threatened to buckle. Her hands covered her face as her body was wracked with sobs. There was nothing to say. He was right. As much as she hated and blamed her mother, he was right. Her mother didn't come over and carry her out of the house. She did the walking all by herself.

Sweat ran down Eli's sides. He shook with anger. For some reason, he looked over at Precious's house, and there she stood at a window.

"Your mother is at the window, watching. She must be enjoying this. Fuck her. I'm done." Without saying another word, he turned and walked away.

Once he turned the corner heading toward school, Eli felt better. He felt relieved. He finally got to have his say. Now he could leave. It was over. Miss Marie was not out on her front porch, but Mrs. Harrell and Cru, her yellow Labrador, were in the front yard. She watered the bush in front and some other plants.

"Hi, Eli! How's the day going, or too soon to tell? If I don't get some water on these things, they are going to dry up and blow away." Cru loped over to say hello and get a pat.

"Hello, Cru," said Eli, stopping for a moment to pat the dog, which calmed him down. Patting and visiting with Cru helped him relax and breathe. Relief flooded through Eli. It was over. He felt better. He was better. He could go on to school and be okay. "Better get going."

"Don't want you to be late. Come on, Cru, you stay with me," said Mrs. Harrell, not wanting Cru to follow Eli to school. Cru trotted back to her. "Have a good day at school."

"Thank you. You have a good day too. Bye."

Mae stood at the window, holding a coffee cup and watching Eli walk to school. She would have waved, except she didn't catch his eye. She gasped when she saw Blair rushing across Booty's yard and Eli rushing over to talk to her. Her hand went to cover her open mouth. "Oh my God! What is he doing?" There was no question that this was a terrible conversation. Eli was obviously screaming at her, and Blair hunched over, covering her face and sobbing. "Oh dear, oh dear, this is terrible. I am so sorry for both of them. Terrible." She slowly turned from the window with Herschel following and walked toward the kitchen. She couldn't watch anymore. This was theirs, and they needed privacy. Tears fell down her cheeks. "It's too much, Herschel. It really is. Ellanor is leaving for New York, of all places, and Eli, poor Eli. What a shame. Wonder how long it will be before he follows Ellanor to New York? I'm going to lose both of them."

★ ★ ★ ★ ★

Eli sat at his desk, staring at his laptop screen as the kids came into class. He could not think of one thing to say to the children; he wasn't in the mood. Blanquitta's notes sat in his desk drawer. He could always see what she had to teach today, but he wasn't in the mood to do that either. He didn't want to think about school. He wanted to think about how soon he could get out of Cedar Springs. He said everything he could think of to say to Blair—for the moment. He was still mad about that, and he was mad that Ellanor had invited himself to live in his apartment.

To Eli's surprise, Ellanor actually did call Christine Klaussen, and what was more surprising, she talked to him. She agreed to meet him when he got to New York City. Eli could not imagine why. He figured she was just being nice, but then she *was* nice. She always was nice to him, so why not be nice to Ellanor?

The class settled down in their seats and waited for Mr. Take to start class. He remained seated at his desk, staring at his computer screen.

Miriam looked over at Clare and mouthed, "What's going on?"

Clare mouthed back, "I don't know."

Miriam mouthed, "Do you think he's all right?"

Clare shrugged and mouthed, "I don't know."

Eli knew he had to do something. He was the teacher. Why couldn't he think of one thing? He was about to check Blanquitta's teaching notes when Betty Ann saved him.

She raised her hand. "Mr. Take?"

"Yes, Betty Ann?"

"Can I go down to the office and ask Miss Pawn if I can rehearse my songs? She told me she wanted to rehearse my songs for the Christmas Extravaganza this morning if you would let me out of class and it's Christmas almost so can I be excused?"

Eli concentrated in following Betty Ann since she talked without commas or periods.

"Miss Pawn was going to take you out of class this morning to rehearse songs?" That made Eli mad, and on top of his morning, the timing could not have been worse. He couldn't believe Lucille put her Christmas program above his class. He was going to have a little chat with her about that. He had already changed the schedule for her so study hall was at the end of the day, in order for the kids to rehearse—and now *this?*

"It is Christmas you know," Betty Ann insisted.

Eli looked at Betty Ann. He was in no mood to hear about Christmas, and then he reconsidered. Maybe that was exactly what he wanted to talk about. Yes, it was, and he smiled. "Christmas," he said.

"Yes, Christmas," said Betty Ann. "You know the birth of our Lord and Personal Savior Jesus Christ."

"Do you want to talk about Christmas or the birth of Jesus?"

Most of the children looked blank, wondering what Mr. Take meant—except A.J., who knew exactly what Mr. Take meant, and he smiled.

Eli walked around to the front of his desk and leaned on it. He folded his arms and said, "Okay, let's talk about how Christmas became Christmas that you celebrate today.

"First you need to know that ancient cultures had celebrations on or around the solstice, which falls on December 21 and is the shortest day of the year. The celebration celebrates the coming of light and the end of darkness. Light triumphs over darkness. From the twenty-first of December on until the summer solstice on the twenty-first of June, which is the longest day of the year, it gets lighter. Don't forget, this was a long, long time before electricity, so you could not come into a room and flip on a switch. It was dark. The world was truly lit by fire. Celebrations occurred on or around the winter solstice to celebrate the coming of light. Days start getting longer after the December solstice. There was an old Roman holiday celebrating the end of darkness and the coming of light, and it is either on December 25, or close to that date. What the early Christians did was to take that Roman holiday and make it their own. They made Christmas to celebrate bringing the light of Christ into the world."

Betty Ann's face turned as red as her hair. She was so shocked that she could not breathe. Hiram was rather hoping she would have a stroke like their grandfather did and die. It would be a wonderful Christmas present to him. He prayed for it.

Lynette Sue's mouth dropped open, and she let out a little scream. The rest of the class—except A.J.—had their mouths open in amazement, for they had never heard anything like this before and didn't know what to think. Could it possibly be true?

Betty Ann said to no one in particular, "What did he just say?" Then her hand shot up, and at the same time, she asked, "Are you saying Christmas isn't Christmas? I don't get it! Christmas is Christmas and everyone knows that and it always has been Christmas!"

Eli looked at Betty Ann, her face still red with anger. "I'm saying that the date of the Christmas holiday comes from many ancient cultures that celebrated the coming of light, mostly on the solstice, December 21 or around that date, which would include December 25. The early Christians simply took a Roman holiday and incorporated it into their own Christian holiday of Christmas."

"*No!* They didn't!" Betty Ann loudly insisted.

"Yes, they did," answered Eli.

"It's true," said A.J. "I've read about it."

Lynette Sue could not help herself and blurted out, "That's not true!"

Quite matter-of-factly, Eli replied, "Yes, it is."

"No, it's not!" Betty Ann seemed to be in a state of shock. "That can't be true. That's a lie! I've never heard anything like that in my life and it's a lie."

"No, it isn't," said Eli.

"You can't say that!" said Lynette Sue. Her bottom lip trembled, and sweat beads broke out on her forehead. "This is blasphemy. I've never heard such blasphemy, not in my whole life, ever! I can't believe I'm hearing this. Whether you know it or not, Jesus was born on Christmas, and that's the truth because the Bible tells us so. What are you, some kind of Muslim? Are you a Muslim? My daddy was right. You can't trust people with those little slanty eyes."

"No, I'm not Muslim, and it wouldn't have anything to do with what I'm saying if I were."

Lynette Sue, chewing on her bright-pink painted fingernails, was unnerved. She would never consciously touch her nails, she so carefully painted, adding just the slightest touch of glitter. Her breasts, which Joe Tom so coveted, heaved with each nervous breath.

Lynette Sue demanded, "Jesus was born at Christmas, and that's the truth, and if you don't believe it, you are going to hell."

Eli continued, "Actually, Jesus was not born at Christmas. According to astrometry records of that period, the stars at the time of Jesus's birth indicate he was born in spring or early summer. The Persians had a vast knowledge of astrometry, and the wise men are thought to be Persians who, incidentally, are not Arabs and live in what is today called Iran."

Eli had certainly captured every child's attention. They all continued to stare at him with their mouths wide open in bewilderment or anger or both—except A.J., who smiled.

Miriam asked in an astonished voice, "Is that true? Are you saying that Jesus wasn't born at Christmastime?"

Eli smiled at her and said, "Yes."

Miriam was amazed at this mind-blowing information; she couldn't quite fathom it. She sat back in her desk chair with her arms folded, contemplating this surprising piece of information. She said, "I can't believe it."

"Believe it," answered Eli. "If you are ever in New York City at Christmastime, go to the Hayden Planetarium at the American Museum of Natural History, and they'll probably show the night sky when Jesus was born. It wasn't a December sky."

A.J. was eating this up; he loved science. "That's great! I'm going to ask my parents to take me."

Hiram simply could not contain himself. He was enjoying this very much because Betty Ann was fit to be tied. She was almost beside herself with anger. He crossed his arms, slouching down in his desk chair, beaming with delight. He knew this was going to send Betty Ann over the edge in fury. He regretted he could not agree with Mr. Take, just to make her madder, but he couldn't. She'd tell their father, who would beat the shit out of him for doing so.

"I'm going to tell my father!" yelled Betty Ann, pointing her finger at Eli. "You just wait. You're going to go to hell! I'm going to tell my father on you. You're teaching blasphemy and I'm going to tell. And he is going to get your ass fired. You are teaching against our Lord Jesus. It's against the law. You are going to go to jail for this."

Eli continued, "I'm not going to jail for practicing my First Amendment right of freedom of speech. As I was saying, the ancients who studied the night sky around the time of Jesus's birth noted an extraordinarily bright star, which the wise men possibly followed, but it wasn't in December. The astrometry journals confirm the star appeared in the spring or early-summer sky. Jesus was born around Easter, rather than Christmas, historically speaking. Of course, it is celebrated at Christmas with the coming of light."

"I think I'm going to faint," said Lynette Sue with great drama. "This is the worst thing I have ever heard. I don't know if I can stand it. This is so terrible."

Eli paid no attention to Lynette Sue's drama and continued. "Easter is part of the ancient tradition of spring celebrations, the rebirth of life coming with spring. Everything seemed dead or lifeless; then spring arrives, and life bursts forth. Jesus symbolized life. Everything the people saw around them was dead, and then with the coming of spring, life resurrected."

"Civilization was born in an agrarian society. Planting seeds occurred in the spring. Rituals and celebrations accompanied this rite of spring, to bless the crops and ensure a good harvest. Remember, there weren't any grocery stores. Survival depended upon a good harvest. Incidentally, in almost every major religion, there is some kind of a resurrection story. It's not unique to Christianity. There was a pagan celebration called Eostre by the Saxons. Again, the early Christians took the ancient Saxon spring celebration and merged it into it what is called today Easter, celebrating the resuming of life after seeming death. This was a celebration of the goddess Eostre in the spring, and the thinking is that the name *Easter* developed from that," said Eli.

Lynette Sue's eyes welled up with tears, and she blubbered, "I don't know how my parents can allow me to stay in this class." The minute she said that, Lynette Sue stopped and tried to regain her composure. She had a major dilemma. She couldn't tell her parents, because they might actually take her out of Lincoln. They wanted her to attend the Christian school over in Athens, and she had battled and begged them not to send her, because of Joe Tom. Reluctantly, they let her finish her sixth-grade year at Lincoln, but if they got wind of this, she would be pulled out of Lincoln. Maybe she wouldn't be allowed to go to Athens Middle School either, and she had to, because of Joe Tom. This was possibly the most horrible day of her life.

Lynette Sue made it her duty never to droop or slump in front of people, but today she couldn't help it; she was too distressed. She slumped down in her seat, and her whole body felt like lead. There was nothing she could do. She didn't have it in her at the moment to perk up. Everything had been too awful. She wanted Mr. Take to be shot for what he said. At the same time, she couldn't tell, for fear of being separated from Joe Tom. There was no question about it—this was the worst day of her life. She hated Mr. Take for doing this to her. Her only consolation was that he was going to burn in hell forever and would never go to heaven. That perked her up a little.

Betty Ann puffed up like an angry toad. She was not going to allow Mr. Take to get away with this. He was not going to spread dangerous, horrible lies! She hated him with a swelling wrath of self-righteousness. If she could have struck him down by lightning or maybe a gun, she would have—for Jesus. She pointed her finger directly at Eli. "Do you know who my father is?"

"Dooley Pastor," answered Eli.

Betty Ann glared at Eli in fury. "Pastor Dooley Pastor! *The* pastor of Holy Jesus Church! Everyone goes to Holy Jesus, and everyone will hear what my father has to say about you, and they will listen!"

"We don't go to Holy Jesus," said Miriam.

Betty Ann glared at Miriam and hissed, "At Holy Jesus, my father preaches against homosexuals. It's against God. You all wouldn't be allowed at Holy Jesus."

Miriam shot Betty Ann a look that could have killed. "And I thought you all were Christians."

"Neither do we," added Clare. "We don't go to Holy Jesus. My mother said that we wouldn't set foot inside the doors."

A.J. announced, "I don't care why Christmas is Christmas. Jesus can be born whenever he wants to. Just so there's Christmas and we get presents."

Betty Ann whipped around to A.J. and said, "Presents are not important."

A.J. looked right at Betty Ann. "Yes, they are. Presents are it."

She sneered at him. "It's about the birth of baby Jesus."

"Right," said A.J. "You keep thinking that."

"Okay, class, that's enough," said Eli, suddenly getting tired of this. "Let's get on with today's lessons."

"Wait a minute!" said Betty Ann a little too loudly. "You can't say what you've said and then just get to today's lessons. This is serious. You have blasphemed my Lord and personal Savior and—"

But Betty Ann didn't have a chance to finish her sentence, because Eli cut her off. "Get out your math books."

Betty Ann's mouth dropped open in surprise. She could not believe that Mr. Take was not taking her seriously. Everyone took her seriously because she was serious. And now! Wait until her father heard about this. He would hear about this, and he would get mad. With any luck at all, she would get Mr. Take's ass fired and have done a good deed. A small, evil-looking smile spread across Betty Ann's face. Okay, she'd study math, but just wait and see who wins, and it won't be that Oriental either. Her father always said you couldn't trust those slanty-eyed Orientals, and he was right. He said that the Chinese were dangerous and trying to take over the world. Just wait until she got to her cell phone and told him. She'd prove her father right. She snorted and smacked her lips.

At recess, Betty Ann wasted no time in telling her father, who immediately called Lucille and told her. Lucille got so upset that she yanked her bun back so tightly, it hurt to look at her. She was furious. She knew she should not have allowed that Oriental boy to teach at Lincoln School—*her* Lincoln School—and now she knew she had been right. That afternoon, in the midst of Eli explaining something to the children, Lucille stormed into the classroom in a fury. She paid no attention to the children, who sat there surprised at her sudden entrance, except for Betty Ann, who smiled with pleasure.

Eli had forgotten talking about Christmas and Easter, so her grand entrance surprised him too.

She zoomed over to his desk, leaning on it and spitting in his face with venomous anger. "How dare you!" she screamed.

Eli sat behind his desk, staring at her. "How dare I what? How dare you come storming into my classroom without even knocking!"

"You know what!"

"No, I don't. Why are you screaming in my classroom? If you have something to say to me, you can wait until after school and talk to me privately."

This almost did poor Lucille in, shocked as she was at his impudence. "Are you telling me I have to wait to talk to you privately?"

"Yes, that's exactly what I'm saying. If you have something to say to me, it will have to wait until after school. This is no time to discuss anything in front of my class while I'm teaching."

"Are you teaching?" she exclaimed.

"Yes, I am teaching. Now go back to your office."

Lucille couldn't believe anyone had the nerve to speak to her like that. She ruled that school, and everyone knew it. When she said *jump,* she expected people to ask how high. This Chinese foreign heathen had the nerve to disobey her and the audacity to tell her to leave the classroom. It was almost too much for Lucille to bear! She wanted to kill him. She gasped at his refusal, sputtering with anger.

He again said, "Leave my classroom, and close the door behind you. Now. You are disrupting class."

Lucille's mouth opened and closed like a fish gasping for breath. She grabbed her heart and glared at him and stormed out of class. A moment later, Lucille opened the classroom door. "You be in my office the minute the last bell of the day rings. You come directly to my office, because I want to talk to you. Right after the last bell, you are in my office!" She grandly slammed the door and marched loudly down the hall, hoping to run into a student out of class so she would have someone to punish.

After the last bell of the day rang and all the children were gone, Eli put on his coat and followed them out the brown metal front doors. Lucille almost fainted from anger after waiting for him to show up for the speech she had prepared. She even raced down to his classroom, only to find it dark and empty. Lucille returned to her office and got on the phone. All the school board members heard in great detail what Lucille wanted done with Eli Take—to have him instantly fired and run out of town. When nothing happened, Lucille got so angry that she broke out in a terrible case of hives. The school board was not going to go against their president and major benefactor of the school, Booty Crutchfield, who backed Eli.

Pastor Dooley Pastor also called every member of the school board, to no avail. He wanted to pull the twins out of Lincoln immediately, and only the tearful pleas of his wife made him leave them there. This was Betty Ann's last year to sing at Lincoln, and they couldn't take her glory away from her. That did not convince Dooley Pastor, until his wife reminded him of Lucille's gift of a new organ to the church. Taking the twins out of school might upset her to the point of canceling the generous gift. They knew Lincoln was her domain and love. This was no time to upset Lucille. Lucille counted on Betty Ann singing in her programs. What Lucille wanted, she got. The twins stayed at Lincoln, despite the pastor's fury.

Lynette Sue's parents heard about it from the pastor preaching against Eli Take and his grave sin at Holy Jesus Church. They were mortified. Only thanks to Lynette Sue's pleas and Lynette Sue's mother being only too happy to see the possibility of her daughter marrying someday into the very rich Herzstein clan did they relent. After all, the school year was half over.

Eli never obeyed Lucille's commands to come to her office. He simply ignored her threatening summons, which exacerbated her already terrible case of hives to the point she considered the unthinkable—going to a doctor.

Chapter 8

Lucille knew that God turned the weather unduly warm as her personal trial. She asked Pastor Pastor to pray for a cold snap, to have a real chill in the air for a Christmas feel. The plumber ended up calling Booty to have him tell Lucille he could not turn the air conditioning on at her every whim. The heating system did not work that way. He asked Booty to tell her to stop calling him all the time. Booty did, but Lucille still bothered the plumber.

Geneva redecorated what would hopefully be Heppy and Isabelle's rooms. Heppy was taking Lorraine's old bedroom, which still had yellow-and-brown cowboy wallpaper that he refused to allow anyone to remove. Geneva figured now that Lorraine was gone, so was his old wallpaper, and it vanished. The interior decorator that Geneva hired (who did all the fashionable houses in Athens) had workers all over the house, especially the upstairs, where Heppy and Isabelle's rooms were being done. Ellanor and a helper were boxing up his things. Some things were being sent to Eli's apartment in New York, to Eli's great consternation, while most of Ellanor's clothes and possessions ended up in the decades-empty maid's apartment above the garages. The big, pink brick house was going through a major interior transformation.

Blair sat at her desk looking out the window at the gray, leafless tree limbs blowing in the wind. The sky was gray, with grayish-black clouds rushing by. Everything looked gray except the dead grass, which was brown. Booty had left for the day. Blair wasn't in a hurry to go home and sat at the desk with her hand resting under her chin. She watched Eli walk by. He always used to glance at Blair's window. He didn't look anymore.

Her cell phone rang, and she looked to see who was calling. It was her mother—as usual—and she ignored the call. She knew what her mother wanted. Her mother wanted her to wear the big diamond ring Bob gave her as an engagement ring. She left it in the top dresser drawer of her apartment. She never had it on her finger, nor did she plan to.

Blair blindly stared out the window and shuddered, thinking about her night out with Bobby. It was enough to make her wince. After much badgering from her mother, she reluctantly agreed to go. Precious knew she could wear Blair down through constant fighting, and Maeva knew how to get to Bobby—money. It was always money. Maeva took his grandmother's big diamond ring surrounded with diamonds and gave it to Bobby for an engagement ring. As she handed it to him, she clinched the deal with an offer he could not and would not refuse: he could have direct access to his trust without his mother's signature, but only if he married Blair Don. Bobby readily agreed to marry her. Why not? It was nothing personal.

Bobby took Blair Don to the best restaurant in Athens. He considered himself quite a handsome stud. Blair was lucky to get to marry him. He thought her foolish not to appreciate how fortunate she was. He would not have considered taking her out in high school, and now she was getting to marry him! Yes, indeed, she was a lucky girl.

Blair disagreed. Every time Blair remembered that awful night at the restaurant, she got more depressed. He got drunk—naturally. She drove them home with him passed out in the passenger seat. The deed was done, and she would be spared Bobby again until the New Year's Eve engagement party. The whole evening was quite revolting. It took some doing for Bobby to get a black velvet ring box out of his pocket, considering how drunk he was. He put the case upon the table and pushed it over to Blair.

"My mother thinks we should get married."

Blair did not answer. She took the ring box without opening it and dropped it in her purse. There. It was done. This would shut her mother up. This is what her mother wanted, and now this is what her mother got. It *should* shut her up, but so far it hadn't. What more could her mother want? Yet the truth was she had not shut up and was still on her, constantly nagging. Blair was tired; she felt dead inside. There was nothing left, no hope. No nothing. Her life was over. Eli was a miracle that came into her life, and she left him. She left him. What a horrible thing to do to someone she loved so much. There was nothing left for her life. Blair stared blindly at the cold, windy day and fought back tears. She was at Booty's; this was no place to break down. She had work to do, and she would do it until she decided what to do. She was not going to marry Bobby Wrightsberg. What to do? That was the question.

The few dead leaves left after the raking swirled in the wind upon the lifeless grass. Blair swiveled her chair a little and continued gazing at nothing. Booty was over in Athens, so she could stare without seeing as long as she wanted. Everything was over.

Eli was proud of how he had quit sneaking glances over at Blair in the window as he walked by Booty's. No, he was not going to look. He was doing just fine. His heart ached, but other than that, he was fine. *Heartbreak goes with being human,* he kept telling himself. Once he got out of Cedar Springs and wouldn't see her every day, he would be even better. She hurt him. She killed his heart. How could he ache for her, for someone who had done that to him? No, he was just fine.

As perturbed as he was at Ellanor, it helped to get some of his thoughts off Blair. Let the silly fool think he could live in New York City. Eli figured if he lasted one month that would be a surprise. Eli smiled at the thought—*he'll never make it.* Ellanor would call Mae and Booty to drive to Oklahoma City and pick him up returning from New York. Eli told Mae not to be upset; Ellanor would be back before she knew it.

Eli couldn't fathom why Christine Klaussen was bothering with Ellanor. They talked on the phone and e-mailed a surprising amount. Christine was handsome, chic, and sophisticated. Eli couldn't imagine how she and Ellanor were becoming friends. Surely she was just being nice to him. Ellanor was getting excited, and that too surprised Eli. Ellanor wasn't the excited type, yet he was acting like a thrilled kid. He couldn't wait to leave tomorrow.

Mae had been busy most of the day, preparing Ellanor's going-away dinner. Eli kept telling her not to think of Ellanor as actually leaving but rather going to New York for a Christmas vacation. He assured her that

Ellanor would never stay. Eli's arguments did not assuage Mae. She knew once Ellanor got to New York, wild horses could not drag him back to Cedar Springs. It saddened her that Ellanor was leaving. Even though Lorraine was just up the street, he was gone from Mae and Booty's lives. They had been with Lorraine and Ellanor all their lives. Mae wiped a tear away and sniffed. She could not be sad; this was Ellanor's time. She hoped this woman Eli introduced him to was nice and they could be friends. Ellanor had never been alone without Geneva, Lorraine, Booty, and Mae. It had never occurred to Mae they would not always be together. Tomorrow they were taking Ellanor to Oklahoma City, to the airport. He really was leaving. Mae was sure Eli would follow. It would just be her, Booty, and Herschel on the front porch when the weather warmed up. Who would have thought it? She and Booty had each other, and thank God for that! They had always had each other.

Mae made a wonderful dinner. Afterward, Mae, Booty, Ellanor, and Eli visited in the den until the inevitable—the night had to end. They walked Ellanor to the front door and stood there, each waiting for the others to say something.

"I'll come over in the morning," said Ellanor.

"No," said Booty. "We'll drive over in the morning so you don't have to walk with your luggage. Just look out the window. We'll wait in the driveway."

"Okay. Why drag my luggage through the dew?"

"Oh, Eli, I forgot to tell you—Christine got us tickets to the Metropolitan Opera for New Year's Eve. Can you imagine? I will be at the Met on New Year's Eve!"

"No," said Eli. "I can't imagine."

"Yes, that's wonderful," said Mae. "You'll have a wonderful time."

"It will be different than spending New Year's here with you all, like usual."

"Yes, it will, dear."

"Not like usual," said Ellanor.

"No. Not like usual."

"You've got the keys to my apartment. You've got all the information," said Eli. Suddenly he felt sad about Ellanor leaving. He was going to miss him.

Ellanor took Eli's hand and looked him in the eye. "Thank you, Eli."

"Sure," was all Eli could think to say. "Sure."

"We'll see you in the morning. Now you get on home. Night, honey." Ellanor leaned down to hug Mae. Mae kissed his cheek and fought back tears.

"I'll say good-bye now," said Eli.

The three walked out onto the front porch, not paying attention to the cold, and watched Ellanor walk across the yard. They stood there until he was through the door and the front light switched off and the big, pink brick house stood dark.

★ ★ ★ ★ ★

Lucille swore this was just too much. She worked herself to the bone every year doing the Christmas Extravaganza, and for what? No one listened to her. If Lucille had time, she would have relished killing Whisper Woman. She very clearly explained to Whisper Woman exactly how to tell the mothers to make the costumes. The red tulle skirts with the red sequined tops for Lynette Sue and Miriam had to be a specific short length. They were backstage the day of the performance, and Lucille knew Whisper Woman did this just to upset her. Whisper Woman was practically in tears.

"You did this to me on purpose," claimed Lucille. Her arms were folded as her foot tapped in anger. "This is just like you to do this to me today."

Whisper Woman was on her knees, trying to stop her hands from shaking and trying not to burst into tears. As carefully as she could, she cut Lynette Sue's skirt to the correct length. Lynette Sue stood with her arms folded, practically in tears, trying to stand still while Whisper Woman cut.

Miriam watched, trying not to smile or look horrified at the outcome.

"It's not my fault," whispered Whisper Woman.

Lucille had no trouble at all hearing everything whispered. "Oh, yes it is."

"No, it's not, Lucille. You know I would never do this."

"Oh, yes you would. You would to spite me and upset me, which you have done many a time. Don't think I forget, because I don't. You finish this up and hurry, because we have a show to put on, and it must be perfect, like all my shows. Don't mess this up."

Having Lucille standing over Whisper Woman was unnerving enough, but then to tell her to hurry and not mess this up was too much for Whisper Woman to take. She was nervous enough, and Lucille knew it; this was too much upset for her. Whisper Woman's heart pounded in her chest.

"Lucille, I'm doing the best I can. It doesn't help having you stand over me," whispered Whisper Woman.

"Where are your scissors?" demanded Lucille. "Why don't you have your scissors? You did this to me on purpose. I know you did."

"You're ruining my skirt!" cried Lynette Sue. "My mother is going to be so upset. You don't know how hard she worked on this costume, and now look what you're doing! It's awful! I can't go out and dance like this."

Lucille gave Lynette Sue a withering look. "Be quiet. You're going to look fine. I wouldn't let you go on stage if you weren't going to look fine, so be quiet."

Lynette Sue loudly sniffled. "My mother is going to be upset."

"If your mother had followed my instructions," snapped Lucille, "we would not have to be doing this right now, so don't give me that."

"My mother—"

Whisper Woman interrupted Lynette Sue. "It's not my fault. Her mother made the skirt too long."

"You told her," said Lucille.

"I told her exactly what you told me to tell the mothers. It's not my fault she didn't do it," whispered Whisper Woman.

"Yes, it is," answered Lucille.

"How?"

"Continue cutting," directed Lucille. "And be careful, for God's sake. Why can't you find your scissors? Where are they?"

"I don't know!" whined Whisper Woman. "Don't you think I'd be using them if I knew where they were?"

Lucille huffed and smacked her lips. "Pinking shears, of all things! You found pinking shears and not your scissors. Impossible."

"At least I found some kind of scissors," Whisper Woman nearly cried.

Lucille smacked her lips and shook her head. "This is going to look awful."

Lynette Sue cried, "I told you it was going to look awful. I don't want to look awful. My mother is going to be so upset."

"Listen to me," snarled Lucille. "This is your mother's fault. Why didn't she listen to my instructions?"

Lynette Sue sniffled. "She thought the skirt was too short, and she didn't want me to look vulgar. She said I'd look vulgar, and I don't want to look vulgar. I want to look nice."

Lucille shook her head. "Your mother should have called me first before she did this."

"My mother did what she thought was right."

"She was wrong," growled Lucille.

"No, she wasn't," cried Lynette Sue.

"Yes, she was, and hush. I'm trying to think."

"Don't move. Stop wiggling," commanded Whisper Woman. "I can't cut straight when you wiggle."

"I can't help it," cried Lynette Sue.

"Yes, you can. Now stand still."

"It's hard to tell how straight it is with pinking shears," said Miriam as she stood and watched.

"We don't need this from you, Miriam," said Lucille. "Hush. Her skirt will be fine. No one worry."

Whisper Woman looked at Lucille, extremely worried.

Lucille pointed to the skirt. "Who is going to know that the skirt isn't supposed to be that way? Whisper Woman, when you finish with Lynette Sue, cut some of Miriam's, and they'll both be alike. Nothing wrong with that."

Miriam did not like that idea one bit. "There's nothing wrong with my skirt. It doesn't need cutting."

"Whisper Woman is only going to cut a little, so the skirts will be exactly alike or as exactly as they can be. They'll be fine. Look on the bright side—if we like the skirts, we'll use pinking shears on purpose next year."

"Hurry up, Whisper Woman," commanded Lucille. "I do have things to do. The Christmas Extravaganza starts in ten minutes and I don't have all day to spend watching you."

"I'm almost finished," whispered Whisper Woman. "Ouch! Damn it! Oh, Lord!"

"Don't you swear in front of the children," said Lucille. "Oh my God, what a mess! You listen to me, Whisper Woman! Don't you dare get a drop of blood on one thing, especially the costumes."

"I think I cut off the top of my finger," whispered Whisper Woman.

"Don't be silly," said Lucille. "There's no time for that now. Hey, boy!" The boys backstage turned and looked at Lucille. "Run over to that cabinet and grab the Band-Aids." No boy moved, because they didn't know to whom Lucille spoke. "Move! Now! You with the red hair, get to the cabinet and get the Band-Aids. Now!"

Hiram jumped up and zoomed to the cabinet, grabbed the box of Band-Aids, and handed them to Lucille.

"It took you long enough." She gave the box to Whisper Woman while taking the pinking shears out of her hand and continued cutting. "Hurry up and patch that thing up and get back here, because I've got too much to do to be wasting my time with this."

"Lucille," whispered Whisper Woman, "I think I cut off the top of my finger."

"That's perfectly fine. Just jam the top back on real tight and bandage it good and tight, and you'll be fine. What's the worst that can happen? You get tetanus. After the show, I'll take you over to the hospital in Athens and get you a shot. Just don't bleed on anything, especially the costumes."

"What about my finger?"

"It will be fine. Don't worry about it. People live all the time without all of their fingers. It's not going to kill you. Just watch the blood please, and hurry up."

"It hurts."

"Really! There's aspirin in my purse. Take some, and you'll be fine. Now hurry up. We don't have time for all this complaining."

"But," whispered Whisper Woman, "Lucille, I really think I need to have a doctor stitch it up!"

"Don't be silly! Now go do something about all this blood before it gets on anything."

Whisper Woman rushed off to the bathroom to repair her finger as best she could. She held it aloft, trying not to get blood on anything, as she ran by Isabelle and Heppy.

Heppy and Isabelle nervously stood together, trying to hide against the wall. They were dressed as Santa's elves in red-and-green costumes. Lucille had commanded Whisper Woman to take care of their costumes. She had elf costumes from years past, so they were elves. Heppy and Isabelle didn't care what they were in the play. What worried them was that they had to go on with Joe Tom, who was Santa Claus, and be in front of people. Always before, Lucille had kept them hidden in back, singing with the chorus. Now they were in front, and people would see them—something they had done their best to avoid. They did not mind when Lucille would not use them in the school plays and let them sit in the audience and watch. They wished she had decided to do that this year, but she didn't for some strange reason they didn't understand.

Lucille also regretted using them in such prize positions in the Extravaganza. She rued the day she told Geneva, after a couple of drinks, about her ideas for the Christmas Extravaganza this year. When Geneva asked and then begged her to use Heppy and Isabelle in plum roles, what could she do? Geneva could show up, and they had to be in some sort of prominent position, at least for a minute. She didn't promise the whole show or even a lot of it. Walking out with Santa Claus was obvious enough and happened at the end, so they wouldn't be on stage too long. Lucille decided it worked out well for both her and Geneva.

Heppy looked particularly sad. "Isabelle, do we really have to sing?"

"Yes," she answered.

"I don't want to."

"Neither do I."

"I bet we could slip out and hide until the play was over and no would know we were gone."

"Heppy, they would know because we're supposed to enter with Joe Tom. If we were back in the chorus, I'd say let's do it, but we can't. We have to. We don't go on until almost the end, and we don't have to sing all by ourselves. Everybody will be singing 'Here Comes Santa Claus.' You can mouth it, and no one will know you're not singing."

"I don't want to," pleaded Heppy.

"Neither do I, but it will be okay."

General noise seeped backstage as children and adults entered the auditorium. Lucille heard it and hurriedly finished cutting Lynette Sue's skirt. She sat back and assessed the garment. *It could be worse,* she thought as she got up and hurried off. Whisper Woman returned with a tightly wrapped finger and promptly forgot about cutting Miriam's skirt, hurrying off to do something else, which relieved Miriam. Lynette Sue's skirt wasn't wonderful, which really upset her. Lynette Sue always wanted to look perfect, and this was *not* perfect. It was her mother's fault. She did make the skirt too long. She told her mother it was too long, but her mother wouldn't listen. She was not going to allow Lynette Sue to be "vulgar," and that was that. Good Christian girls did not wear skirts that short. What was worse for Lynette Sue was that Miriam's skirt was just right. Her only hope was that no one would notice Miriam.

Teachers paraded the lower-grades children into the first rows reserved for them. They had their own Christmas program, in which Lucille had no interest. The Christmas Extravaganza was reserved for the older kids. Everyone else found seats behind them. Eli, Mary, and Prudence came in and found seats on the aisle. Mary had the video camera at the ready to hop up and take every move Miriam made on stage. Since Bobby was not at school as Lucille expected, she asked Dooley Parson to say the opening prayer. Lucille peeked out from the curtain to see the auditorium almost filled with families and their cameras.

She turned to Whisper Woman. "Okay, let's go."

Most of the kids froze when they heard Lucille say that, especially Heppy and Isabelle. Lynette Sue smiled and did a little tap dance. She could not wait. Regardless how her costume looked, she knew she would be the star of the show. She always was.

Lucille thanked God, as she walked out to the center of the stage, that she had thought *before* the show to try on the red satin dress she always wore to the Christmas Extravaganza. She discovered to her horror that she had gained a little weight in the waist, bottom area, and thighs. Her dressmaker told her that this was the last time she could expand the dress. There was no more material to let out, even with a girdle. She couldn't afford to throw her back out again struggling to get all of her bottom stuffed into a girdle and have to be flown out to Houston for surgery. The last time was too painful, not counting the back surgery. Never again.

Lucille stopped at the center of the stage. She had run over to Sister's this morning to get her hair done and took extra care with her makeup. Next year she might chance a little higher heel, she felt so wonderful.

"Merry Christmas, everybody. Thank you all for coming to our Christmas Extravaganza. Before we start, I've asked our good pastor to say a few words."

Lucille smiled, and Dooley Pastor, who had been waiting at the side of the stage, walked over and stood in front of her. She moved to the side so she could be seen.

"Our precious Lord and Savior, Jesus Christ ..." Dooley began.

Prudence looked at Mary, who had the aisle seat. "If he speaks as long as he did last year, I'm going to start screaming."

Mary rolled her eyes. Eli sat next to Prudence and mouthed, "How long?"

"Your life starts to run before your eyes," Prudence answered. "He loves to hear himself talk."

A man behind them coughed and groaned. An old woman sitting in a wheelchair leaned over to the woman next to her and said, "I'm glad I wore my Depends." Then she smiled with relief and went to sleep.

Lucille's foot started to go to sleep. She couldn't stamp on it, not with the pastor praying. If her leg gave way on stage, she would die of mortification. She tried to kick the foot with the other without being noticed. She couldn't walk or hobble off the stage during the pastor's prayer. Dooley was always long-winded, but this series of prayers seemed to be endless. Next year, she could give the prayer, since all of the pastor's children would have graduated from Lincoln, and Dooley had no reason for coming.

Finally, Dooley finished and started walking back to his seat.

"Thank you, Pastor Pastor, for your always stirring prayers. This is the way to start the Christmas season, isn't it! And time to start the show. Just let me get to the piano. You all visit for a moment, and I'll be right there." Lucille could barely walk off stage and out the door to the upright piano at the side of the stage.

The opening chords cued the dark-red velvet curtain to be flung open with a hard tug from Whisper Woman. Children dressed as snowflakes rushed on the stage as family and friends took pictures. Betty Ann stood backstage, scared to death. Lynette Sue was calm and confident, which made Betty Ann jealous, because she was the opposite. Whisper Woman saw Betty Ann standing in the wings, waiting nervously to go on for the next number, and she wanted to do something to help her. She had a Coke in her hand and thought that it might settle her down a bit as she hurried over to the little girl.

"Here," whispered Whisper Woman, "drink some. It will help you."

Betty Ann took the Coke and found it did soothe her parched throat, so she gulped down quite a lot. She handed the almost-empty Coke gratefully back to Whisper Woman.

"Thanks," she whispered.

"Sure thing," Whisper Woman whispered back.

The snowflakes rushed off the stage as Whisper Woman directed them where to go backstage. Betty Ann took a deep breath and smiled as she heard the music to the song she was going to sing. She walked on stage to the applause of her family and over to the mike at the center of the stage with a smile plastered on her face. Today her mother allowed her to wear some rouge, mascara, and a light touch of red lipstick. She wore the green dress her mother had made just for this occasion. The first thing she saw was her father standing at the side, videotaping. She stopped an urge to wave to him. Her mother, aunts, grandmother, even her great-grandmother, brought out from the nursing home just for this, all beamed with anticipation.

Betty Ann heard Lucille play the opening chords for "A Christmas Song." She took a deep breath and began singing. Once she got started, she relaxed a little. The first verse sounded wonderful to Betty Ann's ears, and she sailed into the second verse, when all of a sudden, a terrible, very loud long sound vibrated through the microphone. *What was that?* The stark realization hit Betty Ann. It was a burp, and worse still, it came from her! It was horrifying; she couldn't believe it. She had just burped over the mike, which reverberated loudly throughout the auditorium. Please, Jesus, could she simply dissolve on the spot and vanish forever?

Her mother's head shot up, staring straight at Betty Ann. Suddenly, Betty Ann saw her mother catapulting over people and out of the row. The last she saw of her mother was in daylight when she opened the auditorium door and fled. Betty Ann couldn't recall singing the rest of the song, although she knew she did. Before she knew it, she was off the stage and running to the back to hide. Whisper Woman watched her come off the stage, shaking her head, wondering what had happened. *She never did that in rehearsals.*

The other children who were lined up to follow Betty Ann skipped onto the stage, singing and dancing to "Frosty the Snowman." Lynette Sue really wasn't paying attention to anyone but herself as she waited to go on. She and Miriam were the last—and naturally the best—before Santa Claus. She fretted about her skirt and hoped no one would notice once she started dancing.

After a series of children singing Christmas carols and some dancing, it was time for Lynette Sue and Miriam. Whisper Woman came to get them, ready to follow the kids leaving the stage after singing "Rudolph the Red-Nosed Reindeer" with a little boy dressed as Rudolph.

Lynette Sue's eyes twinkled. She whispered to Miriam, "Break a leg."

Miriam smiled back at her. "Good luck."

Lucille pounded the chords to "We Wish You a Merry Christmas," and out jumped Lynette Sue and Miriam. They quickly did turns and then grandly leaped forward—and the audience gasped. Miriam landed exactly where she was supposed to land, and Lynette Sue rather overshot the mark. She flew through the air, off the stage, landing with a flop in front of the first row of kids. The little children thought this was planned and clapped with heaps of giggles. Lucille stopped playing, which stopped Miriam.

"Oh my God!" screeched Lucille. "Lynette Sue, my dancing angel, are you all right?"

In the meantime, Lynette Sue's mother, father, and family rushed out of their row of seats and over to her. Her mother moaned, "My baby, my baby! Are you all right? What are we going to do? She has to dance again, or what will I do?" Her mother knelt on the floor next to a barely sitting-up Lynette Sue, trying to get her breath back and proceeded to faint.

Lynette Sue sat up with her hands propping her up from behind, looking around, wondering what had happened. She watched her mother faint. "Mama?"

Cries of "Call an ambulance" were heard. Answering cries said, "We already have. An ambulance is on the way from Athens."

Whisper Woman peeked from backstage to see what was happening. "Oh my God!" she whispered. "Lynette Sue's jumped off the stage!"

Joe Tom, dressed as Santa Claus—for that was to be the finale—stood next to Whisper Woman.

"What?" he asked. Then he looked around Whisper Woman to see what all the noise was. When he saw Lynette Sue on the floor sitting up, he rushed on stage. "Lynette Sue," he said.

Lynette Sue watched Joe Tom. If she had been in pain, she certainly did not act it. "Joe Tom! I fell."

Joe Tom climbed off the stage and ran over to her. "Did someone call an ambulance?" He failed to notice Lynette Sue's mother on the floor coming around with her husband kneeling over her.

"Oh, my head," she moaned. "What happened?"

"You fainted," answered Mr. Harper. "Don't worry, an ambulance is on its way from Athens."

"Lynette Sue?" Her mother looked around her. "My baby." When she saw her sitting up, she put her hand upon her heart. "Thank you, Jesus. Thank you."

Lucille saw her Christmas Extravaganza evaporating in front of her. She didn't know what to do. Should she play something? Obviously the show was over. Teachers of the smaller children in the front rows quickly gathered them up and scurried out of the auditorium. The rest of the teachers got up, along with the parents. Families started going backstage to fetch their children. Whisper Woman walked on stage and motioned to Lucille, mouthing, "What should I do?"

Lucille simply shook her head and sat at the piano bench, trying to decide what to do.

Prudence and Mary went over to Miriam, who was still on the stage. Eli watched the whole proceedings and smiled as the paramedics rushed in the auditorium doors.

★ ★ ★ ★ ★

Earlier that day, tense adults bounced in a car down a dirt road marked by deep ruts and ugly potholes. The road ran to a dilapidated frame house that belonged to the White family. Billie Rae, who married Walter Tree, grew up in that house, which at that time had not yet attained its complete state of disrepair that the group bouncing around in the car saw. Plastic covered most of the windows. Rusted red metal lawn chairs sat in the yard, along with an old, tan Ford sedan. Piles of junk were scattered around the barren dirt yard. Garbage piled next to a rusted oil drum rotted while waiting to be burned. A few leafless trees were bent from the Oklahoma winds. A little way off from the house stood a faded red barn. Parked in front of the barn was an old, white Chevy truck. The barn door hung open into darkness. A light shined from the kitchen window; otherwise, the place appeared deserted, silent, and dirty.

The TV was up too loud for Lee Tom to immediately notice the approaching cars. Her pasty, white fat cascaded around her large body as she sat at the kitchen table finishing a cigarette. A small TV tuned to a noisy game show sat atop a greasy, blue plastic tablecloth covering the oval metal kitchen table. She used a plate with the powdered-sugar remains of donuts as an ashtray. The empty donut box on the table was next to a half-empty pack of cigarettes and a Zippo lighter, along with an almost-empty coffee cup. The dregs of this morning's coffee floated in the dirty pot of the coffeemaker. Most of her teeth sat in a half glass of water on a table next to the bed in her room. Her pale, flabby arms fanned out from the short sleeves of a dirty, pink duster that she did not bother to button, revealing a full slip underneath. Her long, sagging breasts hung loosely to the waist. Beige nylon knee hose covered her fleshy calves, and light-blue mules dangled on her feet. Lee Tom was oblivious to the smell of her sour, unwashed body or the rasp in her breathing. Old bacon grease filled to overflowing a light-brown tin canister sat in the middle of the stove. The chilly air rushing through cracks could not dispel the hodgepodge of foul odors hanging in the kitchen.

Car doors slammed in differing rhythms. Lee Tom looked around. She thought—*no.* Did she did hear car doors slamming? *Who in the world?* No one came here except sometimes the postman, and he wouldn't come until afternoon. Someone must be lost, because she knew it wasn't Elmer Jr. He'd been home awhile in the barn as usual. She knew he was home because she had heard him. Lee Tom was positive she was not hearing things, although she did have to think about it. No. She heard doors slam, and that's all there was to it.

"Damn it," she said, slowly extricating herself from the metal kitchen chair. "I'm going to let those people have it. They're at the wrong house and causing me a lot of trouble."

A new silver BMW sedan stopped in front of the old frame house. Four people were gathering together and talking by the car. They turned and started toward the house. Lee Tom gasped. A black woman was among them, and she was not dressed as a maid either. She wore a dark business suit and carried a briefcase along with—*wait a minute.* Lee Tom knew who that man was.

She opened the back door and shouted, "Oliver? Is that you? What are you doing at my house?" Then she spotted Geneva. "Geneva? What are you doing here with Oliver? I haven't seen you all in a hundred years. Oliver, you still look the same, and you've still got all your hair. But my—Geneva, what's happened to you? You've gotten fat. You were such a skinny girl. I don't hardly recognize you. What the hell are you all doing here? You're at the wrong place. Who are you all looking for? Because they're not here!"

Oliver led the way, carefully picking through the ruts in the dirt road, carrying a briefcase. "Hello, Lee Tom."

Her fat body filled the door frame. "Oliver, you're at the wrong house. Who are you looking for? Geneva, what are you doing here? I don't know what you all are doing here! Don't you know your way around out here anymore, Oliver? Has it been that long since you've been out in this part of town? Course, I can't imagine what you'd be doin' out here anyway."

Oliver continued walking toward the house, followed in a line by people carefully trying to avoid the mud.

"Oliver," said Lee Tom, "you all are in the wrong place."

Oliver looked directly at Lee Tom. "No we're not. We're here to see you and Elmer Jr."

Lee Tom had not moved. Her arms were folded; her face bore a permanent frown. "Us? Why?"

"We'll come in and explain," said Oliver.

"Okay, suit yourself. Come on in. You better talk to me first. Elmer Jr. is in the barn. Let yourselves in."

She turned from the door and padded back to her metal chair at the kitchen table. She finished off her cigarette and stubbed it out to join the rest of the butts on the dirty plate, watching uninterested as the four people entered her kitchen. Oliver walked over to the kitchen table and motioned for Norell Hopkins and Geneva to join him. A young, very professional-looking man also holding a briefcase remained standing at the back door.

"We're going to sit here and join you," said Oliver.

Lee Tom gave a mean look at Norell. No black woman had ever sat at the same table with her, much less been there as a guest in her house and not as the help. She didn't approve, and she gave Oliver a look to let him know she did not approve at all. "What do you all want?"

"Lee Tom," said Oliver. "You know Geneva—"

"I certainly do," Lee Tom interrupted. "What are you doing here with them, Geneva?"

Oliver continued, "This is Norell Hopkins. She is a lawyer from Oklahoma City who came down here today, and standing is a lawyer from my firm, Andy Easley."

Lee Tom looked at Andy and Norell. "What are you doing here with so many lawyers? Having a trial?" she joked. She thought she was funny.

The stench was almost overwhelming. Geneva looked around the filthy kitchen. Norell did her best not to gag or show anything, as did Andy. Oliver's face was a blank.

"You need to clean up this kitchen," said Geneva.

Lee Tom looked at Geneva. "Clean up your own damn kitchen."

Oliver did not have time to allow these two women, who had known each other all their lives, to start bickering. He had to control the conversation. He leaned over and turned off the TV. Lee Tom glared at him.

"I was watching that," she said.

"You can turn it back on after we leave. I need to talk to you."

Lee Tom didn't answer. She just glared at Oliver, who put his briefcase on the greasy, blue tablecloth and opened it. He started to take some papers out and then changed his mind and lowered the top of the briefcase without shutting it.

"Norell Hopkins, Andy Easley, and I are here representing Geneva McLish and Ellanor Tree."

"Whoa," interrupted Lee Tom. She sat up straight and pointed her finger at Oliver. "You stop right there. I know why you're here."

Geneva's heart stopped with fear when she heard that. She knew all was lost. It was over, and she was never going to get the children. All of the plans she had weren't going to happen. Lee Tom always was mean. She wasn't going to let them get the children out of spite. She didn't give a damn about the kids; she was just flat-out malicious. Geneva sighed and figured they might as well get up and leave.

Before Oliver could say one word, Lee Tom barreled on. "God damn it! You bring these people in my house and make nice, and all you're after is my land. You can't fool me, Oliver. I know why you're here, and it would be that snake-in-the-grass Ellanor after my money. Well, let me tell you something: that son-of-a-bitch can't have one dime from out here. We don't owe the Trees nothin'—and that's what they're going to get—nothin'. Geneva, you're not part of this. What's your name on this for? You want to try to get your fat hands into my pocket too?"

"Lee Tom," insisted Oliver, raising his voice to get her attention, "what are you talking about?"

"Listen to me, Oliver." Lee Tom hissed like a snake ready to strike. "Don't you and your lawyers think you can pull anything over on me. You want my land. I've got eyes, Oliver; don't think I don't. I see them drilling for oil all over the place. I keep waiting for some oil company to come here wantin' to drill. By God, I don't care if they drill in the damn kitchen.

I wish they would. You don't think I know what's going on around here, but by God I do. They'd drill through their mother's grave if they thought there was oil underneath. That's why you're here. Let me tell you something loud and clear: Billie Rae doesn't have any right to this land. When she left, she left. It's ours now. Whatever oil is here is mine. So you all just get on out of here, because you're wasting your time with me. Do you hear me? Get on out of here! Right now! I'm busy. You tell whatever oil company called you about my land to call *me,* because it's not yours. It's mine. Now skedaddle before I call the police on you for trespassing."

"We're not here about any land," Geneva blurted out. She knew Oliver told her not to say one word, but she couldn't help it. She couldn't let Lee Tom throw them out with being heard about Heppy and Isabelle.

Oliver quickly took over from Geneva. "We are not here about your land. We're here to talk to you about Hepson and Isabelle White."

Lee Tom's face went blank. "Who?"

"First I need to tell you," Oliver continued, "Andy Easley, who is standing behind you at the door, will be both recording and videotaping this interview."

While they talked, Andy put his briefcase upon a small table. He took out a recorder and put it on the table, ready to start recording. He held a video camera.

"Videotaping? What is going on here?" This bewildered Lee Tom. "What do you all want?"

"We are here to talk about your grandchildren, Hepson, who we shall refer to from now on as Heppy, and Isabelle White."

Lee Tom was so astounded by this, she could barely absorb it. "My grandchildren? Why in the world would anyone want to talk about them? Who cares about them? Is there any oil on this property? That's what I want to know!"

Oliver looked at Lee Tom like they were the only people in the room. "I don't know anything about the minerals regarding this property. If there has been any discussion, it has not concerned or involved me in any way. We are here to talk about the children, Heppy and Isabelle White."

Lee Tom stared at Oliver like he must be crazy. "Well, I'll be! Why?"

There were times during Oliver's conversation with Lee Tom that he requested Andy turn off the recorder and the video camera. There are no records of those proceedings. There was a period of time when Oliver and Lee Tom left the kitchen entirely and went into another room, out of earshot of others.

Lee Tom smiled as the group walked out the kitchen door. "Nice doing business with you, Oliver. Go on over to the barn and tell Elmer Jr. I said to sign those papers if he knows what's good for him. You tell him I said to sign them, and I promise you he will. I'll be going to the bank tomorrow, so what we talked about better be there … but I know it will." She closed the kitchen door without bothering to say good-bye—what for? Lee Tom figured everybody was happy. She knew that she was. If Geneva wanted those kids, good luck to her. She had no idea what brats she was getting, but if she wanted them, good riddance. She was glad to have them out of her hair and finally be free of them forever. Thank God!

Lee Tom padded over to the sink and threw open the cabinet under it. She pulled out a half-full fifth of cheap bourbon and gulped it out of the bottle. "I just won the jackpot," she said and drank some more. "Tomorrow I'm going RV shopping and get me one of those fancy RVs with the flat-screen TV I've seen pictures of, and we are out of here. Old Elmer Jr. is going to have to pry his ass out of that barn. We're going to Arizona and retire." Lee Tom laughed out loud. "Oh Lord, I hope there's another bottle of bourbon somewhere, because this one is going down fast. They may have bought the farm, but by God, I kept the mineral rights. We'll see how smart Mr. Oliver Stein is now if they ever find oil on this property and I'm free of those God damn awful brats. Oh Lord, where's the bourbon? Because I am on a roll!"

"Don't say a word," Oliver said to Geneva. "Just get in the car with Norell. I'll put the paper sacks in the trunk."

Norell looked at Oliver. "You don't want me to go with you to the barn?"

She talked to him as he walked around to the trunk to put the two grocery-store paper sacks holding what few belongings Norell and Geneva gathered for Heppy and Isabelle out of their room. He closed the trunk and motioned for Andy, who carried his large briefcase and Oliver's.

"I want to do this fast. Andy, you need to get this recorded and on video. All the papers are ready, and it's quicker for me to talk to Elmer Jr. alone, because he knows me. I want to get this signed and notarized like we did Lee Tom's. It's a good thing you're a notary. Let's get this done and get off the property."

Norell looked at Oliver. "Well done. You said you thought we could do this without having to go to court, and you were right. I really expected to go to court. She couldn't sign fast enough."

"I rather thought Lee Tom would be open to our offer."

"Okay, Andy." Oliver grabbed his briefcase from Andy, and they walked to the barn and through the open door.

It was dark when they entered, and their eyes had to adjust before they could see Elmer Jr. sitting in a lawn chair with an almost empty fifth of bourbon. Elmer didn't notice them until they were standing in front of him.

"Elmer Jr.," said Oliver.

Elmer was skinny. His skin was so wrinkled and dry that it was difficult to guess his age. His face looked ravaged with too much smoking and drinking. His nose was ugly blue-red and had gotten bulbous. He was dirty. His filthy brown hair—what was left of it—was plastered to one side. His eyes looked rheumy.

"Who are you?" Elmer looked around the barn floor. "Where are my smokes?"

Andy's eyes rushed around the barn full of dry hay and wood. He wanted this signed and done so he could get out of the barn. As he got out the recorder and videotape, Andy wondered why this tinderbox of a barn had not already burned down.

"Elmer, I'm Oliver Stein. You remember me?"

It took a minute for Elmer Jr. to get Oliver into focus. "Oliver Stein? I remember you."

"I'm from here, but maybe I've been over in Athens too long. Elmer Jr., I have some papers for you to sign. Lee Tom has signed everything and told us to have you sign."

"Lee Tom's signed?"

"Yes, she has. Also my associate, Andy Easley is recording and videotaping this."

Elmer Jr. smiled. His teeth were so yellow they looked almost brown. "Am I a movie star?"

"Not yet," replied Oliver as he put the papers on a hay bale in front of Elmer Jr.

"Okay," said Elmer Jr. "Am I selling the farm? I can't sell the farm. My daddy told me never to sell the farm." Elmer laughed.

Oliver didn't know whether Elmer was making a joke or was serious. Maybe his father did tell him not to sell the farm. It was too late; it was gone. There were also adoption papers to be signed. Oliver pointed to lines for his signature and handed Elmer a pen.

"I want to explain exactly what you are signing. You need to have all the information and understand what is happening."

Elmer just looked at Oliver like he was crazy. "Shit, no! If Lee Tom told me to sign, I figure she knows what she's doing."

After all the papers were signed and notarized, Andy and Oliver hurried out of the barn into the car and off the property.

As the car bounced off the farm, Geneva turned around to look back. "I hope these kids never see this property again. At least if they do decide to come out here, there won't be one thing to remind them what went on. Oliver, I want you to make sure every building is razed, cleaned up, and gone. You have whoever you hire make sure this property looks natural like it looked before anything was built. I don't care what you have to do or whoever you hire has to do. You tell them to make it like a nature preserve or something like that—natural. They are never going to see the property again like this. Okay?"

"I'll take care of everything, just as we discussed the times you came over to my office," Oliver answered. "Andy, haven't you already started looking into this?"

"Yes. All I'm waiting for is the go-ahead from you. Now that everything is legal and finished, I'll give them a call when I get back to the office."

"Good," said Oliver.

"Good," agreed Geneva. "That's the way I want it."

"It will be," Andy assured Geneva.

"Good. As soon as possible. They have one month to get off the property. I hope they will be gone before that."

"Exactly," agreed Andy. "They'll start as soon as possible."

"Like nothing has ever been here," insisted Geneva.

"That's right," said Andy. "Pristine and back to nature, like the land has never been touched."

"Good." Geneva nodded. "That's real good."

As Geneva walked to the doors of the school auditorium, paramedics rushed by her. She held her large, black leather purse close to her chest. This had been an unnerving day. She had been terrified, sitting at Lee Tom's kitchen table that something might happen. Things could always go wrong, and Geneva would not be able to adopt the kids. Actually, Ellanor, since he was a blood relative. Geneva was their guardian. She didn't understand all of the legal doings, even though Oliver had explained everything to her. She pretended to understand, but really she didn't. She didn't care about that, though. All she cared about was getting Heppy and Isabelle out of that house and legally into hers. Everything else was gibberish, as far as she was concerned.

As scared as Geneva was about not getting the children, she was equally scared about getting them. She couldn't tell anyone that, especially not Ellanor. He would get mad at her, since this was her idea and she forced everything to happen. Ellanor had spent a lot of money. The last thing she could tell him was that she was scared. Maybe she couldn't be a mother. Maybe she didn't want children invading her life, which had always been very quiet and solitary. She had never been around children. What was she doing? *Do no harm*—that was all she wanted. Her life was going to change in ways she could not begin to imagine. Did she really want this? Too late now, because she was on her way into the school to take Heppy and Isabelle to their new home—her home. The children were coming to live with her forever. Well, not exactly forever. They would grow up, and she'd make sure they left home, unlike Lorraine and Ellanor, who she never thought would leave. She never thought Lorraine would leave his bedroom, much less actually move out and get married. No, she wanted these kids to have a life. She didn't know how or what to do, but that's what she wanted for them. Was this the worst day in her life or the best? She couldn't decide; she simply didn't know.

Geneva became worried, watching the paramedics go by her and into the auditorium. What had happened? She hoped Heppy and Isabelle were all right. There must have been some kind of accident; otherwise, why would an ambulance be here? She chewed on her bottom lip in worry as she followed the paramedics into the auditorium. She watched them hurry to the front of the stage. Someone must have been on the floor, because Geneva saw them looking down. Her eyes rushed to the stage. Heppy and Isabelle were not there. Miriam was on the stage, squatting down, talking to Prudence and Mary standing on the floor. *It must not be too bad,* thought Geneva, *because they're laughing. They wouldn't be laughing if something horrible happened.* That thought made Geneva feel better.

Eli saw Geneva enter the auditorium. She was so concerned, looking at the stage area, trying to see what was happening, that she never noticed Eli. She walked right by him.

"Geneva," he said.

She stopped walking and turned toward the voice. "What?"

Eli had gotten up and hurried to her. "What happened? Is everything okay?"

He had been kept informed as to what was happening. When Geneva came to school to talk to the children, Eli carefully guided them to the principal's office, while the other kids ran out for recess. If more time was needed, then he arranged for them to be at rehearsals as the reason for not being in class. Geneva made sure the children were apprised of everything transpiring on their behalf. Most importantly, the children agreed this was what they wanted. Sometimes when Eli walked them back to class, they talked about their concerns. Eli assured them everything was going to work out, hoping that was true.

This was a huge secret. Isabelle and Heppy knew they could not say one word, for fear of ruining everything. They didn't know where they were going, but it had to be better than the way they lived with their grandparents. Isabelle knew that Heppy could not take much more. Events could not happen soon enough, as far as she was concerned. She had never met Ellanor Tree, who very generously had paid for everything. She heard he had gone to New York. Both children only knew Geneva; they liked and trusted her. But they refused to let themselves believe this would actually come true, just in case it didn't. The disappointment would be overwhelming. Isabelle tried to make a plan, in case this did not happen. She had to do something; she had to find some way to get Heppy out of the house. If their grandmother refused to let them go with Geneva—and knowing their grandmother, that was a real possibility—there had to be a plan B. But what? That was the question. What? And that, Isabelle did not know.

No one paid any attention to Isabelle and Heppy as they huddled together on stage with the rest of the kids who came out from backstage to see what was happening. They were scared to death; they knew today was the day. They did not know any more than that. Did Geneva and the lawyers go out to the farm and talk to their grandmother? Their grandfather would do whatever their grandmother commanded. Their grandmother was the question. What would she do? They didn't know, and it scared them. When they left the house this morning, neither looked back as they got in the old white pickup with Elmer Jr. and drove away.

When all the commotion occurred, Isabelle and Heppy looked at each other. Heppy's eyes got big. "What's happening?"

"I don't know," answered Isabelle.

Whisper Woman peeked out from behind the curtain. "Oh my God! Lynette Sue jumped off the stage!"

Isabelle looked at Heppy. "What are we going to do?" he asked.

"I'll look." Since there was so much hubbub backstage after Whisper Woman said that, she knew no one would notice them moving.

Joe Tom almost ran into Isabelle as he rushed by her to the stage. She looked up at him as he brushed her going by. "Watch it." Isabelle was amazed she had the nerve to say that to Joe Tom. He was one of the popular boys who never gave her the time of day. She didn't like being pushed like that. Isabelle took Heppy's hand and led him on stage. Was Geneva there? If she had not arrived, that meant their grandmother had refused. Their grandfather would pick them up as always, and if that happened … Isabelle shuddered to think about the consequences when they got back. One thing she could count on was her grandmother being mad. She was always mad, but this would really make her furious. Isabelle's heart pounded. What was happening? Where was Geneva? How could she tell Heppy their grandfather was there instead of Geneva? She had told him not to get excited. Isabelle told him over and over, don't get excited, but he did. She knew he did. It gave him hope. Isabelle wanted to cry, she was so upset, but she knew she couldn't. Later, when she was in bed, no one would hear her cry. Not now.

Isabelle looked out again at the audience and gasped. Heppy heard her, she gasped so loud.

"What?" he asked. "What is it?" He was afraid to ask if Geneva was here. He didn't think he could face his grandfather but if he had to, he had to. He would think of something. He always did while he was being beaten. Usually he sang to himself. He could do that again.

"She's here." Isabelle was so scared and excited, she barely got the words out. Her heart beat so hard, she wondered if it would jump out of her chest. To her surprise, her knees were shaking.

"What?" Heppy was afraid to believe what he heard.

"She's here," Heppy said, looking at Isabelle with wide, unbelieving eyes. He could not believe what he was seeing.

Geneva and Mr. Take were walking to the stage. They were walking to them. Heppy and Isabelle looked at each other, not knowing what to do.

"What should we do?" asked Heppy. He was stark white with fear and could barely swallow.

"I don't know."

Isabelle watched Geneva and Eli a moment longer. "Maybe we should go meet them?"

"I'm afraid to."

"So am I, but it's either stay here or go meet them. I think we should go meet them."

Heppy looked at Isabelle with terrified eyes. "I don't want to."

"We can't stand here for the rest of our lives. I think we ought to go meet them."

"I can't move," said Heppy. "I'm afraid. I've never slept anyplace but the farm in my life. I don't want to go."

"Neither have I. I've never slept anyplace but the farm either. Don't you think I'm scared? I am. Listen, Heppy, we have to go. It's better than going back to the farm. Anything has to be better than that. Geneva seems nice. I don't think she'll hurt us. I really don't. This is a miracle, Heppy. We're getting away. We have to get out of there. *You* have to get out of there for sure."

"I'm okay. I'm fine at the farm."

"No, you're not. Come on."

"I'm afraid. I don't want to go."

"Heppy, I'm afraid, but we're going. We're going right now to meet Geneva and Mr. Take."

Isabelle grabbed Heppy's hand and led him off the stage and out the stage door.

They walked by as the paramedics were putting Lynette Sue on a stretcher and her mother on another one. Mrs. Harper kept insisting she was fine and would not faint again, although she was a little worried about her heart. She'd had such a scare. "You never know what that will do."

"It hurts!" cried Lynette Sue, holding her ankle.

"Give her a shot," demanded Mrs. Harper. "Help my baby. She's in pain. Help my baby."

"We already have given her something for pain," one of the paramedics told Mrs. Harper. "We need to get her to the hospital. It looks like her ankle is broken."

"Broken?" wailed Mrs. Harper. "My baby's ankle is broken. Oh my God! Oh my God! What will I do? I think I'm going to faint again. I need one of your pain shots. This is all too much for a mother to bear."

The paramedics took Mrs. Harper first and hurried her out of the auditorium to the ambulance. She cried and moaned all the way out the door.

Joe Tom held Lynette Sue's hand as she lay on the stretcher. The narcotic they gave her began to kick in, and she was feeling no pain. She smiled and looked down at the red tulle skirt. "My skirt is ruined," she told Joe Tom.

"It would be," answered Joe Tom, full of sympathy and concern. "You fell off the stage. You'll get a new skirt that's better than this one."

"I better. I'm never wearing this one again."

Joe Tom patted her hand. "Of course you're not. Are you in a lot of pain?"

She looked up at him from the stretcher with a big, toothy smile. "No, I'm fine. I feel great."

"Good. That's good."

Lynette Sue looked around and saw Miriam. She yelled, "Hey, Miriam! Want to finish our dance?"

Miriam, Prudence, and Mary stopped talking when they heard Lynette Sue shout. "No," answered Miriam. "You have to go to the hospital."

Lynette Sue looked at her. "No, I don't. I feel great. I wanna dance."

Joe Tom watched the paramedics return for Lynette Sue. "Here are the people to take you to the hospital."

"Why?"

Joe Tom patted her hand and walked out with them as the paramedics rolled Lynette Sue out of the auditorium. She waved at everyone as she rolled by. Her father handed her a bunch of long-stem red carnations he brought to give her after the show. She pulled one out of the bouquet and put it sideways dangling from her mouth.

"Bye-bye, you all. I broke my ankle. I feel great. Bye-bye. I'm going to the hospital. Come see me at the hospital, okay?"

Heppy and Isabelle arrived about the same time as Geneva and Eli Take, at the point when Lynette Sue was being wheeled out of the auditorium.

"Oh my goodness," said Geneva, equally as startled as the children were. "Here you all are. I can't believe it. I just can't believe it." This had been an overwhelming day for her. She looked at the two children dressed as Christmas elves and didn't know what to do. The Tree family was never effusive. She, Lorraine, and Ellanor had never hugged each other in their lives. The only family member Geneva remembered hugging was Billie Rae, but everyone thought Billie Rae was crazy. She probably should hug the children. Geneva stammered. She genuinely didn't know how. She didn't know what to do.

The children stood there, not knowing what to do or say.

Eli stood watching, aware of their uncertainty. Geneva froze. The kids stopped and waited. Eli had to do something. They could not stand there, staring at each other, not knowing what to do; on the other hand, Eli didn't know what to do either. His family had never showed emotion. He couldn't invite everyone over to Mae's for cocktails—which, for some reason, flew into his mind. That certainly would not do. *These are children. What should I do?* He had to do something.

Laughter erupted from Miriam, Mary, and Prudence as they helped their daughter off the stage. People were talking and leaving the auditorium. Lucille still sat at the piano, staring helplessly as her grand Extravaganza turned to shreds. Whisper Woman ran around telling those who wore costumes owned by the school that they had to return the costumes. They weren't theirs! People barely heard—or at the moment cared—about Whisper Woman's threats and warnings about the costumes.

Whisper Woman, completely oblivious to the life-changing drama in front of her, whirled over to Geneva, Heppy, Isabelle, and Eli.

"Those aren't yours," she whispered.

Geneva looked blank. "What?"

Whisper Woman shook her finger at the children. "Those aren't your costumes."

"What are you talking about?" Geneva asked, taken aback by Whisper Woman's insistence.

"They belong to the school. You can't have them," she insisted.

"I don't want them," said Geneva.

Whisper Woman suddenly realized that Geneva was there. "What are you doing here? I wasn't talking to you. I was talking to these children. They are wearing property that belongs to Lincoln School. You kids have to give those costumes back. Do you hear me?"

They barely heard Whisper Woman whispering, but they knew what she was saying. They didn't know what to say except *okay*.

The sudden and unexpected confrontation with Whisper Woman shook Geneva and brought her back to the present. No longer frozen, she was mad at Whisper Woman for interrupting what was probably the most important moment in her life.

"Come on, children," announced Geneva. She'd had quite enough of Whisper Woman. "We're going home."

Geneva grabbed the two children's hands and marched them out of the auditorium.

Whisper Woman's mouth dropped open. "Wait a minute."

She turned to Eli, who remained there. "What was Geneva doing at Lincoln, and what was she doing with those kids? Since when does Geneva know them, of all people? Geneva doesn't know them. She can't just walk out of the school with two children. You can't do that. They don't belong to her. I'm going to go do something! You just can't come into a school, pick out two children, and leave. This isn't a department store, you know. Just what does Geneva think she's doing? I'm calling the police."

"They do belong to her," answered Eli quietly. "They are her family now, and she's theirs."

Whisper Woman glared at Eli. "Just what do you mean by that? No, they are not. They are no more her family than the man in the moon. You don't know, because you just came here. I've lived here all of my life, and I know who is related to whom."

"Yes, they are. She is their legal guardian."

Whisper Woman jammed her hands on her hips and puffed up. "She is not!"

"She is too."

"No she's not."

"Yes, she is."

"I've known Geneva McLish all of my life, and believe me, she isn't anyone's legal guardian. She's an orphan."

"Geneva is their legal guardian. Call Oliver Stein if you don't believe me."

"Oliver? What does he have to do with this?"

"He's their lawyer. Call him. I'd call him before I called the police."

"How can Geneva be their guardian when I don't think she knows those kids?"

"Billie Rae White Tree is their great aunt."

That stopped Whisper Woman. She had to think for a moment. "Well, good Lord! That's right. I forgot Billie Rae was a White. I'm sure my mother told me that Billie Rae Tree was a White, but my God, that was a hundred years ago. Who would ever think about Billie Rae being a member of that horrible White family? I have got to tell Lucille. She needs to know those kids left with Geneva, of all people. Lucille won't believe it. What if their whoever-it-is comes to get them?"

"Lucille already knows, and their grandparents won't be coming for them."

"Lucille can't know!"

"She does."

"She can't know because she would have told *me,* and I didn't know."

"She knows."

"I don't believe it."

"Okay then. Go ask her."

"That is just what I'm going to do."

Whisper Woman strode over to the piano where Lucille sat. Eli strolled out of the auditorium and down the hall. He gathered up his things in the classroom, turned out the light, and closed the door.

Chapter 9

Booty and Eli's faces felt chilled as they slowly rocked back and forth on the front porch swing, but they didn't care. An almost-empty bottle of champagne stood in easy reach of Booty for refills. They were getting drunk. They knew they were getting drunk, and they didn't care. They enjoyed the crisp air and dreamily gazed at the stars that glittered like diamonds against the black sky.

After dinner, Mae had said, "If you all want to catch your death of cold sitting outside, be my guest. Go ahead, freeze to death; see if I care. I'm going upstairs to my nice, warm bed and maybe stay awake to watch the ball drop in Times Square. If you all wanted to be civilized and go to the den and watch the ball drop, I'd be with you, but sitting outside in the cold is not my idea of fun."

"Oh, come on, Mae," said Booty. "We're going to bundle up. It's such a pretty night."

"I don't give a damn if Jesus Christ decides to resurrect right now on the front yard. I am not freezing to death sitting outside. Why? I have a perfectly good house that is warm. You all have fun. I love you both. Happy New Year. I'm going to bed."

Eli and Booty went over to Mae. She gave them both a kiss, waved good-bye, and headed for the stairs. "Come on, Herschel. Let's go to bed."

The dog looked longingly at Booty, because he wanted to join them in the cold. But instead he dutifully followed Mae upstairs and into the bedroom.

Booty grabbed and opened another bottle of champagne and two champagne flutes and headed to the coat closet in the hall, followed by Eli.

Except for his face, Eli wasn't the least bit cold. Booty insisted he wear Mae's full-length mink coat, warm gloves, and a hat. Booty wore his overcoat, gloves, and a hat, and they were bundled under throws taken from the den. All in all, Eli thought it was quite pleasant, except for the noise of people leaving the party.

Precious was throwing a New Year's Eve party to introduce the newly engaged couple to the society worthies. Cars were parked up and down the block and overflowing the Blairs' driveway. Every light in the house was on. So were the twinkling white lights circling the trunks and the limbs of all the leafless front-yard trees. A spotlight lit the huge red-and-white neon OU sign on the roof with a Santa Claus on either side waving. White-flocked Christmas trees with twinkling white lights stood on either side of the front door.

A couple of weeks before the party, Precious had called Mae to ask if the guests might use the driveway at Booty's house and at her family's house.

When the phone rang, Mae was surprised to hear Precious's voice on the other end. "Mae, this is Precious."

Precious never called Mae, so she must want something. What did she want?

Precious's voice was syrupy sweet. "Are you all going to be home New Year's Eve?"

Mae had heard about the party at the beauty parlor. She sucked in her breath with surprise and couldn't believe Precious was actually calling to invite them. "We always stay home New Year's Eve. I don't like being on the highway to go over to Athens for dinner."

"Too many drunk drivers," said Precious.

"Yes." Mae waited.

"Mae, since you all will be home and you aren't needing to go in and out of the driveway, I was wondering if I could use your drive and the Crutchfield house's drive for New Year's Eve?"

Mae felt her face flush with anger. She knew Precious was rude and mean. Out of curiosity, Mae waited without saying a word. Would Precious not even invite them after asking to use their drives for parking?

"Well since you'll be home with your cars in the garage, why let the drives sit empty? That's what I was wondering."

"No."

"Why not?"

"I don't want to."

"At least let me use Booty's. I don't see why I can't use that one, since it is right next to my house and couldn't be more convenient."

"No. Good-bye."

"Mae, I don't understand why you have to be like this."

"You're asking to use my driveways for parking to a party that Booty and I aren't invited to. No."

"I don't see why you have to be so rude, Mae. I'm free, white, and twenty-one. I get to invite who I want to my parties. I don't see what that has to do with me using empty driveways."

"Good-bye, Precious."

"I always thought you were nice, Mae. I see I was wrong. Good-bye."

Booty watched the people park in his driveway. He knew Precious would tell them it was okay. Never mind it was a lie. Precious had no problem with lying. He should have thought to put up some kind of barrier to keep people out. He leaned down and grabbed the champagne bottle. "Hand me your glass."

Eli dutifully obeyed. "Shall I go in and get us another bottle?"

"Absolutely. There's one in the fridge."

"I know."

"God damn that Precious," said Booty.

"She's a real piece of work," said Eli as he wandered into the house. "Be right back."

"If she does this again next year, I'll put up barricades to make damn sure she can't use my property for her guests," Booty said to himself, since Eli was not in earshot. "All my life she's been hateful to me and to Mae; thinking she's so much better than anybody else. Racist, horrible woman. Horrible family. Horrible, all of them. Blair was such a fool ... such a God damn fool."

Eli strolled back to the porch with an open bottle of champagne. "Blair was a fool," he said as he returned to the swing. "Blair was a fool, and she's mean."

"Blair *was* mean," Booty agreed. "The whole family was mean."

"She left me without so much as a note telling me she was leaving. Nothing. Can you believe that?"

"Yes," answered Booty.

"Yes?"

"Yes."

"Why?"

"Because of the whole God damn family, that's why. I had hoped Blair was different."

"Why did you hire her?"

"Because I hoped she would be a better person than any other member of her family. I needed someone, and she was there and qualified. Seemed like a good idea at the time. She's very capable; I'll say that for her."

"Capable of moving out on me. How would you feel if you came home one day and Mae had vanished? Just how would you feel?"

"I don't know. Mae's never done that."

"Let me help you. It hurts. I never want to have that happen to me again." Eli took a long drink and continued, "Makes you lose faith in humanity."

"I would think so. Just like that jackass Precious makes you lose faith in humanity. Can humans act human, or is Precious acting human? If that is humanity, there isn't any."

"What?"

"Oh never mind ... who gives a shit?"

Women's laughter drifted through the air. Cars were jammed up and down the block. The glow from the moon highlighted the guests leaving Precious's house. Booty and Eli watched them walking down the block, talking and looking for their cars. No one seemed to notice or care about the two men rocking on the creaking porch swing.

"Do you think you'll stay after this school year ends?" Booty asked.

"No. I don't know if I'll finish the rest of the year."

"Really? I figured you would leave, but I thought you'd finish out the school year. What are we going to do for a teacher? Damn, don't do that. Lucille was hounding me about some cousin wanting to teach at Lincoln. The cousin teaches in Athens and is commuting from here."

Eli interrupted, "That's a commute?"

"Lucille thinks so. She got mad at me when the board hired you instead of the cousin. Thank God we had you to hire. The last thing I want is Lucille's cousin."

"Any relation to Lucille, I can understand why you wouldn't want to hire them."

"Right."

"So Mae thinks I'm going to leave?" asked Eli.

"What do you think, after Blair pulled that number?"

"I don't want to hurt Mae, but I can't stay."

"We both know that. Don't worry about Mae. She'll be fine."

They rocked back and forth for a while in comfortable silence.

"There goes a shooting star."

"Where?" asked Eli.

"You missed it. It was over there, close to Orion."

"Booty?"

"Hum?"

"Maybe I'm seeing things, but I think there's someone walking toward us."

"Probably some drunk wandering around lost. We'll turn them around to head back to Precious's house. I hope whoever it is doesn't throw up on my bushes, or worse yet the front porch. Maybe I should have gone over and turned some lights on."

Eli continued to watch the figure walking in the dark. "It's a man, and I'm telling you he is coming this way, to this house."

"Can't be to this house," said Booty. "Who'd come over here? Some drunk got lost from the party; that's all it is."

"Booty, no person walks that straight while drunk. Someone is heading to this house."

"Impossible." Booty sat up, looking hard into the night.

Just then, a tall, lanky man came into view in the light from the living room's long windows.

"Good God! What are you doing here, Lorraine? Why aren't you at your own party? Didn't Precious invite you either? She didn't invite us. She invited us to let her use our driveways for your guests. We said no, and she did it at my house anyway."

"Lorraine," said Eli, "what are you doing here?"

Lorraine strolled up the front porch stairs like he had just been there ten minutes ago instead of months. "Here." He handed Booty a chilled bottle of Dom Perignon.

"Wait a minute," said Booty. "I still have this bottle open. Keep that bottle for you."

"No, I'll take the open one, and you open this bottle."

"Okay, except Eli has the bottle."

Eli dutifully exchanged bottles with Lorraine, who wandered over and grabbed one of the wicker chairs pushed against the house. He dragged it close to Eli and Booty and then plopped down and chugged a good deal from the bottle. "Fuck. I hate parties."

"You've always hated parties, and you're having one big party," said Booty. "My God, how many people did Precious invite? The whole town of Athens and those deemed socially acceptable from here are at her house. Old Precious is doing your money up proud, serving Dom Perignon. That must have cost a damn fortune."

"I have the most expensive caterer from Oklahoma City, no less, serving up God knows what."

"Then why didn't you bring us a plate?" asked Booty. "What are you doing here?"

"Yes," said Eli, "don't you think she'll miss you? You're the host. Aren't you supposed to be at your own party?"

"No. Can you believe I stood in a damn receiving line for what seems like years? It was horrible. Precious kept telling me who the people were, because I'd never have known. And they kept telling me how good it was to see me. Probably what they meant was they didn't know I was still alive. I saw people tonight that I didn't know were still alive."

Eli leaned over, looking at Lorraine. "How did you leave your own party?"

"Precious probably doesn't know I'm gone. She was so busy talking. I just walked through the kitchen and out the door."

"Nobody said a thing?" asked Eli.

"I'm paying them."

Booty looked at Lorraine. "Lorraine, you're in a tux! You're having a party and in a tux! My God, this is shocking. I'm sorry Mae went to bed. She would love seeing this."

"That's not funny."

"Oh, yes it is."

"It's not my fault. Precious made me wear it."

"You look very nice," said Eli.

"Shut up," said Lorraine and gulped from the champagne bottle. "I haven't had a God damn drink all night. Precious wouldn't let me. You still have the bourbon in the wicker cupboard, or did you clear out the bar for the winter?"

Booty glanced over at the cupboard. "I don't know. Go see if Mae emptied it for the winter. If she did, you know where the bar is. Go inside and grab whatever you want, because I'm not getting up."

Lorraine got up and went to the cupboard, where there was a brand-new, unopened fifth of Jack Daniel's bourbon. "There is a God." He grabbed the fifth and a paper cup and returned to the wicker chair. He flopped down, opened the bottle of Jack, poured it to the top of the tall paper cup, and gulped.

Lorraine relaxed back into the chair. "I suppose the cushions are put away for the winter like always?"

"Of course," answered Booty. "They're back in the storage area in the garage. Go get one if you want it."

"No, too far. The last receiving line I stood in had to be Mother's funeral. Booty, do you remember Sally Ann Gowan? Of course her name isn't Gowan anymore and hasn't been since the Flood. It's whatever it is, and who cares? The point is you won't believe her now. Remember her? The fat, ugly, pig-faced girl looked just like a pig. You remember her from grade school? Looking at her made you believe in evolution, and she evolved from pigs."

"I remember the name. I do remember her now that you mention it. Her face did look like a pig—little, short nose like a snout. She was round as a ball and conceited. Of all people to be conceited, but she was. Why?"

"I couldn't believe it when Precious introduced me. She looked great. Precious told me she had every kind of plastic surgery known to man, and it worked. I told her so too. I said, 'My God, Sally Ann, you look great! I would never have recognized you. All that plastic surgery Precious told me you had really worked. You stick with that doctor.' Then Precious got mad at me. What did I do? I thought women liked hearing they look great, especially someone who evolved from a pig."

"I don't know what the hell women want," said Eli. "God forbid I should ask, but did you see Blair?"

"Of course. She was in the receiving line. Looked like shit. Maybe she was sick. I'd be sick if I were going to marry Bobby Wrightsberg. Conceited bastard, just like his father, and I never liked him either, that son of a bitch. Just as well he hung himself in the front yard."

Eli leaned over and looked at Lorraine. "He hung himself in the front yard? That's fucking great."

Lorraine shrugged. "I know. Generally speaking, I'd say it was thoughtless to hang yourself in the front yard for all to see, but in the case of the Wrightsbergs, I'd say it was perfect. Booty, don't you remember hearing how Maeva drove in the driveway from picking up the kids at school, and there old Wrightsberg was, hanging from a mulberry tree in the front yard? I thought it was great. Don't you remember, Booty?"

"Yes. Mae said that Maeva nearly died from embarrassment because she thought it scandalized the family. I don't think Maeva gave a damn he was dead. Mae thought Maeva couldn't stand him. She heard old Wrightsberg beat up Maeva, and he was a notorious womanizer, just like his son. It probably upset the kids, but I would think Maeva was relieved except for the front yard part."

"Probably," said Eli. "I would think seeing your father hanging would upset the kids."

"Why?" said Booty. "Wrightsberg was a real bastard. I don't think anybody missed him."

"I certainly didn't," said Lorraine.

"You wouldn't," said Booty. "You didn't have to deal with him because you lived in the bedroom."

"If you really want to know the truth, the whole reason for this marriage is to salvage the Wrightsberg name. I happen to know this because Maeva and Precious talk in front of me. They think I'm not listening. Idiots."

"Tells me right there how much they don't know you," interrupted Booty. "You're the worst gossip I know."

"Anyway, they planned the whole thing. The deal is Blair Don marries the sleaze. She gets his money—read that most likely Precious gets the money—and he gets to marry into the fine, upstanding Blair family, which Maeva thinks will make the scandal disappear. Good luck on that one, since we forget nothing here. I rather underrated how much Precious loves money. How would I know that?"

"Anyone not living in their bedroom knew that," said Booty.

"What fine, upstanding Blair name?" asked Eli.

"All I'm doing is reporting," said Lorraine. "I've never been able to stand any of them. Since when does being in the Ku Klux Klan trump hanging yourself in the front yard? That's one hell of a statement, and everyone knew Judge Blair and his father were members. Plus I always wondered about the judge having a stroke over the crepe myrtle bush—speaking of dying in the front yard. Everyone knew he was a drunk. I always thought the old fool got drunk and passed out and died. A stroke, my ass."

"That's what Mae thinks," said Eli.

"Mae's right, but Precious will go to her grave with what really happened. And she lies. I never knew Precious lied."

Booty interrupted. "You're the only one that didn't know. And you married her."

"Oh, that's right! I did."

"You forgot?" asked Eli.

Lorraine gave Eli a stern look and took another swig of bourbon. "We all make mistakes."

"Yes. We do," agreed Eli.

They sat in silence for a moment and drank while watching and listening to people leaving.

"My God, I had a big party. No wonder it cost so damn much. Why aren't they all gone by now?"

"Precious was a bitch to call Mae to borrow the driveways and not invite us; not that we would have gone, but it was the principle of the thing. Did you know she did that?" said Booty.

Lorraine nodded as he drank. "Yes. I told her don't do that. She doesn't listen to me. I just write the checks. And speaking of checks, guess what I bought, or rather what Precious had me buy?"

"I'm afraid to ask," said Booty. "What?"

"I bought that white elephant, the Herman H. Green house in Athens."

Booty sat up in the swing. "You didn't."

"Yes I did. I bought that hideous, giant, white stucco monstrosity. It is such a period piece, the only thing missing are silent screen stars playing croquet on one of the lawns."

"I've seen pictures of those old movie stars playing croquet," said Eli.

"It's going to cost you a fortune," said Booty. "I don't know how long that house has sat empty."

"I don't want to think about it. It's got a solid copper ceiling in the dining room with some kind of design etched in it."

"Do you have to polish your ceiling?" asked Eli. "Excuse me, I have to go polish my ceiling."

"That's not funny, and I don't know. Who polishes a damn ceiling? To top it off, the whole house is painted a nauseating pea green. Makes you want to throw up."

"How lovely," said Eli. "Thank God I'll never be invited."

"No," answered Booty, "I'll drive you by so we can laugh at how much money Lorraine is going to have to spend to get that old house up and going."

"That's not funny, Booty," said Lorraine.

"I didn't mean to be funny. I mean you bought a bottomless pit."

Lorraine sounded sad. "I did, and that house is big. You've never been inside. There are big yards and a big swimming pool and a big pool house and big garages, and I forgot what else. It is big."

"It's going to cost a fortune to run," said Eli.

"I know it," agreed Lorraine. "A God damned fortune. Specifically, *my* God damned fortune, and I don't even like the house. I like my house here."

"The pink palace? You like that ugly, pink brick house?" said Booty. "Maybe it wouldn't be so bad if it wasn't pink."

"You know I do. I love that house. It's my home, and Geneva took down my wallpaper. Did you know that?"

"No," said Booty. "But Lorraine, think about it. It's about time. I remember that wallpaper when we were boys. You're too old for cowboy-and-Indian wallpaper."

"I would never have taken it off," said Lorraine.

"Geneva did a good deed," said Booty. "It deserved a rest. Why did you buy the house in Athens? You would never live in Athens."

"Precious said it was a perfect house for entertaining."

"Perfect," said Booty. "You're going to have a lot of fun entertaining, Lorraine."

"Shut up. That's not funny."

"I know it's not funny. It's also not you. So what are you doing?"

Lorraine turned his head toward Booty and said, "I have a plan."

"Now I believe you. You're not going to live in that monstrosity in Athens."

"No. Money will buy you a lot. You ought to know that better than I, Booty."

"What's your plan, other than buying Precious off? She won't divorce you, you know."

"Oh, no. She won't kill the golden goose with some kind of divorce settlement. She thinks she will be a rich widow and inherit, and she is wrong. I had Oliver make damn sure of that. She is in for a big surprise. She is so screwed."

"That makes me happy," said Booty.

"Me too," agreed Eli. "Fitting justice, I call it."

"So you're buying Precious off with the house and staying here," said Booty.

"Where is it written in stone we have to live together? Nowhere."

"Mae will be glad to have you back."

"Ellanor really went to New York? He didn't even say good-bye to me."

"He hates Precious. Always has. You know that. Her mother was hateful to your mother, and Precious was always a rude shit to all of us. And you married her. There wasn't a whole lot to say to you. Ellanor's gone."

"Do you really think he's gone for good?"

"I sincerely hope not, since he's in my apartment," said Eli. "No. He won't last in New York."

Booty was silent for a while. "I'm not so sure about that."

"What?" said Lorraine. "You think Ellanor won't return here?"

"He better not think he can stay in my apartment. What if I want it?"

"You think that, Booty?" asked Lorraine.

Booty nodded. "I wouldn't be one bit surprised. I don't think he will ever come back, and I can't say I blame him."

"Booty," said Lorraine.

He didn't have a chance to finish his sentence because Eli interrupted. "I can't believe I'm saying this: I'm hungry."

"I haven't eaten dinner," said Lorraine. "I forgot that."

Booty looked at Lorraine. "You mean to tell me you didn't eat at your fancy party after spending all that money on your Oklahoma City caterer?"

"I just didn't want it. Is there any fried chicken?"

Eli smiled. "Yes. We had it last night, and tonight we had beef tenderloin and there's some left, plus chocolate pie. I want some more chocolate pie."

Before anyone knew it, they were out of their chairs and heading for the nice, warm kitchen.

The next morning when Mae came downstairs, she discovered a mess. She knew Booty had not come to bed and wasn't in any of the guest rooms, so she figured him to be downstairs, probably with Eli. She walked to the den door, and sure enough, there was Booty, asleep on the couch, snoring away. Eli was sound asleep in a wingback chair with an ottoman pulled up for his feet. Mae decided to let them sleep and walked into the kitchen to let Herschel out in the backyard. When she saw the kitchen, her hand went to her mouth in surprise. After letting Herschel outside, she sat in a chair, inspecting the damage.

"Oh my lordly Lord, what a mess! At least they put food back in the fridge, but how many plates did they use?" Mae looked around at the plates and realized there was three of everything. She shook her head, wondering who else was here. Who could it have been? Surely Blair did not come to her senses and come over. Besides, if it had been Blair, she would still be here. She couldn't very well return to her house, because Precious would be on the warpath. It wasn't Blair. Who's left? Lorraine? No, it surely couldn't have been Lorraine. Mae cleaned up the kitchen then walked to the front door to look at the porch. Did they leave a mess there?

She opened the front door, and the first thing she saw was a wicker chair. Next to the chair, on the floor, an empty champagne bottle rolled around. Standing next to the champagne bottle was a Jack Daniel's bottle about three-quarters empty. Mae's eyes got big.

"Oh my God! Lorraine was over here!"

Mae was so surprised that Lorraine had actually come over that she sat in the porch swing for the longest time, not noticing the chill in the air as she wondered what went on last night. Lorraine had come over. A tear crept down her cold cheek.

★ ★ ★ ★ ★

The strong Oklahoma winds, which usually blew in from the south, had turned and were blowing from the north. Gusts of arctic air ripped through Eli as he trudged to school, fighting against the bitter wind. His black felt hat was jammed hard upon his head so that it rested barely above his eyebrows. The collar of the black woolen overcoat was turned up, and his gloved hands were jammed into the pockets. Mae's Christmas gift of a long, red cashmere muffler snaked around his neck and mouth. He felt like a turtle peering out from under his winter garb. Two pairs of wool socks tried to keep his feet warm in the old Canadian snow boots he had bought years ago. Thank God he insisted upon dragging them around with him.

He argued with himself about why he refused to take Mae's car to school instead of walking and decided that pride was not going to win again.

Eli sat at his desk, pretending to read school assignments as the children dribbled in for their first day back after Christmas vacation. Some were happy to be back. Others slowly shuffled back into the classroom frowning at the thought of being stuck there until the next vacation. Eli tried not to look as shocked as he felt when he saw Heppy and Isabelle. They were still terribly thin, but they looked different. For one thing, Geneva had gone shopping for them in a big way. Their clothes were new and expensive. They were clean and their hair bright. Eli relaxed and smiled to himself when he saw them. They were going to be all right. His throat tightened. Quickly he had to concentrate on class before he started to cry.

"All right. Settle down," Eli said. "I hope everyone had a nice holiday. How was everyone's Christmas? Would someone like to tell us about your holiday?"

Lynette Sue couldn't wait to raise her hand. "I want everyone to know that I am just fine after my terrible fall off the stage at the Extravaganza. I knew you all would be worried, but I'm fine—really. They thought I broke my ankle, but I didn't. Praise Jesus."

Eli completely forgot that she had leapt off the stage. He stuffed down a tremendous urge to laugh, forcing himself not to think about her flying through the air and the shocked expression on her face. It was very funny.

"Anyway," Lynette Sue continued, mercifully unaware of Eli's determination not to laugh, "I just wanted you all to know I'm fine. Nothing broken. We're not going to sue the school, even though my mother really wants to."

"Good. We're glad you're fine."

"Thank you, Mr. Take," said Lynette Sue. She was well on her way to developing into a young woman and she knew it—and used it. She flashed Eli such a smile that it surprised him.

A.J. held up his hand.

"Yes, A.J.," said Eli. "Did you enjoy your Christmas?"

A.J. was very serious. "My part of the Herzstein family is Jewish, so we don't have Christmas. We have Chanukah and a Chanukah bush, which is really a tree, but we call it a bush, except we didn't have one this year. My mother took us kids to Hawaii for the holiday because our daddy is having an affair with his secretary."

Eli looked around, not knowing what to say.

Clare turned white and gasped. "A.J., I can't believe you told that! My mommy said that your mommy wasn't ready to tell anyone yet." She turned to the kids in the class. "Listen, you all—you did not hear that. A.J. and his family except his daddy went to Hawaii on a vacation, and that's all. Nobody is divorcing anybody, and A.J.'s mother and the kids are not moving back to St. Louis where she's from, so don't believe that."

A.J. glared at Clare. "That is not what my mama says, and you know it. If what you say is true, then why is my mama going to St. Louis next week to look at schools for us, huh? Anyway, it wasn't my mother who got so drunk on New Year's Day that she nearly burned down the house because she left bacon cooking in the broiler and forgot, huh? It was *your* mother. And I heard there were flames as tall as the ceiling, and the fire department had to be called. So don't tell me what I can say and what I can't. You're not my mother."

Before Clare could pounce on A.J., Eli jumped into action. "That is quite enough, Clare and A.J. You can settle your differences later and not in this classroom."

Clare's face was bright red. She mouthed to A.J., "I'm going to fucking kill you."

To this, A.J. smiled and mouthed, "Fuck you."

Clare mouthed, "I hate you."

A.J. mouthed back, "I hate you too, and I hope you die."

Clare was not about to quit and mouthed back, "I hope *you* die."

Miriam looked straight at Betty Ann and said, "I saw a TV program on PBS about Mars."

Eli was relieved the subject changed. Anything to get away from Clare and A.J. mouthing back and forth, thinking he didn't see what was happening. "Oh, good! That's interesting. Hopefully in my lifetime, and I would think yours for sure, there will be a manned mission to Mars."

Joe Tom looked at Lynette Sue and said, "I'd like to be an astronaut and go to Mars."

That got Clare's attention. Joe Tom was not considered to be the brightest bulb on the block. The Herzstein family had a lot of money and heavily contributed to the private Episcopal school in Athens, plus the Herzstein children who did not go away to boarding school always graduated from there. The school and the Herzsteins had too much invested in each other not to let Joe Tom in. Besides, they could use him on the football team.

"You'd be an astronaut?" asked Clare surprised he knew that word.

Joe Tom looked at Clare and in all seriousness replied, "Yes. I can if I want."

Miriam thought even with all his family's money, they could not buy him that. She liked Joe Tom. She thought him rather dumb, which explained his taste in girls like Lynette Sue. "The program said that where there's water, there's life. There very well could be some form of life on Mars."

Miriam was being naughty. She said that on purpose, knowing how mad it would make Betty Ann Pastor. She could not stand Betty Ann or her holier-than-thou family, except for Hiram. He was okay because he couldn't stand them either. On Christmas Eve, she and her mothers wanted to go to church, except they couldn't. They should have gone earlier to a church in Athens that welcomed gay couples, but they didn't, and by the time they decided to go to the later service, it was dark and cold. The road to Athens would be icy, especially on the return trip. There was Holy Jesus in Cedar Springs, but they knew they wouldn't be welcome. Mary and Joseph had found a place, but they knew they wouldn't, not at Holy Jesus, the way Pastor Pastor preached about "ho-mo-sex-uals." He drew the word out and spat it. They decided to stay home instead, listening to Christmas music and singing carols around the fire, which Prudence proclaimed so much more comfortable. This way they could roast marshmallows and sing, which they could not have done at church. Next year they would plan better and go to an early church service in Athens. Miriam loved her mothers very much and couldn't stand to see them hurt. She would make Betty Ann pay.

"Oh no, there's not!" Betty Ann slammed her hand down hard upon the desk.

Eli had no idea what was going on. "What?"

Betty Ann was about to explode. "Miriam, let me tell you something, and if you would ever come to church, you'd know, but you don't, so you don't know. There's no life on Mars. The Bible says we are the only life there is."

Eli was astounded at her outburst. "I didn't know the Bible said that! Does the Bible say that? Even if the Bible says something like that—and since I've never read it, I don't know—but I do know that the Bible was written before modern physics. Although that is not entirely true, considering the discoveries of the ancients."

"What?" interrupted Betty Ann.

"Mr. Take, sir, you don't want to do this." Suddenly, Miriam felt guilty about bringing in Mr. Take, whom she liked. She was simply trying to get at Betty Ann. She had not planned on Mr. Take getting involved.

"What?" Eli said.

But it was too late. Lynette Sue said, "I can't believe you haven't read the Bible. I thought everybody in the whole world had read the Bible at least once. I remember my grandmother sitting in her living room by the window in her black dress reading the Bible all the time except when she was watching Lawrence Welk on TV. My mother said that my grandmother read the Bible and prayed especially for my uncle to quit drinking, which he didn't. He went out back of her house into the alley and blew his head off."

Eli was so astounded that he had no idea how to reply.

Miriam saw that Mr. Take was clearly in over his head. It was her fault to start this. She had to save him. "Mr. Take, we went to Oklahoma City for a few days. We went to the art museum and the cowboy museum, where there's lots of Western art. My mother said what a fine Western art collection it has."

Betty Ann glared at Miriam. She knew Miriam brought the subject up to goad her, because her father and the whole parish had tried to get her lesbian mothers fired from teaching at Lincoln. Her father preached that no homosexual should be allowed around children, much less allowed to teach children. "*Which* mother?" Betty Ann hissed.

Miriam ignored Betty Ann.

A.J. was still fuming at Clare and decided he was not through. "I heard my mother saying on the phone how glad she was we were in Hawaii and didn't have to go to Oklahoma City over Christmas with your mother and father and that group. She said that they were at some expensive restaurant in Oklahoma City, and your mother got up to go to the bathroom and was so drunk that she passed out on the table next to them, and she had dessert all over her front. The maître d' called an ambulance because he thought she had a heart attack and gave her artificial respiration, pumping her heart and—"

Clare jumped in and shouted at A.J., "Listen, you creep, you shut the fuck up!"

All heads quickly turned to Clare. Some gasped and a few laughed. "She said that word in front of me!" Lynette Sue whined. Eli tried to restore order.

"My father didn't start a fight at a restaurant like yours did just because some man said something and your father didn't like it. What was it your father poured over his head, wine?" Clare screamed. "So don't you talk about my mother! You can't move to St. Louis soon enough. I hope you go tomorrow."

A.J. glared back at Clare. "I hope I do too, so I'll never have to see you again."

Betty Ann would have none of Clare and A.J.'s argument. "We are here, right here on earth, and that's it. There's no need to go to Mars or anyplace else, because I'm telling you right now there's nothing there but rocks."

Eli could not help himself. "You're kidding."

Betty Ann looked at Eli like he was daft. "No, I'm not."

"Mr. Take," said Miriam, "Betty Ann never kids."

"I never kid."

"You mean to tell me," said Eli, "with a sky full of stars—and that's just what we can see with the naked eye, not to mention the pictures we've seen of multiple galaxies from the space telescope—when you look out there, you have never wondered?"

"I have," said Hiram.

Betty Ann's head snapped around to him. "You better not have wondered. I'm going to tell my daddy you said that, and I'm going to stand right there and laugh when he gets out his belt and whips the shit out of you."

Heppy's head snapped up, and he stared at Hiram. He thought he was the only one who was ever beaten. He never knew it happened to other kids too. Hearing this was a revelation. It made him like Hiram.

"I certainly have," announced Miriam. "What about you, Joe Tom?" She did that to make Lynette Sue mad, which it did.

Lynette Sue's eyes flashed to Joe Tom as she held her breath. "Joe Tom, *no!*" She prayed a little too loud.

Joe Tom looked around, befuddled by the question. "I don't know."

Lynette Sue loudly sighed with relief. "Thank you, Jesus. Thank you, Jesus."

Even Isabelle and Heppy, who rarely said anything in class, agreed with the possibility of life out there. "I like to look at the stars," Heppy said. "I think they're pretty. I hope there is life out there, and I hope there's lots of it, because it has to be better than some of the life here."

Betty Ann folded her arms and glared at the class and Mr. Take. "I'm going to tell my daddy. You all are going to go to hell, and that includes you, Hiram, and I can't wait."

The first day back after vacation was not going quite as Eli had planned. His head began to ache. Maybe he was not approaching this correctly and not being understood.

He blithely continued. "Let's try a different approach and look at it this way. Scientists discovered the *possibility* of water on Mars."

"No, they didn't!" interrupted Betty Ann.

"Yes, they did," answered Eli.

"Mr. Take is right," said Miriam. "They talked about it on the news. And where there is water, there are microbes, and that's life."

If looks could kill, Betty Ann's glare at Miriam would have zapped her. "You just wait," she hissed. "You and your mothers are going straight to hell, and I'm not kidding."

Hiram was smiling like a Cheshire cat. "I've watched reruns of all of the *Star Trek* shows, including *The Next Generation* and *Deep Space*

Nine. They go through wormholes to different universes. I want to be an engineer, just like Scotty, and beam up."

Betty Ann glared at Hiram. "I'm going to tell my mother and my daddy you said that. I've heard my daddy say that you're on the computer too much, and when he hears what you've been watching, no more computer for you. You're so stupid, Hiram."

"No, I'm not," he replied. He couldn't wait until he was bigger than Betty Ann (he prayed that he would grow bigger than she) so he could beat the shit out of her, just like she did him.

Isabelle and Miriam looked at Hiram at the same time. They had known him all their lives and considered Hiram nothing more than a talking nonentity. Who knew his aspiration was to be a spaceship engineer?

Miriam said to Hiram, "Then you better study math more and make good grades."

Hiram looked at Miriam. "I will."

Joe Tom was doing his best to follow what was being said. He wanted to show the class that he knew what they were talking about. "My mother told me and my brothers that we were creating new life in our swimming pool because it was so dirty."

Everyone stopped talking and arguing and stared at Joe Tom.

Joe Tom was proud that he had captured their attention. "While the pool was still open, before we closed it for the winter, when my mother was gone to play bridge, my brother went to the grocery store and bought a lot of bottles of bleach, and we poured it all into the pool, then we went swimming. When my mother got home, she said that the pool sparkled. My little brother wanted to cut off frogs' heads on a raft in the pool, but we wouldn't let him, not after we just cleaned the pool. We made my little brother go around to the side of the house to cut off frogs' heads with his toy guillotine that's real, so he wouldn't get frog blood in the pool and get it dirty again."

Eli's mouth dropped open. He could not decide what was more surprising—that someone would swim in a pool full of bleach or that the younger Herzstein boy was a psychopath.

"Speaking of life," said Betty Ann a little too nicely, "Miriam, I heard that your old dog finally died. Is that why your mothers took you to

Oklahoma City? Because you were so upset because your dog died? You know that dogs don't go to heaven, don't you? Only humans have souls and go to heaven, so if you think you are ever going to see that old dog again, you're not. He doesn't have a soul. He's dead and gone and rotting." Betty Ann smacked her lips, tilted her head, and smiled at Miriam.

Miriam actually started to get out of her seat but then thought better of it. She knew Betty Ann was trying to hurt her, and she was not going to let her do that. She knew it wasn't right to hate people, but she hated Betty Ann with a passion. Her mother told her not to hate people and to pray for her instead. Miriam could not pray for Betty Ann. She tried to please her mother. Maybe at some point in the far, far distant future, she could pray for her, but not anytime soon.

"Oh," crooned Lynette Sue, "I didn't know your old collie died. I remember him when we were over at your house at cheerleader practice. He was so sweet. Oh well, I'm sure you'll get another dog. Like my mommy says, it's just a dog. Like Betty Ann said, only us humans have souls. Have you ever thought that maybe it was God punishing you about your mothers?"

Heppy watched this whole thing. Miriam had always been kind to him, whereas neither Lynette Sue nor Betty Ann had ever given him the time of day. He figured they did not know he existed, but Miriam was different. He thought he was secretly in love with Miriam. No one would ever know that. Heppy swore he would never tell that to anyone. It took all of his nerve to go up to her later at recess and tell her how sorry he was that her dog died. He assured Miriam that her dog did have a soul and was in heaven, no matter what Betty Ann said.

By the end of the day, Eli's head was pounding. After the final bell, when the room sat empty, he remained at his desk for the longest time, staring blankly out of the long window, watching the wind whip around the barren branches of the trees. January's sun sank into the horizon, bringing dusk early to the afternoon. It was dark by the time Eli roused and headed home. A blast of cold slapped him in the face as he pushed open the steel door. He didn't care how cold it was; he just wanted to go home. Eli was tired, hungry, and mad at the world in general. He jammed his hat on tighter, wrapped the red muffler around his face like a mummy, and trudged into the icy, howling wind. By God, tomorrow he was going to take Mae's car to school. The sidewalks were glazing over. No one dared go out unless they had to be in the elements. Booty's house sat dark. Blair wasn't at the window working.

Lights glowed in Mae's kitchen. Eli looked at his cottage, dark and cold. His hands and feet felt frozen. He didn't want to be alone, so he turned toward Mae's back door.

Mae stood at the stove as Eli walked into the warm, cozy kitchen. The wonderful aroma of food cooking soothed his frayed, chilled nerves. She took immediate care. "Honey," she said, "you look half frozen. Come on in right now. Booty's in the den watching the news with that big, old shaggy dog. Let's get you in there in front of the fire and get you thawed."

"I hope you don't mind," said Eli, obeying her guidance.

"Oh honey, you know I don't mind. We love having you. Let's get you warm before you catch your death. What have you been doing at school so long? I thought you'd be home long before now. Geneva drove by with the kids awhile ago."

"It was horrible. How would I know that Betty Ann didn't believe there was any other life form in the entire universe? Who would know people believe that? Then Betty Ann told Miriam that dogs don't have souls and don't go to heaven, and poor Miriam's dog just died. Why? Why would she do that to Miriam? What did Miriam do to her to elicit such mean behavior? Nothing. And for Betty Ann to say that? I don't understand. I don't understand at all. Betty Ann told the kids they were going to hell, except for Lynette Sue. She even told her brother Hiram. It's crazy! I think she enjoys telling kids they are going to burn in hell."

"I wouldn't say the Pastors were the most open-minded people in the world," answered Mae. "That's what I've never understood about people going around saying how Christian they were and then be so hateful and mean. What's Christian about that?"

Herschel got up and greeted Eli as Mae led him into the den. "You go on in and get warm. Booty, why don't you make Eli a nice something to drink to warm up his bones?"

"Hi, Eli," said Booty. "You look like death warmed over. Go on and sit down. I'll bring you just the thing to warm you up and make you feel better."

Eli did exactly as he was told as he slowly wandered over to an overstuffed chair near the fire. He flopped down after shedding his Canadian snow boots and propped his cold feet on an ottoman in front of the fire. He grabbed the thick mohair throw behind the chair and threw it over his slowly warming body. For the first time that day, he relaxed.

★ ★ ★ ★ ★

January was a cold, savage month. Snow blasted the small town and then turned into sheets of ice. Icicles hung from houses like stalactites. Everything closed because of ice on the roads. The town was frozen shut and silent. People huddled in their homes. At Mae's insistence, Eli stayed with them in the big house. She did not want him alone down at the cottage in this dangerous cold snap. Tree limbs glistening with ice threatened to break off and fall on electric lines. Power would be lost, which scared and concerned all those stranded in the terrible, relentless cold. School was out for a whole week. Life seemed to be at a dead stop, but it wasn't. People stayed in touch by phone to make sure everyone was all right. Blair called to make sure they were okay. Mae talked to her, saying how she made Eli move in with them just to be safe. Blair tried to tread across to Booty's, just to get out of her own house, but it was too icy, and she barely made it back up her stairs to the apartment.

After what felt like an eternity, the ice melted. Power was never lost, even though tree limbs covered the area. The roads were cleared, and life resumed. In the lingering cold, people waddled around in thick layers of clothes. True to Oklahoma weather lore, which says to wait five minutes and the weather will change, it did. The end of January arrived on a surprisingly warm and windy day. The warmth soothed the chill away, tantalizing the buds to open. Winter's first flowers fought their way through the brick-hard ground, bringing much-needed color to otherwise bleak light. Everyone knew this was only a short reprieve from another blast of winter's loud winds refusing to leave so soon.

Chapter 10

Life's routine chugged along into February without much notice. The trees still appeared lifeless. Heavy drizzle from last night's rain left droplets clinging like tiny, glittering crystals on branches. A flock of birds darkened the sky. They flew by, made a U-turn, and retreated. The day before, on the evening news, the redheaded weatherman had predicted a snow and ice storm traveling through the area would hit tomorrow.

Eli found the prediction hard to believe as he strolled home. The wind was gentle and soft. Eli looked over at Blair's house. The lights downstairs were ablaze, and Lorraine and Blair's cars were in the driveway. Precious must still be wherever she was. Eli guessed she was still over at the Herman H. Green house. Mae told him that she heard at Sister's that Precious had workers going at top speed. Sister told Mae that Precious wouldn't tell exactly how much money she was spending. All she would say was the renovation probably would cost about a million dollars when everything was said and done. She said that the interior decorator was the most sought-after in Athens—even more so than the one Geneva used and much more expensive. Only the very best of everything would be used.

Eli could not help but smile at the thought as he passed the Blair house, where Lorraine was in residence. He wondered what Lorraine's plan was to avoid actually living in the white stucco money-eating monstrosity. On Saturday, Booty had driven Eli over to Athens, where they had lunch. Then they drove to the Herman H. Green house, up the long, winding drive filled with workers' cars. He stopped for a moment so Eli could take in the mansion.

"My God," said Eli, "you were right. It looks like someone plucked a big, white stucco house from 1920s California built for some silent screen star and dropped it in Athens, Oklahoma. Amazing. It really is a period piece."

"Isn't it, though?" agreed Booty.

"It's going to cost Lorraine a fortune."

"Yes, it is," said Booty, smiling. "Serves him right for marrying Precious."

"Yes, it does," agreed Eli.

Eli smiled, thinking about the white elephant of a house Lorraine was renovating. He wondered if he really would have the nerve to stay in Cedar Springs and not follow Precious to Athens. Eli looked up at the clear sky full of billowing clouds. The day was so lovely. He could not imagine a snowstorm coming. He wandered in front of Booty's house, and there was Blair. He stared at her through the long window, as she sat at the desk. Just looking at her made his heartache and his stomach tighten. Suddenly he didn't feel well, but he knew he was not getting sick. He missed her. How could he miss someone who had hurt him so terribly? Yet in spite of that, he missed her, and that made him mad. Damn her. He would never forgive her—never. Damn her. Damn her. Damn her. Eli just wanted out of this town and away to forget everything. Maybe he should reconsider what he told Booty, that he would stay until school was out. Maybe he just couldn't do it. The more he thought, the madder he got, until suddenly his feet were taking him to Booty's house. He stopped in front of the white double doors, trying to decide what to do. Go in and bawl her out or keep walking and go back to his cottage, get on his computer, and look for a car to get him out of here? Booty had reimbursed him for his now-dismantled Honda. All he had to do was find a car, buy it, and he was gone.

Blair saw him stop in front of Booty's house; watched him storm up to the porch in anger. A lump was so big in her throat that she thought she would choke. Tears rolled down her face. She had to get out of Cedar Springs. Had to, and soon. Her heart was breaking. She and Eli had found each other. They had each other, and then she walked out. What a thing to do. Without standing up to look out the window, she knew Eli was on the front porch. What was he going to do? What was *she* going to do? Maybe run out the back door? She turned off her cell and tipped the landline phone off the hook. Her mother better not decide to call. If he does come inside, her mother will not interrupt them. Blair will not allow it.

Eli stood frozen at the front door, wondering what to do. He had vowed never to talk to Blair again. He hated her. He should leave. Instead of leaving, he watched his hand open one of the white double doors, and then he walked into her office.

When Blair heard the door open, she jumped out of her chair and walked toward the door. Her knees felt weak. There was Eli standing in front of her.

"Eli." She barely got his name out.

"Yes." Eli stood there, wanting to tell her exactly what he thought of her, when suddenly his mind went blank. He could not think of one thing to say. Not one thing. How horrible, when moments before he knew exactly what he wanted to say, itching to scream at her about his pain and how she caused it, and now ... what? What was he doing there?

Blair's mind was equally blank. She was shocked he actually came in. They both stood dumbly staring at each other.

Someone had to break the awkward silence. It certainly did not look like it was going to be Eli, so Blair took it upon herself. "Booty isn't here. He went over to Crutchfield Oil in Athens."

Eli just stared. To top everything off, he now felt like a complete fool. Why had he gone in, especially if he could not think of one thing to say? Why couldn't he get mad? He had been mad. He *was* mad. So say something! Nothing. Without a doubt, this was becoming one of the worst moments in his life.

Blair stared at Eli, hoping he would say something. Anything. Scream at her. Get mad. God knows she was mad enough at herself. As she looked at him staring dumbly at her, Blair got perturbed. Why was he here?

Eli thought the same thing. Why was he there? This was ridiculous.

Blair did not know what to do. Should she ask him to sit down? No. She couldn't do that. What would he think? She wanted to tell him what a fool she had been to leave and how sorry she was. How much she regretted it. How leaving him was the biggest mistake of her life. What a cowardly thing to do and how much she loved him. She certainly couldn't tell him she loved him. Words begged to spill out of her mouth. She yearned to say all of those things to him and more, but she was too afraid. Blair was too afraid, and so was Eli.

The prolonged silence neared being painful, it was so unbearable. Until finally Eli said, "Okay then."

"Okay." Blair felt so helpless. She didn't know what to do or to say. Was there anything to do or say?

"Okay," Eli repeated.

"Okay."

Eli started toward the door and then suddenly stopped. Blair was behind him, following. He quickly turned and kissed her. She was so surprised that it took a moment to realize what was happening. Then she knew. She loved him with all her heart and soul and always would.

Eli was equally surprised by what he did. What had he done? Better yet, why? He was not going to allow himself to be hurt anymore. He hated her. No. He didn't. He loved her, and that was not allowed. He had to get out of there.

"Okay. Good-bye."

Blair watched him rush out the door. "Good-bye."

The snowstorm arrived as predicted. Eli stayed with Mae and Booty until the world around them unthawed and life resumed. He tried not to think about how he made such an ass out of himself with Blair. What was he thinking, and why did he kiss her, of all things? Plus now, when it was too late, he could think of a lot of things to say to her. He had to leave town, and that was all there was to it.

★ ★ ★ ★ ★

Valentine's Day turned out to be cold but surprisingly pretty with a clear, blue sky full of white clouds that looked like cotton candy. Eli walked to school carrying a huge heart-shaped box of chocolates. Mae bought it for him to put on his desk for the children. He remembered to order a dozen red roses for Mae from the florist in Athens that Booty told him to use.

The minute the school bell sounded, Lynette Sue raised her hand. "Mr. Take."

Eli looked at her. "Yes?"

"Mr. Take ... you know."

Know what? Eli looked blank. He had no idea what she was talking about.

Miriam saw Eli's confusion. Her hand shot up. "Mr. Take, it's Valentine's Day. Usually the first thing we do is to open our valentines. I see there's a big heart-shaped box on your desk. Is it for us?"

Eli looked down at the box he put on his desk without thinking and preceded to forget all about it. "Right. Yes. It is for all of you." He fumbled opening it and slid it to the corner of his desk. "Please have some."

"Mr. Take," answered Miriam, "could we please get our valentines and read them?"

Eli could not think of a reason to say no, although he wanted to. Seemed like a waste of school time to him. "Okay."

"You might want to open yours too," said Miriam, trying to cue him what to do.

"Mine?"

"Look at your desk, Mr. Take. There are cards." Miriam pointed.

Eli looked down, and sure enough, envelopes were on his desk next to where he opened the chocolates, and he had not noticed. "Oh, look." He stared at the different envelopes. "You brought me valentines." Eli stared at the bright envelopes. "Sure. You all go ahead." He could not remember the last time anyone gave him a valentine. Had anyone ever given him a valentine? He couldn't remember. He was surprisingly touched and had to sit down. Mae had gotten him chocolates for the kids, knowing he never would have done that—and he wouldn't. He didn't think about valentines. How long had it been since he gave anyone a valentine? Yes, he got Mae flowers. He should do that. He knew to do that, but a real valentine? He couldn't remember. He tried to shoo away the lump forming in his throat and the strange feeling in his nose and around his eyes ready to issue tears. This was no time for that.

A wild commotion erupted as the kids ran to their folders, gathered their valentines, and then hurried back to their desks. The room was uncommonly quiet as the kids and Eli read their valentines.

Lynette Sue squealed, "Oh! Joe Tom!" She looked over to him and smiled as she held up a gold heart dangling from a gold chain necklace. "Is it real?"

Joe Tom's eyes appeared blank. He had no idea whether it was real or not. He asked his mother to get something for him to give to Lynette Sue for Valentine's Day, and the rest he left up to his mother. She knew more about what to get for a girl than he did. He simply smiled, and that seemed to be enough for Lynette Sue, who giggled and put it on.

Clare turned to Hiram. "Thank you, Hiram." She held up a card and a small, heart-shaped box of chocolates.

Hiram could not help it and blushed, turning bright red, which almost matched his hair. He had always had a secret crush on Clare and never had the courage to give her a valentine, much less chocolates. This year, for some reason, he did, and he was glad.

Betty Ann glared at Hiram and hissed, "I can't believe you did that. Who gave you the money to buy that box of chocolates?"

Hiram sneered at her. "Wouldn't you like to know!"

Betty Ann snarled, "I can't believe you gave that to a Herzstein. I'm going to tell my mother."

"She already knows," said Hiram, and he smiled at her.

Betty Ann very much disapproved of the Herzsteins. Her father's bigotry was certainly no secret. He blamed the Jews for Jesus's death. Betty Ann could hear her father saying, "They murdered my precious Lord and personal Savior Jesus." She hated Jews too, because her father did, and she could not wait to tell him about Hiram's chocolates for Clare. This was for sure going to get him beaten but good, and that made Betty Ann happy. She would also get her mother into trouble, because where else would Hiram have gotten the money for the candy? She had seen her father hit her mother, and this would make him mad enough to hit her again. Betty Ann knew her mother deserved it.

Miriam smiled at Heppy and mouthed, "Thank you."

Heppy nearly fainted; he was scared to put the little box of chocolates and valentine Isabelle picked out for him in Miriam's folder.

Isabelle leaned over to Heppy. "See, I told you she'd like it."

Isabelle got a bunch of heart-shaped red lollipops wrapped in a big, red ribbon, and a valentine from A.J., which surprised her. She waved and smiled at A.J. She liked him. She heard that his mother was probably moving the kids to St. Louis after school was out. Isabelle was sorry, because she was just getting to know A.J. He was sweet.

Betty Ann was so mad, she was afraid her face was turning red. No one gave her a special valentine. It humiliated her, and she hated everyone. She told herself that she didn't care and didn't want a boyfriend anyway. She hated valentines. She decided to beat Hiram up in the holly bushes behind the church after school.

Eli never expected the children to give him valentines. Miriam, Isabelle, and Clare wrote especially nice things. His heart was so touched that he considered staying at Lincoln and teaching next year.

As he walked home from school by Booty's, there was Blair at work. To his surprise, she looked at him. Neither acknowledged the other, and he continued on to the cottage.

That evening, Booty and Eli waited patiently in the den for Mae to finish dressing. When she walked through the door, both men smiled. She looked radiantly happy in a beautifully tailored red wool suit and a double strand of large pearls with a sparkling diamond clasp. She took both their arms and walked out the door.

Fresh flowers in small vases sat on each table at the new restaurant that just opened in Athens. White tablecloths with expensive china and silver covered the tables. Money had been put into this restaurant, and it showed. The maître d' expected them and put them at a good table. Crutchfield Oil Company was well represented, with different high-ranking employees making the pilgrimage over to Booty's table to pay court.

Some tables away sat a rather large party of old Athens society, and among the group sat Precious gleaming and Lorraine squirming. It was obvious from the loud laughter and talk they were already pretty drunk. Neither Precious nor Lorraine acknowledged Mae, Booty, and Eli as they walked by their table; nor did they acknowledge Precious and Lorraine. It was as if they were strangers.

Dinner was surprisingly good, and after dessert, the three enjoyed coffee. It had been a wonderful evening, which Eli enjoyed more than he expected. He had had a delightful day with the children's valentines and a lovely dinner with good company. Even seeing Blair did not upset him, which was pleasantly unexpected. For the moment, he was not even mad at her. As the evening progressed, Lorraine and Precious's table got louder and louder and drunker and drunker. All the diners in the packed restaurant, including Mae, Booty, and Eli, did their best to ignore them.

Upon Mae's return from a trip to the bathroom, she said, "You'll never believe who is sitting behind us in one of those dark corner booths in the back."

After sitting down, Mae continued, "If you all will just glance a little over that way," and she quickly pointed, "you'll see the school principal, Bobby Wrightsberg, being shall we say quite overt with a young blonde woman."

"What?" both Eli and Booty said. They hurriedly looked over to the corner table.

"Well, I'll be damned," said Booty. "Bobby's with the new bank teller. I've seen her at the bank. If she's twenty-three, I won't believe it."

"Younger, I'd say," said Mae. "If she is twenty-one, I'd be shocked. She looks right out of high school to me."

Booty continued as if Mae had not interrupted. "They certainly are going at it. I think they should leave the restaurant if they are going to act like that. This is most inappropriate for Lincoln School's principal. I'm going to bring this up with the board. We can't have the school principal acting like that in public. And what is he doing with her? I'd heard he was dating the bank manager."

"That seems to be common knowledge, that he's dating the bank manager. Everybody at the beauty parlor knows it, I bet, including Precious," said Mae.

"What's he doing?" asked Eli who could not quit staring. "I didn't know that he was dating anyone but Blair. Where is Blair? I thought he and Blair were engaged. Why doesn't anyone tell me anything? Are he and Blair still engaged?"

"Of course they're still engaged," said Mae. "I'm telling you, he is just like his father. Just like the old, sleazy bastard alley cat. I bet Maeva wanted to hang him herself on the front yard tree—of course, she would have chosen the backyard. The front yard is too public for that sort of thing. I know I certainly would have wanted to hang him."

"Bob is engaged to Blair and has no qualms about doing *that* in public?" said Eli. "I didn't know he was going with the bank manager! That's terrible to do to Blair. Mae, you have to keep me informed about this kind of thing."

"Really, Booty, this is most inappropriate. Look at them! Vulgar, that's what it is. Why doesn't the restaurant do something before they start taking off their clothes?" said Mae. "Booty, you have to do something about Bobby. He is a blight on Lincoln. The school can't have the principal going around acting like that. Why don't they go someplace? Here this nice restaurant just opened. I hope it doesn't hurt the restaurant's reputation. Athens has so few good restaurants. It would be a shame to lose this one, especially after it just opened. I'm telling you he has to go from Lincoln."

"Oh, he's going," answered Booty.

"Do you think Precious has seen them?" asked Eli.

"No," said Mae. "If she had, the whole restaurant would hear about it. If Lorraine has seen them, he's smart enough not to say a word. Precious is going to have a fit if she finds out, and so will Maeva. Sister told me at the beauty parlor this was Bobby's last chance. I don't believe it. Maeva worships him. As bad as he is, he still can't do any wrong in her eyes. My God, look at him! He's gotten fat. He used to be so thin and nice looking, and now he's ballooned out. Wonder if it's from all the whiskey? According to Sister, Maeva won't let him touch the trust money unless he marries Blair. Sister said she knows all about it since she's done Maeva's hair forever. Maeva is going to keep Bobby on a tight lead. I always did think she had control issues. My goodness, I think they need to leave this restaurant if they are going to act like that in public. Booty, this really is most unacceptable behavior."

"Why would Blair marry someone like that? I just don't understand!" said Eli.

"Obviously you don't know Precious Blair Mason," said Mae, making a face like she had smelled something unpleasant. "She is a nasty piece of work. Honey, she may tell you Jesus is her personal Lord and Savior like they do so much around here, but don't you believe it for one minute. Her personal Lord and Savior is money—green money. She and Maeva made a deal. If Blair actually goes through with it and marries that bastard, I'll eat this table, I'll be so shocked. She is not going to marry him. I don't know how she's going to get out of it, especially with her mother constantly on her heels about it, but mark my words she will. You watch."

Eli thought this was the most they had talked about Blair since she left him. His emotions were mixed—horror at the principal's behavior, satisfaction that Blair deserved this for leaving him, and sorrow for her situation.

Bobby wasn't paying the slightest bit of attention to anyone in the restaurant. He was completely captivated by the voluptuous blonde. He was drunk and fawning over her. She appeared to be just as drunk, and she fell into him as they kissed passionately. He had his hand down her low-cut royal-blue dress. One very large breast was about to pop out.

"Oh my God," Eli, Mae, and Booty said at the same time.

"She's about to expose herself," said Mae.

"Certainly looks like it to me," agreed Eli.

"Booty!" exclaimed Mae. "This is entirely too much."

Booty nodded. "It certainly is. Wonder if any of the staff are going to do anything about it?"

"Booty," said Mae. She was looking around the restaurant to see if anyone else saw what was going on in the corner booth. "Booty."

"Hmm?"

"Booty, look at that woman over there staring at them. Now that is one mad-looking woman. Good Lord, is that—"

Booty followed Mae's look. "Oh, my God!"

"What?" asked Eli.

"That's the bank manager," answered Booty. "She's with the man who bought the GM dealership in Athens. She's better off with him than Bobby. I heard he's newly divorced."

"Booty," said Eli, "you know everything that's happening around here."

Without taking her eyes off the drunken, fawning couple, Mae said, "Honey, Booty knows everything that is going on around here, including how much money everybody has."

"I just hear things, like the Wrightsbergs don't have the money they used to have, which Precious doesn't know, and I heard the bank manager plans to marry Bobby Wrightsberg."

"See. I told you Booty knows everything."

Eli interrupted. "Does she know Bob is engaged?"

Booty looked at him. "Don't be naïve. Do you really think she cares? Besides, Bobby has been going out with her for I don't know how long. Look at the way she looks at the bank teller. If looks could kill! To think the teller is her employee. That job is not going to last long. Why would Bobby bring her here of all places tonight? Surely he had the sense enough to know a bunch of Athens and Cedar Springs people would be here."

"Bobby doesn't have a lick of sense," said Mae. "Besides, he's a drunk. What drunk thinks?"

"Or has morals," said Eli, glaring at the couple at the table. "He doesn't care about anybody but himself."

"Of course he doesn't," said Mae. "Oh my, would you look at that bank manager! Oh, Lordy, is she furious. She certainly is an attractive woman. That's a lovely black suit she's got on—very chic. Has to be designer, and I'm telling you right now, I bet it came from Neiman's. Her date is attractive. Looks prosperous, and he's noticing how mad she is. This is inconvenient. Her date is so much better looking than that drunk making an ass out of himself with the teller. This woman is making a big mistake."

"Women make big mistakes," agreed Eli.

"So do men," said Booty. "Worst things about making these big mistakes is that there is usually so much bad blood spilled, there's no going back."

"What are you talking about, Booty?" asked Mae.

"Life."

"Oh well, there is that," agreed Mae.

The waiter held a silver coffeepot. "More coffee?"

Booty replied, "The check, please."

Mae quickly interrupted. "Yes, I think we will have more coffee. Thank you."

Booty looked at Mae and then shrugged. "Why don't you bring us the check, and we'll have more coffee." As the waiter walked away, Booty said to Mae, "Okay, we'll see what happens, but I want to be ready to leave if the fireworks start."

"Fireworks?" said Eli. "You really think it will get to that?"

"I don't know, but I want to be ready to leave, just in case."

Mae kept looking over to the table with the bank teller and Bobby. "I don't know how you can say that. This might be fun. When was the last time we had any excitement in our little burg? Yes, one of the Herzsteins got shot in the stomach when the neighbor rancher came over and shot him. I never did find out exactly what that argument was about. I'll have to remember to ask Sister; she'll know. She does a bunch of the Herzstein women's hair. Anyway, he didn't die. He was okay enough to drive himself over to the hospital in Athens. You know how he always drove white Lincolns. I wondered if all that blood ruined the upholstery of his car. I bet it was a brand-new car too. They always drive new cars. I'm sure the upholstery was leather. Does blood wash off leather, or do you think it would stain?"

Eli looked at Mae. He was aghast hearing this. "Wait a minute. Did the neighbor rancher get charged with—wouldn't that be attempted murder? He just went over to his ranch and shot him?"

Mae patted Eli's hand. "Honey, you haven't been here long enough."

"What does that mean?" asked Eli.

"Just that," answered Mae.

Booty acted as interpreter, since Eli was not getting what Mae said. "No, the neighbor was never charged, and nothing was ever said about the shooting. Besides, he lived. There really wasn't too much to say."

"The guy was never charged?" asked Eli.

"Certainly not," replied Mae. "No one would have done a thing like that."

"Even if he died?" Eli was continually amazed with the thinking here.

"Probably not," said Mae. "There wouldn't be any point if he died. He's dead. I'm sure it was a perfectly valid argument to make one rancher get in his car and drive all the way over to the other ranch just to shoot someone. It's quite a way between those ranches. They're big. You have to get on the highway. Anyway, it's not like those two oilmen from Athens, when a bunch of the old Athens socials rented a train to take them to an OU football game. Now that really *was* rude. They were more than likely drunk, although I never heard for sure, but I'd bet money on it, knowing them. Well, these two men got in some sort of argument, and one man pulled out a gun and shot the other one. Had to stop the train to get the one who was shot off and to a hospital. Plus everyone was so mad at old Bug-Eye—that was the shooter—they threw him and his wife off the train too. I want you to know that man looked exactly like a frog, bug eyes and all. Except for his mouth, and that looked like a fish, and his head looked like a fish's head, now that I think about it. He was stop-a-clock ugly, kind of a cross between amphibian, fish, and human—not what I would call a pretty combination. So old Bug-Eye shot this pompous ass with a little, thin pencil mustache and slick-back, thin, dyed-black hair. He dressed impeccably and went to Harvard for all of one year, then returned with—of all things—an English accent. Frankly, shooting the pretentious son of a bitch with the pretend English accent was too good for him. Worse part was that Mr. Pretend English Accent didn't have the decency to die and put us all out of our misery having to listen to him. Shooting him did ruin old Bug-Eye and his wife socially in Athens and after building that big pretty house and all. I thought it was a shame, since the wife planned to entertain. She had a whole set of vermeil everything: knives, forks, plates, goblets—you name it and she had it. I hope she got to use it. Wonder if it can go in the dishwasher. Well, Good Lord—" All the time Mae was talking, she kept her eyes on Bobby's table.

"What?" asked Eli.

"Oh, dear," said Mae. "Mercy me."

"What?" asked Eli. "What?"

"Use your eyes," she said.

"What?"

"I told you we should have left," said Booty. "This is not going to be good."

"No, but it is going to be fun," said Mae. "Oh, Booty, I'm so glad we came here for dinner. Thank you."

251

Now Eli saw what they were talking about. "Oh my … what is she going to do?"

The tall, handsome bank manager, expensively dressed and slim with perfectly groomed hair, strode across the restaurant. Her date watched her with disgust, slapped his napkin down on the table, and then got up and left.

It was unfortunate timing, because Bobby had just finished paying the check and was attempting (being drunk himself) to lead his drunken date from the booth across the room to the door.

Precious and her group were enjoying the evening. Since Precious had her back to Bobby, she had no idea he was there. Lorraine, on the other hand, faced Bobby and his date. His eyes darted from Precious to them and back to Precious. It was obvious that Lorraine was extremely uncomfortable, although no one at his table noticed. They were drunk and laughing way too loud to notice anything except themselves. Precious was especially drunk and having a marvelous time, having placed herself among the cream of old Athens society. As far as she was concerned, she had made it, moving to Athens into the old Herman H. Greene house, which everyone knew was big and expensive. They also knew she was spending a bunch of money on renovations. Now she had the money and mansion to vie for a major position in old Athens society. Until now, she had only danced on the periphery. This was her moment.

As Bobby drunkenly maneuvered through the restaurant to the door, he was so engrossed with the lovely young teller that he never noticed the bank manager (also his girlfriend) in a fury on her way over to cut him off from the exit door. The confrontation unfortunately happened right at Precious's table, with her back still to them.

The sophisticated bank manager completely lost her cool. She rushed up to Bobby and proceeded to haul off and slug him while screaming, "You two-timing son of a bitch!"

"My God," said Eli. "What a hit."

Bobby immediately fell back upon Precious. "What the hell?" she exclaimed. She looked around, patting her hair back into place. "Bobby, watch what you're doing." Then Precious grasped what was happening. "Bobby! What the hell do you think you're doing?"

Bob righted himself without noticing Precious and glared drunkenly at the bank manager, who was panting in fury. "You hit me!" he said, quite confused. "Why did you hit me?"

"You fucking bastard," she said and slugged him again. Except this time, he was ready for her and punched her back. She fell into a man at the next table who had been watching the fight and caught her.

One of the socials at Precious's table gasped and proclaimed, "She used the F word!"

The bank manager moaned and rubbed her eye and forehead. The skin was broken, and a thin trickle of blood dripped down her face. "You bastard! You hit me! You son of a bitch, God damn, fucking bastard! Oh my God, I'm bleeding. If this ruins my brand-new God damn expensive suit, you will pay for it!" She struggled to get upright with the help of the man at the next table whose wife slapped her napkin on the table, got up, and said, "Get home yourself." Then she walked out of the restaurant, pulling the car keys out of her purse.

The bank manager's chest heaved in fury. "How dare you be with that little whore!"

"Who is she calling a whore?" asked the drunk bank teller, confused by what was happening. "Is she calling *me* a whore? Who's the whore? I'm not a whore. *She's* a whore."

Bob reeled back and forth and was unprepared when the bank manager got the energy to slug him again. Shaking her sore hand, she said, "Shit! I broke a nail!"

The bank teller was in the depth of drunken confusion. "Who is she calling a whore? Me? Is she calling me a whore? I'm not a whore. I'm almost a virgin. I'm not a whore. She is a whore, and I know it. She can't call me a whore! We go to church. I don't feel good. I have to go home."

Precious was watching in horror and quickly moved as Bobby fell on the table. Everyone jumped up. Some of the ladies screamed and covered their mouths with their hands, mumbling, "This is horrible. Get me out of here. I have to go home."

The bank manager's date opened the door and walked out. He never looked back.

"My God," said Eli, amazed. "Where did that woman learn to punch like that?"

Mae watched the bank teller as she staggered to the door, opened it, and left. "Booty, look at her. Oh my goodness! Look at her. Do you think?"

Booty thought Mae was talking about the bank manager. "I never knew she had such a punch. She always seemed so quiet and reserved. Very professional. Wonder if she will lose her job. I know the bank president, and I don't think he will take this lightly. He's very conservative. I don't think he will like his bank manager going around punching people, even though the Wrightsbergs aren't very big customers."

"No, not the bank manager. I'm not talking about her. But if she were my employee and beat up Bobby Wrightsberg, I'd give her a raise. No. I'm talking about the teller," said Mae. "Damn! Oh, it's too late."

"I can't believe he hit her back!" said Eli. "He actually slugged the bank manager."

Booty shook his head. "Bobby is going to have to be fired for this."

"Oh, I hope that blood doesn't get on her nice black suit. It might ruin it. What a shame. I'm sure she spent a lot of money on it too," said Mae.

"She looks fine to me except for maybe a cut," replied Booty. "Bobby looks in worse shape."

Precious was furious with Bobby and mortified at the thought what this might do to her aspiring social standing in Athens. She and Lorraine had asked these couples out to dinner. It was their party, and now it might be ruined because everyone knew Bobby Wrightsberg was engaged to her daughter and it looked terrible. Precious was shaking in anger. Couldn't he keep it in his pants until after he married Blair Don? He had to be the most spoiled, thoughtless bastard who ever lived. If this ruined her wedding (for that is exactly how she considered Blair's wedding—*her* wedding), Precious would not know what to do. Possibly she could turn what would have been a fabulous wedding reception on the lawns and gardens into a garden party. Some relief assuaged Precious, because that might work. All she had to do was to change the wedding and groom's cake into regular cakes, and everything else might work. She still was furious at Bobby for causing her so much trouble and falling on her, messing up her hair, not to mention falling on the table. She straightened her dress and said, "Why don't we all sit down and have a nice little drink? I think we need one."

Everyone at Precious's table looked shocked at the fight going on. Lorraine motioned to a waiter for the check. Bobby had gotten himself off the table and was going after the bank manager as best he could, considering how drunk he was. Four waiters and the maître d' ran over to the couple slugging each other and screaming obscenities, grabbed them both, and dragged them out of the restaurant. They were put in separate taxis and sent on their way after being barred from the restaurant for life. The new chef/owner was beside himself, terrified that this business venture was deemed a failure before it had a chance to start. He stood in front of shocked clients ready to stampede out of there.

He shouted to get their attention. "Please! Just a minute! Just a minute, please. Let's try to put this little interruption behind us." As he spoke, waiters streamed out of the kitchen, holding trays of champagne and desserts. "Please sit down and enjoy the champagne, chocolate truffles, and desserts being passed with my compliments." He tried to look upbeat as he returned to the kitchen. The moment the kitchen door swung closed, he collapsed at a table and put his head in his hands. All he could do now was hope the restaurant would be saved.

Precious cajoled her guests to enjoy the champagne and desserts. Lorraine was still pale and shaken from witnessing what had happened right in front of him. He sat as instructed and drank. This was too much. He had not liked the guests Precious invited. Dinner had been a trial, struggling to make conversation with a boring, inflated, rich woman telling him the square footage of her new house. Precious was spending his money like water with this dinner, and then there was the Herman H. Green disaster. He wiped his brow with a handkerchief.

"Oh, poor Lorraine," sighed Mae. She was the only person in the restaurant who smiled through the fight, enjoying it thoroughly. "Bless his heart."

"Bless his heart?" said Eli. "What about us? We had to sit through it."

Mae turned to Eli and patted his hand. "Bless your heart. You're not used to this."

"You don't get used to this," said Booty. "I can't stand scenes."

"But they happen, honey," Mae said. "Look on the bright side. No one had a gun."

★ ★ ★ ★ ★

Also having Valentine's dinner at the restaurant was a childhood friend of Blair's. She saw the whole thing and knew all of the participants, especially Bobby, with whom she too had grown up. She told her husband, who had taken her out for what he hoped would be a romantic evening and instead turned into a brawl, that this was one of the most enjoyable evenings she had in a long time. Her husband shook his head in amazement how his wife of this many years still continued to surprise him. Maybe they would have sex tonight, like he hoped. He also knew Blair and watched as his wife quickly texted Blair a blow-by-blow account.

Wave upon wave of relief swept through Blair. She was free, and she knew it. It was over. Every bit of the madness caused by Bobby, her mother, and Maeva was over. She participated in the whole despicable affair too. Blair knew that as well as anyone and had blamed herself. Her knees felt weak at the thought of how close she came to having to do God knows what to get out of this mess. Thank God for Bobby being despicable. In his crazy way, he saved her. "Thanks, Bobby."

Blair had a bottle of champagne in the fridge, saving it for some special occasion. This certainly merited it. She opened the bottle and grabbed any old glass. Somehow she had acquired a tall glass with a big, colorful balloon attached to a basket soaring away. Under the basket were the words "The Albuquerque Balloon Festival." Blair filled the glass to the top and started dialing the phone. She had friends to talk to right now.

The next morning, Blair called Booty and told him she would be late to work. Mae was dying to know what Blair thought about the fight at the restaurant. Naturally Blair knew. Nothing was a secret in this little town. There was never a question in Mae's mind that Blair was being told as it happened. Mae would quickly have to make a hair appointment at Sister's to find out what was going on. She had to know if, when, and preferably how Blair broke off the engagement.

The minute Blair hung up with Booty, she rushed to her car and drove over to the grand Victorian monster of a house that was the Wrightsberg family home. Bernice, the black maid, dressed as usual in a starched sparkling-white uniform, answered the front door. She had been with the Wrightsbergs for years, since the children were small. She and Maeva had aged together.

"Blair Don," said Bernice, surprised to see her, "you're here early." Bernice, as a member of the family, knew everything. Maeva had heard last night and told Bernice the first thing when she came to work this morning.

"You didn't waste any time getting over here," said Bernice. "I wondered how long it would take you."

Blair strode in the open door past Bernice. "Where is she?"

"Honey, where you do you think she is? She's upstairs in bed, having her coffee. She's had quite a night. I wouldn't advise you going up right now. She's in one of her moods."

It was too late. The moment Blair heard where Maeva was, she rushed up the wide staircase. Bernice watched her leaping up the stairs and shook her head. "Oh dear, this is going to be bad. Bobby always was such a bad boy, and now he's done it for sure. All I can say is it's a good thing he didn't come home last night."

Blair loped down the hall to the master bedroom at the end of the dark hallway. For the first time in a long time, there was color in her cheeks and she felt great. She felt alive.

She went through the alcove to the bedroom. Maeva was propped up on a powder-blue reading pillow with her initials scrolled across the back in large, white, flowing script. She had a silver tray on the bed with a small silver pot of coffee, some coffee in a china cup, a silver sugar bowl, and a small silver cream jug. Crumbs from a piece of toast were scattered over a white china plate with gold trim. She was reading the paper and frowning. She wore glasses and had on a white satin quilted bed jacket that was open, showing her sagging breasts in a lacy powder-blue nightgown. She had not bothered to get up and brush her teeth, wash her face, or brush her hair. Her eyes went up when Blair walked into the overheated bedroom, so hot that Blair could barely breathe. It was nauseating from the heat and Maeva's unwashed body.

Maeva lowered the paper, placing it on the bed. She glared at Blair as if this whole thing was her fault, which Maeva believed it was. "It's too early. Go home. I'm not receiving. If you must, come back later or just call if you have something to say to me."

"I don't have anything to say to you." She walked over to the bed and simply dropped the diamond ring used for her engagement on the silver tray. It clanged as it hit the metal.

"You could have scratched my silver tray! Blair Don, what are you thinking? This was my husband's mother's diamond, and you could have hurt it, not to mention the tray." Maeva glared at Blair like she wanted to kill her, which she did.

She could feel Maeva's anger. As she dropped the big, heavy ring on the silver tray, followed by the velvet ring box, Blair quietly said, "Here. I wanted to make sure I gave this to you personally, so we both know you have it."

"Just what do you mean by that?"

"Just that," answered Blair. She quickly turned around and headed out of the stifling bedroom.

"Wait just one minute, Blair Don! You come back here right now! I have not finished with you! This is all your fault! Do you know that? If you'd stayed with Bobby all of the time, this never would have happened. And now look what you've done! You might as well keep this, because you and Bobby are getting married. Do you understand me? Did you hear me! Blair Don, you come back here right now. Do you hear me? You come back here. I have not finished talking to you. Come back here right now, or I'll get mad and call your mother!"

It was too late. Blair nearly broke into a full run down the long, dark hall to the wide staircase and hurried down. The sound of Maeva's voice became fainter and fainter as she rushed out the front door, allowing it to slam behind her.

Bernice opened the front door. "Maeva is yelling for you. You better come on back in."

Blair got into her car, gave a short wave to Bernice, and zoomed out of the driveway. As she sped away, she did not bother to look back to see Bernice standing by the open front door, shaking her head and smiling.

Blair knew what to expect, and she was ready. Late in the afternoon, Precious's car screeched into Booty's driveway. She slammed the car door and angrily strode into Booty's house. Before she had gotten to Blair's office, she was yelling.

"Blair Don—you've done it now! God damn it! Do you hear me? Have you lost your mind? How dare you go over to Maeva's house at the crack of dawn and just drop old Mrs. Wrightsberg's beautiful diamond ring on her breakfast tray like some old thing! I can't understand you, I really can't! What in the world do you think you're doing? Maeva was furious, and I don't blame her one bit, not one bit. You invaded the inner sanctum of her bedroom, of all places. I told Maeva when she called me that I didn't understand it. I really didn't. You're brought up better than to do something like that. You know not to call on people before ten o'clock in the morning and certainly not go over unless you call first. I told Maeva that. I told her you were brought up better than that, and I didn't understand what you were doing. I figured you lost your mind. I told her that you didn't mean it, so you go on over there right now. Bernice has the ring and is waiting for you to come over and pick it up. Now you get on over there before Bernice leaves, or you'll have to bother poor Maeva, who has taken to her bed. I think Maeva has been through quite enough today, don't you? So you get on over there right now, and you apologize to Maeva if you see her, and you write her a nice apology note on your good stationery and get it in the mail immediately, even if it means you have to drive over to the post office in Athens. Do you hear me?"

Booty was in his office and heard the whole thing. He got up and walked into Blair's office, where Precious was standing screaming at her.

"Precious, Blair is at work," Booty calmly said. "You go home now. Don't ever let me hear you speak that way to Blair again. Not in my house. I won't have it."

Precious exploded. "How dare you speak to me like that! What nerve! You're aiming way above your station in life, boy! Blair Don is my daughter, and I can speak to her any way I want to, and it is none of your damn business."

"It is my business when you are speaking to her like that in my house. I suggest you leave, Precious. And never ever refer to me as *boy* again."

Precious's eyes became wild with fury. She was aghast that Booty, a black man, had the nerve to speak to her like that. Then she looked around as if she had just realized where she was. She was standing inside Booty Crutchfield's house, and she was horrified. When it hit Precious where she was, she automatically backed up as if to get away from a horrible stench. Thank the dear Lord she was finally moving away from the Crutchfield house and Booty Crutchfield. She was going where she belonged. There were no black families in the area of Athens where she was moving. She was going to a nice neighborhood with nice people.

Anger and revulsion burst forth from Precious. "How dare you talk to me like that! How dare you! How dare you! How dare you! Blair Don, I don't want you in this house one minute longer. You have just quit this job. I don't want you to work anyway. Nice girls don't work. I want you to stay in bed until ten o'clock every morning, like women of your place in society are supposed to. I should never have allowed you to come into this house and work for that man. I must have been crazy at the time to let you do it. Black people work for us. The Blair family does not work for them."

Blair sat up straight, staring in quiet fury at her mother. A rush of anger ran up her spine. Her head pounded with anger.

"Did you just hear what I said to you, Blair Don? Get out of that chair right now, and you come with me if you know what's good for you! Don't you sit there looking like that at me! Who the hell do you think you are? You are my daughter, and you will do as I say! Do you hear me? Get out of that chair and come on. I want to get out of this house. You come with me right now! If you want me to treat you like a child and drag you out, I damn well will."

As she started to walk over and grab Blair, Booty calmly walked over to Precious and took her arm. "It's time for you to leave my house."

"Ahhhh! Just what do you think you are doing? You're touching me! How dare you touch me! Don't you touch me! Do you hear me? You do not touch me. You're not allowed! You listen to me. If my father and grandfather were still alive, they'd have you strung up for touching me. My grandfather and everybody else was right. We never should have allowed people like you to move here. You belong on the other side of the railroad tracks, not in this neighborhood. My grandmother always said that Able Crutchfield and W.D. Hoover should have been shot, and she was right! Don't touch me! Blair Don, are you going to allow this man to manhandle me? Blair Don! You better be careful who you are touching! My family still has power, and I'll get you good for this. You need to be run out of town, and Mae Hoover needs to go with you. It used to be against the law for a white woman to live with—or worse yet, marry of all things—a black man, and it still should be. They should shoot you both or string you up."

Blair did not say one word. She was mortified and embarrassed by her mother.

"My, Precious! What a Christian thing to say," said Booty.

"Don't you dare say that to me, Booty Crutchfield! The fine Blair family has always been good Christians. Why, I just joined a fine church in Athens, where all the nicer people go. No God damned blacks go there or Mexicans or homosexuals, for that matter. None of that sort of thing happens in my church."

"Well, that certainly is Christian of you, Precious. I'm sure Jesus would have been very proud how you are applying His compassion."

"There's nobody more Christian than I am, God damn you! Look how many Mexicans I have working on my house. Blair Don, where are you? Do you understand that I am leaving right now? You better come here this instant if you ever want a dime of my money."

Booty said, "Don't you mean Lorraine's money?"

"It's mine! And it is not going to be yours when I die, Blair Don, if you don't come here right now."

"I've had enough of this. Precious, you are leaving my house right now." Booty took her arm and escorted her out the front door.

"You listen to me, Booty Crutchfield," Precious screamed in his face. "There was a time when I could have had you hung for touching me. My family is important! Do you hear? *Important!* Blair Don, you come here right now! She does not work for you anymore. Blair Don, you come with me right now, or I'll come back and drag you out of this house. You are never to set foot in here again or you will regret it for the rest of your life, and I am not kidding. Blair Don! Blair Don—answer me!"

There was no answer from Blair. By that time, they were at Booty's heavy double front doors. He opened a door and escorted her out.

"Don't ever come into my house again," said Booty. As he was returning to his house, Booty stopped and turned to Precious. In a cold voice that brought chills to her because she knew he meant it, he said, "Precious, I am sick of you. I am sick of your family. I'm sick of what your family did—like scaring my grandmother away from this house so that my grandfather was left alone. He was not about to leave, regardless of your grandfather and father's threats and membership in the Ku Klux Klan, and they were very much members. I know, Precious. I don't forget. I also know you don't have any money. You don't have any power to do anything to me. Don't make me mad, Precious, or *you* will regret it the rest of your life. You do not want me as your enemy. You really don't. Now, I am sick of you. Get off my property, and never get on my property again, or I will call the police and have Oscar Stein, who is my lawyer and no longer your lawyer, screw you so badly that you won't have a dime left, or Lorraine to save you, or want to stay in Oklahoma after what will get out about your family. I will ruin you. You get the hell off my land. Now." Booty calmly walked back into the house and shut the door in Precious's face.

Precious was beside herself with fury. She was not about to tolerate Booty telling her where she could and couldn't go. She was free, white, and twenty-one, and she could damn well go anyplace she wanted. She was going back into that house and telling him *exactly* what she thought about him, his color, and his family! They should all rot in hell! Precious tried to open the door and screamed in fury when she discovered it was locked. "How dare you lock the door on me! You open this door right now!" She kept trying the door, which steadfastly remained locked. "God damn you, Booty Crutchfield! God damn you!" She stormed to the long window where Blair sat and pounded on it.

"Blair Don, you come outside right now. You open that front door and come outside! Do you hear me? You come here right now! I have to talk to you. You don't know what trouble is if you don't do as I say! Do you hear me? You better believe that my will is going to be rewritten if you don't come outside right now."

Booty walked over to the window and pulled the cord, closing the curtains. Precious felt her heart; she thought she was going to faint. She pounded on the window. "You're going to end up a poor, old, lonely woman with nothing, living on the street, and it's all your own fault. You remember what I am saying to you. End up on the street for all I care.

You're throwing away everything. You are crazy, Blair Don. You really are. You need help. You come with me. Do you hear me? Do you?" She continued to pound on the window. Finally she got tired out and decided if she died of a heart attack, it was all Blair Don's fault. Blair Don always did hate her.

After Booty closed the drapes, he looked at Blair. They heard Precious pounding on the glass and shouting. "I was not going to allow her to talk to you or to me like that," said Booty.

Blair slumped over the desk and rested her head in her shaking hands. "Thank you, Booty. I'm tired. I am so tired."

"Did you really go over to Maeva's and drop that ring on her tray?"

Blair looked up at Booty, smiling as if life had just reentered her. "Yes. Right on her silver breakfast tray. You should have heard that thing bounce and clang. I wish you could have seen Maeva's face. She turned red as a beet, she was so mad. For a moment, I thought she was going to have a stroke."

They both laughed a laugh of relief.

"I'll wait until later to sneak into my apartment; although it really doesn't matter when, because my mother will be lying in wait for me. You know I'll never hear the end of this, but it was worth it."

Booty sat down in a chair in front of Blair's desk. She looked up at him surprised, wondering what he was doing, since she expected him to return to his office rather than sit down with her.

"You're not going back to your apartment. Well, let me restate that. I am going back with you, and we will gather up whatever you need. You can return later, when you know your mother has gone and it's safe to finish packing. You're moving over here into this house."

"What?"

"Yes, you are. Why not? The house certainly is big enough for us to have an office down here in this area and for you to have the rest of the house. You have the whole house to yourself, and your mother does not have the keys, nor will she. You stay here as long as you want. Forever, for all I care, since no one has lived in the house for years. It's good for me because someone is living here, and it gets you out of your house. What do you say?"

She was astonished. What a wonderful idea. She had never thought about moving in here, but it was the logical thing to do, at least until she decided where to go. She was not returning to her mother's. This was a great idea. Relief washed over her, and she slumped back into her chair.

"I like it, Booty." Blair barely got the words out.

"Good. I hoped you would. Now let's go over to your apartment and get what you need."

As quickly as the relief came, it vanished. Terror spread through her, and her first thought was to run. "I can't."

"Why not?"

"I can't do it." Fear paralyzed her. "She'll kill me. I can't go over there. I can't."

Booty just looked at Blair. Suddenly he felt angry and disgusted and did his best not to show it. "Blair, you either do it now or not at all. I'm here to walk over there with you. Your mother is a coward. I doubt if she'll have the nerve to yell at me, and if she does, I will stop her. She will not yell at me. She knows that she does not want to take me on. She really doesn't. This is not about your mother. It's about you. Do you want to stop this or not? If you go back there alone, you will stay. In your heart, you know what I am saying is true. I will help you if you want my help. Once I go into my office, I'm done. Throughout the years, my family has taken a lot off of your family. I am willing to help you, if you are willing to break away. This is your choice. I don't care. I won't offer again. Now is the time if you're going to do it."

Blair felt like she was being torn apart. A terrible cold ran through her veins. She knew this was it—either she decided to leave or not. Something deep within her pulled at her to go with Booty to her house, but if she did … if she really did, her mother would never forgive her. This was the unforgivable move. She had had enough trouble and fights in order to go to the University of Oklahoma, since her mother had wanted her to go to school closer to home. Then, when she married and moved to Dallas, it was another big fight. To move to Booty's would be worse. Members of her family fanatically hated the Crutchfield family for one reason: they were black. This step would alienate her mother and most probably the rest of the Blair family. She was doing the unthinkable. Blair felt ripped apart. Was she going crazy? Moving to Booty's would mean being friends with Mae. The Blair family historically hated the Hoover family because they brought the Crutchfields into the neighborhood and "ruined it." Plus, they made a lot of what they considered to be dirty money by supplying liquor to the bootleggers when the state was dry. Then there was Eli. She knew this might bring Eli back into her life. Her mother hated him too. He was Oriental. Precious actually knew nothing about him, so she made up his history and believed what she made up. She decided he was poor, Oriental white trash, and his family had sneaked into this country illegally on some boat. He was definitely after Blair's money and status, and besides, Precious didn't like his smile and the way he looked. She thought he was ugly and shuddered when she spit out his name.

Blair heard Booty talking. She did not want to make this decision now; maybe later, when things were all right. Booty was telling her she had to decide now; she didn't want to, but she had to if she wanted his help. She wanted and needed his help. She had to have it. Booty was right; she would never have the courage to move over to his house alone. He was giving her a place to live, and it was a beautiful place to live for free for as long as she wanted. Why was Booty making her choose right now? Why couldn't she wait? She hated decisions. This was too big of a change, and she hated change. She did not want to make this decision, because it was too final. She did not want to make any kind of final decision. They were so final.

"Blair," said Booty, "are you listening to me?"

She looked into his eyes.

"Did you hear me?"

"Yes."

"What are you going to do? Because if you're not going to do it, I'm going back into my office. I have work to do. If you want me to go with you, let's go. If not, then let's get back to work and forget about it."

"I have to decide."

"If you want me to help you, you do."

"She'll never forgive me."

"Then don't do it if you care about that so much. It's okay. I don't care what you decide. Just decide."

"I don't know if I can do it to my mother."

"Okay," answered Booty. He turned to go into his office.

"Booty!"

"What?"

"Maybe I'll decide later."

Booty shook his head.

"Booty!" She knew this was it, and it made her sick to her stomach. He was right. If she went home, she would stay. She knew that, and it turned her blood cold. She knew herself well enough to know she would not leave. She would move with Lorraine and her mother over to Athens. With Bobby Wrightsberg out of her life, Blair knew what her mother would decide. She would move into the guesthouse in Athens and take care of them until they died. She felt her heart pounding in her stomach. The chance to change was right here, right now, beckoning her. Could she do it? What she *should* do fought with what she *wanted* to do. Blair was mad at Booty for forcing her to make a decision and refusing to help her later if she decided to move. It was his fault she had to decide right now. Why couldn't she wait until later, when the time was right? Suddenly a thought burst into her mind. The information was from her soul. It was absolute. It was the truth. She knew. She knew from the depth of her being. And the thought was she did not want to die, before she had a chance to live. And she wanted to live.

Tears ran down her face as she stood up. Blair walked steadily and with purpose to the front door.

Booty followed her out.

Chapter 11

March came in like a lamb, but no one believed that for a moment. It was tornado season—oh, yes—and it was spring. Tulips forced their way through the rock-hard soil, followed by daffodils and hyacinths. Throughout the years, Mae's constant change of mind as to what color tulips to plant resulted in a blast of uncoordinated color. She tried to be an organized gardener, but it just was not in her—rather like her hair, which refused to remain coifed and ended up in disorganized, fluffy, white curls. She wanted to make the backyard into a meadow of daffodils. Every year she planted more and more daffodils, so that now the backyard was flooded with them. The problem was, how do you mow? She didn't. The daffodils were surrounded by long, uncut grass. Bradford pear trees, other flowering trees, and bushes burst into pastels as the hardness of bleak winter light softened. Crickets and frogs began to return after a quiet hiatus, bringing music once again to the evenings. Slowly but surely, as the sun started to set later and the undercurrent of warmth overtook the cold pushing it away, life—in spurts and starts—resumed on the front porch.

Eli strolled home after a surprisingly eventful day at school. He had made everyone so mad that he could actually have gotten himself fired before the end of school and break his contract. If that happened, he was out of here. Even though Blair moved into Booty's house, it didn't mean he talked to her. He saw her at the window every day as he walked by, but she never invited him inside. Eli felt relieved. If she didn't want to have anything to do with him, that was fine. Eli was sure he was over her and could drive away from Cedar Springs without looking back. There was a bounce to his step. He chuckled, thinking about the day.

Easter was approaching, and Betty Ann had been particularly excited. She announced to the class how this was the most important Christian holiday in the year, and if they didn't believe her, they could just ask her father. All the kids, with the exception of Lynette Sue and Hiram (who had the good sense to stay out of it), told her she was wrong. Christmas by far was the most important, because Santa came and you got presents. Eli knew not to get involved, but he could not help himself. Betty Ann was such a self-righteous little prig that it gave him a perverse joy to upset her firmly laid-out, unquestioning, static world.

Betty Ann's deep-red hair was swept back into a tight ponytail. She was smacking her lips in disdain at the children who insisted Christmas was the most important Christian holiday. *Really,* she thought. *What idiots!* Even though she was only eleven years old, she possessed the scorn of a sour, old woman. Eli looked at Hiram, who pretended to be studying the fresh, green leaves fluttering in the wind, ignoring his sister as best he could. He was morose that she was still taller and bigger than he was. She was such a bully, relishing beating him up after school in the holly bushes behind the church. He was beginning to give up believing that there was a God, no matter what his father preached. If there were, then why was she still bigger than he? He prayed all the time, and still she outgrew him. He sighed.

Eli glanced at Betty Ann, who seemed to be taking a break in her conversion strategy, to the relief of the class. A voice in his mind told him not to say it. *Don't do it, don't do it, don't do it,* the voice repeated. *They are going to get mad.* It made him gleeful at the prospect of rattling their world and reconciled it as his job. He was a teacher.

"Class," Eli said. He forced back a grin. All eyes were upon him. "Just to give you some historical perspective on the celebration of Easter. The word *Easter* is derived from the Celtic spring goddess Eostre. Her festival was celebrated the first full moon after the spring equinox, and her symbol was the hare or rabbit, as you might know it, which symbolized mating. The egg was coupled with the hare, and it symbolized new life. Hence, today we have the Easter bunny that brings what? Easter eggs! Isn't that interesting? And the Catholic Church—"

Betty Ann blurted out, "They are *not* Christians!"

"What?" said Eli, quite astonished by that statement. "What do you mean they're not Christians?"

Betty Ann folded her arms and looked at Eli like he was the dumbest person on earth. She shook her head. "Mr. Take, are you a Muslim?"

"Am I a Muslim? No, I'm not Muslim. What does being Muslim have to do with anything?"

Lynette Sue thought she was helping Eli when she said, "Because you'd have to be a Muslim to think Catholics were Christians."

"I don't see what being Muslim has to do with Catholics. It doesn't."

Miriam clearly saw that Eli was not tracking. She knew because she had heard this all her life. "Mr. Take."

"Yes?" said Eli.

"Betty Ann and the church she goes to do not believe Catholics are Christians."

"We don't," Betty Ann said smartly. "They are idol worshippers."

Eli could not contain himself. "That is the dumbest thing I have ever heard. Number one: Who do you think were the first Christians in Europe? Catholics were. Catholics were the Christians in Europe until 1517, when Martin Luther, who was a monk at the time, nailed his ninety-five theses on the door of Castle Church in Wittenberg, Germany, which started the Protestant Reformation and got him excommunicated. Everybody in Europe who was Christian was Catholic until then. Because of the invention of the printing press and Martin Luther knowing how to use it for mass communication, Protestantism was born. St. Peter would certainly be shocked to learn the church he started in Rome is not considered Christian by some churches, because that is exactly what the Catholic Church is. It is Christian! And what is this idol crap?"

Lynette Sue gasped and said, "Mr. Take swore in class. You said a word my mother would never let me say."

Clare turned to Lynette Sue and said, "Oh, please! That is not swearing. *This* is swearing—shut the fuck up!"

Eli saw this was getting out of control and had to do something. "Clare, please, we do not use language like that in this class or in this school. Do not use that word again."

"Betty Ann means saints," clarified Miriam.

"Saints?" asked Eli.

"They're idol worship," said Betty Ann proudly.

"Oh my God," said Eli. "I have never heard anything like that in my life."

"That's why you have to be a Muslim," said Betty Ann.

"No," said Eli. "That's why you need to learn history. You listen to me. The Catholic Church is the first Christian church in Europe, founded in Rome—and that is in Italy, and that is in Europe, from where a great number of your ancestors emigrated. And odds are many of your ancestors that immigrated to America were Catholic."

"Not any of *my* ancestors!" proclaimed Betty Ann. "My mother's family came from Ireland. My grandmother told me so."

Eli looked at Betty Ann. "Right. Irish and not Catholic. Well that's certainly possible, but I doubt it."

"We are not Catholic, and I'm going to tell my daddy what you said."

"Please do," replied Eli. "And to continue, if you knew history, you would know that the early Christians more than likely took the name of the Celtic goddess Eostre, and the hare, and the egg, which evolved into what you know as Easter. Rebirth. Regeneration. Resurrection. That which appeared dead in winter came to life in spring. Look outside the window. Do it. Look! The trees that had no leaves on them, appearing dead, now have leaves and are very much alive."

Everyone in the class sat staring at him, their mouths wide open in shock at what he just said. This was not the least bit interesting to them; it was horrible. It was blasphemy. Betty Ann was sure this was a sin of the highest sort. Lynette Sue mouthed, "Just wait until I get home" to Betty Ann, who nodded knowingly. Isabelle and Heppy, who thought Mr. Take could do no wrong, immediately changed their minds. Their backs were plastered against the back of the chairs in fear and quandary as to what to do. Should they tell Geneva? That might get Mr. Take into trouble, and they did not want to do that. On the other hand, Geneva was sure to hear about it. Maybe they should tell her first, before she found out from someone else? She for sure was going to get mad. The question was, what would she do? They usually got beaten, especially Heppy, when adults got mad. Geneva had not shown any signs of beating or hurting the children in any way. Would this be enough to make her that mad? Their eyes shot back and forth to each other in worry. *Why did Mr. Take do this?*

Miriam sat back in her chair, surprised and wondering if what Mr. Take said was true. The first thing she planned on doing after getting home was getting on the Internet. The business about the Easter bunny and the eggs blew her away. She wondered what her mothers would say.

Joe Tom kind of missed the whole thing and did not quite get what all the upset was about. The minute he heard *Easter bunny,* his mind jumped to chocolate. He hoped his mother got Lynette Sue something good for Easter. He dreamed of losing his virginity with Lynette Sue. She had allowed him to touch her budding new breasts, which made him happier than he had ever been in his life. Now he wanted more.

Clare was also curious like Miriam and wondered if it was true. She too planned to immediately check the Internet when she got home. She had no plans to tell either of her parents. Her father was always traveling, and her mother would not care enough to listen. Her mother was more interested in playing bridge.

A.J., like Joe Tom, did not really listen to Mr. Take. Unlike Joe Tom, he would have immediately understood. His mind was too preoccupied. During their early spring break, his mother had again taken the kids back to St. Louis. There was no question in his mind, even though no adult had said so, that his mother was leaving and taking the kids with her. She showed them a house she was going to buy. It was in the same expensive old part of St. Louis where his grandparents lived. He and his brothers and sister had interviewed at a private school there, which to him seemed pretty final.

Some of his cousins went to that school where his mother had gone. All of his mother's family stayed in St. Louis. A.J. knew that everything was very nice. The school was nice. The new big house was nice. It was not that. He did not want to go. He liked where he was and had looked forward to going to school in Athens. This was his home, and he was leaving it, and he was not quite sure why. Why did his father have to have an affair with his secretary? He overheard his father telling his mother he wanted to marry the secretary. Why? Why would he want to do that when he had his mother and them? Maybe it was A.J. Did he do something that made his father want to leave their family? Maybe. A.J. could not understand and sat worried about what was going to happen. He knew there was a big hubbub in the class over what Mr. Take said. He did not much care; he had much bigger things to worry about than what Mr. Take said. Who cares about Easter anyway, when most of the Herzsteins were Jewish? They were interested in Passover.

The class was in a buzz the rest of the afternoon and rushed out the minute the last bell of the day sounded. Eli sat back at his desk and knew he was in trouble. He didn't really care. They needed to have their world rocked a little. Besides, he wasn't staying. So what if everyone got mad? It only gave him more of an excuse to want to leave Cedar Springs. They were a bunch of narrow-minded bigots. He was sick of the way Lucille smacked her lips at him and looked down her nose, making a face like he was a bad smell. She said he was the first "Oriental" to whom she had ever spoken, and he believed it. She did make an exception for placing orders to the employees at the Chinese and Vietnamese restaurants in Athens, but that did not count as actually talking to an Oriental.

Eli strolled down the uneven sidewalk of the brick street after school. New leaves fluttered in the breeze still a bright green before the hot sun scorched the brightness away, turning them dull. He passed by Mrs. Harrell and wondered if she had heard yet. News traveled fast here. Eli liked her; she had always been pleasant to him. Mrs. Harrell was on her knees, working hard at a bush in her front yard. Dirt plastered the knees of her slacks.

"Afternoon, Eli," she said. "This bush will not budge. Probably because it's older than I am, and that means ancient. I'm going to cut this thing back if it kills me. I've had it with the thing. It's not a bush, it's a tree, and I've had enough. I've been fighting with it for years. See my Cru on the front porch?"

Eli looked over to the front porch, where a big yellow Lab lay on a blanket. When he saw Eli looking, his strong tail beat back and forth on the wood floor of the porch.

"Hi, Cru," said Eli. "What's wrong with Cru?"

Mrs. Harrell sat back. Her garden gloves were as dirty as her pants. She wiped a tear from her eye, streaking her face with dirt. "The vet told me to fix Cru. That damn man in the house behind me complained. His little ick of a dog was in heat, and Cru won't shut up howling. Why doesn't he fix that ugly little thing of his? Who wants more of those? One's ugly enough. Cru got snipped this morning, bless his heart. It made me so nervous that I almost had a fit in the vet's office. I told the vet that without a doubt, I was going to have a nervous breakdown if he didn't give me a tranquilizer right now. I couldn't sleep last night. I was so worried about Cru. They had to put him under, and dogs can die under anesthesia. Well, I couldn't stand it. I sat there at the vet's, sobbing and telling him that I was going to pieces, which he could easily see. I mean to tell you I thought I was going to die right then and there, my heart was beating so bad, and the surgery hadn't even started. I've known the vet since he was born. He was holding Cru, and I already was going to pieces, crying. I told him that if he didn't give me something, I'd never make it through the surgery. He left with Cru, and I thought that was it. I knew I was going to keel over; then the vet walked out. He handed me a pill and a paper cup of water and told me if I ever told anyone he gave me a dog tranquilizer—as he didn't have any human ones—he could get in big trouble. I said I'd never tell anyone and I appreciated his kindness to me. It was the easiest surgery I've ever been through, and Cru is just fine—maybe not a happy camper, but he's fine."

"I'm glad to hear it, Mrs. Harrell. Cru's a good boy."

"Yes. He is." She wiped another tear beginning to form, smearing more dirt on her pretty face.

"Didn't you tell me he's four years old?"

"Yes. Cru's four now."

"He's young. He'll be fine."

"I'm going to get that damn bush."

"Good. That's a good thing to do."

She picked up some sharp hedge scissors. "See you later."

"Okay, Mrs. Harrell. Bye."

"Listen," Mrs. Harrell said.

Eli stopped.

"You don't worry one bit about what people say about you. Honey, they're not worth shaving your legs for."

Eli did not know what to say. *Okay,* he thought since he didn't shave his legs. "Okay."

She returned to the bush, enthusiastically whacking away at it.

Eli watched her for a moment, smiled, and then strolled down the block. *The news was already out.*

Miss Marie rocked in a swing on the front porch. He said, "Hello, Miss Marie. It's a nice afternoon."

She smiled back and shook a fat finger at him. "Naughty boy," she said.

"I know, Miss Marie. I know."

Eli continued by Booty's house. The drapes were drawn, and the house sat empty. Eli knew that Blair was in Oklahoma City, staying with a friend to help her while she was recovering from breast-cancer surgery. She had been gone a couple of days. Eli wondered if she already knew about his teaching disaster. If she did not know now, she would soon. It was just a matter of time. Eli had caused a scandal.

"Eli, you have caused a scandal," said Mae. After dinner, they sat on the porch, enjoying a lovely spring evening.

"You really have," agreed Booty. "Why?"

"I couldn't help myself."

"I understand that," answered Booty. "But why?"

"That's the truth. I couldn't help myself. Betty Ann got on my nerves too much."

"I understand *that*. If she's like her parents, she would get on my nerves too," said Mae.

"I just got sick of her self-righteous ignorance," answered Eli.

"Do you know how many phone calls I've gotten today about you?" asked Booty.

"No. I figure a lot."

"A lot."

"I'm sorry about that."

"Not half as sorry as I am, since I had to talk to them. I thought Lynette Sue's mother and Betty Ann's were going to froth at the mouth. They're out for blood. They want you fired."

Eli looked at Booty. "What did you say to them?"

"I told them you are not going to be fired."

"Booty, I'm sorry I caused so much trouble for you. I'll quit, if it's easier for you. I wouldn't mind."

Mae's stomach tightened when she heard Eli say that. She knew he was waiting to leave, and quitting would hasten that. She did not understand what Blair was doing. Why hadn't she said anything to Eli? Why was she avoiding all of them? Mae had invited her over for dinner, and she declined. She didn't want to come over to visit. She didn't want to have anything to do with any of them, so Mae left her alone. Blair could make him stay—maybe. Maybe it was too late. Mae wrung her hands. She got cold chills, even though she was not the least bit cold.

"I don't want you to quit. I'm not doing this for you; I'm doing it for the school. We cannot have our teachers run out of teaching because of what they say or for their sexual preference or for anything else other than gross misbehavior as in sexual abuse. If I let them run you off, Mary and Prudence will be next. You have to stay. They're not withdrawing their kids. It's too late in the school year. The kids will graduate soon enough and then be out of Lincoln forever."

"You want me to stay?"

"I insist on it, for the sake of the school," answered Booty. "However, you will have to deal with Lucille. She demands that you be called into the principal's office for 'a stern talking to' as she put it."

"Bob is going to talk to me? What does he, of all people, have to say? More than likely, he wasn't at school when it happened."

"I'm sure Lucille is counting on him not being at school, which is why she insisted upon you going to the principal's office. She wants to let you have it."

"Do I have to let Lucille bawl me out?"

"How you handle Lucille is none of my business. I'm telling you what is going to happen. How you deal with it is your business."

"Damn," said Eli.

"Yes. Damn," agreed Booty. "Why didn't you keep your mouth shut?"

"I'm a teacher. I'm supposed to educate the uneducated."

"Good for you," said Mae.

"Well, next time *you* talk to Betty Ann's and Lynette Sue's mothers," said Booty. "I'm sick of them."

"Then don't talk to them," said Mae. "Who said that you had to talk to them? Refer them to Lucille. And why is Bobby still at school? I thought after the Valentine's Day brawl, you were going to fire him?"

Booty sighed. "The board wants to let him finish out the school year. Believe me, I was not for it, but we don't want to pay off his contract, and the school year is almost over."

Mae huffed and then was quiet for a minute, thinking. "It's a beautiful spring evening."

"I agree," said Eli. "It's time to change the subject."

The next morning was lovely as Eli walked to school. He knew Lucille planned to demand his presence.

Miss Marie was already ensconced in the swing. She held a cup of coffee warming her hands.

"Good morning, Miss Marie," Eli said politely.

She smiled at him. "Lucille is waiting for you at school."

"I know."

She continued smiling as he walked on to Mrs. Harrell's. Neither she nor Cru was outside. Her car was gone from the driveway. Cru slobbered on the closed living room window and barked at Eli as he walked by the house.

When Eli saw Cru, he waved at the big yellow Lab. "Hi, Cru."

The dog barked back. The dog wasn't mad at him, Eli thought. Cru did not care what he said in school. Eli considered how much nicer Cru was than Lucille would ever be.

The more he thought about Lucille in wait for him at school, the madder he got and the faster he walked. Who the hell was Lucille to bawl him out? She was the school secretary, not the principal, even though she thought she was. She had no right to say anything to him; it wasn't her job. He didn't have to listen to her at all. The trepidation nagging at Eli faded away as his pace quickened. He was not a naughty little boy. He was a teacher Lucille Pawn was trying to censure, and that was not going to happen. By the time he got to school, he was in such a mood that he strode with his jaw clenched, down the hall to the classroom. His steps loudly slammed against the floor, echoing though the hallway.

Eli sat at his desk, pretending to be busy as the kids entered the classroom. Some said hello, and some walked past him. Betty Ann made sure her nose was in the air as she shot him a look, which Eli shot back as she marched by his desk. Lynette Sue stood at his desk for a moment. Eli thought she might say something, but she didn't. She dramatically turned and walked to her desk.

Hiram was funny when he came in following Betty Ann. He smiled at Eli and shook his head, mouthing, "Lucille's after you."

Eli nodded back knowingly and smiled.

Isabelle and Heppy had had a strange night. For the first time ever in their short lives, an adult was angry and did not hit or hurt them in any way. They didn't know what to make of it. They waited for the other shoe to drop, for Geneva to get mad and do something to them. Nothing happened; she was mad, but not at them. She was mad at Mr. Take. She was on the phone a lot last night. They overheard her talking to the headmaster at the Episcopal school in Athens they were attending next year. It was too late to transfer; the school year was nearly over. Geneva sighed when she hung up the phone with him. They knew Lucille was on the warpath. She assured all of the outraged parents that she would make that little Oriental son of a bitch rue the day he was born.

They didn't want to see Mr. Take get into trouble, yet there was nothing they could do. They hoped he would not get fired; they liked him. Both children wanted to warn him about the oncoming attack of Miss Pawn, but they could not figure out how to do it. Poor Geneva had been so upset! They planned not to tell her, knowing how upset she would get, except unfortunately Lucille called. Geneva wrung her hands as she talked to them. She had never heard such a thing in her life, and she didn't know what to do. She tried and failed to get them out of Eli Take's classroom immediately. Lucille couldn't transfer them into the other sixth grade, because it was full, and besides Geneva wasn't sure she wanted to do that. Wasn't it like going from the frying pan into the fire? Miriam McKeen's mother, Mary, who taught the other sixth grade class, was a … Geneva could not bring herself to say the word.

They say that Mary McKeen was perfectly nice, but—and there was always a *but* in Geneva's mind. Eli Take, Mary McKeen, and Prudence

Carpenter were heathens and going against the Bible's teaching. Of that she had no doubt. She wrung her hands and worried. She needed to talk to Pastor Pastor. Just because Heppy and Isabelle were being taught by a man of immoral beliefs, did that mean the children would go to hell with Eli Take? She had gotten them to accept Jesus Christ as their personal Lord and Savior. Surely that was enough to protect them from the Eli Takes of the world. Geneva wrung her hands, which were wet from fear. She had had no idea what Eli Take was like, except by looking at his friends. He was a friend of Booty, Mae, Ellanor, and Lorraine before Precious saved him. They were certainly suspect, making Eli Take suspect. Geneva had never trusted Ellanor. She secretly suspected him of having dangerous beliefs, and his taking off for New York City confirmed she was right.

Geneva, like Lucille, had a terrible crush on Dooley Pastor and hung on every word he said. His pronouncements were the gospel. She wrung her hands as her mind shot to the pastor telling her not to send "those children to that Episcopal school" because they would not receive the correct teachings about the Bible and our Lord Jesus Christ. Geneva wholeheartedly agreed. She would never in a million years have sent the children to the Episcopal school. She wasn't sure Episcopalians were actually Christians, since they were considered close to Catholics, and she'd never forget the sermon Dooley preached about Catholics not being Christians. But what could she do? She explained to Dooley that she had no choice in the matter, since Ellanor was paying for everything. Ellanor had a real thing about Holy Jesus Church. When she tried to broach the subject with Ellanor about sending them to the Christian school where Dooley wanted them to go, he had a fit. Geneva chewed her bottom lip and worried. Her eyes shot around the room as if searching for an answer from the walls. This was all getting to be too much for her. She told the children that she had to sit quietly for a spell and think. Isabelle and Heppy worried about Geneva because she was so upset. They did not know what to do. They fervently wished Lucille Pawn had not called.

None of the Herzstein parents got upset or called anyone. Perhaps it was because none of them cared or had been told by their children. Mary and Prudence joined Miriam at the computer, reading in surprise and fascination, having never heard anything like this before in their lives.

Eli simultaneously felt excited to take on Lucille the bitch and scared because he did not like confrontation. This was going to be a confrontation. He wished Lucille had forgotten about it. Not a chance. Lucille forgot nothing that angered her.

As Eli was about to tell the children to quiet down and open their books, the classroom door swung open with a bang. Standing there glaring at him, puffed up with vengeance, was Lucille. Her tiny teeth clicked. Her bun overflowing with brownish-gray curls was yanked painfully tight atop her head, and her eyes shined with victory. Cowering behind Lucille stood Whisper Woman. Her eyes darted around the room in fright, knowing Lucille was on the warpath. She grew up with Lucille warring against her or one person or another. She could not stand Lucille in her furious rampage threatening all sorts of nasty things. It scared her.

Whisper Woman never quite got over being scared since she, Lucille, and her mother had discovered her brother hanging at the top of the stairs. She never liked her brother and always thought him odd, especially after he went after their mother in the kitchen with the scissors. What was really scary, hanging right next to him, was an effigy of their mother, hung with ketchup as blood poured all over her. Now that really did scare her. Whisper Woman considered him crazy, but this was unnecessarily thoughtless and greatly upset their mother. Lucille flew into command of the situation then, just as she did now.

When Lucille had commanded last night that Whisper Woman was coming to school with her, in order to take Eli Take's class while she had a little talk with him, Whisper Woman obeyed, because it was the easiest thing to do.

Whisper Woman dared not argue with Lucille. She was too afraid of her and her anger. She really did not want to do this, not today. Today was an important funeral that Whisper Woman had been awaiting forever, since she heard a big, rich queen of Athens society had a stroke and was likely to die. She waited patiently, combing the daily obits. When the woman had the good sense to finally die, she so looked forward to attending the funeral. Whisper Woman's passion was attending funerals and rearranging the flowers. It did not matter whether or not Whisper Woman actually knew the dead person or their family. She went anyway, and it was one of her few real joys in life. She couldn't tell Lucille that today was the day of a particularly important funeral that she was looking forward to attending. Her heart fluttered with joy every time she thought about all the flowers that would be there. Whisper Woman's heart saddened to a tired, slow thump, thump, thump because there was nothing to be done. Lucille told her she had to be at school today, and that was all there was to it. Whisper Woman peered around Lucille at the children, hoping they wouldn't be any trouble. Whisper Woman did not like trouble.

"Mr. Take," Lucille commanded. Her voice demanded complete, utter attention and obedience. It reverberated off the walls down the hall. If her voice consisted of bullets, Eli Take would be dead.

The children jumped in their seats and sat straight up. Most looked around scared. Betty Ann snickered, relishing how Lucille Pawn was going to let him have it as he deserved.

Eli looked at her without replying. He determined to hold his own and not fold. He was not going to be intimidated and controlled by this bully of a woman. The problem was that his heart pounded in his chest, and he burst out into a sweat. His mouth was bone dry. His voice had to sound firm and strong.

"Come with me. Immediately," demanded Lucille with the expectation of utter obedience. "Miss Pawn will take over your class." She whipped around to Whisper Woman, which made her jump with the sudden movement. "Go to his desk."

Whisper Woman scurried around Lucille, over to Eli's desk. She stood there not knowing what to do, since Eli Take did not move or appear to be about to get up. She looked to Lucille for help.

Lucille was furious. This was not what she expected. No one went against her orders, and she had ordered that Oriental boy to get up and come with her. This insubordination would be severely punished. Her hands rushed to her bun and gave it a sharp, tight pull. She cleared her throat. Her eyes narrowed into angry slits. Her tiny teeth clicked.

"You. Come here. Now!"

Whisper Woman turned pale and felt weak with fear, to the point that she thought her knees might give way. She stood by Eli's chair helplessly, not knowing what to do. Why didn't he do as he was told and get up so she could sit down before her knees gave out?

Eli's heart pounded in his chest. He neither moved nor said anything.

The children were frozen in terror. No one refused Miss Pawn—ever. Mr. Take was doing the unthinkable. For Betty Ann and Lynette Sue, it was a shock. Some in class were bewildered, and some, even though frightened, enjoyed the standoff.

Whisper Woman balanced from one foot to the other. She worried that this was not good, not good at all. No one disobeyed Lucille. How would Lucille be at home tonight? She prayed Lucille would not take her fury out on her. A shudder ran through Whisper Woman's body at the thought of it.

Eli looked straight at Lucille, refusing to show fear. He had to remember to breathe.

It was a stare down. Eli sat in the chair and did not budge. Lucille shook in rage. She could not believe this was happening to her. Words shot out of her mouth one after another like a machine gun. "You come to my office right now! *Right now!* Do you hear me? Don't think there is a choice, because there isn't one. Now, to my office. Now! I won't have this."

Calmly Eli answered, "Upon whose authority am I to go to your office?"

Lucille actually thought she might faint and wondered what it felt like to have a coronary, because she might be having one. No one ever questioned her. She wanted to grab her heart but refused to give him the pleasure. "I don't need authority. I *am* authority! My authority is whose authority. My authority!"

"You're not my boss. You don't have authority over a teacher. The principal does. If Mr. Wrightsberg wants to see me, he can tell me. Until I hear from the principal personally, I don't believe there is anything more to be said. If you and Miss Pawn would leave, I have a class to teach."

Betty Ann's face went from a smart-alecky snicker to absolute shock. Her mouth dropped open. No one ever disobeyed Lucille. Wait until her father heard about this! Everyone knew Lucille Pawn ran the school. She ran off principals because it was *her* school. She prided herself in bullying them out of their job. Everyone was afraid of her.

Eli's whole body relaxed when he realized she could not make him do anything. It was wonderful. First he found the courage to leave his job and his father in New York City. Now, to his surprise, he refused to obey Lucille Pawn. Eli was amazed. He felt great and turned to Whisper Woman, who was so surprised at the happenings that her eyes were as big as saucers. She had waited to see this all of her life, wondering if she ever would, and now Eli Take was refusing Lucille's orders. This was certainly one of the best days in her life. For some strange reason, she had a strong urge to dance, and she really wanted to. This was marvelous, simply marvelous.

"Miss Pawn," Eli said to Whisper Woman, "would you please leave my classroom?"

"Don't you dare move!" shouted Lucille.

But it was too late. Whisper Woman left Eli's desk and swiftly glided to and then out the door. She proceeded down the hall, singing to herself, hoping to make it to Athens in time for the funeral.

Lucille watched in fury as Whisper Woman walked past her and down the hall to the front doors. She whipped around. "Just where in the hell do you think you're going? Whisper Woman! Whisper Woman, you answer me right now, or you know when you get home, there will be hell to pay! Whisper Woman! Whisper Woman, you wait just a moment. Whisper Woman!"

Lucille's face was bright red with anger. She rushed down the hall, yelling after Whisper Woman. She stood looking at the closed front doors as Whisper Woman walked with a bounce to her car, got in, and drove away.

She had disobeyed Lucille for the first time in memory and wasn't the least bit scared. Whisper Woman heard Lucille yelling at her, throwing threat after threat, but she didn't care. Who knows? Maybe she wouldn't return home tonight. Her crazy brother who hung himself left all of his money solely to Whisper Woman, which made the rest of the family furious, and that was more than likely why he did it. She had her own income; she didn't need to live in the family home with Lucille. If she lived in Athens, she would be free to attend all the funerals she wanted and not have to do everything Lucille wanted all the time. She might even go on a cruise! She always wanted to go on a cruise, but Lucille refused to go because she was afraid she would get seasick. She glanced at the time; there was time to make it to the church after all.

Lucille stood at the brown metal front doors, shaking with rage. Punishment would be rendered upon Whisper Woman. The question was what kind. Whisper Woman would never disobey her again after she was through with her. She panted, her cheeks bright red. She chewed her bottom lip so that most of the red lipstick was gone and a spot of blood appeared. She leaned on the bar that opened the door and nearly fell out when it suddenly opened, which gave her a start. At first, Lucille thought it must be Whisper Woman coming to her senses and begging for forgiveness, but it wasn't. A man Lucille thought she might know came in the door, followed by a very pregnant young blonde woman.

What the hell are these people doing here? thought Lucille. *I don't know them. What are they doing here in my school? Let the pregnant woman come back when her kid is ready for the first grade.* She looked scornfully at the older man and huffed. *Another one of these men old enough to be the woman's father.* She sniffed as she looked disapprovingly at the pregnant young woman.

"Do you know where the principal's office is?" asked the man.

Lucille glared at him. She very much disapproved of this old man fathering a child with the young woman. She was not about to help the old letch. He should be with someone his own age. "Of course I know where the principal's office is," she snapped and then turned and marched off, leaving the man and woman in her wake.

Lucille stomped into the office, and to her genuine surprise, Bob sat at the desk in his office. This was too much for Lucille. *What's he doing here? He's never here, and today of all days he is here, just when I planned to have a good talking-to with Eli Take in his office.* He had his nerve to show up. She stormed into his office. Bobby had his back turned to the door with his feet on the desk, talking on a cell phone and staring blindly out the window.

Lucille jammed her hands upon her hips. "Just what are you doing here?"

Bob ignored her. He was too involved in his conversation and did not want to be interrupted.

"Yes, sure. I can be in Oklahoma City tonight," he said.

"Bobby!" she demanded.

He refused to pay attention to Lucille and gave a sexy laugh at something said to him on the phone. "Sure," he answered. "I can't wait."

Lucille would have none of this. She'd had quite enough disobedience for today from Eli Take, not to mention her own sister. She was not about to take anything off Bobby Wrightsberg, whom she had known all his life. He was a spoiled-brat child who grew into a spoiled-brat adult. Lucille stomped her foot. "Bobby! Get off that phone right now! I have to talk to you. Bobby!"

At all the noise, Bob reluctantly turned to Lucille. "What do you want?"

"Get off the damn phone! I have to talk to you right now! We've got a big problem—"

But while Lucille was talking, the outer door to the principal's office opened, and the pregnant young woman and older man walked into Lucille's office. Bob could easily see them, and he gasped.

Lucille was so busy talking to Bob that she had not noticed them come into her office and then on into the principal's office. She still had her hands on her hips, commanding what must be done.

"Bobby! Are you listening to me? You have a major problem with one of your teachers, and he needs to be fired immediately! Bobby! Are you listening? We don't need to call a board meeting or anything like that. You can do it. This is an extraordinary circumstance. I'll back you up with Booty. Don't worry about him. I'll take care of him and the board. And I'll take care of the teacher. Bobby! Are you listening to me?" Just then, Lucille noticed the man and woman walking past her toward Bob's desk.

"Hey," Lucille said as she was moved aside, "just what do you think you are doing? You can't just walk in here. You have to go through me first, and I'm busy, so go away. Go home. Call and make an appointment. Can't you see I'm busy?"

They ignored Lucille, which made her madder. "Hey!"

Bob turned white. He mumbled something into the phone and hurriedly hung up, sitting straight up, at a loss as to what to do. He wanted to make a run for it, but that was impossible, since Lucille and the man and woman blocked the only exit. He burst out sweating. He wanted to call his mother. She had always gotten him out of everything, and he knew he needed help immediately.

They walked up to Bob's desk and sat in the two empty chairs facing him.

Bob could not speak. For once in his life, he was at a loss for words. He simply stared.

Lucille could not get over how rude those people were to ignore her and walk right into Bob's office. They sat down like they owned the place. She was about to walk right over and tell them what she thought about their rudeness, and she was in the mood to do it too.

"Bob Wrightsberg?" the man said.

"Yes," answered Bob, barely audible. He felt sick. This was the worst day in his life. He just knew it. Why didn't she come to him? Tell him she was pregnant? He would have taken care of everything. Why did she do this to him?

"It's obvious you know my daughter," the man continued.

"Your daughter?" said Lucille. "I thought that was your wife."

The man turned and looked at Lucille. "That's not my wife. My wife is my wife." He shook his head and returned to Bob.

"Do I know you?" asked Lucille.

He turned again to Lucille. "No."

"Why don't I know you?" asked Lucille. "How old are you?"

"Lady, I am trying to talk to this man."

"I don't understand why I don't know you, since we're about the same age, and I know everyone from around here. Are you from around here? Who are your parents?"

"My parents have nothing to do with this," the man snapped at Lucille.

"Well, I think they do, since you're here, aren't you?" Lucille folded her arms and tapped her foot. She knew she was absolutely right in her questions and was not about to be dissuaded.

Bob had a terrible urge to pee in his pants, which shocked him. He had not done that since he was in the first grade here at Lincoln, when he had to go to the bathroom. He had been too afraid and embarrassed to ask to be excused and peed right in his pants as he sat at the desk. It was horrible. He had never been so humiliated. Oh God, he could not do that again, and certainly not right now. He wondered if he could be excused to go to the bathroom, and then he could slip out after that.

"Lady, do you understand that my daughter and I are not here to talk to you, and it doesn't matter where I'm from?"

"Yes, it certainly does matter where you're from," corrected Lucille. "You must not be from here to speak to me that way. People from here know better than to speak to me that way."

"Daddy," cried the young woman.

Her father gently patted her. "You're right, honey." He faced Bob, who squirmed in his seat. "Now listen to me, Bob Wrightsberg—that's what my daughter tells me your name is, since she never saw fit to introduce her parents to the man that got her pregnant. You're coming with me, and you're coming with me right now. You and my daughter are going to get married. We don't cotton to things like this. We are a good Christian family, and we don't abide by this behavior. Men marry their women, and by God, you're marrying Penny."

"Penny who?" asked Lucille. "Who's her family?"

Bob had not spoken a word because he couldn't speak. His mouth and throat were too dry.

"Now you come with me, and let's make this nice and easy," said the man. "We're not having any bastards in our family. Our girls get married."

"Daddy!" Penny cried. "Don't say that word."

"I'm sorry, honey. I didn't mean to upset you. We've got business to do and this man to be doin' it with." He turned to Bob. "Now you get out of your chair and come along. Penny's mother is in the car, and she is pretty darn upset about all of this. We had high hopes for our Penny, and now that's not to be. She's going to be marrying you, and you're going to be good to her, or I'll shoot off every limb of your body and finish with your head. Do you understand what I'm saying?"

Bob pushed against the back of the chair as if it could save him. He cried and whimpered.

"Penny's mother and I kept thinking you were going to do the right thing by her, but you didn't. You can see there's no time left."

"Bob, I'm sorry!" she cried. "I kept thinking you'd call like you used to do, and you didn't, and I couldn't tell you because you didn't call me, and you told me never to call you, so I didn't." Penny gasped for breath, having said that in one long sentence, and being so heavily pregnant, it was hard to breathe. "I almost called you, even though you told me not to, but I almost did, and then it got so late, and my mother and daddy kept asking me where you were, and I had to tell them, because, Bob, you told me that you loved me. You said that you loved me. You said. Bob, you said that, then you quit calling, and I didn't know what to think. Then I discovered I was pregnant, and my mother liked to have died with shame, and I kept telling her that you loved me, and I didn't understand why you didn't call when you said you would. Why didn't you? I could have told you if you called, but you didn't. How come? My boss got so mad at me for getting pregnant with your baby that she up and fired me from the bank the minute I told her whose child it was. She really got mad, and it's not my fault. Daddy said that we're going to sue the bank for firing me 'cause I was pregnant. You can't do that. She liked to have had a fit when I told her it was your baby, but it *is* your baby. I think she got mad because she thought she was going to marry you herself, but she's not. I am. I love you, Bob."

"Now you just wait one minute," said Lucille. "Who did you say you are, and where do you come from?"

"Lady, this is none of your damn business. So get your nose out of it," said Penny's father.

"It is too my business!" exclaimed Lucille.

"It is not!"

"Daddy, Mama's waiting in the car. We've got to get to the judge's office 'fore it closes. We told him we'd be there, so we better be there 'cause he said he couldn't wait. He's got some dinner or something to go to, and I'm not feeling too well."

"Come on, boy. Get out of that chair and get going. I'm calling you Bob. You call me Mr. Price, because I'm mad at you and I'll never forgive you for doing this to my daughter. If it weren't for my daughter loving you so much, I would have killed you. Now get going. Come on."

"Price?" said Lucille. "Let me see. What Prices do I know? I don't know any. I don't know any Price family that I can think of off the top of my head at all. Bobby, who is this family you're marrying into? Does your mother know? I don't know the Prices, so they can't be from around here, or I would have at least heard of them, but I haven't. I haven't at all. Where is your family from?"

Tears ran down Penny Price's pretty face. "Bob, don't you want to marry me? If you say you love someone, that means you want to marry them. You said that you loved me, so how come you're sitting in that chair? How come?"

"Don't you worry, honey," said her father, getting up. "We're taking care of this. If you want this boy, you can have him, if that makes you happy."

"Thank you, Daddy," she said, smiling.

"Who are you people to think you can just marry into the Wrightsberg family?" insisted Lucille. "You can't marry into the Wrightsberg family without Bobby's mother's permission, and she is not likely to give it—not likely at all. In fact, I'll go so far as to say Maeva Wrightsberg won't allow it. Bobby can't marry just anyone. He has to marry *somebody*. Since I haven't heard of your family, I think—as rude as it might sound—that you are a bunch of nobodies." Lucille smacked her lips with finality and folded her arms. As far as she was concerned, she had taken care of this for Maeva, who could thank her later for saving her son from such terrible misfortune. It would be nice to have Maeva—that bitch—beholden to her.

Mr. Price glared at Lucille like she was crazy. He pointed his finger at her. "Lady, shut up. This is none of your business. Stay out of it and go away."

Lucille gasped. "Well, I never!"

Mr. Price ignored Lucille. He was a tall, sturdy man with a big, solid barrel chest. He wore a cowboy hat, dark-brown boots, pressed jeans, and a long-sleeve pressed and starched white shirt. He quickly walked to Bob's chair and grabbed him by his shirt at the throat, dragging him up.

"Ahhhh," said Bob as he was being yanked out of his chair. Fortunately, the back of his pants was not wet, although Bobby wondered whether it might be, he was so nervous.

"Come on. You're coming with me to make an honest woman of my daughter. Right now. I told you that we're good Christian people. We don't take to having kids out of wedlock, and I'm not waiting any longer.

You've upset my wife, you've upset my daughter, and most importantly, you've upset me!"

Bob looked at Mr. Price. "But—"

"Listen to me, son. There are no buts about it. We are going right now. Aren't we, honey?"

"Yes, Daddy." Penny struggled to get out of the chair and waddled after her father, who was leading Bob out the door and down the hall.

"Hey!" shouted Lucille after them. "Where do you think you're going?"

Bob turned and looked to Lucille for help.

"Don't you worry one bit, Bobby. I've never liked you, but that doesn't mean I won't help your mother. I'll give her a call, and we'll fix things up for you. She won't want you marrying into some no-account family, no sir! I know she did not raise you for that. Don't you worry one bit. Maeva will fix everything up just fine like always. You'll see."

That was the last thing Bob heard as Mr. Price led him out the front door, followed by Penny holding her stomach. The door slammed behind them to silence. Lucille had followed them to the door, which slammed in her face. She quickly turned and marched back to the office. There were calls to make. Bobby Wrightsberg was marrying into some family she'd never heard of. Who were they anyway, and where did they come from? Maeva would have a fit. Just the thought of the fit Maeva would have made Lucille actually feel joyful. Eli Take and Whisper Woman faded away for her. She forgot her anger at them. She had been front row center for a major scandal and gossip. She got to pay back Maeva Wrightsberg, who always had acted so high and mighty toward everyone, like she was better than they were. Like she was beyond normal human bodily functions and didn't go to the bathroom or anything unmentionable. Just wait until everyone heard about *this!*

Lucille stopped for a minute, thinking, and then she smiled. Talking to herself as she slowed from a march to a stroll back to her office, she said, "I think I better make some other calls before I bother to call Maeva. I mean, what's the rush? Maeva will find out when she finds out. It's not like there's a fire. Who knows? By the time Maeva hears, with any luck at all, Bobby will already be married into that horrible family. Maeva is going to get the vapors so bad, she'll take her bottle of bourbon to bed with her for a year to try to get over it 'cause there is nothing she can do. I don't think Maeva's money is going to make this go away like it didn't happen. Mr. Price was real mad, and he said what Christians they were. He's going to make damn sure Bobby makes that little girl an honest woman. Oh, yes he is."

She sashayed back to her desk and grandly took her seat. *How lovely these calls will be,* she thought, and that brought joy to her heart. The question was, who to call first? Should she call Precious or Sister at the beauty parlor? Come to think of it, Precious had always been such a bitch to her and didn't deserve the first call with this valuable piece of gossip. Lucille enjoyed her power and giggled. She patted the bun atop her head, opened the top desk drawer, pulled out a mirror, and looked in it. She patted her hair again and then smiled into the mirror and rubbed her finger across her front teeth to clean them. She quickly leaned down, grabbed her purse, yanked out a lipstick, and glided the red lipstick over her lips. She smiled once again at herself in the mirror before returning it to the desk drawer.

Lucille had decided on the all-important first call. She would give a call to Sister to alert her as to what was up, and then she would call Precious. This should be particularly fun, since Precious was still trying to figure out how to get Blair Don and Bobby back together. Lucille giggled at how Precious was still after the Wrightsberg family money and knowing marrying Blair to Bobby would do it. Precious was such a greedy bitch. Maeva's life was centered on reclaiming the grandeur of the Wrightsberg name, previously soiled by her thoughtless husband's hanging in the front yard. Lucille had heard all about that and was gleeful when he did it in the front yard. Lucille knew Maeva and Precious still schemed to merge the families, and now it was over. Even they couldn't lie to themselves about this.

Lucille giggled again, a nasty little giggle. She was having such fun, and to think how furious she was earlier at Eli Take, who always infuriated her anyway, and Whisper Woman, who was crazy. She didn't pay much mind to Whisper Woman. What was it she was so angry at Eli about this time? Lucille quite forgot in all the new excitement. This had turned out to be an absolutely wonderful day—just wonderful for her. What fun to be the bearer of good tidings of a major scandal! How lovely! She picked up the phone and called Sister.

"Oh, Sister, I am so glad you answered the phone. We have a little emergency on our hands, and I know you are the one to talk to about it." Lucille told Sister everything in great detail. Sister had to stop cutting a woman's hair, and she gasped in glee.

Chapter 12

The news of Bobby and Penny's wedding at the judge's office spread like wildfire. Mrs. Harrell was over in Athens to do some errands and to attend the social queen's funeral, where Whisper Woman gloriously rearranged all of the flowers. One errand was to pay a speeding ticket that had insulted her no end. How dare a policeman be between the vet's office and Cedar Springs when everyone knew people had to speed to get to the vet's? Mrs. Harrell happened to be standing in the cashier's line when she saw Bobby Wrightsberg being led upstairs at the courthouse, where the judge's chambers were located. Behind Bobby was a big man in a cowboy hat, leading him, followed closely by a very pregnant young woman who, upon looking closer, Mrs. Harrell recognized as the nice young bank teller, holding arms with an older woman who was crying. Mrs. Harrell figured her to be the mother. At first, she started to say hello to Bobby and the bank teller, but upon reflection seeing their expressions, she decided not to say a word to them.

When it was Mrs. Harrell's turn at the cashier's window, she was pleased to see that she knew the cashier, who had grown up in Cedar Springs. Mrs. Harrell's curiosity was simply too much. She asked the cashier if she knew what was going on with Bobby Wrightsberg and who those other people were. The cashier made it her business to know what was going on at the courthouse, so when the judge's secretary told her in strictest confidence that Bobby Wrightsberg was scheduled to be married to Penny Price—you know, the nice young bank teller whose family owns the cleaners—in the judge's office, she smelled a scandal in the works. The cashier's mother was an old friend of Mrs. Harrell's, so she felt perfectly comfortable explaining to Mrs. Harrell about the Prices.

The cashier leaned forward, and Mrs. Harrell leaned in so she would not miss one word.

Mrs. Harrell quickly asked, "Okay, so who are the Prices, other than they own the dry cleaners? Do I know them?"

The cashier shook her head. "No. You would never have known them. They're new in Athens. They've only been here about twenty years."

Mrs. Harrell shook her head in agreement. "Uh huh."

The cashier went on to say, "The way Mr. Price had his hand on Bobby's back, making damn sure he wasn't going anywhere but up those stairs to the judge's office, and how pregnant that girl looked, I'd say Bobby is going to be a daddy and soon."

Mrs. Harrell said, "I'm not the least bit surprised, not in the least. Just like his daddy all over again. I wouldn't trust him as far as I could throw him. What surprises me is that it didn't happen sooner. If it did, Maeva got him out of it, just like she'll get him out of this."

The cashier folded her arms, nodding her chin at the stairs where Mr. Price had led Bobby, followed by a very pregnant Penny Price and her mother. "I don't think so. By the way Mr. Price looked, I don't think Jesus resurrecting right here on this spot could get Bobby out of this. Who I feel sorry for is the girl."

Mrs. Harrell looked at the empty staircase and shook her head. "If this marriage lasts, I'll eat my purse."

The cashier smiled. "The judge's secretary told me she goes to church with the Prices, and that church does not believe in divorce. Mr. Price will kill Bobby if he pulls something."

"You see, there always is a bright side. Here's my credit card. I'll be sure to tell your mother what a nice visit we had."

Lucille couldn't remember the last time she'd had so much fun. She loved hearing Sister's reaction, which was just as she figured. At that moment, she knew there was a God, because all her life she dreamed of screwing Maeva and Precious. They were such shits to Lucille, from the playground at Lincoln School on. Even if Maeva succeeded in buying Bobby out of this, everyone would know the truth, thanks to Lucille, who was an eyewitness. Lucille clicked her little teeth and shook with excitement. What a wonderful day.

It just so happened that the woman sitting with a wet head in Sister's chair getting her hair cut was a childhood friend of Blair's. They talked on the phone almost every day, and upon hearing the conversation Sister was having with Lucille, she had to call Blair immediately.

While Sister was on one phone, so absorbed in her conversation that she forgot about finishing the woman's hair, the friend reported a blow-by-blow account of their conversation to Blair.

Suddenly Sister whooped, "Oh my God! Maeva is going to have one of her nervous breakdowns and disappear again. The next time we see her. She'll have another facelift. Please, God, may it be better than the last one. What a shame her top lip went one way and the bottom another. Oh Lord, and there's that expensive mother-of-the-groom dress she got at Neiman's, and it's been altered. She can't return it. She'll have to find someplace to wear it. Now, who are the Prices? I don't know the name."

The woman reporting to Blair gasped when she heard Sister say the name. She knew who the Prices were. She used their cleaners over in Athens. *Oh my God! Bobby Wrightsberg married the cleaner's daughter!* The friend interrupted talking to Blair to explain to Sister who the Prices were. They owned the dry cleaners in Athens. Upon hearing that information, Sister and Lucille launched into an in-depth discussion about Maeva's drinking. There was no question that Maeva would take to her bed. The question was for how long.

Blair's heart had never felt so light, maybe never in her whole life. She cried in relief and joy. There was absolutely nothing her mother could do to change what had happened. The undercurrent of fear that nagged and tickled at her insides disappeared. Blair was truly free. Maybe it was time to call Mae. She needed to talk to Mae, to see if there was anything she could do about Eli. What did Mae think about her inviting Eli over? Or calling him? Or should she/could she do anything? Was all lost with him? Blair was afraid it was. It didn't hurt to ask Mae. She could always talk to Mae. Blair needed to get off the phone and call her right now.

Lucille tore herself away from talking to Sister. There were just a few short calls she had to make before calling Precious and then Maeva. By calling the other ladies first, Lucille deemed herself the bearer of good news, like shouting out the gospel, since most of the ladies in town couldn't stand either Maeva or Precious. Then it was time to call Precious and then Maeva. Lucille's tiny teeth clicked with excitement when she dialed Precious. She called her cell figuring Precious would be over in Athens at the Herman H. Green house. Lucille was right. Precious was, in fact, in the middle of having a major fabric discussion with the interior decorator and was annoyed at Lucille's interruption. Only at Lucille's insistence that Precious would want to hear this did she listen, but not before demanding to make it quick because she was busy.

Lucille did her best to sound somber. "Precious, Bobby Wrightsberg got married today. I thought you would want to know. Bye."

"What!" yelled Precious into the phone. "Don't you dare hang up on me, Lucille Pawn! What the hell do you mean Bobby got married? He better not have gotten married! He can't just get married! If Blair Don decided to run off and marry him just to spite me out of having my big wedding, she is wrong. There will be a big wedding. I'm going to call her right now. She did this to spite me, and by God, she will be sorry."

"Precious," said Lucille, smiling as she patted the bun atop her head, "Blair Don didn't marry Bobby. Honey, the bank teller did. Her family has the dry cleaners in Athens."

It took a moment for Precious to actually grasp what Lucille just said. "What?"

Lucille smiled graciously. "Bobby married the bank teller today, and I know it because her daddy came to the school to get him. He had his daughter with him. Did you know her name is Penny? And Maeva is going to be a grandmother very, very soon. Isn't that sweet?"

"Bobby was at Lincoln?"

"Yes, he was. He did pick a bad day to show up for work, didn't he? Bobby was sitting right at his desk when Mr. Price went into his office and grabbed him up out of his chair by the neck of his shirt. Did you hear me say Penny is pregnant? She's as big as a house. Mr. Price wanted to make sure Bobby made an honest woman of her. I hope they'll be very happy."

"Bobby can't marry anyone but Blair Don!" Precious screamed.

"Well now, Precious," Lucille said, smiling sweetly, "it seems that he did."

"He can't do that!"

"Precious, I have to go. I just thought you might like to know."

"You can't hang up on me now!"

"Bye-bye, Precious."

"What?"

"Bye, Precious. I have to go."

Lucille dialed Maeva. She had to get to her before Precious did.

To Lucille's joy, Maeva answered the phone. Lucille could tell by her voice she had not heard. Otherwise, she would never have sounded so good.

"Oh, Maeva," said Lucille, trying to appear concerned, "you haven't heard?"

"Heard what?" answered Maeva. "I have an appointment at Sister's, and I have to go. Let me talk to you later." Maeva did have an appointment with Sister but not at that moment. She didn't want to talk to Lucille.

"Okay," answered Lucille, "so you don't want to hear that Bobby got married today and not to Blair Don?"

It gave Lucille such joy to hear Maeva shriek. "God damn it! You better be joking, Lucille!"

Lucille patted her bun. "Do I joke?"

Maeva knew Lucille lacked a sense of humor. Her knees felt weak, and she collapsed on the chaise longue in her bedroom. When she answered, her voice had lost its verve and wobbled. "How do you know this, Lucille? You better be wrong!"

"It happened at Lincoln, and I am not wrong. I was a witness."

"They did not get married at Lincoln. Now I don't believe you."

"No. They didn't get married at Lincoln," snapped Lucille. "Mr. Price and his very pregnant daughter came to Lincoln to get Bobby."

"Who is Mr. Price?"

"I don't know who the Prices are other than they own the dry cleaners. I asked him who they were, and he didn't answer me. I've never heard of the family. They're your new in-laws, that's all I know."

"Wait a minute," interrupted Maeva, daring to feel hope again. "Was Bobby at Lincoln?"

"Yes he was," Lucille answered proudly.

"What was he doing there?"

"Maeva, he works here."

Maeva's heart dropped. She could barely talk. All the energy drained out of her body, and she felt weak. She whispered, "Lucille, you tell me what happened right now."

"I told you. Mr. Price and his very pregnant daughter came here. Mr. Price pulled Bobby out of his chair and marched him out the door. He said that a judge was waiting to marry them, so for all I know, they're married by now."

"Oh no, they are *not* married! I'm calling Oliver right now. He'll do something. I'll buy them off, and it will be done with."

"Maeva, from what I could tell of Mr. Price, I don't think he can be bought off."

"Lucille, don't be silly! Of course whatever his name is can be bought off! Everybody can be bought off. All you have to do is make it worth their while. Believe me, I can make it worth a dry cleaner's while in a minute. No one turns me down." Maeva's voice rebounded to its strength again. She was back into action without a worry. "I've got this under control. Lucille, I've had problems, and this is not one of them. A dry cleaner … please. Believe me, if Bobby was stupid enough to get married, I'll get him a divorce before the ink is dried on the marriage license. I have to go Lucille and call Oliver. Bye."

"Maeva," said Lucille, "I don't think you are going to get Bobby out of this."

"Don't be silly. You always are so negative, Lucille. Of course I will."

"I'm not being negative, Maeva. I saw Mr. Price's face. This man meant business. You're not—"

Lucille did not get a chance to finish her sentence, because Maeva interrupted. "Oh, Lucille, don't be so tiresome. I have to call Oliver. Good-bye."

But Lucille turned out to be right. Maeva called Oliver Stein the minute she hung up with Lucille, only to discover, to her horror, that

Oliver wanted no part in it. He had gotten Bobby out of messes and was through with him and with Maeva. When Maeva threatened to take her business elsewhere if Oliver didn't get Bobby out of this, Oliver asked where he should send her records and hung up. Maeva immediately called another lawyer in Athens, to whom she offered a lot of money. The lawyer dutifully called Mr. Price with an offer he was sure to accept, except to the lawyer's surprise and Maeva's shock, he refused. And that was when Lucille correctly predicted Maeva taking to her bed with the vapors and a fifth of bourbon for an indeterminate period of time.

Precious was much more resilient. She had always thought she could force Blair to come to her senses and marry Bobby. Now she knew there would not be a wedding. All of her efforts were wasted because Bobby was such a fool. It was okay, though. Precious would be fine. The caterers were hired, the date planned. Her fallback plan of a garden party would be just as lovely. After all, the whole point was to show off her newly redone fabulous house. It would no longer be known as the Herman H. Green house. It was now all hers.

Blair was getting ready to call Mae when Booty walked in from Athens. "Booty," said Blair, barely able to contain herself.

Booty took one look at Blair and knew something had changed. "What happened?"

"Booty, Bobby married the nice, young bank teller."

"How do you know?"

She relayed everything to Booty, who smiled and laughed, saying, "Well, isn't that wonderful! Not for the poor young woman, though. I feel sorry for her. Does Mae know?"

"Not that I know of. I was just getting ready to call her."

"Were you?"

"Oh, yes. I knew she would want to know."

But just as Blair was getting ready to call Mae, the phone rang. It was Mae calling Booty. The minute Mrs. Harrell walked away from the cashier, she called Mae, who was an old friend. Mrs. Harrell knew that Mae would want to know this immediately, and she was right. After an extremely detailed conversation, hashing over and digesting every bit of gossip, Mrs. Harrell headed back to Cedar Springs, and Mae dialed the phone. What news! She could not wait to tell Booty.

The minute Mae heard Blair's voice, she started talking. Mae was so excited. "Oh my God, Blair, I just heard the greatest news! Bobby married the nice bank teller. Well, I guess it is not such great news for her. She had to marry the bastard, but for everyone else it is."

Blair's heart sank, not because Bobby got married. That thrilled her. Rather, now she did not have a reason to call Mae. She planned to use the news about Bobby to evolve the conversation into Eli and what she should or could do, if anything.

"Oh yes, Mae, I heard from my friend who was having her hair done at Sister's when Lucille called. The young woman and her father picked up Bobby at Lincoln—"

At this point, Mae blurted, "Bobby was at Lincoln? What was he doing there? I didn't think he ever went to work."

Booty stood listening to everything and said, "My God, Bobby actually was at work?"

Blair smiled and continued, "He picked a fine day to show up. According to my friend, who heard from Sister, who was talking directly to Lucille, who was there and saw the whole thing, the father jerked Bobby right out of his chair and hauled him out of Lincoln to Athens and the judge's office. And the girl is very pregnant, so this is a rush."

"I knew she was pregnant. I was trying to tell Booty that night at the restaurant, but she had walked away from us, and I forgot with all the excitement of the fight. I knew it! I knew she was pregnant. She looked it to me. Anyway, you know Maeva will buy the father and her off."

Blair answered, "According to Lucille, she doesn't think the father can be bought off."

"That's what I heard too," said Mae. "They go to a church that doesn't believe in divorce."

"Perfect," said Blair.

Before she had time to say anything else, Mae interrupted. "Can I talk to Booty?"

"Oh, of course. Here he is." As she tried to hand Booty the phone, he motioned to his office that he would take the call in there.

Blair turned to look out the window and tried to think. *Now what?*

Eli had no idea any of this was happening. He had been at school all day without talking to anyone. All day he waited and wondered where Lucille was. Would she make another grand appearance with Whisper Woman, demanding he follow her to the office while leaving Whisper Woman to take over his class? Eli tightened his jaw when he thought about his decision not to leave the class. He was not going to allow Lucille to bully him. In some ways, he yearned for Lucille to reappear, so he could stand his ground with her again, which was fun.

Lynette Sue and Betty Ann waited and wondered the same thing. Where was Lucille, and why hadn't she returned? Lucille did not give up. She did not forget. She hounded people until they were worn down and relented or left the school.

The rest of the day, nothing happened with Lucille, and neither Eli nor Betty Ann nor Lynette Sue could figure out why. At recess, the two girls made sure to walk past the principal's office and found Lucille on the phone. They tried to go into the office just to say hello, and she shooed the pair away. Neither girl could understand why. This was not like Lucille at all. Why wasn't she still after Eli Take? Betty Ann couldn't wait for the school day to end so she could get home. She had to talk to her father. He would straighten Lucille out. Hopefully tomorrow they would see Mr. Take get what he deserved.

Lynette Sue and Betty Ann were not the only students concerned about what was happening. Isabelle, Heppy, and Miriam also worried. All of them liked Mr. Take, and all knew what a shrew Lucille Pawn was. Isabelle and Heppy heard Geneva on the phone until late into the night, talking about Mr. Take and what to do about him. They knew Geneva talked to Lucille several times over the course of the evening. They knew Lucille was out to get Mr. Take and planned to get him to the principal's office, where they would be undisturbed, since Bob Wrightsberg was never there. Then Lucille would give Eli Take a good talkin'-to like he never had before and with any luck at all run him out of town. Isabelle and Heppy worried for Mr. Take. He had been instrumental in saving their lives by getting them away from their grandparents. In their years at school, he was the only teacher to take an interest in them and do something. He told people about the abuse and how the children suffered. They did not want anything to happen to Mr. Take. Yet there was nothing they could do except watch and hope. Geneva was really angry with him.

Miriam's mothers liked Eli. He had opened Miriam's mind and consequently opened theirs too. Miriam couldn't wait to tell them when they got home about Lucille coming into class and what had resulted. They wouldn't believe how Mr. Take took on Lucille and refused her command. The night before, they had talked about how Lucille would attack Eli Take. The last thing any of them wanted was for Mr. Take to be the butt of Lucille's wrath. He was too nice. Yet there was nothing they could do. All day, Miriam expected Miss Pawn to return to their classroom with guns blazing, to get Mr. Take and leave that spooky Whisper Woman, the other Miss Pawn, to take over the class. Lucille's non-appearance worried Miriam, because it must mean something really bad. She could not wait to graduate from Lincoln and get over to Athens to the Episcopal school and get away from the terror of Lucille Pawn.

Eli was uneasy the rest of the day. Lucille was not one to give up so easily. He had stood his ground with her, and she was furious about it. If that was the case, then what happened? He had been so proud of himself for standing up to her. All day he waited for the other shoe to drop, and when it didn't, he worried. Maybe she had something bigger in store for him? Surely it could not have been that easy to stand up to Lucille. Could it? Had it been that easy? Really? Could he truly hold his own that easily and, to his surprise, feel better for it? Amazing—simply amazing.

The last bell rang. After all the kids left, Eli walked down the empty, quiet hall. For a brief time, he considered sneaking by the principal's office, just to see if Lucille was there. This was so unlike her that it crossed Eli's mind to wonder if something had happened to her. Was she still at school, or had she been carted off to the emergency room? No. He wasn't going to push his luck. If she happened to be at her desk and saw him, the battle might begin again. He had won. He'd savor his victory rather than push it.

Time to leave school while he was ahead, which he did.

Eli walked home over the ancient, cracked sidewalk like he always did. When spring had arrived, he appreciated the unfurling of the new leaves from the old trees lining the blocks, shading him from the relentless Oklahoma sun. He watched as the fresh, green leaves started to dull with the advent of the summer heat and the incessant sun. School wasn't even out, and it was already hot. Just wait until summer really got started, when it got almost too hot to go outside because your skin felt like it was being broiled. Eli stopped at that thought, since he did not plan to experience the terrible heat. He would be long gone from Cedar Springs by then. He promised Booty he would stay on until school ended, and he would. Then he was off to—where? He had no idea. Even though Blair had moved to Booty's, Eli still believed in the end she would more than likely get married to that shit, Bob Wrightsberg, who never bothered to show up at school. Talk about someone who should be fired. Eli reminded himself that it was none of his business. He was out of here. Bob and Blair could live happily ever after, for all he cared.

Mrs. Harrell was outside, attacking the overgrown bush. Cru had better sense and stayed in the shade of the front porch, napping. Every so often, the yellow Lab raised his head to check on his mistress. Seeing she was okay, he would fall back to sleep. Mrs. Harrell was a pretty woman and so alive.

"Hello, Mrs. Harrell," said Eli as he strolled by.

She looked up at him and shielded her eyes from the sun. "Can you believe I'm still after this bush? It's either going to be the bush or me."

He stopped for a moment, not in any hurry to get back to the cottage. "Why don't you hire someone to do that?"

"Hire someone?"

"You could get rid of the bush or cut it back."

"And miss all this fun? I'll get this bush if it kills me or I kill it first. I've let this bush sit and grow for years. I looked out at it a while ago and thought that I'd had enough of it. I don't care if my late husband's ashes are in it. I didn't mean to put him there in the first place. The Lab I had before Cru—Cruella was her name because she was a girl—did it. Cruella joined my husband there after she died. I figure why not let them be together, since she put him there in the first place. It was my fault. I wasn't paying the slightest bit of attention at the time, although I can't for the life of me remember why. Anyway, I was going to scatter him out where we'd go fishing at the lake. The blue velvet bag was sitting right there in my open purse on the dining room table, with me not thinking one thing about it. Before I knew it, there's ashes on the Oriental rug, and I'll be damned if Cruella hadn't opened the screen door and trotted out with him to the front yard. She'd opened the blue velvet bag with the gold cord and gotten out my husband's plastic bag. First—I'm sorry to say—she put him on the Oriental rug, where she had a little snack of him.

"Well! I gathered up what I could from the rug and tossed him in the azalea, which has long since died. I couldn't throw out the azalea's soil—that would be terrible. I couldn't throw out my husband. I'd feel awful about that. I did the only thing I could do. So part of him is in the geranium pot. Cruella trotted right out to the front yard with the plastic bag of him, and the next thing I knew, he was in the bush. I almost called the vet because Cruella ate so much, but I didn't. I mean, what could the vet have done? And Cruella had eaten whole lot worse things than ashes in her life. I was really worried when she ate that dead rabbit. Who knew if the rabbit had rabies? The vet told me not to worry about it, since Cruella had her rabies shot and she'd be okay. He said that the worst thing would be diarrhea, but that didn't happen. She didn't get sick at all, although it scared me to death, her eating that rabbit, and I know—you don't need to tell me—she's a dog.

"Anyway, my husband's been dead since before Methuselah was born, and it's time for him to go on and do whatever it is he needs to do if he hasn't done it already, and it's time to cut this bush back so I can see the street. How was school today?"

"Your husband is scattered in that bush?" asked Eli.

"Not scattered, I would say. I'd say more like spilled. He's here and in the Oriental rug, except probably not so much, since the rug's been vacuumed, but the geranium is doing fine. I haven't been able to move. How could I move? I can't leave my husband and Cruella, but that's fine since I haven't wanted to. I'm just fine right here.

"At least I know where he is, not like my poor sister-in-law, who still thinks my brother is in the urn sitting on her piano. I couldn't ever tell her that she's got ashes from our barbecue in there. She'd die. He had pancreatic cancer, and when they said he had about six months to live, they weren't kidding. Bless his heart. Anyway, after the funeral, I thought it would be nice to have a little going-away party for him here at my house. Thank God my sister-in-law was inside the house and never knew a thing. Of course, she was drunk as a skunk and couldn't get out of that wingback chair in the living room if you paid her. The truth is, unfortunately, we all were a little bit drunk. We probably should have eaten lunch before the funeral, but no one felt like it. We were sitting outside, and because my brother had loved to sit outside, we brought him with us. To this day I don't know how my son did it because to tell you the truth I wasn't paying the slightest bit of attention until he screamed, 'Oh my God!' I thought, *my God, what's happened?* Anyway there are my brother's ashes in the grass all over the place, and we couldn't gather him up to save our lives. My son felt terrible about the whole thing. We had to do something. It would just kill my sister-in-law to know my brother's ashes were in the backyard and not in the urn. So we did the only thing anyone could possibly do. There were ashes sitting right in front of us in the barbecue from the hamburgers we had for dinner the night before. So my son grabbed the plastic bag and filled it with the ashes from the barbecue, and really who knew the difference? No one. He still felt awfully guilty—bless his heart—so he went to the funeral home in Athens and bought the most expensive urn they had and put the plastic bag with barbecue ashes in it. My sister-in-law was so appreciative because it was much nicer than she could have afforded. You know, she never said a word about the barbecue smell that came from the urn.

"There's my brother in the backyard and Cruella and my husband in the bush. So you can see why I can't move, even though my children who live all over the place with families of their own want me to."

Eli didn't know quite what to say except, "Okay."

"So what'd you think about school?" Mrs. Harrell asked as she returned to cutting the bush.

"What about school?"

"You know," she said. "What do you think about Lucille and everything?"

"Oh, about Lucille. I didn't let her get to me. She tried to have Whisper Woman teach my class and take me down to the principal's office, but I refused." Eli fully expected Mrs. Harrell to be surprised at his boldness against Lucille.

Instead of saying anything, Mrs. Harrell sat back and thought. "Oh, that's right ... Lucille was out for your blood. Oh well, that's behind us now. You're all forgotten. You and Whisper Woman."

How could that be, thought Eli, *when yesterday I was the town's gossip? And what about Whisper Woman?* "Whisper Woman?"

"My God! I was over at that big funeral in Athens today, and as I rightly predicted, it wasn't worth shaving your legs for. There was Whisper Woman, big as life, rearranging the sprays that were all lined up. You would have thought she was the florist, how particular she was about those sprays, and then there were the flowers. Some of us were in the church reception room visiting before the funeral, and there she was as busy as ever with those flowers. When we all went into the church for the funeral, Whisper Woman went right along with us like she knew the dead woman, but she didn't any more know her than she knew Adam. She sat in the pew right behind me and sniffed."

At one point, Eli would have thought this conversation odd, but now that he had been in Cedar Springs a little while, he thought nothing of it. "I better be going."

"Okay," answered Mrs. Harrell, busy with the bush. "Let me know tomorrow if Bobby shows up at school. I'll bet money Lincoln won't see him again."

Eli looked at Mrs. Harrell and thought, *Why would Bob be at school? He's rarely at school. Why would tomorrow be any different?* He said, "He's almost never at school. Why would he come tomorrow?"

Mrs. Harrell's attention was back on the bush. "Maybe to get out of the house?"

Eli shrugged. He didn't know what Mrs. Harrell was talking about, but then he didn't know a lot of the time what many of the people in Cedar Springs were talking about. "Okay. Bye."

"Bye-bye," she hollered with her head in the bush.

Eli continued up the block, where Miss Marie sat on the front-porch swing. She was busy talking on the phone with such concentration that all she had time to do was to wave as Eli walked by. He waved back and then turned the corner. Eli strolled past the Blair family house. He knew Blair lived at Booty's, but he still looked back to her apartment. Her car was no longer in the driveway. It was now parked in one of Booty's garages. Lorraine's car sat in the drive. Precious's was gone as usual, since most of her time was spent in Athens, hounding the workers at the Herman H. Green house.

Eli wondered what Lorraine did with his day. He often thought that as he passed the house. Lorraine used to look out the window a lot when he lived at home in the pink brick house. Eli had not once seen him at a window since he moved in with and then married Precious. He thought Lorraine surely must be lonely. All of his friends were gone from his life. Ellanor was in New York City, having the time of his life. Because Precious could not stand Booty or Mae, Lorraine no longer was allowed to have them as friends. He must sit at the computer all day, or ... who knows what?

He got to Booty's white mansion with the columns running across the long front porch. He tried not to be obvious, glancing over at the house, and started to speed up a little.

"Eli."

He knew it was Blair's voice. Should he stop or hurry on? He started to pick up his pace again.

"Eli."

He stopped and looked. The front door stood open, and Blair was on the porch. She looked beautiful. Her hair drifted in the breeze. He did not know what to do or say. There wasn't anything to be said. Everything was over.

Her voice was rich and strong. She felt alive and happy. "Eli, won't you come up here?" She motioned to him.

He stood and looked. What did she want? Why would she want him to join her? What was there to say? Nothing. Best to leave it and move on. He turned to leave. She ran over the grass to him.

"Eli."

"What?" Eli tried to keep his voice civil.

"Come in. I want to talk to you."

"There's nothing to talk about. Anyway, you're supposed to be at work. Where's Booty?"

Blair's heart sank. Suddenly she felt sick and leaden. All the wonderful thoughts, her lightness, her happiness vanished in a heartbeat. Of course he's heard about Bobby marrying the bank teller. Everyone in town heard about that, and nothing had changed between them. She was silly to think maybe it would change things between them. How could she have been so blind not to see that Bobby getting married changed nothing between them? It was her fault. Everything was her fault. She broke it off. She hurt him. She left him. Why would he forgive her? "Oh. I had hoped—"

"What? What had you hoped? What do you want of me? You're getting married in—I don't know when, but you will. Your mother always wins. It is none of my business. I don't see there is a whole lot to say." He started to walk on.

She looked at him. "Eli?"

"What?"

"You don't know?"

"Know what? Did something happen?" Suddenly Eli got worried. Did something happen to Mae or Booty? Is that why Blair stopped him to talk?

"Bobby married the bank teller today."

"Bob married the bank teller. Bob married *what* bank teller? Are Mae and Booty all right?"

Blair looked at Eli oddly. "Mae and Booty? Of course they're all right. They went over to Athens. You know the bank teller that Bobby had dinner with at the restaurant Valentine's Day? The Valentine's Day brawl, that young woman. Bobby got her pregnant. She and her father went to Lincoln today. Her father escorted Bobby out the school door and over to Athens to a judge's office, where they got married."

"Wait a minute. Bob was at school today?"

"Yes. He picked quite a day to finally show up."

"How do you know this?"

"Lucille saw everything. She called Sister. My friend was having her hair done and heard everything Sister said on the phone to Lucille. Then my friend called me."

"So *that's* what happened to Lucille?"

"What?"

"She was out for my blood this morning when she came in the classroom with Whisper Woman. She demanded I follow her to the principal's office and leave Whisper Woman to teach my class. I refused."

"You refused?" asked Blair. "You actually refused a summons by Lucille?"

"I did."

"How wonderful! I wish I could have seen it. I bet she could have shot you, she would have been so mad."

"Yes. I'm sure she would have enjoyed shooting me. The funny thing was that I waited all day for her to come back. I expected her. And now I see why she never came."

"Bobby and his new wife upstaged you."

"Yes, thank God they did."

"Lucille would rather gossip than breathe," said Blair.

"Lucille is a horrible woman. Have you heard from your mother?"

That comment struck Blair. She tried not to let it show. "No. There's nothing to say."

"I have to go."

"Please—don't."

"God damn it, Blair! What do you want me to say? Why did you stop me? What do you want?"

"Eli, I made a terrible mistake."

"Yes, you did. It's a little late. Why would I ever trust you again? How would I know that your mother won't call again with some idea and you go sneaking away, leaving me? How would I know that? I can't go through that again. I never want to go through that again, and I won't."

"I understand. I'm so sorry."

"I'm sorry. I'm sorry? I'm sorry is no excuse."

"There is no excuse," she said. She had lost. She lost him. She saw it in his eyes. "All I can say is that I am sorry. It was the biggest mistake I ever made."

All of the pent-up rage burst inside and rushed through him. "What the fuck did you think I was going to do?"

She simply looked at him. There were no words.

"God damn it!" He was screaming. His insides were hot. Heat ran up his spine and ruptured in his head, almost blinding him with pain. "Do you know what you've done? Do you have any idea what you have done to me?"

"Yes," she answered quietly.

"God damn you!" His head throbbed. His face felt scalding hot. "God damn you! It's too much! You casually sneaked away, leaving an empty house, and you left me—"

"It wasn't casual," Blair interrupted, to no avail.

Eli didn't hear her in his fury. "You didn't have the God damn decency to talk to me—to tell me! You fucking ran off and let me walk into an empty, dark house without even a note. How could you honestly tell me that you loved me and then run off and vanish without a word? How could you do that to someone you're supposed to love? I don't get it. I'll never understand how you could have done that to me. It's cruel. I would *never* have done that to you. I respected you. I thought we could talk to each other. I thought we *were* talking to each other. The worst part is that I trusted you. I really trusted you." He gasped for breath, heaving and trembling. He wanted to cry. His mind screamed, *Get out of this place! Go anyplace, just get out of here!*

Blair watched his fury, knowing there was nothing she could do. Tears streamed down her face.

The bright happiness in her eyes when she walked out on the porch was long gone. Her body felt dull, weak, empty, and hopeless. "Eli, I just wanted you to know before you left here that I am truly, deeply sorry. I will never forgive myself for hurting you. It was cruel. I was a fool. It really was the biggest mistake I have ever made in my life. That's it. That's all."

It was over. She turned and slowly walked back to the house.

Eli felt sick. He felt sick about everything that had happened. All he wanted was out of this little town. He strode back to the cottage and closed the door.

After Blair closed the front door, her legs gave way, and she collapsed to the floor. She leaned back against the old, solid-wood door and wept.

Chapter 13

Lucille sat at her desk, supposedly typing but actually thinking. *Who would take Bobby's place as principal?* She knew the board had sent Bob a letter telling him that his contract was not going to be renewed. She applied for his job. It was about time she became the principal of Lincoln School. She ran the school, and she deserved the title. She knew the school better than anyone, and no one deserved the job more than she did. Lucille made it her business to know there were other applications, and that was what worried her. She chewed on her bottom lip worrying and glanced into the principal's office and shook her head.

Bobby sat at the desk, hunched over, pretending to work. He was depressed and mad. Ever since he married Penny Price, he had been at work. It was the only way to get out of that tiny house and the loud, crying baby. They lived in a tacky rental house in Athens, the likes of which Bobby would never have chosen, and he hated it, his situation, and that his mother refused to help him. His contract was not renewed as principal, which was okay, since he didn't like children. He rented a small office in Athens, and the minute school ended and he got his last paycheck, he would work there as an attorney. It was all he could do. Having to actually make a living had never entered his head previously, since he always counted on his mother doling out the money, and upon her death, he would finally get his part of the trust. For the first time in his life, he was on his own and had to make money, and it terrified him. What if he didn't get any clients? No law firm in Athens would hire him—nor anyplace else for that matter—because his reputation preceded him.

His mother had taken to bed with a fifth of bourbon and refused to talk to him, proclaiming that he was no longer her son and making damn sure her will reflected that. He had no access to the trust and its money. What also drove him crazy was that Penny cooed with happiness, since all she ever wanted was to be a wife and mother. Marriage and a family was the last thing Bobby ever wanted. Plus her cooking was awful. He yearned to run off, but he needed her income. Penny joined the family dry-cleaning business, and she hounded him to join it too, so they could be together all the time. He considered disappearing, but if he did, Bobby knew Mr. Price would hunt him down and kill him.

His only hope was to get back into his mother's good graces, so she would write him back into her will. Even if he did get back into the will, his chances of getting the money soon were not good. His mother was not likely to die in the near future. In spite of her hypochondria, she was healthy as a horse, and she had great genes. Her mother lived until she was ninety-eight, drank bourbon like a fish, was hugely fat living on boxes of Russell Stover chocolates, never lifted a finger to do anything (since that was the help's job), and was never sick a day in her life until one day her body just died. None of this was good news for Bobby, who currently chewed on his fingernails worrying.

★ ★ ★ ★ ★

Eli sat at his desk watching the kids complete a test. He smiled. The year was almost over. He had fulfilled his bargain with Booty to stay until school was out. Blanquitta wanted her sixth-grade class back. Her mother would take care of the baby while she was at school. She and her husband needed the money. His job as the organist and choir director at a church in Athens wasn't enough, and teaching at Lincoln would ease the strain of the house payments and other bills. Truth was, it was fine with Eli. Let Blanquitta have her class back. He didn't want it … or did he? Surely not. Eli shrugged at that thought. He glanced back at the class. No. It was time for him to leave Cedar Springs.

The only sound in the classroom was the air conditioner chugging. Outside Eli's classroom windows, the once-green grass had faded into heat-baked dull brown. The oaks planted when the school was young had grown big and tall, giving much-needed shade from the relentless Oklahoma sun. Suddenly a booming clap of thunder got the attention of Eli and the class. All eyes shot to the long windows. Layers of thick, black clouds churned in what only a short time ago was a clear, bright-blue sky. The wind quickly picked up, shaking the oak leaves. Eli looked at the class, who in turn looked back at him.

"I didn't see any storm warning. Did you?" he asked.

"No," said A.J. He whipped out his laptop and went immediately to an Oklahoma City TV station. He pointed to the screen, where the red-haired weatherman stood before a map of Oklahoma. "Look at this."

Everyone including Eli gravitated to A.J.'s desk, watching the screen in silence and listening carefully to the weatherman.

The sky outside the long windows was black, illuminated only by flashes of lightning, followed by close, loud bangs of thunder.

Heppy stared out the window. "The thunder is too close. It's right on top of us."

"It sure is," said A.J., staring at the computer screen. "Look at this." He pointed to the computer screen. "There's the hook echo. The storm is headed right at us."

Betty Ann said, "I have to go home."

"No you don't," said Eli. "No one is going anyplace. You're safer inside. You know that."

Heppy added, "More people get killed by flying objects than the tornado itself."

Isabelle looked at Heppy and said, "Thanks, Heppy. That makes us all feel a lot better."

"Well, it's true," he replied. "You've got boards and glass and everything flying through the air at a high rate of speed."

Eli looked at Heppy and Isabelle. It was amazing how fast they had changed. They didn't look or act like the same children who had started the sixth grade with him. They had gained weight, lost their gaunt appearance, and probably for the first time in their lives were healthy and happy. Eli was proud of Heppy. He had failed the sixth grade twice and was not going to fail again. His grades had shot up. He would be a fine student at the Episcopal school in Athens. It was wonderful to see the work Geneva had done with the children. Eli thought how giving them love and safety had changed them to a remarkable extent. They no longer lived in fear, and it showed. His mind wandered to Blair. He wondered how she was.

Sharp bangs of thunder rattled the windows. Flashes of lightning came fast and furious, turning the world an eerie white. Branches tapped frantically against the windows from the howling wind. Gradations of pitch-black clouds covered the sky with small funnels dangling from them.

"Hey, guys," said A.J. His eyes were glued to the computer screen, as were everyone else's. "Look."

At the same time A.J. told everyone to look, the red-haired weatherman announced, "Tornado on the ground. Take your tornado precautions immediately." Kids had already turned on their cell phones, which began ringing. The helicopter pilot came on TV. "I have to move away because I'm being sucked in. It's too strong. I have to move." The pictures of the tornado that he had been showing stopped as the helicopter turned to fly away in the opposite direction. Weathermen riding with the storm chasers approached the scene. One stood outside the truck, reporting. Another reporter had to jump back into the truck and get away from the tornado heading down the highway directly toward them. The only thing he had time to say before hurrying back into the truck was, "It's a big one. Looks a mile wide, from what I could see. I'd say probably EF4 or maybe five. It's dangerous. Everyone get to safety. Get underground if you can. If you're in a car, get out and get to a ditch for safety. Don't stay in your car under an underpass. Tornadoes suck people out of their cars. Get to a ditch and lie as low in it as you can."

As he said that, Lucille came on the school intercom. "You all get away from the windows right now and into the hall. Right now! We're in a tornado alert. Don't forget some kind of identification so they can identify your body." Tornadoes scared Lucille half to death. She quickly grabbed the bottle of Valium that was always in her purse and popped two into her mouth, washed down with some of the cold coffee sitting in the cup at her desk. She was furious with Bobby, who the minute he saw the sky getting dark ran out of the door.

He jumped into his car and sped over to his mother's house to take refuge in the basement. He still had the keys to her house and ran first to the bar, where he grabbed a fifth of vodka, and then to the basement. He doubted if his mother would know he was there, since she was ensconced on her powder-blue chaise longue with a fifth of bourbon. She wouldn't care what hit the house.

Lucille called him a coward (not to his face) because like a captain going down with the ship, he should have stayed at school and been blown away with the rest of them. She was also mad he left, because had Bob done the honorable thing and stayed at school, she could have left and gone home to *her* basement shelter. Now she had to stay since that coward deserted. She was left alone, and someone had to be in charge of the school. Lucille vowed if she lived through this, she would kill Bobby.

The minute Lucille told everyone to get into the windowless hall, Eli directed the kids to take their possessions and follow him. The wail of tornado sirens was almost drowned out by the pounding wind, the torrential rain, and the thunder. Eli directed the children, who walked dutifully in a line into the long, dark hall, away from a door. After making sure all of the children were out of the classroom, he followed them, closing the door behind him. Suddenly the electricity went off, silencing the chug of the air conditioner. Cell phone reception and Wi-Fi were lost. They were cut off from the outside world. The kids sat on the floor on either side of Eli. Every so often, someone would start crying and then stop. Eli wondered what to throw over the children for protection. Since it was getting close to summer, no one had heavy coats they could use.

"Don't forget," said Heppy with assurance, "it's the flying objects that get you, so watch out. Remember, a man's head was cut completely off by a flying board. His head was found in one place and his body in another."

"Heppy," pleaded Isabelle, "come on."

"I was just trying to be helpful," he said.

"Thank you, Heppy," said Eli. "We appreciate the warning." Eli studied the hall for anything that could become a lethal flying object.

Clare sat next to Isabelle. They had become good friends. She leaned over Isabelle to Heppy, who sat next to Mr. Take. "Heppy," she said, "no more flying-objects warning unless you see something coming toward us, okay?"

Lynette Sue sat next to Betty Ann. She smacked her lips. "My mother was taking me over to Athens shopping after school today. I have to get a graduation dress, and we were going to get it today. Do you think we'll still go? It's not that bad, do you think? I want to go shopping, and I need to get my dress today. We might eat dinner over in Athens. Do you have your dress yet? It has to be white, you know. Miss Pawn said so. All the sixth-grade girls have to wear white dresses. I hope we don't have trouble finding a white dress I like. My mother said that she hopes people don't think we're Catholics buying a confirmation dress, because they're white too. That's what worried my mother. People are going to think we're Catholics, and we are *not* Catholics. We are Christians. What are you going to wear? I hope it's not a dress one of your sisters wore. Everyone's seen it."

"It is," Betty Ann answered, "but my mother is completely remaking it so it will be like new. Besides, I love the dress. It's so pretty with all of the lace. I just love it, and I want to wear it."

Lynette Sue shot her a look. "Okay. I just wondered. You don't need to get mad."

"I'm not mad," snapped Betty Ann. "I would have asked to wear that dress even if my mother hadn't said anything. It's special. It's historical. And the boys have to wear pants, so you can't wear blue jeans, Hiram." She jabbed him hard in the side.

"Oh, come on, Betty Ann," he said. "I didn't do anything to you." Hiram moved down out of her jabbing range, hoping that if they did have a tornado, it got her.

They sat in the windowless hall with the classroom doors shut, listening to the tornado siren's wail piercing through the blinding rain, the whips of the wind, and the ear-splitting crashing thunder.

"I have to go to the bathroom, Mr. Take," said Betty Ann.

"Me too," echoed Lynette Sue.

"No," answered Eli. "We all stay together."

"But ..." whined Betty Ann.

"No buts," interrupted Eli. "No one leaves my sight until I give the all clear."

"But, Mr. Take, what if I can't hold it?" said Betty Ann.

"This is an emergency. You have to hold it. If I see other teachers allowing the kids to go to the bathroom, I'll let you join them. No one is moving, and neither will you. It will be clear shortly," Eli said, hoping that was true.

"I don't think it will be clear anytime soon," said Heppy, attempting to be helpful.

"Nah, I don't think so either," agreed A.J.

Clare looked at both boys. "Thanks, you all. This is just what we needed to hear."

A.J. looked at her. "Well, it's probably true. If we're not blown away first."

"Come on," said Isabelle, clearly worried. "Do you think Geneva is driving over here to get us? I tried to call her before we lost reception. I left a message for her not to get in the car. We're okay. Do you think she got my message?"

Clare looked at Isabelle and shook her head. "I don't know. Adults know not to get into cars during a tornado. A car or a mobile home is about as dangerous as you can be."

"Where there's a hook echo, there's a good chance of a tornado," A.J pronounced. "I'd say a tornado is coming right toward us. I sure am going to miss this when I move to St. Louis. I hope they have tornadoes there. I bet they don't have weather coverage like we do. If we don't get killed, I want to be a weatherman and a storm chaser. I've seen a storm chaser's truck, and it looks like space age. I want to do that. Looks great."

"That's the last thing I'd want to do," said Isabelle.

Heppy said, "Don't worry about it, because if the tornado is as big as that weatherman said, we're all going to be killed. Anyone above ground will probably be killed."

Eli listened to the kids and felt sick. He was never going to leave Cedar Springs, because he was going to die here with his head cut off. Hopefully they would find his body. This was terrible. He would never leave now. Would his father know he was dead? Would he care? His stepmother certainly wouldn't. Ellanor knew to leave here and go to New York City. Why didn't Ellanor tell him about tornadoes and insist he go with him? Eli had to keep himself together. He had to be brave for the children. How would it look if their teacher went to pieces? He couldn't. He had to keep it together for them. Why did his car have to break down in Oklahoma? Why not some safe place without tornadoes? He was going to die. Eli just knew it.

Lynette Sue started to cry. "I'm not going to get to go to Athens today and get my graduation dress."

"Don't worry," said A.J. "You won't need it, since we're all going to die."

"A.J.," snapped Isabelle, "don't say that. You don't know we're going to die."

"If we take a direct hit," said Heppy, "our chances of survival are slim to none, being above ground."

Betty Ann whimpered, "I want to go home."

Eli wondered why they did not build a basement when they built the school. The thought that there wasn't a basement in a school made him mad. Irresponsible, and now it was too late. How could anyone build anything in Oklahoma without a basement or a safe room? Eli felt depressed. He hoped that Mae and Booty would recognize his head and body and put him back together again before cremating him, which he forgot to tell Mae he wanted.

Isabelle looked at him and worried. "Mr. Take, are you all right?"

"I'm fine," he answered.

Betty Ann whimpered, "I think we ought to pray."

Lynette Sue got on her knees and put her hands together in prayer. "Dear heavenly Father—"

Eli interrupted her, "Pray to yourself, not out loud."

Lynette Sue glared at him. "I thought I would give us comfort, since we'll all be with Jesus soon."

"I'm not planning on going anyplace. Jesus will have to wait." As Eli was saying that to Lynette Sue, he was thinking, *We are all going to die.*

Miriam's mother Mary sat across the hall with her sixth-grade class. She motioned for Miriam to come sit with her.

"Mr. Take, asked Miriam, "may I go sit with my mother?"

"Yes, of course," answered Eli.

317

Miriam grabbed her things and hurried over to huddle in her mother's arms.

Prudence sat down the hall on the floor among her third-grade students. She quietly looked at Mary and watched Miriam rush straight across with her backpack to Mary's waiting open arms. There was nothing she could do. She could not join Mary and Miriam. According to California law, she and Mary were married, and according to Oklahoma law, they were not. All Prudence could do was catch Mary's eye and say good-bye. She could not leave her third-grade class alone. She put her arms around the two children sitting on either side of her and comforted them.

Joe Tom watched Miriam rush across the hall. He wished he had talked to her. Lynette Sue had made him sit next to her. "I want us to die together," she commanded. He did not want to die with her. He did not want to die at all. He wanted to go to the Episcopal school and play football.

Eli thought about Blair. He was going to die with her thinking he was mad at her. It was too late. Damn it. Booty's house had a basement, so she would survive. He was glad about that.

Lucille sat at her desk after announcing on the intercom for everyone to get into the hall. She watched the trees bend like they were rubber in the blowing wind and rain. This was about the worst storm she could remember seeing. It didn't seem to her that storms used to be this bad. She had agreed with the pastor when he told the congregation in a powerful sermon on Sunday how the Devil was making up stories, telling people there was global warming. He said that climate change was a lie. Lucille looked out the window. When lightning lit the sky, she saw the billowing layers of black clouds. There was a sickening yellow color mixed with the black. It didn't look good. She wondered again about all this talk about climate change. One thing for sure—storms were worse, bigger, and coming at times of year when they shouldn't be coming. She used to never hear about EF4 tornadoes and certainly not EF5. The last thing she heard before they lost contact with the outside world was the red-haired weatherman saying an EF5 was on the ground and heading straight for Cedar Springs.

The window glass shook. There was no question the storm was worsening. The question was, what was she going to do? Should she go into the hall like she told everyone to do or stay here and watch the storm? What if she got blown away? Somehow her feet refused to move. She should at least close the blinds and the curtains to protect her from flying glass, but she didn't. She walked into the principal's office and sat in the big, brown leather chair. She opened the desk's bottom drawer. Good old Bobby. She could count on him to have a fifth of vodka in there. And he didn't think it made him smell like liquor. She laughed. Yes, it did. She always knew when he'd been drinking. Now she needed a glass. Just because she was about to be blown away didn't mean she could drink straight out of the bottle. She was brought up better than that. She looked over his desk. No glass. That meant Bobby drank straight out of the bottle. Shame on him. His mother brought him up better than that, and if she lived through this, his mother would hear about Bobby's lack of manners. Damn. She had to go to her office and grab her coffee cup on the desk. Well, she simply had to do it. Lucille got out of the leather chair and hurried back to her desk, grabbed the cup, and then rushed back to the chair.

Lucille held the fifth of vodka and coffee cup and looked around the large room. Should she hide under the big, heavy wooden desk? No, too uncomfortable. Lucille sat in the chair and rolled it between the file cabinets and the wall and watched the storm. She lost track of exactly how many Valiums she had taken, but it didn't matter. She felt fine.

★ ★ ★ ★ ★

When Mae saw the sky changing color, she immediately turned on the TV to see what was happening. Just as she suspected, a storm was brewing—a bad storm. Why hadn't the weather people seen this coming? She had not heard about any storm for today, and yet right on the TV's radar, she saw a severe storm heading toward Cedar Springs. This was not good. Quickly she called Booty, who was over at the office in Athens.

"Booty," she said, trying to keep her voice level.

"I know. We have the TV on. You get down to the basement. You've got Herschel. Get down there."

"Yes, I will. What about you? You're not going to be here." Mae felt her voice about to lose control, and she could not allow that. "Booty, I do not want you on that highway. You stay put. I don't want to worry about you trying to get home on the highway. It's too dangerous. You promise you will stay right where you are. There's a basement at Crutchfield Oil, so get down there. Will you? Do you promise me? Please, Booty, please. Do this for me. Please. I don't want to live without you. I need you to take care of yourself and get down to the basement. Please do this for me."

Booty heard Mae's fear. He had always been with her in storms. He knew how much Mae was scared of storms. Being stranded in Athens with Mae in Cedar Springs was terrible. What could he do? He couldn't get to Cedar Springs, even if he tried, since the police closed the roads. No one was going anywhere. The roadways were being cleared for the emergency vehicles to be able to get through. He was helpless to do anything.

"Booty, promise me you'll stay in the basement until this is over. You won't try to get on the road."

Booty looked around his office. Everyone stared at the TV, listening carefully to what was being said. There was no question about it: this storm was bad. People were going to get hurt or killed. The question was how many. This was his company. He could not have run back to Mae. He had to stay here and make sure everyone was safe. When the building was built, a basement was included for safety. Mae was right; it was time to get the employees down to the basement. He had to make sure everyone was all right.

"Okay, we are heading to the basement. You and Herschel go on downstairs and take care of yourselves. I'll come home when it's safe to get on the highway." He stopped for a moment and was quiet. "Mae, do not ever forget I love you."

"Booty," cried Mae.

There was a steady calmness in his voice. "You and Herschel go on down to the basement. Right now, Mae."

"Booty," cried Mae.

"Right now, Mae."

"I love you, Booty. I always have, and I always will."

"I'll be home, Mae."

Booty watched the people around his office finishing their phone calls. Phone reception could be lost at any moment. Everyone knew it was time to go to the basement.

Mae hung up the phone and wept. Rain beat against the window. She hated storms and patted Herschel, who stood by her. This was no time to be alone. She called Blair.

"Hello?"

"Come over right now," said Mae. "Come on. This is no time to be alone. Come be with Herschel and me. Come to the front door, and hurry. We need to get to the basement—quick."

Blair didn't want to be alone. She was sitting at her desk, staring at the oncoming storm, wondering what to do.

"I'm coming."

"Blair," said Mae, "is Lorraine alone over at your mother's?"

"Yes. I saw Mother drive out earlier, going over to Athens. I'll call him to go over to your house."

Blair called Lorraine the minute she hung up with Mae.

"Hello?" he said.

"Lorraine, it's Blair. We are going over to Mae's and get in her basement. She said to go to the front door. Now!"

"Yes." He had been following the storm. He knew how deadly it was, and he did not want to be alone. Not now. He wanted to go home.

Blair jumped out of the chair, grabbed a raincoat, and then ran out the door into the pounding, blinding rain. She could barely see her hand in front of her face, much less if Lorraine was near. She headed for Mae's against the howling wind and the beating rain. Sheet lightning lit the yards between the houses. The electricity had gone off, and the houses were dark. Water rushed down the street. Tree limbs snapped, and Blair prayed not to be hit by one with the wind. A tornado siren could barely be heard through the storm.

Mae held the door open as Blair ran into the house. She was drenched and shook with a chill that permeated her bones.

Mae took off her soaked coat and threw a blanket around her. She handed her a flashlight, a warm sweater, and socks. "Get down to the basement. I've made Herschel stay there. Both of you stay there, and I'll be down as soon as Lorraine gets here. Now hurry. Lorraine is coming, isn't he?"

"Yes. He's on his way."

"Good, good," said Mae, nodding. "Now go on. Take care of Herschel. He gets scared in storms." She almost pushed Blair toward the basement door. "Hurry."

Mae stood at the front door. Torrents of rain blinded any chance of seeing anyone. Cold spray from the rain covered her. Shivers ran through Mae's body. She strained to see through the pounding rain. Lightning flashed, illuminating the yard an eerie white. Mae desperately searched for Lorraine.

"Lorraine!" she shouted.

"Mae!"

"Lorraine?"

"Mae, I'm coming."

Mae burst into tears of relief when she saw the lanky man climbing up the porch steps, holding a flashlight. Water poured down him. He had not thought to put on a raincoat, which was typical.

"Oh, thank God, Lorraine! Thank God," cried Mae as she threw a blanket over him, pushing him inside.

"I'm all wet," he said.

"I know. I brought some of Booty's clothes in case you needed something. Come on, hurry. You can change in the basement bathroom. Blair's already down there. Use your flashlight; it's dark. Be careful of the stairs."

"Mae, I do know this staircase." He started down with Mae right behind.

"Yes, yes. I know you know. Just be careful anyway."

Blair had the battery-powered TV on the Oklahoma City station with the red-haired weatherman talking. She also had the portable radio's NOAA weather station turned on.

A loud crash of thunder shook the house.

"Jesus," said Lorraine.

"The weatherman said it's an EF5, Mae," said Blair.

"Oh, my God!" said Mae as she sat on the couch with Herschel sitting on her feet in front of her.

"Damn," said Lorraine.

"I talked to Booty after you talked to him, Mae," said Blair. "He was heading for the basement with everyone. He'll be fine."

"I hope so, honey."

"He will, Mae. He'll be fine."

The different voices from the TV and the radio talked at once. Blair and Mae were on the couch. Lorraine took one of the comfortable chairs. As soon as Lorraine sat down, he hopped up and walked to the bar.

"Who wants what?" he asked. His voice had a cheerful quality. He could not remember when he last had fun. He was having fun.

Blair turned to Mae on the couch. She placed her hand on top of Mae's. "The school doesn't have a basement."

"I know."

"Why didn't anyone ever build a basement in the school? With all the work that's been done over the years, why wasn't a basement put in? Why?" Blair's voice cried as she spoke. "I don't understand it."

"What does anyone want to drink?" Lorraine asked. He grabbed a tall glass and added a little ice and mostly bourbon and swirled it around. "Anyone want anything? I highly recommend having a drink because, by God, we might need it."

"I don't want anything," said Blair, staring at the TV.

"Me neither," said Mae. "I'm too worried to drink. I need to keep my wits about me."

"Why?" asked Lorraine.

"What if something happens to Booty? I have to be prepared to get over to Athens as quickly as possible. I have to have a clear head."

"Why? All the more reason to drink," said Lorraine.

"No," replied Mae, "I don't want anything."

"Not even a Coke?" asked Lorraine. "You always want a Coke. There isn't any iced tea."

"I'll have a Coke," said Blair. "My stomach needs settling."

"So does mine," said Mae. "Lorraine, I'd like a Coke too."

"Okay. Thank God your father believed in keeping his basement survival-ready with cases of bourbon and toilet paper. The only things in life needed to survive. I always did like your father, Mae."

"Come on back and sit down. Oh my God, this is a bad storm." She pointed to the map of Oklahoma on the TV. "Look where it is."

A weatherman stood outside a truck, holding on to his baseball hat to keep it from flying off as he talked into the microphone. He pointed to a huge tornado eating everything in its path. Debris flew into the air.

"It's a good mile wide," said the man, standing on an empty two-lane highway, pointing toward the storm.

"Yes, I see," said the weatherman back at the station, looking at different screens. He had been at the television station for so long, he spanned generations and had seen it all. He spoke in a calm, reassuring voice, never with alarm or panic.

"You must take your tornado precautions now. Get below ground if at all possible. You people in Lone Mill, if you're not at your place of safety, get there now, because this is outside your town. Your town is directly in its path. Get below ground."

Mae, Lorraine, and Blair sat up and looked at each other. Their eyes were wide with horror.

"That's right outside town," Blair said so softly that she was barely heard. "Oh my God." She put her head into her hands. "Please, God, spare the school. Please." She turned to Mae. "If we get through this and the school survives, you have got to build a basement, and that's all there is to it. We cannot have a school without an underground shelter. It's terrible, terrible. They have to have protection."

"I agree," answered Mae. "I'll talk to Booty. I agree that it must be done."

Blair nearly cried. "It's not fair to do this to the parents."

"Or the children," said Mae.

Blair repeated, "Or the children."

"Or the teachers," said Mae.

"Or the teachers," repeated Blair.

The helicopter had returned. Pictures were being transmitted of the tornado going through the town of Lone Mill, just outside of Cedar

Springs. Pieces of what was a quiet town's life were flying into the air. Anything not in its path remained untouched and unharmed. Three reddish-brown cows with white faces stood in a field, watching the storm, and then returned to grazing after the tornado passed the area.

Lorraine pointed to the TV. "Lone Mill is being leveled."

"In all my life," said Mae, "I've never seen anything like this. Poor Lone Mill. Poor, poor Lone Mill."

"The funeral homes are going to be filled up tonight," said Lorraine.

"Lorraine!" said Mae. "You don't know that. That's not a very nice thing to say."

"All I know is what I'm seeing on TV, and from what I see, my guess is that there's no room in the inn at the funeral homes tonight."

"I hope you're wrong," said Mae.

"The hospital will be filled, I bet," said Blair, staring at the screen. "That's assuming the hospital in Athens won't be hit."

"Look at that," said Lorraine.

They watched with horror as the tornado drove through the center of the town that was just outside Cedar Springs.

"Oh, Booty!" exclaimed Mae.

"Booty will be fine," said Blair.

"Especially if it veers off and doesn't hit Athens. What I don't know is about us," said Lorraine. "We might not be so fine."

It was curious how neither Lorraine nor Blair thought about Precious. She never entered their minds.

★ ★ ★ ★ ★

A sudden calmness came over Eli that he could not understand. He did not feel any panic at all, whereas only a moment before, he had felt like screaming. He felt the rain pounding on the roof and heard the wind howling, mixed with thunder that shook the building. He knew in his innermost being that whatever happened, he would be all right, even if they all got killed. That profound information shocked him. What happened? He did not know, but something certainly did. Something shifted within him. He felt no anger at all toward Blair and worried if she was all right and in a safe place. Booty's house had a basement, and so did Mae's. He hoped Blair went over to Mae's and was not alone.

"I'm cold," fussed Betty Ann. "Aren't you all cold sitting on this cold floor? I'm cold. I need to go to the bathroom too. I hope I don't burst. I could burst and die."

"You'll be blown away first, so don't worry about it," said A.J.

"Shut up, Betty Ann," said Clare. "Everybody's cold and has to go to the bathroom."

"I don't," said Hiram just to make Betty Ann mad.

"Most of us then," said Clare.

"Joe Tom," cooed Lynette Sue, "I'll just cuddle up to you to stay warm. Okay?"

Joe Tom wasn't paying attention to Lynette Sue. He worried about the ranch, his family, and his horse. Were they all right? Surely the ranch hands and family got all of the horses into the barns, but what about the cattle? Right now, he didn't give a damn about Lynette Sue. She annoyed him. Was the ranch going to be destroyed? The family lived in a compound at the ranch. What about his house? He worried if his mother was at home or over in Athens. His older siblings were at the Episcopal school in Athens. He hoped they were all right. And where was his father? Surely his father was at the ranch. This was the worst storm he had seen in his life, and it scared him. He wanted to go home.

"Joe Tom," insisted Lynette Sue, "I want you to put your arm around me."

"Not now," he answered.

Lynette Sue's bottom lip started to tremble. "Okay, Joe Tom, if that's the way you want it to be, then we'll break up, if that's what you want."

"What?"

"We'll break up, if that's the way you want it," said Lynette Sue bravely.

Isabelle and Clare couldn't help but hear everything, and they rolled their eyes.

Clare leaned into Isabelle so no one else would hear. "She doesn't ever stop, does she? Not even when we're all about to all be blown away."

Isabelle answered, "Drama queen."

What was happening around them was far too serious for Lynette Sue's silly little games. Joe Tom usually thought her flirty, cute, and sexy, but not right now. "Come on, Lynette Sue. Not now."

She sat up away from him and folded her arms. "Okay. If that is the way you want to be." She sniffed, fought back tears, and loudly pouted.

A.J. put his head against Eli, who had his arm around him. "Where is the tornado?"

"I don't know," answered Eli quietly.

"Last we heard, it was an EF4 or five." A.J. sniffed, holding back tears. "Do you think we're going to die?"

"I don't know," answered Eli.

A.J. smiled a little and looked at Eli. "Well, if we do get killed, that means I won't have to move to St. Louis."

"I drove through St. Louis driving out here. It looked pretty. It's a big city. You might like it. There will be lots of things to do."

"But the ranch won't be there or any of my friends or the rest of the family. I don't want to go."

"There are things in life we have to do that we don't want to do. We do them anyway and try to make the best of it. Mae says that you can make it hard or you can make it easy. Might as well make it easy, since you have to do it anyway."

"You think I might like it?"

"Sure I do. I think you might like it a lot."

"Really?"

"Yes, really. I came from New York to here, and I really didn't think I would like it, and I like it very much. It has been the best thing that ever happened to me. I love it here. I feel at home." Hearing the words come out of his mouth shocked Eli. He certainly did not know he felt that way. He thought he could not wait for school to end and get out of Cedar Springs as fast as possible and never look back. What had he just said?

A.J. certainly had no idea how astonished Eli was by what he just said. "So you think maybe it will be okay to move?"

"What?" asked Eli, still amazed by what he had said.

"So maybe you think it will be okay to move?" A.J. repeated.

"Of course. You get to meet new people and have an adventure. It's terrific."

"If we live," said A.J.

"Yes, there is that," said Eli, nodding. "If we live."

The storm raged around them. Since the pupils and teachers sat on the floor in the windowless hall huddled together, Lucille was the only person at the school to see out the windows at the sudden stillness. The air felt charged. Lucille did not have a radio or TV. She didn't need to. She knew. She felt it through the blur she tried to create with the Valium and the vodka. She knew when everything stopped. She waited for the sound of a freight train. That was what she had always heard—tornadoes sound like a freight train coming toward you. No freight train. No nothing. She knew. Somewhere very close, this monster tornado was tearing up and killing everything in its path. She held her breath, waiting. Nothing happened. She could not see anything. Nothing. Suddenly the wind blasted, shaking and blowing everything. The panes in the windows shook to the point that Lucille believed they were all going to fly out. She wondered if she should move under the desk. Tree branches broke and flew all over the place. A large tree snapped and fell on top of a car, crushing it.

The teachers and kids did not know about the sudden stillness. Later, some described the air as charged with electricity. They held on to each other as they heard the sounds of breaking along with the howling wind and the bangs of thunder. Eli told the children to lie down as flat as they could. He lay between them, trying to shield the children as best he could with his body. If anyone was going to be blown away, he was going first. Lynette Sue screamed. Betty Ann cried and screamed, joining Lynette Sue, trying to get Joe Tom to shield them. Joe Tom looked disgusted at both girls. He couldn't wait to get away from both of them next year.

"Cover your heads with your hands," instructed Eli. The truth was, he had no idea what to do, since he had never experienced anything like this in his life. "Keep your head down."

"The floor is cold," whined Betty Ann.

"The floor is cold for all of us," snapped Isabelle. "Get over it."

Heppy peeked around. "If the walls fall inward, they'll collapse on us and kill us. We'll be crushed."

"Shut up, Heppy," said Isabelle.

"Shut up, Heppy," Clare agreed. "That's enough of that. We're going to be okay."

"You don't know that," snapped Heppy.

"Well, you don't know we're going to be killed, so shut up," argued Clare.

"Let's be quiet," instructed Eli.

"And pray," said Lynette Sue.

"Whatever you want," said Eli.

★ ★ ★ ★ ★

Blair, Lorraine, and Mae sat mesmerized, watching the storm on the TV. It was frightening, and they were helpless to do anything except watch.

One of the weathermen following the storm stopped in Lone Mill, which had been devastated. The reporter stood in front of demolished buildings that once made up Lone Mill's downtown. As he reported, people started slowly coming out from their shelters. They were bewildered, looking around in shock at what used to be their town. Some were injured. Almost all were crying.

The reporter talked to the camera. "I have to stop." He looked around, surveying the terrible scene behind him. "People need help. No ambulances have made it here yet, and we have first-aid equipment. I'm signing off so I can help." The reporter stopped transmitting. The head meteorologist back at the studio quickly went to another reporter at a different location.

The helicopter hovered overhead, zooming in on the devastation. Mae, Lorraine, and Blair strained to see what if anything they recognized of the town was still standing. The small town of Lone Mill had taken a direct hit. The south side of Cedar Springs and everything in that area had been in the tornado's path. The mobile home park was destroyed. Houses were flattened. In one block, no houses were there; only exposed foundations told where houses once stood. Everything was gone, as if a gigantic bomb had hit. Roofs were torn from walls that were still holding up what was left of the houses. A bathtub rested among branches of a tree. People were being told to stay off the roads, to keep them clear for emergency vehicles.

Blair turned to Lorraine. "Maybe I do need a drink."

"Okay. I'll get it for you."

"Not too strong, Lorraine."

★ ★ ★ ★ ★

Eli felt his heart beating in his chest. He was calm and afraid at the same time. No one knew what to do, so they remained on the floor.

"I want to go home!" screamed Betty Ann.

Hiram looked at his twin sister. "Stop it! There's nothing your crying will help, so shut up." Hiram was sick of Betty Ann. For once in his life he was not going to listen to her. He wondered if they had a home to go to.

His response shocked Betty Ann so much that she quit crying. She was too scared to be mad at Hiram. Where were her parents, and were they okay?

Lucille stared at the clearing sky. "My God, I'm alive." Her head ached, and she felt terrible. "I need some aspirin." As she crawled over to the desk to help herself get up, she continued to stare at the sun shining through the window. "It's over. She stood on wobbly legs and pulled the intercom over to her. "Listen here, everyone," she announced.

Upon hearing Lucille's voice echoing through the hall, everyone sat up, alert and listening.

A.J. turned to Eli. "Is it over?"

"I don't know. Let's listen."

"Okay. The sky is blue outside. I don't know what happened. All I know is that the storm isn't over us anymore. I don't know where it is, but it isn't here. Thank you, Jesus!" And she whooped.

"Praise Jesus!" cried Lynette Sue. "We made it. Thank you, Jesus. Thank you, Jesus."

"Shut up, Lynette Sue," said Betty Ann. She was in no mood to hear Lynette Sue chirping about Jesus—or anybody, for that matter. She was too tired. Betty Ann leaned back against the cold wall and closed her eyes.

It was over. The air cleared; the storm passed. It felt strange when teachers and children looked into classrooms bright and filled with sunshine coming through the long windows that somehow remained intact, as they had through years of storms. A teacher got up and opened the big, brown, metal front doors to the school, letting in the sun that warmed their chilled

330

skin. The sky had transformed from frightening, black, churning clouds to bright blue with big, white, fluffy clouds. Looking at the sky, one would not think anything had happened—that is, until they looked around. Around them, damage was everywhere. Tree limbs and debris filled the streets and yards. One of the big, old oaks had succumbed to the storm, completely destroying the car upon which it fell. Sirens from different emergency vehicles wailed. Everyone wondered where they would go and who was hurt and what was gone.

★ ★ ★ ★ ★

Mary McKeen was very much a take-charge woman. She had applied for principal's position. When Lucille saw her application, she rolled her eyes. Never would Lincoln School give a lesbian the job of principal. Lucille thought Mary had real nerve applying for the job in the first place, when she should know she never would get it. If it were up to Lucille, neither Mary nor Prudence would have their jobs as teachers, and for Mary to apply for principal was the height of nerve.

When Mary realized the storm had passed, she immediately recruited Prudence and Eli to help her assess the damage. She told the other teachers to make sure everyone stayed put until Mary was positive it was safe. She, Eli, and Prudence first went to the cafeteria, because that's where Mary wanted everyone relocated. Mercifully, it was intact, as were the classrooms. The school had been spared. They were too busy to think about Lucille or check the principal's office. Someone had seen Bob drive off the minute the storm threatened. They knew that he was not at school and had not been for the duration of the storm.

★ ★ ★ ★ ★

As Blair and Mae slowly walked up the basement stairs, they felt drained. "I feel like I've been run over by a truck," said Mae.

Blair nodded. "So do I."

"I don't think I've ever been so tired in my life."

"Me neither," said Blair. She followed Mae to the front door and stood on the porch, assessing the mess outside.

They walked to the sidewalk and started down the block. Booty's house had lost a lot of tree branches and some bushes. Other than that, the old house had withstood another storm. They stopped at the Blair family home.

Blair's hand rushed to cover her mouth. "Oh my God," she said slowly. "Oh Lord! It's ruined. I don't know what can be done!"

"I don't know either," Mae echoed.

A giant tree had fallen on top of the home, crashing through the roof. Much of the roof had caved in, destroying the middle and front parts of the house.

Seeing the destruction of the house reminded her that she had not thought about her mother. "When Mother gets back from Athens—if she makes it here today at all—she'll have a fit. I don't know what she'll do."

"She ought to pull the old thing down," said Mae. "Maybe you could save the back half. I don't know. That midpoint to the front looks pretty much gone to me. Your frame house has looked weak to me for years. It's a wonder it didn't happen sooner."

"I know," Blair agreed. "I've been in that house when the wind was so bad, I thought it was going to blow the house down. It scared me the way the house shook so badly. I thought the place would collapse or be blown off the foundation. It's a wonder that it lasted as long as it has. No substantial work has been done on it for years, maybe never. All Mother ever did was cosmetic repairs."

"I believe that."

Blair looked around. "Where's Lorraine?"

Mae followed her, looking around for Lorraine. "I don't know. He might well still be in the basement. He did have quite a lot to drink. He's probably having a little nap. We'll leave him to it."

Blair folded her arms, staring at the destruction. "Just as well my mother planned to move to Athens. They can't live in this house."

Mae said, "Lorraine isn't moving to Athens. He's no more going to live in the Herman H. Green house than I am."

Blair turned and stared at her. "Really? How do you know?"

"I don't know for sure, except I know Lorraine, and he is not going over to Athens. I don't believe it."

"You think?"

Mae nodded. "I do."

"Mother will have a fit."

"I doubt it."

Blair went back to studying the house. "You're right. She won't care. I'd just tear that old house down and to hell with it. I never liked the house."

"Neither did I."

★ ★ ★ ★ ★

Mary had gathered all of the children and the teachers in the cafeteria. Those who needed to go to the bathroom could, but they had to return to the cafeteria. No one was quite sure how long it would take the parents to make it over to the school through all of the destruction in the streets. There was plenty of food in the cafeteria if the teachers needed to prepare sandwiches.

She went up to Eli and Prudence, who had settled their classes. "Don't you think it's strange we haven't seen Lucille? She should be here trying to run the show, and she's nowhere in sight."

"Well, where is she?" asked Eli.

"That's what we need to find out. Come on." Mary led them out of the cafeteria and down the dark hall to the principal's office. "If she's not in the office, then we'll check the auditorium," said Mary. "I can't think where else she'd be."

They walked into the front office used by Lucille, which sat empty, so they continued through the principal's door into the office. There, face down on the floor, was Lucille, moaning.

"Oh my God," said Prudence as she rushed over to Lucille. "Look." She pointed to a leg that was laying in such a way that it had to be broken. "She's broken her leg. Lucille! Lucille! Can you hear me?"

Lucille only moaned.

Eli knelt beside her. He leaned down to take a closer look. "She's drunk."

Mary and Prudence looked at each other.

"You're kidding," said Mary.

Prudence looked around the room. "Eli's right. Look here." She leaned down and picked up an empty fifth of vodka rolling around the floor. She looked over at Lucille, still moaning on the floor. "Lucille, you old hypocrite! You! If you'd caught any of us drinking—much less drunk—at school, we'd be fired—except for Bobby, of course. I've been in here when he reeks of alcohol, and you've done nothing because of his mother. This bottle is our evidence, and I am keeping it. Lucille." She leaned down and talked straight into Lucille's face. "Lucille! Wake up! Can you hear me?"

Lucille peeked up at Prudence and moaned. "I need help."

"You sure as hell do. Here's the thing, Lucille: Eli, Mary, and I are the only people who know you're here, and you have been a real shit to us. I have to think about what we want to do. You might want to be a little nicer to people, because you never know when you might need them. Looks like your leg is broken."

"My leg," she moaned.

"Yes, it's your leg," replied Prudence. "And it is not at all in a very pretty position. I don't think legs go in that direction. You need medical care, so now you concentrate real hard on what I'm going to tell you. Do you hear me? Answer that you hear me."

Lucille nodded.

"Okay, here's the little deal we're going to make: We'll call an ambulance to take you to the hospital in Athens, and you will never try to fuck with Eli, Mary, or me ever again. You will not fight our contract renewals, like you have with Mary and me for years, and now you won't fight Eli either. You also won't fight when we come up for raises. You will leave us alone. Agree?"

Lucille lay on the floor thinking. She could always lie, but Prudence had the bottle for evidence. She hated Prudence. She never wanted to know anyone like her or Mary, much less have them under the same roof where she worked. If she got the job of principal like she deserved, Lucille planned to fire all three of them.

On the other hand, how long could she hold out waiting for someone else to find her? She was in a lot of pain. This was horrible. She hated all three of them. She also could not stand the pain much longer. Why did they, of all people, have to find her?

"Oh look, Lucille," said Prudence. "You've got your red lipstick smeared all over this nice rug. What will Booty think when Eli tells him about you being drunk and maybe ruining the rug? Eli and Booty are real good friends, aren't you, Eli?"

Eli and Mary were enjoying this. "Yes we are," he answered proudly. "I know how upset Booty would be to hear that you, the school secretary, were drunk on the job, especially in this dangerous storm, when everyone needed their wits about them to take care of the children."

"I don't think that is being responsible," said Mary.

"No. It is not responsible at all," Eli agreed. "Dangerous."

"Very," Mary added.

"I think we need to be checking the rest of the school," said Prudence. "Okay, Lucille. Surely someone will find you later. Hope your pain doesn't get too great, since you've drunk all the liquor."

"Wait!" screeched Lucille. "You can't leave me."

"Yes, we can," said Eli.

"What do you want?" she moaned.

"You not to bother us again about anything ever, including our contracts and raises," demanded Prudence. "I'm not in a friendly mood, Lucille, so I suggest you take it, or you might lie here for hours before someone thinks to look in here again. Maybe not even for the rest of the day. Give you time to sleep off your drunk."

"I hate you all," Lucille growled through her little teeth.

"What a shame," said Mary. "And I always thought you liked us."

"See you, Lucille," said Prudence, getting up.

"Wait!"

"Lucille, we have to see how the rest of the school is," said Eli. "If you have anything to say to us, now is the time, because you will not see us again. Wonder how long it takes for gangrene to set in?"

"I don't know," replied Mary. "It certainly is a thought."

"Okay," screeched Lucille, furious. "Okay, okay, okay! You win. I agree. I agree. Just call the damn ambulance."

"Lucille," said Eli, "I know you think you will screw us. We know you're lying. You can't screw us as much as you want to, because we can prove that you were drunk in your beloved school during a serious crisis. I will be watching you, Lucille, so don't even think about trying anything. Don't fuck with me, or you will be very, very sorry. I have nothing to lose in this community, and you have *everything* to lose. Don't worry. I'll keep reminding you."

"I hate Orientals!"

Mary asked, "What are we going to do with her?"

"The landline works," said Eli holding the phone. He called 911. "I've got a woman with a broken leg at the school in Cedar Springs," he told the emergency operator.

After listening, he replied, "Okay. I understand. Yes. We'll try to get her over there. I understand. That's right. Okay. Thank you. Bye."

Eli turned to Prudence and Mary. "All of the emergency vehicles are over in Lone Mill, which took a direct hit. There are a lot of serious injuries there that have to be taken care of before they can get over here."

"That makes sense," said Mary. "How are we going to get Lucille over to the hospital in Athens?"

Eli asked, "What about Whisper Woman? She's her sister. Does anyone know their number?"

"Are you kidding?" said Prudence.

"Give me some paper and I'll write it down," hissed Lucille.

Eli handed her paper he found in the desk and she quickly wrote down the numbers.

"The cell towers are more than likely down," Mary said.

He dialed Whisper Woman's number, and to his surprise, she answered. She whispered, "Hello?"

Eli could barely hear her. "Whisper Woman," he said, "this is Eli Take over at Lincoln School. Your sister has had an accident and needs to get to a hospital. All the emergency vehicles are in Lone Mill, and the emergency operator said we had to get her to the hospital. I don't know how passable the roads are. Can you get over here? She is on the floor in the principal's office."

He strained to hear her. "What? You want to do what? God damn it! I don't have time for this shit. Talk in a normal voice so I can hear you. We have a cafeteria full of scared kids, and I don't have time for this. God damn it! No! You have to. None of the teachers can go. They have to stay here. Do you understand we have kids here who can't be left just because you are afraid to drive on the highway! How do you get to the funerals over there? Walk? Yes, you can come out of the house. Listen to me, God damn it! So what if you don't have any makeup on! For God's sake! No one cares. We have just survived a major tornado, and I heard that Lone Mill is destroyed."

He listened and then screamed, interrupting her. "No taxi is going to be available to drive over here and get your sister! Jesus Christ! And I don't think a funeral home has time to rent you a driver and a limousine. They are busy dealing with a tragedy. I'm afraid people have died." As Eli listened to Whisper Woman, he was grateful she was not in front of him, because he would have strangled her and enjoyed doing it. No wonder her brother hanged himself, if that was the only way to get away from the family. Eli wanted to cry out of frustration. His eyes joined Prudence and Mary's as they looked to see who walked into the outer office.

"Hello?" said Mary.

"Hello," said Pastor Pastor as he walked into the principal's office with Hiram on one side and Betty Ann on the other, clinging to him as she cried.

"Wait a minute, Whisper Woman," said Eli.

"I just wanted to let you all know that I've got my young ones, and we're going home. Everything is all right, praise Jesus! The church is saved and our home and children."

"Wait a minute," said Eli.

The pastor stopped and stared at Eli with contempt. "What?" Dooley Pastor hated all people other than white Evangelicals. Orientals were never to be trusted since the Pearl Harbor incident, plus they all looked alike, and there was something not to be trusted in that.

Eli continued. "Lucille Pawn has had an accident."

That was the first time Dooley Pastor bothered to look around the principal's office, and sure enough, there was Lucille, moaning on the floor.

He looked at Eli. "What happened to her?" he demanded as if Eli were the culprit.

"It appears she broke her leg. She must get to a hospital, and none of the teachers can leave the school. Whisper Woman can't come over because she doesn't have any makeup on. Would you take Lucille to the emergency room?"

"Makeup? Why can't Whisper Woman come over and get her?" demanded Dooley Pastor. "I've got to get home. Their mother is worried to death. Somehow I've got to get over to Athens to pick up the older kids at school, and I don't know how, since we're not supposed to use the highway. I'll have to go the back road, which will take longer, but I have a better chance of actually getting there."

"If you're going to Athens anyhow," said Mary, "why can't you drop Lucille off at the emergency room at the hospital?"

Dooley looked down his nose at Mary. "No. I don't have time."

Mary glared at Dooley. "How much money has Lucille given you and your church, and you can't do this for her?"

Dooley glared back and went over and knelt beside Lucille, who continued moaning. "Lucille," he said too loudly, "it's your pastor."

"Dooley, help me," she moaned.

"Lucille, listen to me. What's wrong with you?" He could not understand why he was not getting through to her. She always responded to him. He was well aware that she had a terrible crush on him, and he used it to get her money. Dooley looked up at Eli, Prudence, and Mary. "What's wrong with her?"

"Other than the fact her leg is busted," replied Mary, "she's drunk."

Dooley sat back and stared at Lucille, then at Eli, Mary, and Prudence, and then back at Lucille. "She is not."

"Really?" said Mary.

"Smell her," said Eli.

He leaned down and took a whiff of Lucille. "I don't smell anything," Dooley lied, incensed at their accusation of one of his best donors.

Hiram and Betty Ann stood at the entrance of the principal's office where Dooley had left them. "Daddy," whined Betty Ann, "I want to go home. I want my mama."

Hiram rolled his eyes and shook his head when she said that.

"I know, honey," said her father. He was in a quandary as to what to do. The last thing he wanted was to deal with a drunk Lucille with a broken leg. The problem was, she gave him any amount of money he wanted anytime he wanted it. It was not a good idea for her to think he didn't care—which he didn't. "You said Mama is waiting for us at home," whined Betty Ann. She loved to nag. Betty Ann made nagging an art form. "Come on, Daddy. You said Mama wanted us to come home. I'm cold. I have to go to the bathroom."

Hiram looked at her in disbelief. "You do not. You just went."

"I do too. You don't know if I have to go to the bathroom or not, and anyway, I have to go again!"

Dooley was stymied. He wanted to take the kids home and get to Athens to pick up the rest of the kids at school there. His phone rang constantly since the storm was over, with people and their problems and fears. One of his biggest challenges being a pastor was that he lacked patience and didn't like being kind. He wanted to slap people upside the head and scream at them. An idea itched at him of joining his uncle in the funeral-home business in a town about one hundred miles from Cedar Springs. Growing up, he had spent summers working for the family funeral-home business, helping with dead people. He was already familiar with that, and the best part is that dead people can't talk. He wouldn't have to placate anyone anymore for any reason, and he could quit having to be at church every Sunday and Wednesday night and all the other times. He could send his wife and children to church and stay home to work on his cars in quiet. An additional wonderful, merciful perk of moving one hundred miles away was that he could finally get away from his mother-in-law, who, if he weren't a preacher, he would enjoy murdering.

"Daddy!" cried Betty Ann. "I want to go home!"

"Betty Ann," said Mary, "you know where the bathroom is. Just go and come back here when you're through."

"I don't need to go to the bathroom that much. I want to go home."

Hiram snapped, "I knew you didn't have to go to the bathroom."

"I did too, then. I just don't anymore. I want to go home."

All this time, Whisper Woman waited on the other end of the phone, overhearing the entire conversation.

Eli returned to her. "Whisper Woman, you have to take her to Athens."

Dooley quickly looked at Eli. "Is that Whisper Woman?" He smiled and thanked Jesus. He could get Whisper Woman to do anything he wanted.

He rushed over to the phone. "Whisper Woman, this is your pastor speaking. I need you to come over here right now and get your sister and take her to the hospital in Athens. Please, for Jesus and me."

After listening to Whisper Woman for way too long, Dooley interrupted her. "Now you listen to me. I am done with this. I don't give a damn how you're dressed or whatever it is. I have to get my kids back home and deal with their mother and my mother-in-law, then drive to Athens and get the rest of the kids and come back to listen to my mother-in-law, who's mad that I don't have a safe room. Let her pay to build a safe room. Do you know how much they cost?"

Whisper Woman must have interrupted him, because Dooley's face turned bright red as he listened. He lost whatever patience he had left and his temper.

"Now you listen to me and you listen good. Get your ass over here right now and pick up Lucille, who is drunk as a skunk, and get her over to the hospital." Evidently, that did it, because Dooley relaxed, smiled, and hung up the phone.

"Come on. We better be going before your mother gets more worried than she already is. You know how she breaks out in a rash and throws up and pulls her hair out of her head or gets out the scissors and cuts her hair. Remember how scary she looked the last time she had a fit and cut her hair? We don't want that, do we?"

"Whisper Woman is on her way over here to get Lucille," he said as he walked with the children out the door.

Eli, Prudence, and Mary all looked at each other and laughed.

"That was great," said Eli.

Lucille moaned, which reminded them that she was still there.

Prudence leaned down to her. "Lucille! How did you fall?"

She muttered, "I don't know. I fell and I'm sick."

"Uh huh," said Prudence.

"I'm on the floor," she moaned.

"Just stay there," said Prudence. "Here." She moved the wastepaper basket within reach of Lucille. "If you're going to throw up, throw up in the basket."

"I can't move," moaned Lucille.

"Good," answered Prudence. "Don't move. Whisper Woman will be here soon to take you to the hospital in Athens."

As clear as anything, Lucille said, "No! I am not riding in the car with Whisper Woman! She's a horrible driver. She's even worse sober. If you want me to ride in the car with her driving, then you tell her I won't get in unless she wears her glasses! She's too vain to wear her damn glasses, and I am *not* riding in the car with her unless she does!"

Prudence got up from leaning over to talk to Lucille. "You tell her that yourself. We have to get back to the children."

"Don't you dare leave me," Lucille tried to command. "I could be dying!"

Eli said as they headed to the door, "We should be so lucky."

"My leg hurts!"

"It ought to hurt. It looks broken," said Mary as they walked out of the office.

"I don't break legs," Lucille moaned. "It's my head that's killing me. It's a brain tumor. That's it. I'm going to die, because no head could hurt this bad and not be a brain tumor."

"Fine," said Eli as they left Lucille babbling to herself and screaming invectives at them for leaving. The teachers hurried down the hall back to the children.

Finally the children under Eli's care were claimed by relatives or friends. After seeing the last child off, he stood in the cafeteria exhausted. Mary and Prudence were staying until every child had a safe place to go. Mary insisted Eli did not need to stay with them and he should go on home. He slowly walked down the hall, where hours before they had sat in terror, believing they might die. He felt wrung out and emotionally exhausted. This had been a terrifying experience, one he never wanted to repeat. He pushed open the metal doors and walked out into the afternoon sun. "My God, it's still daylight!" he said to himself, standing and looking at the blue sky. He felt like he had been at the school so long, surely it was night. The destruction took Eli back. An old oak succumbed and crushed a car. It was a miracle it fell the opposite direction of the school. Trees, branches, bushes, and things from people's homes and yards littered the streets. He walked slowly down the block, surveying the damage.

Mrs. Harrell and Cru stood in the front yard. "How are you, Mrs. Harrell?" asked Eli.

"What a mess. Have you ever seen such a mess? Well, it could be a lot worse. Look at those poor people in Lone Mill. It's blown away. It always was an ugly little town, but it didn't deserve to look like an atom bomb hit it. All I have is a mess, so I should be grateful. I was about to decide to put shutters on the house. I always thought windows with shutters looked so pretty, but not now. It's just one more thing to blow off. The storm tore off a bunch. Look at that branch that broke off my old used-to-be-pretty tree blocking the driveway. What a mess! The good news is that it didn't hit the house. Look what survived untouched." She pointed to the bush. "Can you believe that bush did not lose one leaf or branch or anything? How could it be untouched? But it sure was. Cruella and my husband in there must have protected it."

"It is a comfort to know that you and the bush rode through the storm together."

"Yes, it is."

"Do you know how things are on my street?"

"Everything is a mess. The Blair house looks bad. I just walked down to take a quick look. I didn't have time to really see what happened."

When Eli heard the Blair house, he felt a chill of fear. What if Blair had gone home to ride out the storm? "What happened? Is anyone hurt?"

"Looks like the house is a goner. I don't think anyone got hurt."

Eli looked to Miss Marie's house. "How's Miss Marie? Is she okay?"

She's over at her brother's. I saw him pick her up before the storm got bad. I'm sure they're fine. Almost all of these older houses have basements. Why they build new houses in Oklahoma without basements is beyond me."

"I better be going. Bye, Mrs. Harrell."

"Bye, Eli. See you. Are you all going to have school tomorrow?"

"I don't know. I didn't think to ask. I'll find out later. Is the electricity back on?"

"Mine came on about ten minutes ago. They need to bury all the power lines under the ground. I don't know why they don't, especially in Oklahoma."

"Glad you made it through the storm."

"It was scary," said Mrs. Harrell. "I'm not one to believe in God. My mother always said that nice people don't believe in God. I'm telling you this. I thank God we made it through. It's a miracle we weren't hit. People get blown away all of the time, standing outside and watching. What do you think is going to happen if you stand outside and watch a tornado? And they're surprised they die? Stay inside, and if you get blown away, you'll go with the house. To think that all the funeral homes in Athens are full. It's a shame. Sad. It's terrible. I didn't know anyone from Lone Mill, except I had a yardman from there once, but it's still terrible."

"I'm glad you're okay."

"I'm glad we're all okay."

Eli walked on, and when he turned the corner, he wondered what he would see. Everything was a mess. He didn't see any big trees uprooted until he got to the Blair family house. When he reached the front of the house, Eli stood staring. "My God."

★ ★ ★ ★ ★

Blair slowly rocked on Mae's front-porch swing, waiting frantically for Eli to return. She knew Lincoln made it through the storm. The minute Geneva thought it was safe, she jumped into the car and headed for the school. She was scared to death something had happened to the building and was so nervous, she could barely drive. Blair and Mae stood in the front yard, assessing the Blair family house's damage and watched her drive by and waved. Geneva was so scared, she could not take her hands off the steering wheel and simply nodded a hello. This had been a horrible day, especially when Geneva realized that she could not make it to the school to pick up the children. She knew Lincoln did not have a basement. There was no safe room. The children were exposed, above ground. If the school took a direct hit, there was no question in Geneva's mind that they would die. Hot tears ran down her face, and her lips trembled.

She was in a state. During the storm, all she could do as she sat in the basement was cry and pray. She was helpless to do anything else.

The minute the sky cleared, Geneva was getting to that school—period. If the damn car got ruined, then it did. She didn't care if she tore the whole bottom out; she was getting to that school. It never occurred to her to walk. She drove everywhere, even down the block to visit Precious.

Geneva was so scared and worried that she did not remember parking the car on the curb, leaping out, and running down the hall of the school. She heard voices in the cafeteria and headed toward it. Nothing had changed much since she went to Lincoln, so she knew exactly where the cafeteria was. Heppy and Isabelle saw her run in the door, and they leapt up and ran over to her. The three of them stood at the door and cried.

Blair watched Geneva's car return creeping down the street into the driveway and the garage. The moment Blair saw Geneva's car, she took off running over to the pink brick house. Mae was startled how fast Blair zipped away, and she remained in the yard watching.

"Geneva!" Blair yelled. "Geneva!" She saw the children in the back seat, which told her Isabelle and Heppy were safe, so maybe Eli was too.

Blair ran up panting as Geneva helped the children out of the back seat, talking to them.

"Geneva!"

The children saw Blair standing there, but Geneva was so emotionally overwrought and focused on the children, she didn't notice. When she heard her name, she jumped. "Oh my goodness." Geneva's hand held her heart in surprise. "Oh, dear me! You gave me quite a start!"

Words poured out of Blair's mouth. "The school! The school! How is the school? How's Eli? Is Eli okay? What happened? Is Eli okay? Tell me. Please tell me." Blair was in tears.

Isabelle had climbed out of the car and stood next to Blair, who was shaking. Geneva was too rattled to deal with anything or anyone and had scared Isabelle to death, the way she drove back home.

Isabelle took Blair's hand. "Mr. Take is okay."

Blair looked at Isabelle. Tears flowed down her face. "He's okay?"

"Yes, he's fine. Everyone is okay. The only injury I heard about was when Mr. Take told another teacher Miss Pawn broke her leg because she was drunk and fell."

When Geneva heard that, she stood straight up and stared at Isabelle in complete surprise. "What? That can't be true. Did you say Lucille was drunk?"

"Yes," answered Heppy, "that's what Mr. Take said, because he saw her. She was on the floor, and he said her leg looked broken."

Lucille was a dear friend of Geneva's. She would never get drunk at Lincoln. "That's quite impossible. I don't understand," Geneva stammered. "It can't be true. It can't!"

Heppy shrugged. "I don't know. That's what we heard. We weren't allowed out of the cafeteria."

"Oh, my Lord." This day had been too much for Geneva, who lived a nice, quiet, routine life, trying to avoid any upset. She wrung her hands in worry. "Oh, dear me! I don't know what to do! I can't leave poor Lucille on the floor at Lincoln when she might need medical care. Oh dear, I am really not up to driving back to Lincoln at all. On the other hand, I don't know what to do. I can't leave her there."

"Oh, no, you don't have to go," said Heppy. "Mr. Take told the other teacher Whisper Woman was coming to take her over to the hospital in Athens. All the ambulances are in Lone Mill. Did you know Lone Mill took a direct hit? Nine-one-one told Mr. Take he had to get her to the hospital. Mr. Take said that it took the pastor to make Whisper Woman get out of her house, because she didn't have any makeup on, and come get Miss Pawn."

Geneva was bewildered. "What was the pastor doing at Lincoln?"

Blair instantly answered, "You know Dooley has twins in Eli's class."

"Oh yes, of course, of course," muttered Geneva as she wrung her hands, flustered. "I don't understand. You mean that Whisper Woman is driving Lucille to Athens?"

"That's what we heard Mr. Take say," said Isabelle. She was concerned how upset poor Geneva was. "Geneva," Isabelle said softly, "I think we should get you into the house. How about I make you a nice cup of tea, like you showed me how to do?"

"A nice cup of tea?" Everything was just too much for Geneva. She was a fragile soul.

Isabelle took her hand, leading her into the house.

"Wait!" exclaimed Geneva to Blair. "We can't let poor Lucille ride all the way over to Athens with Whisper Woman. I'm sorry to say this in front of the children, but Whisper Woman is crazy. She drives awful. She's dangerous. Lucille won't make it alive over to Athens. She can't go with Whisper Woman."

"Geneva," said Blair, "there is nothing we can do. Lucille is probably already on the road with Whisper Woman. Let Isabelle take you in the house. She'll make you a nice cup of tea; then you take a little rest."

Geneva looked at Blair and rubbed her forehead. "Yes. This has been a little much for me today, with the storm and all and now poor Lucille. It is all a little too much. I think I need to sit down."

"Yes, you do. You just follow Isabelle on in the house and have a little sit-down."

"Yes. Yes, I will."

"Good. Isabelle, can I help you?"

Isabelle had Geneva's hand. "No, we're okay."

Heppy had walked on by them into the house.

"When do you think Mr. Take will be home?" Blair asked, her heart pounding.

"I don't know. I heard Miss McKeen tell him to go on, that he didn't have to stay with them."

Blair walked to Mae's house. Mae was on the front porch. "How's the school? How's Eli?"

Blair smiled. "He's fine."

"Thank you, God."

Blair fell into the swing. "I'm tired."

Mae joined her on the swing. "What a day. And those poor souls over in Lone Mill. What a tragedy."

"Awful," said Blair, looking at the blue sky. "Isabelle overheard Eli telling a teacher that Lucille was drunk on the floor, probably with a broken leg."

Mae stopped swinging and looked at Blair. "There *is* a God."

"Isn't it wonderful!"

"Yes, it is!"

"Almost redeems the day."

"Yes, it does," Mae said with a big smile.

"Whisper Woman is driving her over to the hospital in Athens, since all the ambulances are in Lone Mill."

Mae smiled. "Oh dear, they probably won't make it with Whisper Woman driving. I'm amazed she would drive over there. I thought she only braves the highway for funerals."

"The pastor talked her into it. He was there getting his kids. I guess they had to get him to intercede."

"That's the only way she would do it," said Mae.

"That is the only way she did do it."

"And Lucille was drunk?"

"That's what Isabelle said that Eli said."

"Marvelous," said Mae, smiling.

"Yes, it is," Blair agreed. "I'm going to wait on the swing and watch for Eli."

"I'll go inside and check on Lorraine. Last I noticed, he was still passed out on the couch downstairs. The landlines are in service. If you need me, I'm going inside and wait to hear from Booty."

Blair was so concerned about Eli, she had not thought about Booty. *Oh my God, is he all right?* "Let me know when you hear. I want to be sure he's all right."

Mae chewed her lip, worrying as she walked in the door. "I'm sure he's fine," she called back to Blair.

Blair stared straight ahead, waiting. She was afraid to blink in case she missed Eli walking down the block. She didn't care how long it took; she was not leaving the swing until she saw him. Blair scarcely noticed the birds had returned from their shelter during the storm. She barely heard their songs. All she knew was that she had to see Eli. She had to make sure he was all right; then she could relax, but not until she saw him. What was she going to do when she saw him? She didn't know. Probably not let him see her and sneak back to Booty's house. She had to know he was okay; then she could leave the swing. She strained to see the end of the block. Was it a speck she saw? Was that Eli turning the corner? Her stomach tightened, and she could not breathe. Was it? Yes. She knew his walk. She knew him. Eli was there. He was there, and he was alive and all right. Tears streamed down her face. "Eli!" Before she knew it, she was running down the sidewalk toward him.

★ ★ ★ ★ ★

Eli stood looking at the devastation of the Blair family's house. It was destroyed. The old tree had collapsed the roof, and the walls gave in around it. They might as well pull the whole thing down. Then he thought, *where is Lorraine?* All these old houses had basements, and Eli hoped Lorraine had the sense to get in this one, but where was he? The storm was over. If Lorraine had been in the house, he certainly could not be there now. Unless something happened to him, but then surely Mae, Blair, and Booty would be here, and no one was there that he could see. Then he heard running and looked to see Blair coming to him.

"Eli," she said, out of breath, "you're all right."

"Yes, I'm fine. Where's Lorraine? Is he all right?" he asked, looking at the destroyed house.

"He's at Mae's. That's where we rode out the storm. He's probably still in the basement, asleep on the couch. That's the last time I saw him."

"Booty wasn't there?"

"No. He's over in Athens. Mae is waiting to hear from him. The landlines are working."

Eli was exhausted from the day, which seemed so long that the storm felt like years ago, not just a few hours. He stood looking at Blair. "It was horrible."

"Yes, it was."

"I thought we were going to die."

"I was afraid *you* were going to die. That damn school doesn't have a basement. Why doesn't it have a basement? I told Mae they have got to put in a basement. She said that they had to. They have to! We can't go through this again. You have to keep safe." The fear made Blair feel completely wrung out and exhausted. Tears cascaded down her cheeks, and she was shaking. "Eli, I was so scared you were going to be killed. I've never been so scared in my life. I didn't know what was happening. I didn't know how you were. I didn't know if you were alive. I was so scared. Eli, if you had died, I didn't know what I would do! And that damn school doesn't have a basement, and you could have died. Oh, Eli—"

Eli grabbed her and kissed her. They held each other as tightly as they could, touching each other, kissing each other to make sure they were really there and alive.

"I'm not going through life without you," said Eli.

"I love you, Eli. I love you. I love you. I love you."

Mae wandered into the living room with a cup of tea and sat in a comfortable chair, looking out the window, waiting to see Booty's car. She saw Blair run up the block to Eli.

Mae's bottom lip trembled, and tears came to her eyes. She sniffed and took a Kleenex out of her pocket and wiped her nose. Then she watched as they walked into Booty's house, holding on to each other. Her cell phone and the landline phone sat silently upon the table next to her. Where was he? Who could she call in Athens that might know? Mae's mind was blank; she couldn't think of one person to call. Was Booty all right? Of course, he was all right, she told herself. Otherwise she would have heard. Someone would have called—surely. Someone would call her if something had happened. The tornado came close to Athens, but she didn't think it got into the town where the Crutchfield building was located. She thought the building was all right. That's what she had to believe unless and until she heard otherwise, and she would hear—surely. Someone would think to call her—surely.

Lorraine came into the living room and sat down with Mae. "My head aches," he said.

Without taking her eyes off of the street, Mae answered, "I'm sure it does."

"I think I have a hangover."

"I'm sure you do. There's some aspirin in the kitchen drawer. You know where it is. Go take a couple. There's one of those ice packs in the freezer if you want one."

"Okay," murmured Lorraine as he got up and wandered into the kitchen. "Maybe I'll go in the den to the bar and have a little hair of the dog that bit me."

"That's fine. Do whatever you want to do. You know where everything is."

Mae chewed on her bottom lip, worrying and wondering what she could do. Should she call the hospital in Athens? Wait. Call Crutchfield Oil? Maybe someone will answer the phone. Maybe. Her mind went blank. She knew the number as well as she knew her name, but the day had been too much. She was too scared to think. She ran into Booty's office, frantically looking for his Rolodex. Where is the number for Crutchfield Oil? This was ridiculous. Why couldn't she remember the phone number? But as much as she tried, she couldn't.

Lorraine walked into Booty's office as Mae was frantically going through his desk, looking for phone numbers. He was holding a drink.

"What are you doing in here? There's fried chicken in the fridge. What are you looking for?"

"Where's Booty's Rolodex or wherever it is he keeps his numbers?"

Lorraine walked over to the desk and picked up a Rolodex, which was behind the phone on Booty's desk, right where Mae was looking. "Is this what you're looking for?" he asked, holding up the crammed file.

"Good Lord, Lorraine, I'm glad you're here. It was right in front of me, and I didn't see it. You can see how I am."

She took it and quickly looked through the numbers, shaking.

"Who's number are you looking for?" asked Lorraine.

"Crutchfield Oil."

Lorraine took the Rolodex out of Mae's trembling hands. "Here, you'll never find it." He flipped through and found it. "Here's the general number for Crutchfield Oil." Lorraine automatically picked up the phone and dialed. "It's ringing."

Mae's hands covered her face in fear.

The phone rang a long time. Finally, a woman answered. Her voice shook from the fear of the day. "Hello?"

"Is this Crutchfield Oil?" asked Lorraine. Mae listened intently, ready to grab the phone out of Lorraine's hands. "Good, good. Are you all all right?" He listened for what Mae thought was too long a time. She tried to grab the phone away from Lorraine, but he would not let her. "Good, that's good. Trees can be replaced. Is Booty Crutchfield there?" As Lorraine listened, Mae's cell rang.

She grabbed her cell. "Booty! Booty! Are you all right? Lorraine is on the phone with Crutchfield Oil. Are you all right? Did anyone get hurt? Oh, Booty, I was so worried!" Tears flowed from her eyes, and she could barely talk. She gasped for breath. "Oh honey. Oh honey, where are you?" She listened. Tears ran over her pink cheeks. "Booty, please come home, please." Mae looked at Lorraine, who watched her. He was worried too. Her fear turned into anger. "They would never have done that for you! You know they would never have stopped for you or for me, for that matter! That was kind of you to get Lucille to the hospital. Now you come home. You got her to the hospital. Please come home, please! There's stuff all over the roads. I'm worried about you. The highway is closed. You'll have to take the back road, and it's two lanes and curvy and dangerous, and who knows what's lying across it, and it's dangerous. Please come home. Please, Booty." As she listened, Mae got mad. "God damn it, Booty! You let Whisper Woman handle it. She can handle it. She's crazy, but she's not dumb." Lorraine took the phone out of her hands. Mae snapped, "Lorraine, just what do you think you are doing?"

"Mae, sit down."

"No! Give me back the phone!"

"Booty," said Lorraine.

"What are you doing at my house?" asked Booty.

"Mae called, or maybe it was Blair. Anyway, we were in the basement. What about Whisper Woman? Come on back. Mae is really upset, and I have a headache."

"God damn it, Lorraine, give me back the phone!" Mae grabbed it out of his hand, glaring at him. "Booty, what the hell are you doing at the hospital with Lucille and Whisper Woman? Get on home! I'm tired of this."

"I was on my way home," explained Booty. "You have to take the back road because the highway is closed."

"I know it," interrupted Mae. "Come home!"

"I was driving when I saw Whisper Woman pulled over to the side of the road with Lucille in the back seat, drunk. She had pulled off the road because she got scared, and Lucille was screaming at her, and she couldn't function."

"Whisper Woman can't ever function," Mae interrupted.

"Yes, I know," answered Booty. "I couldn't leave her there, wringing her hands, standing at the side of the road by her car. I had to do something, so I stopped and ended up putting Lucille in the back of my car, because Whisper Woman was too nervous, driving with her, and Lucille would not shut up. I put her in the back of my car, and Whisper Woman followed me, and we're at the hospital. Lucille broke her leg in two places. It's quite a severe break. The hospital is trying to get hold of the orthopedic surgeon to return. She needs surgery, but they can't get hold of him. All of the doctors are over to Lone Mill."

"Listen to me," demanded Mae. "You have done everything you can do. Let Whisper Woman sit with Lucille. You got them to the hospital, and that's all you can do, so come home right now—and I mean it—or you'll have to take me to the hospital, because I am going to have a heart attack if you don't come home right now. Booty, please!"

"Yes, you're right. I've done all I can do here. I'll be home as soon as I can."

"Thank you, dear. Now be careful." Mae hung up the phone and slumped into the chair. "This has been an awful day," she said. "I'm exhausted. Let's go in the kitchen, so I can make a cup of tea and turn on the TV. I want to see how Lone Mill is."

As she started to get up, the phone rang. It was Geneva calling Lorraine. Mae handed him the phone and continued to the kitchen, followed by the white, shaggy dog.

"Geneva," said Lorraine.

"Precious called here looking for you."

"Why? I wouldn't be at your house, which is actually my house."

"There's no one at Precious's house, and there won't be anytime soon, because the thing is destroyed."

Since Lorraine had not made it outside, he had no idea the house was destroyed. "The Blair house is destroyed? How? We're fine here."

"A tree fell on it, and I told Precious, and she said to tell you to get in the car and come over to the Herman H. Green house, because that is where you are going to live from now on. It's livable, and you have to go there right now."

Lorraine suddenly got mad. He was sick of Geneva; she always was so bossy. And he was sick of Precious, who was even bossier than Geneva. He was not about to go live in Athens and certainly not in that hideous house. Lorraine had had enough of Geneva and especially of Precious. She spent a colossal amount of his money, and he was sick of the whole thing. "Geneva," Lorraine interrupted her, "I want my house back. I am not moving to Athens. I want to move back home, and you and the children have to move. Go find a house in Athens. That's best for the children anyway, since they will be in school over there. I will buy it, so go find what you like, and it better be available immediately, because you are moving there. I'll live wherever I can find until you are out of my house, but be out soon. I want my bedroom back, and I want to go home, and that's that."

Mae moved from the kitchen to the den and sat on the couch, watching the red-haired weatherman on TV talking about the storm, which was continuing to cross the state. She sipped hot tea without taking her eyes off the TV.

Lorraine entered the room. "I went to the kitchen."

"I moved."

"I see. Want a drink? I think I'll have another." He made himself a drink and flopped down in what had always been his chair. It was as if he'd never left.

Mae spoke without taking her eyes off the TV. "It's torn up everything in its path, and the thing is still traveling across the state. It's still as big as it was and hasn't lost any energy. It's terrible. God knows what the death toll will be when it's over. What did Geneva want with you?"

"She delivered a message from Precious. Did you know the Blair house was destroyed by a tree?"

"Oh, yes. I forgot to tell you. That ugly, old house needs to be pulled down and carted off. I don't know how it stood for so long."

"It's a piece of shit," said Lorraine.

"Looks it. So what did Precious demand? You all can't stay there anymore. Does she want you over at the Herman H. Green house?"

"I'm not going. I might as well move into a mausoleum as move into that house. I want my house back."

"You'll have to move Geneva and the children out, because you don't want to live with them."

"That's exactly what I offered to do. I told Geneva to buy a house in Athens. It's better anyway, since that's where the kids are going to school."

"Geneva is not going to use her money to buy a house."

"I know it; that's why I told her I'd pay for it. Just do it and soon."

"Are you and Precious going to get a divorce?"

"I don't know. She won't miss me."

"Will you miss her?"

"I don't know."

"Geneva is not going to find a house tomorrow afternoon. It may take time."

"It better not take a lot of time."

"Where will you stay? You really can't stay in that house. It's destroyed."

"I'll stay in Blair's old apartment."

"Is it livable? The back of the house appears to be unharmed, but who knows? I wouldn't want to stay there."

"Surely it won't take her long. If I know Geneva, she's probably had her eye on a house in Athens since Precious got the Herman H. Green house. That would be like her. Wherever Precious goes, Geneva is soon to follow."

"You're going home?"

"Yes."

"Will you miss Ellanor?"

"Probably."

"I don't think he's coming back from New York. He's having a wonderful time and really likes the woman Eli introduced him to. I think Ellanor is happy for the first time in his life."

"He's not coming home?"

"No, Lorraine, I don't think so. You'll be okay without him?"

"I have to be. Being home is better than living in the Herman H. Green house. I think that would be really lonely."

"Yes." Mae got up. "I'm going to sit out on the porch and watch for Booty."

"Okay. I'll stay in the den and let you know if anything happens with the storm or a damage report from Lone Mill."

"Yes. Please do." Mae turned to walk out of the room and then stopped. "Lorraine."

"Yes?"

"I'll be willing to bet that my grandmother's cottage behind this house will be free. You can live there until Geneva is out of your house."

"What about Eli? I don't think he wants me living with him. You better ask him first. I thought he was leaving Cedar Springs after school finished."

"I don't think Eli is leaving Cedar Springs, and I strongly suspect he won't be back to the cottage. I think he and Blair will be living over at Booty's."

"Really? Eli and Blair? I didn't know they were back together. Precious won't like that."

"Precious doesn't like anything except the Herman H. Green house, money, and Athens society."

"She can have it."

"Yes, she can," Mae agreed.

"I'm not going there," said Lorraine, staring at the TV. "So you think the cottage is available for me to move in? And you think Eli and Blair are back together? Since when?"

"Since now," replied Mae as she strolled smiling to the front porch.

Epilogue

The sixth-grade students had finished their tests. Everything was complete; school was over. All that was left was the final ceremony. This sixth-grade class was leaving for other schools. The school board met with Lucille and gave her a choice: she could get fired without any benefits and lose her pension, or she could retire with full benefits. The result was Lucille's announced retirement. Bob Wrightsberg was asked by the board not to return to the school. After the tornado, he came back to clean out his desk, and that was the last anyone saw of him at Lincoln.

Mary immediately assumed the job as principal, even though she still had to balance it between finishing the year with her sixth-grade class. Blanquitta asked Mary to consider hiring her husband, David, as her secretary. Both of them could work in Cedar Springs, which would save money on the commute to Athens every day. He worked his way through school as a secretary and acted as the church secretary in addition to being the choir director. David would be a natural to take Lucille's job. Mary and the board agreed.

Lucille tried to stay in control. She had a wheelchair, which allowed her to be mobile with her broken leg. She zoomed up and down the halls, attempting to give orders. This was her last graduation ceremony, and it was going to be quite grand with her favorites Lynette Sue and Miriam, giving their final dance performance at Lincoln School. It didn't happen, though. Mary overruled her. The graduation ceremony was to be simple.

Eli walked to school and greeted Miss Marie, who was spread out on her swing, and Mrs. Harrell working in the flower garden before the day got too hot to be outside. Mrs. Harrell no longer tried to demolish the bush that housed her husband and her dog's ashes.

Mrs. Harrell told Eli, "I don't care if the damn bush takes over the whole front yard and I can't see a thing out the windows. I'm not touching it ever again. Just the thought of losing my husband and my dog and the bush to that storm scared me to death. I put all my coffee grounds in it to keep the bush healthy. I can't let anything happen to it. I don't care if we need a machete to get to the front door."

She waved at Eli as he strolled by her house. "Last day?"

"Yes," he answered and continued on toward Lincoln.

Eli smiled as he approached the old, yellow brick building. Next year, he would teach Mary's sixth-grade class, since she would be the school's principal. It seemed perfectly natural that he move into her class, since he had already taught the sixth grade. Blanquitta would return to her original sixth-grade classroom, because that's what she wanted, and Eli didn't care. It did not matter in the slightest which room he taught the sixth grade in. What mattered was that he taught at Lincoln.

He and Blair lived at Booty's big, white southern colonial house, and that pleased Booty to no end. There was plenty of room for Booty and Blair to take care of the foundation and for Blair and Eli to live in the house. Would they stay there forever? They didn't know. What they did know is that they were going to be together for the rest of their lives, which was all they cared about.

Eli had asked Blair to marry him, and she said yes. When they were actually going to get married they didn't quite know. Probably this summer, maybe on the front porch at Mae's. The point was they were together.

The trees shaded Eli's walk over the cracked sidewalks. It was already hot, which was why the graduation ceremony was planned for earlier rather than later in the day. School was out, so the only people in the auditorium today were the sixth graders, their families, guests, and their teachers. Lucille had already commanded the girls to wear white dresses. Mary decided that would be enough. They didn't need to pull out the old moth-eaten purple gowns and mortarboards with the gold tassels. This wasn't a high school graduation, at which wearing the robes would mean so much more. The sixth graders were off to a different school in Athens. Their lives as schoolchildren in Cedar Springs were over.

A.J. Herzstein would not be at Lincoln graduation, since the minute his tests were over and he passed, his mother took all of the children and moved back to St. Louis, where her family lived. Gossip was A.J.'s father had already moved his secretary into their house out at the ranch compound before the ink on the divorce papers was dry.

Lynette Sue planned a dramatic and tearful farewell to Joe Tom at the graduation party, but the truth is, he didn't care. He was more excited about going to football camp. Geneva, Isabelle, and Heppy were having a graduation party for all of the sixth graders tonight at the Whiz Bang Café in the party room that was rarely used nowadays. There would be music and hamburgers and dancing.

Geneva found a big Tudor house in one of the best neighborhoods in Athens, close to Precious holding court in the Herman H. Green house. Heppy and Isabelle were leaving Cedar Springs, which had held such terror in their short lives, and moving on to new adventures. Geneva was scared to leave the safety of the big, ugly, pink brick house where she had lived since her parents died. She was doing it for the children, she said.

Lorraine couldn't wait for them to move. The sale was almost complete, and he could return to his childhood home. Ellanor wanted no part of coming back to Cedar Springs and said that he didn't care if he never saw the town again. He had become a New Yorker.

Everything had been cleaned up, leveled, or repaired since the horrendous tornado. The big, old tree in front of Lincoln was gone because of the storm. A new oak was planted in its place. Eli wondered if he would live long enough to see the new tree reach maturity into a grand old oak, giving much-needed shade to the school.

Eli opened the front doors and walked into the empty hall. He felt a blast of cold air from the air conditioner as he strolled to the auditorium, where people were coming in those doors. Excited children, all of whom he knew, ran toward the stage that had large baskets full of dyed purple and gold carnations standing on either side. A purple satin banner with *Lincoln School* written in gold script covered the top of the stage. The newly tuned piano echoed through the empty school hall. Blanquitta's husband played the piano for the graduation ceremony, starting a new tradition. For the first time in anyone's memory, Lucille was not at the piano. Eli entered the auditorium and went up to his seat, next to Prudence. The children sat on the stage. Mary sat next to a table, holding rolled certificates. She smiled. To the surprise of everyone, Lucille came in her wheelchair and sat in the back row next to Whisper Woman, who had driven her. The minute the ceremony ended, she sped out in her wheelchair with Whisper Woman hurriedly following, without saying good-bye to anyone.

All the girls on the stage looked bright and pretty in their white dresses. The boys wore their Sunday suits, looking polished and clean. Mary prepared a short speech to the parents, families and friends, and the graduating class. Then she called each student's name to come up and receive his or her diploma. Blanquitta's husband smiled and started playing "Pomp and Circumstance." The song filled the auditorium. People dabbed their eyes. Eli patted Prudence's hand. They looked at each other and smiled as Prudence's bottom lip quivered. Her and Mary's daughter, Miriam, was growing up and leaving childhood at Lincoln School in Cedar Springs. It was a new beginning for all of them. Eli's eyes filled with tears. He always did cry when he heard "Pomp and Circumstance."